CHILDREN'S PEER RELATIONS

CHILDREN'S PEER RELATIONS

From Development to Intervention

Edited by
Janis B. Kupersmidt
and Kenneth A. Dodge

American Psychological Association, Washington, DC

Published by
American Psychological Association
750 First Street, NE
Washington, DC 20002
www.apa.org

To order
APA Order Department
P.O. Box 92984
Washington, DC 20090-2984
Tel: (800) 374-2721; Direct: (202) 336-5510
Fax: (202) 336-5502; TDD/TTY: (202) 336-6123
Online: www.apa.org/books/
E-mail: order@apa.org

In the U.K., Europe, Africa,
and the Middle East,
copies may be ordered from
American Psychological Association
3 Henrietta Street
Covent Garden, London
WC2E 8LU England

Typeset in Century Schoolbook by World Composition Services, Inc., Sterling, VA

Printer: Data Reproductions, Auburn Hills, MI
Cover Designer: Go! Creative, Kensington, MD
Technical/Production Editors: Casey Ann Reever and Tiffany L. Klaff

The opinions and statements published are the responsibility of the authors, and such opinions and statements do not necessarily represent the policies of the American Psychological Association.

Library of Congress Cataloging-in-Publication Data

Children's peer relations : from development to intervention / edited by Janis B. Kupersmidt and Kenneth A. Dodge.
    p. cm. — (Decade of behavior)
  Includes bibliographical references and indexes.
  ISBN 1-59147-105-2 (hardcover : alk. paper)
    1. Interpersonal relations in children.   2. Rejection (Psychology) in children.
    3. Conduct disorders in children.   I. Kupersmidt, Janis B.   II. Dodge, Kenneth A.
  III. Series.

BF723.I646C48 2004
155.4′18—dc22   2003026066

British Library Cataloguing-in-Publication Data
A CIP record is available from the British Library.

Printed in the United States of America
First Edition

APA Science Volumes

APA Decade of Behavior Volumes

Contents

Contributors

Catherine L. Bagwell, University of Richmond, VA
Antonius H. N. Cillessen, University of Connecticut, Storrs
John D. Coie, Duke University, Durham, NC
Conduct Problems Prevention Research Group, Duke University, Durham, NC
Philip Costanzo, Duke University, Durham, NC
Carolyn Pape Cowan, University of California, Berkeley
Philip A. Cowan, University of California, Berkeley
Karen F. Dearing, University of Delaware, Newark
Melissa E. DeRosier, University of North Carolina at Chapel Hill
Kenneth A. Dodge, Duke University, Durham, NC
Mary E. Gifford-Smith, Duke University, Durham, NC
Christina L. Grimes, Duke University, Durham, NC
Magaretha G. Hartley Herman, Duke University, Durham, NC
Julie A. Hubbard, University of Delaware, Newark
Tovah P. Klein, Barnard College, New York, NY
Janis B. Kupersmidt, University of North Carolina at Chapel Hill
Lara Mayeux, University of Connecticut, Storrs
Shari Miller-Johnson, Duke University, Durham, NC
Martha Putallaz, Duke University, Durham, NC
Marlene J. Sandstrom, Williams College, Williamstown, MA
David L. Rabiner, Duke University, Durham, NC
Marion K. Underwood, University of Texas at Dallas
Donna-Marie C. Winn, Duke University, Durham, NC
Audrey L. Zakriski, Connecticut College, New London

Foreword

In early 1988, the American Psychological Association (APA) Science Director-ate began its sponsorship of what would become an exceptionally successful activity in support of psychological science—the APA Scientific Conferences program. This program has showcased some of the most important topics in psychological science and has provided a forum for collaboration among many leading figures in the field.

The program has inspired a series of books that have presented cutting-edge work in all areas of psychology. At the turn of the millennium, the series was renamed the Decade of Behavior Series to help advance the goals of this important initiative. The Decade of Behavior is a major interdisciplinary campaign designed to promote the contributions of the behavioral and social sciences to our most important societal challenges in the decade leading up to 2010. Although a key goal has been to inform the public about these scientific contributions, other activities have been designed to encourage and further collaboration among scientists. Hence, the series that was the "APA Science Series" has continued as the "Decade of Behavior Series." This represents one element in APA's efforts to promote the Decade of Behavior initiative as one of its endorsing organizations. For additional information about the Decade of Behavior, please visit http://www.decadeofbehavior.org.

Over the course of the past years, the Science Conference and Decade of Behavior Series has allowed psychological scientists to share and explore cutting-edge findings in psychology. The APA Science Directorate looks forward to continuing this successful program and to sponsoring other conferences and books in the years ahead. This series has been so successful that we have chosen to extend it to include books that, although they do not arise from conferences, report with the same high quality of scholarship on the latest research.

We are pleased that this important contribution to the literature was supported in part by the Decade of Behavior program. Congratulations to the editors and contributors of this volume on their sterling effort.

Steven J. Breckler, PhD
Executive Director for Science

Virginia E. Holt
Assistant Executive Director for Science

Preface

Prior to the past decade, psychologists (and laypersons alike) assumed that when psychologists referred to children being rejected or victimized that they meant that the child was rejected or victimized by a parent. No one thought about rejection or victimization by peers at the time, nor was it considered to be a serious problem. Similarly, when a child had behavioral, academic, or emotional problems, it was assumed that his or her parents—most often the child's mother—were ultimately the cause. These assumptions were challenged and the field of child development underwent a transformation from a narrow focus on the effects of parents, and more particularly, mothers, on their children's development to a consideration of other contextual factors in the development of the child.

This book aims to provide an overview of the main areas of research on peer relations conducted by John D. Coie and his students and collaborators over the past 30 years. Coie's work put a human face on the problem of rejection by peers. By conducting ongoing interventions with children who are socially rejected, both funded and not funded, he was able to learn about individual lives as well as normative processes. Our goal in creating this volume was to honor John D. Coie and his work as a scientist, clinician, mentor, and teacher. It is with respect, pride, and warmth that we present this volume. Coie's early research was instrumental in calling attention to the profound impact of peer relations on children and through his attempts to develop a methodology that would reliably and validly assess peer problems.[1] He was successful in these efforts, and this methodology took the field by storm and finally provided researchers with a definition and understanding of the important developmental construct of peer rejection.

During much of the 1970s and 1980s, research in clinical psychology focused on the development of effective treatments for childhood disorders, with an increasing emphasis on cognitive–behavioral interventions. By understanding the roots of conduct problems, Coie was able to develop a model and perspective for bringing prevention into this realm of study. Finally, as research in developmental psychology and child clinical psychology melded into a new field of developmental psychopathology, Coie's research was exemplary of research that began to reveal the processes by which normal development went awry. The chapters in this volume began as Festschrift presentations held in May 2000 honoring John D. Coie. This volume serves as a historical document reflecting three decades of work on peer relations as well as a discussion of current findings and theories related to problems of peer rejection. In addition,

---

[1]Asher, S. R., & Coie, J. D. (Eds.). (1990). *Peer rejection in childhood*. New York: Cambridge University Press.

it demonstrates Coie's pioneering work and lasting contributions to the field of child development and gives readers a glimpse into the exciting and important directions for future research.

Organization of the Volume

The volume is divided into five parts. The parts mirror in some ways the research path taken by Coie from more basic research on the study of peer relationships, their correlates, and consequences to intervention and prevention studies. The first part, titled "Peer Status in Context," contains three chapters. The first chapter by Cillessen and Mayeux is an update and extension of a chapter in *Peer Rejection in Childhood*, which focused on the behavioral correlates of sociometric status. In addition to this literature review, these authors introduce important methodological issues in measurement of behavior and status; subtypes of rejected and popular sociometric status groups; and moderators between status and behavior such as gender, ethnicity, age, and social context. In chapter 2, Underwood examines the role of gender in the study of children's peer relations. She critically reviews the theory and data related to the theory that boys and girls grow up in two disparate peer cultures. The first part concludes with a chapter by Bagwell on the relation between children's friendship characteristics, features, and qualities and the development and maintenance of aggressive and antisocial behavior.

The second part addresses social–cognitive and emotional processes and examines the subjective experience of peer rejection. Chapter 4 by Gifford-Smith and Rabiner provides a review of the literature on the relations between social information processing (SIP) patterns and children's social adjustment, with a focus on several important questions. They discuss the role of prior experience in SIP, the malleability of SIP, the relation between SIP and emotions, the roles of development and gender in moderating the relations between SIP and adjustment, and the relations between the SIP model and other forms of behavioral adjustment besides aggression. In chapter 5, Hubbard and Dearing review the role of emotional knowledge and regulation in contributing to peer problems. Their discussion builds on the foundation of a recently proposed model of affective social competence. In chapter 6, Sandstrom and Zakriski review the literature on the subjective experience of peer rejection with a discussion of the relation between peer problems and internalizing symptoms, attributions, and self-perceived social acceptance. In addition, they discuss the appraisal of the rejection experiences with peers as a causal mechanism between social experiences and negative internal experiences. In chapter 7, Kupersmidt and DeRosier provide a brief review of the literature on the relation between problematic peer experiences and negative outcomes and propose an integrative mediational model to explain these relations. This model includes negative social experiences, social–cognitive deficits, and unsupportive contextual factors. Their discussion of social–cognitive deficits focuses on the child's database, including social self-discrepancy theory, rigid or distorted cognitions of others, and cognitive deficits in coping with stress.

The third part, on family influences, consists of two chapters. In chapter 8, Grimes, Klein, and Putallaz review how parents' relationships with their own parents, past and current, influence their own parenting. They also review research on how parents' childhood and contemporary peer experiences affect their parenting and their children's development. Cowan and Cowan in chapter 9 examine the unique contribution of early peer rejection to antisocial behavior in later elementary school. Then, they report on the results of an intervention program with couples who have preschool-age children with the goals of enhancing marital and parent–child interactions and improving social and behavioral adjustment in children in kindergarten and first grade.

Three chapters in the fourth part address intervention and prevention. Chapter 10 by Coie's colleagues in the Conduct Problems Prevention Research Group provides a review of the literature on the consequences of peer rejection, causes and correlates of peer rejection, early interventions to improve social skills and reduce aggressive behavior, and an extensive discussion of the background, design, intervention model, and outcomes of the Fast Track experiment. Miller-Johnson and Costanzo in chapter 11 discuss a peer-based intervention designed to reduce antisocial and other risky health behaviors in adolescents. In chapter 12, Winn and Herman discuss practical issues including processes used and barriers encountered in trying to disseminate effective programs in community-based settings. They review the initiation, implementation, and conclusion phases of the dissemination process.

The final part consists of a chapter by Coie that provides an overview and integration of research on peer relations in relation to antisocial behavior. Because his contributions in peer relations have been so wide-ranging, no single chapter fully captures the scope or import of this body of knowledge. This volume, taken together, stands as a testament to the breadth and depth of his contributions.

Acknowledgments

Many authors of this volume, including ourselves, were very fortunate to have had Coie as our research and clinical mentor in graduate school. There is a consensus that Coie is a scholar with a brilliant and disciplined mind, high scientific standards, and clinical acumen. In addition, he was an empathic, compassionate, and supportive mentor. Despite his many accomplishments, Coie remained a humble, yet confident, person. He showed great respect to all he met regardless of rank or position, and it is these personal qualities that engendered such affection and loyalty from others.

We are grateful to the American Psychological Association Science Directorate for its generous support in making this Festschrift for John D. Coie possible. We also thank Susan Roth, chair, Department of Psychology: Social and Health Sciences at Duke University, for additional support of conference-related activities. We thank the Center for Child and Family Policy and the Terry Sanford Institute of Public Policy at Duke University for hosting the Festschrift in its beautiful building and providing crucial financial support.

We are very grateful to Barbara Pollock, assistant director of the Center for Child and Family Policy, for administrative and planning leadership and to Lynda Harrison for conference management. Finally, we extend our thanks to Mary Lynn Skutley and Tiffany Klaff for their assistance in the preparation of this volume.

Part I

Peer Status in Context

1

Sociometric Status and Peer Group Behavior: Previous Findings and Current Directions

Antonius H. N. Cillessen and Lara Mayeux

Researchers have long acknowledged that peer relationships form an important developmental context for children (e.g., Hartup, 1983). Although researchers have known this from a conceptual and theoretical perspective (e.g., Sullivan, 1953), recent empirical research on peer relations grew exponentially in part because of the presentation by Coie, Dodge, and Coppotelli (1982) of an improved method to study peer relations in groups. This new method was based on, and combined, essential elements of previous sociometric methods to study children's peer relationships. One of the most frequently studied topics in this new wave of research was the relationship between sociometric status and concurrent social behavior. The purpose of this chapter is to review this research on the concurrent behavioral correlates of sociometric status, to summarize past findings, and to examine in more detail the new developments and directions that are currently taking place in research on this topic.

To successfully examine the concurrent behavioral correlates of sociometric status, we need to establish what time frame is meant by the term *concurrent*. For practical purposes, the term concurrent here refers to the associations between sociometric status and social behavior when both have been assessed within the context of the same school year, typically in the same semester. It also includes studies in which sociometric status was assessed in the spring of the school year and behavioral measures were assessed at some point during the summer months immediately following that school year, usually in contrived playgroups in a lab setting. In the concluding chapter of Asher and Coie (1990), Coie introduced the terms *proximal* and *distal* to distinguish the immediate and long-term parts of a developmental time frame and applied these terms to both causes and consequences of peer relationships in childhood and adolescence. The frequently used term *concurrent correlates* in the peer relations literature coincides with the proximal (behavioral) causes and consequences of sociometric status. Distinguishing causes from consequences in this context, and the larger issue of causality per se, are discussed in the "Causality" section as one of the current directions in peer relations research.

Because the association between sociometric status and social behavior has been studied so frequently, the findings from this research may be perceived as well-known and well established. We demonstrate, however, that these findings are not always interpreted correctly. In addition, we point to and describe a series of interesting recent developments in the study of the association between sociometric status and peer group behavior that deserve our attention. Our discussion of these issues clearly demonstrates the important contribution that Coie has made to each of them. This chapter is structured around the discussion of five key issues in research on the status–behavior link. First, we address what is known from initial research on the behavioral correlates of sociometric status. Second, methodological issues relevant to current research with sociometric methods are discussed. Third, new research perspectives and current directions regarding the behavioral correlates of sociometric status are presented. Fourth, the association between sociometric status and social behavior varies across groups of children and social contexts and we discuss these moderators of the social status–social behavior link. Finally, the issue of causality in the association between peer status and behavior is addressed. We conclude with remarks pertaining to critical needs and directions for future research.

Sociometric Status and Social Behavior

The association between sociometric status and social behavior has been addressed in a large number of studies throughout the history of social development research since the 1930s, beginning with Koch's (1933) article on the patterns of playgroup behavior of preschool children of varying social status. Some book chapters included review sections of this literature (e.g., Hartup, 1983), but the first chapter devoted solely to this line of research was authored by Coie, Dodge, and Kupersmidt (1990). They provided a comprehensive review of the behavioral correlates of sociometric status, examining behavioral data derived from peer reports, teacher reports, and behavioral observers in experimental and field settings. A large number of behaviors were included in the review and summarized under three general categories: aggressive-disruptive behavior, withdrawn behavior, and peer sociability. The generalizations that the authors were able to make about children of different status types constitute the behavioral descriptions that researchers have used for years. Popular children were described as helpful and considerate, following the rules that regulate peer interaction and demonstrating academic and athletic competence. Rejected children were aggressive and disruptive and violated social rules. Neglected children were involved in more solitary play and less aggressive interaction than other children. Controversial children were highly active and aggressive. This pattern of behavior could easily provoke anger in the peer group under certain conditions. The disruptive activities of these children were also often seen as humorous by their peers (but not by their teachers, who would reprimand them).

An important feature of the Coie et al. (1990) review is its sensitivity to age differences in the association between behavior and peer status. The authors considered findings from three age groups (preschool, elementary school, and adolescence) separately. Thus, age was introduced as a moderator of the link between sociometric status and behavior, although the age comparisons were indirect rather than direct. The age comparisons were typically between different studies, not of various age groups compared directly and empirically within the same study. This made it somewhat difficult to reach general conclusions. An additional complicating factor is that the amount of data available for the different age groups was not identical. Specifically, much more was known about the behavioral correlates of sociometric status in middle childhood than in preschool or adolescent groups.

An occasional study in the Coie et al. (1990) review investigated the role of gender in the status–behavior link. But, as for age, the number of direct comparison studies was small, and most conclusions were based on indirect comparisons of results from different studies. In general, these findings suggested that aggression was a more important determinant of peer rejection for boys, whereas social withdrawal was a more important determinant of peer rejection for girls. These conclusions were based not on a direct test of moderator effects, but on an indirect comparison across studies. In addition, the studies reviewed were conducted before more refined distinctions were made between multiple forms of aggression (see Underwood, Galen, & Paquette, 2001, for a review) that have changed our perspective on the association between gender and aggression.

The narrative review by Coie et al. (1990) provided the basis for the next step of research in this field. Newcomb, Bukowski, and Pattee (1993) pointed out that it is difficult to conduct a narrative review in a research area where a large amount of information is available. Therefore, they conducted a statistical meta-analysis of the link between status and behavior using the same database used in the Coie et al. review, expanded to include recent studies. Further additions were made. First, the meta-analysis included self-report data that were not examined by Coie et al. Second, a fourth broadband behavioral category was added to the three examined by Coie et al. Although Coie et al. occasionally discussed academic abilities, Newcomb et al. added an explicit analysis of cognitive abilities to their meta-analysis.

For each of the four broadband categories, Newcomb et al. (1993) computed effect sizes (across studies) for the behavioral difference between each of the sociometric status groups—popular, rejected, neglected, and controversial—and the average group. Of the four broadband categories—aggression, withdrawal, peer sociability, and cognitive abilities—the largest effect sizes were found for aggression, emphasizing the importance of the study of antisocial behavior in childhood social development (Coie & Dodge, 1998). With a few exceptions, the resulting behavioral profiles of each status group were not surprising. Children of popular status were in general less aggressive and withdrawn, and more sociable, than average children. They also had stronger cognitive abilities than the average group. Neglected children were less aggressive and sociable than average, and the most socially withdrawn of all groups.

Rejected children demonstrated higher levels of aggression than average, the weakest cognitive abilities of all groups, and the lowest level of peer sociability. Controversial children had high levels of sociability as well as the highest levels of aggression of any status group.

Because Coie et al. (1990) had argued for the examination of specific behavioral categories rather than general categories alone, Newcomb et al. (1993) repeated their meta-analytic group comparisons for narrowband behavioral categories within the initial broadband categories. They examined three subcategories of aggression: disruptive behavior, physical aggression, and negative affect. Three narrowband examples of withdrawal were considered: loneliness, anxiety, and depression. Seven subtypes of sociability were examined: social interaction, communication skill, problem solving, positive social actions, positive social traits, friendship relations, and adult interaction. The differences between status groups for these narrowband categories replicated the findings for the broadband categories, with some detailed differences that are beyond the scope of this chapter (see Newcomb et al., 1993).

An important feature of the Newcomb et al. (1993) review is its focus on effect sizes. Consistent with recent statistical and conceptual guidelines, the focus on effect sizes rather than significance testing is an important goal for peer relations researchers (e.g., Thompson, 2001; Wilkinson & APA Task Force on Statistical Inference, 1999). By using effect sizes, Newcomb et al. have documented the robust relationships between sociometric status and social behavior. The findings are mostly consistent with and confirm what was found by Coie et al. (1990) in their narrative review. However, two findings in the Newcomb et al. review stand out as being less in line with the typical way sociometric status groups are described and that are often ignored in the peer relations literature. First, both reviews concluded that controversial children are highly aggressive. Researchers typically emphasize that rejected children are aggressive at levels over and above those exhibited by the children of other status groups. Although there is obviously an important correlation between rejection and aggression, the high aggression scores of the controversial group are often ignored. The high aggression scores of the controversial group can be explained by the association between peer-perceived popularity and aggression, which is discussed in the "Subtypes of Popularity" section.

The second finding to be emphasized from the Newcomb et al. review is that the neglected group, although less aggressive and sociable than average, is not characterized by especially high levels of social withdrawal. In fact, the average effect size for withdrawal for the neglected group was almost zero, making this group indistinguishable from the average group. Thus, the typical description of the neglected group as socially withdrawn does not fully describe the behavioral profile of this sociometric status group. The final word on the behavioral characteristics of the neglected group, however, may not be in. The behavioral profile yielded by sociometric studies may vary depending on how sociometric neglect is measured, for example, as low social impact (as was done in most recent studies) or as defined more strictly by exactly zero nominations received as liked-most and liked-least (as was done in the original studies).

Methodological Issues

In studies on the relationship between sociometric status and social behavior, a variety of different research methods have been used. There is variation in the methods of data collection, as well as in the methods of quantification of scores derived from them. Regarding this variation in methodology, three issues in particular deserve further consideration: (a) variation in the measurement of social behavior, (b) variation in the measurement of sociometric status, and (c) the use of categorical status types versus continuous dimensions of peer status.

Issue 1

Does it matter how social behavior is measured? Typically, four sources of information are considered in peer relations research: peer-, teacher-, and self-reports and detailed observations of behavior. Newcomb et al. (1993) analyzed these different sources directly in their review and found that source of information has some effects on the status–behavior link. In particular, they found that results using these different sources of information are more convergent for the behavioral correlates of the rejected and popular groups than for the neglected and controversial groups. In addition, although there is much consistency among results from peer-reports, teacher-reports, and behavior observations, the results of self-report data are in less agreement with the other three sources of information. The main reason for this is that self-report data show less variability, and therefore fewer distinctions, between the sociometric status groups than do the other three sources. Thus, self-reports seem less suited for examining behavioral characteristics associated with social status, although they are obviously essential for the assessment of internalizing behaviors that cannot be assessed as adequately with the other data collection methods.

Setting self-report data aside, Coie and Dodge (1988) conducted a direct comparison study of the behavioral correlates of sociometric status determined by peers, teachers, and observations. They compared status group differences according to the three sources of information and found both concordances and differences in the comparison of status groups. In general, however, information from the three sources was positively correlated. Coie and Dodge argued for the usefulness of each data source: peers are important because they provide the "inside view" of the peer group, and teachers provide their own unique adult perspective on the social behaviors of children they interact with almost daily. Observations by trained coders are important because they are not subject to the same biases that influence peers and teachers. This final source of information is perhaps the most important one, as previously argued (see, e.g., Coie, 1990; Coie & Dodge, 1988, 1998). It is also clearly one of the most difficult, logistically challenging, and time-consuming methods of data collection, but the use of observational methods in combination with experimental playgroup settings in the laboratory remains of primary importance for the peer relations field. With the initial playgroup studies he and his colleagues conducted (Coie

& Kupersmidt, 1983; Dodge, 1983; Putallaz, 1983), Coie created a high standard for the field and a tradition of observational lab studies that is continued even today by those he trained (see, e.g., Bagwell, Andreassi, & Keeley, 2001; Hubbard, 2001; Sandstrom, Cillessen, & Eisenhower, 2003; Underwood & Bjornstad, 2001; Zakriski & Coie, 1996).

Issue 2

Does it matter how sociometric status is measured? Clearly, it matters that peers assess sociometric status. As Cillessen, Terry, Coie, and Lochman (1992) demonstrated, judgments by teachers cannot replace the sociometric status information provided by the peer group. Terry and Coie (1991) demonstrated that different methods of using these unique peer assessments yield converging results. Although teachers cannot be used as an alternative to evaluations by peers, researchers are investigating alternatives to the traditional sociometric methods. There are various reasons to develop these alternative methods. One reason is that researchers have begun to apply sociometric methods to older age groups in which they have been used only infrequently in the past, such as in the middle school and high school context (e.g., Poulin & Dishion, 2002). The reference group for sociometric assessment in these grades is larger, requiring different methods of assessment, such as the use of unlimited nominations (Terry, 2000), the selection of expert nominators (Prinstein & Cillessen, 2003), or randomized subsets of votees (Gorman, Kim, & Schimmelbusch, 2001). Another reason for the further refinement of sociometric methods is that researchers conducting large-scale intervention studies need cost-effective methods that are proxies for full status assessment in large numbers of classrooms. Thus, sociometric methods have continued to evolve since the renewal of the method by Coie et al. (1982). The degree to which these new methods will change our perspective on the relationship between social status and behavior, as well as the relationship between status and social-cognitive and emotional variables, is unknown at this time. Future research on alternative methods to assess children's and adolescents' sociometric status will reveal the answers to this question.

Issue 3

Twenty years after the rediscovery of sociometric status types (Coie et al., 1982; Newcomb & Bukowski, 1983), an issue that is sometimes considered is whether the use of continuous dimensions of sociometric status should be preferred over the use of categorical status types. Typically, information present in continuous scores is lost when they are dichotomized. This principle also applies to the dimensions of social preference and social impact that underlie most modern sociometric classification systems. This statistical principle is reflected in the fact that the short-term and long-term stability of sociometric status categories is modest, whereas the stabilities of the underlying continuous dimensions are higher and comparable to the stabilities of the most stable dimensions in the social development field, such as aggression (Cillessen,

Bukowski, & Haselager, 2000; Coie & Dodge, 1983). Indeed, continuous scores for acceptance, rejection, preference, impact, or popularity have the advantage that they can be used more easily in certain statistical analysis techniques, such as growth curve modeling (Coie, Lochman, Terry, & Hyman, 1992; Coie, Terry, Lenox, Lochman, & Hyman, 1995) or structural equation modeling (Cillessen, Bryan, & Mayeux, 2003).

In spite of these advantages, the use of sociometric status types continues to be important. Types remain an important tool for the prediction of negative outcomes, especially when the types have been assessed more than once. For example, a large literature demonstrates that rejected status significantly predicts negative outcomes (see chap. 7, this volume). Moreover, classification of children as repeatedly rejected within the context of one school year significantly improved the prediction of negative outcomes one year later in fifth grade (Cillessen, 1999), a fact that could not be achieved easily by using the underlying continuous dimensions. Similarly, repeated assessments of peer rejection over consecutive school years, enabling the identification of chronically rejected peers, was also clearly related to the occurrence of externalizing and internalizing problems (DeRosier, Kupersmidt, & Patterson, 1994). Thus, the use of sociometric status classifications should not be discarded for both research purposes and clinical or intervention purposes. However, researchers do need to continue to investigate the methodological innovations that can optimize the reliability and short-term and long-term stability of sociometric status types.

New Perspectives on the Relationship Between Sociometric Status and Behavior

Subtypes of Rejection

The identification of subtypes of peer-rejected status (based on its behavioral correlates) is important for a number of reasons. In their meta-analysis, Newcomb et al. (1993) recognized that children of rejected status, as a group, were above average on both aggression and withdrawal, indicating behavioral heterogeneity. From the perspective of establishing a behavior—status link, it is quite obvious that not all children who are disliked by their peers are aggressive, disruptive, and aversive in social interaction (i.e., the typical stereotype of a peer-rejected child). Such behavior in children and adolescents is relatively rare, with only about half of rejected children being characterized this way (Cillessen, van IJzendoorn, van Lieshout, & Hartup, 1992). This characterization begs the question of what behaviors or characteristics the remainder of peer-rejected children have that contribute to their low status. French (1988, 1990) published the first typologies of rejected girls and boys based on factor analytic procedures of peer nomination and self-report data. For boys, two subtypes of rejected status emerged: an aggressive group and a withdrawn group. For girls, aggression did not play a strong functional role in distinguishing types of rejection. French identified one subgroup of girls he called "more deviant" in regard to their social and academic functioning than the second subgroup, but neither group was particularly aggressive in comparison to their peers. This focus on girls was especially important given the relative neglect of the topic of aggressive girls in the literature, although this situation is changing (see chap. 2, this volume).

Cillessen et al. (1992) replicated and extended the findings of French by both identifying four subtypes of rejection in boys and examining the stabilities of the four subtypes. The largest subgroup of rejected boys, comprising 48% of the main group, were aggressive, impulsive, and uncooperative. Furthermore, these boys were most likely to remain rejected one year later. A smaller subgroup of 13% was characterized as shy, withdrawn, and uncooperative. These boys also appeared to be most sensitive to their status as disliked. The two remaining rejected subgroups were not particularly deviant socially, although one group was more likely to endorse antisocial solutions in a hypothetical social problem-solving measure. These two groups of boys were neither aggressive nor withdrawn, yet scored low enough on social preference to be categorized as peer-rejected. These findings reemphasize the need for investigations of other behaviors and characteristics, above and beyond aggression and withdrawal, that are associated with being peer-rejected.

A study by Bierman, Smoot, and Aumiller (1993) may shed light on this issue. Bierman et al. similarly categorized boys as aggressive-rejected and nonaggressive-rejected, while adding a third group, aggressive-nonrejected, for further comparison. These authors found distinct clusters of behaviors that were associated with each category, with the profile of nonaggressive-rejected boys being especially informative. These boys, surprisingly, were no more shy and passive than average boys. They were, however, described by peers as socially awkward and incompetent, and as being insensitive to group norms, such as by having poor hygiene, exhibiting immature behavior, or having unusual habits. Thus, although these boys were not aversive in social interaction in the same way that an aggressive or disruptive peer might be, they were sufficiently socially inept to interfere with their peer relations. These behaviors may have characterized the nonaggressive and nonwithdrawn subtypes of rejected boys found in the Cillessen et al. (1992) study.

Further, Bierman et al. (1993) found that both aggressive-rejected boys and aggressive-nonrejected boys were significantly more physically aggressive than average boys, but the rejected children were also more argumentative and disruptive, as well as exhibiting more attention and social perception problems. These findings suggest that although it is possible to be highly aggressive and yet maintain high peer acceptance, the task becomes more difficult when a constellation of behavior and conduct problems that affect social interaction is present.

An issue related to the behavioral characteristics of subgroups of rejected children is their self-perceptions and interpretations of that rejection. An important issue surrounding the study of rejected children is that of distinguishing between *having* rejected status and the *experience* of being rejected; one would expect those children who are both rejected and aware of their rejected status to be quite different from those children who are rejected but not aware of it or, indeed, not rejected but perceive themselves to be so. Zakriski and Coie (1996) conducted a series of studies with fourth-grade children to examine these issues in the context of the aggressive-rejected versus nonaggressive-rejected dichotomy. They found that while nonaggressive-rejected children were generally realistic in their assessments of their own status, aggressive-rejected children overestimated their status. Moreover, both subgroups of rejected children were very accurate in assessing the social status of their peers (in some cases, more accurate than children of higher sociometric status), suggesting that the social perception deficits of aggressive-rejected children pertain only to social information directed at themselves, rather than social information in general. Indeed, in a separate experimental study, aggressive-rejected children rated self-directed rejection feedback more positively than other-directed rejection feedback; this self–other discrepancy was significantly greater than that of nonaggressive-rejected or average children. Zakriski and Coie argued that their results support the notion that aggressive-rejected children lack awareness of, and thus escape the lowered self-esteem and loneliness associated with peer rejection because of a tendency toward ego-defensiveness and denial of the true meaning of the social information directed at them.

The stability or chronicity of peer rejection can also be viewed as a means of creating subgroups of rejected status. Extreme cases of chronic rejection are interesting from the perspective of identifying the types or developmental pathways of behaviors that contribute to rejection over the long term. In a unique study, four subgroups of rejected boys were identified based on their behavioral and sociometric trajectories over a five-year period (Haselager, Cillessen, Hartup, van Lieshout, & Riksen-Walraven, 2002). Two groups showed relatively stable rejection. The first was characterized by average and stable levels of both aggression and prosocial behavior. The second was high on aggression but low to average on prosocial behavior. The two remaining groups showed improvements in their rejected status over time. Improvements in sociometric status were associated with a decrease in levels of aggression for one group, but the second "improving" subgroup was never particularly aggressive to begin with and showed no specific prosocial or antisocial changes that were obviously associated with their status improvements. Haselager et al. speculated that this subgroup was composed of boys who were initially rejected because of their shyness and withdrawal, and whose status improved when they became more assertive in their interactions with peers.

Subtypes of Popularity

Behavioral characteristics have also been found to distinguish children and adolescents belonging to two distinct groups of children and adolescents having popular status. Recent research has increasingly focused on the difference between peer popularity as a measure of social preference (*sociometric* popularity; e.g., Coie et al. 1982) and peer popularity as a measure of social visibility (*perceived* popularity; e.g., Parkhurst & Hopmeyer, 1998). The two conceptualizations of high-status children have roots in different research traditions: Sociometric popularity, from a developmental psychologist's perspective, refers to the level of acceptance of a child by his or her peer group, whereas studies of perceived popularity were initially conducted by ethological researchers in the sociology of education who were interested in the dynamic nature of high-status children's social groups.

The children and adolescents who belong to these two status groups have been shown to be quite different behaviorally. Adolescents nominated as sociometrically popular are described by peers as kind, trustworthy, coopera-tive, and sociable (LaFontana & Cillessen, 1999, 2002; Parkhurst & Hopmeyer, 1998). Those nominated as perceived popular, however, are characterized as athletic, cool, dominant, arrogant, and both physically and relationally aggressive by their peers and teachers (Parkhurst & Hopmeyer, 1998; Rodkin, Farmer, Pearl, & Van Acker, 2000; Rose, Lockerd, & Swenson, 2001). Perceived-popular children and adolescents who also belong to the sociometric-ally popular group are typically not described as aggressive or arrogant and are also nominated as kind and trustworthy (Parkhurst & Hopmeyer, 1998); the two conceptualizations of popularity are not mutually exclusive. Thus, although sociometrically popular youth are typically prosocial in their behavior toward peers, perceived-popular youth sometimes exhibit behavior that has a significant antisocial edge. Perhaps most important, the perceived-popular individuals often form the peer cliques that attain the highest status, social network centrality, and influence within their grade. This potential to influence and shape the behavior of others makes the behavioral developmental trajec-tory of perceived-popular children and adolescents an important area of study.

The pattern of behaviors associated with perceived popularity also calls into question the traditional assumption that popularity is an index of social competence—or, at least, calls into question researchers' notions of what social competence actually is. The often manipulative, Machiavellian nature of perceived-popular adolescents' social dealings cannot be called socially *in*competent if the end result of their behavior—their high status—is taken as a measure of its effectiveness. However, manipulation and aggression (either overt or indirect) are universally considered to be maladaptive in the developmental literature. If the distinction between sociometric and perceived popularity in peer relations research has accomplished anything, it has been to remind us that antisocial behaviors sometimes can be used in very adaptive ways.

The few existing studies of perceived popularity raise more questions than they answer. How do perceived-popular children obtain (and maintain) their high status? It does not appear to be through prosocial behavior that these children attain popularity, if their peers' and teachers' characterizations are any indication. How does physical and relational aggression play a role in becoming (or remaining) such a high-status member of the peer group? Why is it that children ascribe popularity to antisocial peers—indeed, do they even truly view them as popular? Given the reputational and image-related nature of perceived popularity, it is worth investigating the true nature of their peers' attitudes toward perceived-popular children. For example, LaFontana and Cillessen (1998) found that young adolescents were more likely to attribute hostile intent to hypothetical peers of perceived-popular status than to hypothetical peers of neutral status. These findings, in combina-tion with the unflattering characterizations of perceived-popular children by their peers (e.g., "stuck up"), suggest that "perceived popularity" might not really be a type of popularity at all, but rather an indication of social dominance (see Parkhurst & Hopmeyer, 1998). The answers to these questions and others are vitally important to our understanding of how social behavior relates to peer status, especially among adolescents.

Other distinctions within the construct of popularity have been identified as well. Just as groups of rejected children are heterogeneous in their composition, sociometric popularity is also associated with multiple behavioral profiles. In one of the first studies to focus on this heterogeneity, Rodkin et al. (2000) identified two subtypes of popular boys in early adolescence. Those popular boys who were aggressive, cool, and athletic were called "tough" by the researchers; those who were friendly, prosocial, academically oriented, and athletic were dubbed "model" boys. Similarly, Hartup, Cillessen, Haselager, Scholte, and van Lieshout (2002) identified three subtypes of popular boys in middle childhood and early adolescence. "Average" popular boys showed average levels of cooperation (compared with the other two subgroups of popular boys), below-average levels of aggression, and average levels of peer acceptance. "Stable high prosocial" popular boys were analogous to Rodkin et al.'s "model" boys, showing high levels of cooperation, very low levels of aggression, and high levels of acceptance. "Increasing antisocial" popular boys showed below-average levels of cooperation, high levels of aggression, and lower levels of acceptance. In addition, they found that each subtype of popularity was associated with its own unique developmental trajectory of status and behavior. For example, boys in the "increasing antisocial" group became less cooperative and more aggressive, yet more accepted, over time, whereas boys in the "stable high prosocial" group remained relatively stable on all measures over a five-year period. Thus, evidence is also emerging on heterogeneity of the popular status group. It remains to be seen whether a similar heterogeneity can be found for girls and whether the difference is the same across various age groups.

Moderators of the Association Between Sociometric Status and Social Behavior

Is the social status–social behavior link constant? Coie and Cillessen (1993) argued that the sociometric status of a child in the group reflects both the person and the situation. According to this point of view, one may expect that both individual characteristics and situational characteristics moderate the relationship between social status and social behavior. From an individual perspective, characteristics such as gender, ethnicity, and age can be distinguished. From a situational perspective, one can identify various social contextual factors that may moderate the status–behavior link, such as group norms or other aspects of classroom context.

Gender

The role of gender in the status–behavior association is a topic that has been the focus of much research over the past decade, especially with respect to gender differences in subtypes of aggression. A robust finding in the literature is the higher rate of physical aggression in males and relational aggression in females. This higher rate has been demonstrated in terms of the mean levels with which these behaviors occur in boys or girls. For example, Crick and Grotpeter (1995) found grade-school girls significantly more likely than boys to be nominated as relationally aggressive. Compare this with the many studies that have found boys to exhibit more physical and overt verbal aggression than girls (e.g., Coie et al., 1982; Maccoby & Jacklin, 1974). However, the identification of mean levels of these behaviors needs to be distinguished from the identification of predictive effects. Crick (1995), for example, found that relationally aggressive girls were more likely than nonaggressive girls to be peer-rejected; similarly, physically aggressive boys were more likely than non-aggressive boys to be peer-rejected (e.g., Coie et al., 1982). However, studies involving both relationally aggressive girls and boys and physically aggressive girls and boys are needed in order to test for the moderating effects of gender in the relationship between these types of behavior and peer status. One such study of early adolescents found that relational aggression increased the likelihood of being rejected for girls, but not for boys (Kaplan, Cillessen, & LaFontana, 1999). Another study found no such gender effect for either relational or overt aggression (Rose et al., 2002).

Ethnicity

The use of ethnicity as a moderator in the status–behavior link can answer questions about the role of race and ethnicity in both ethnically diverse and ethnically homogeneous schools and classrooms. The role of ethnicity, therefore, can be viewed as both an individual-difference factor and a contextual one. In this section, we address the role of ethnicity as both an individual characteristic that moderates the relationship between social behavior and peer status, and a contextual one. Thus, the first question is, does ethnicity influence the relationship between status and behavior when ethnic groups are represented relatively equally? In a sample that includes 40% African American and 60% White children, Cillessen (1994) found that leadership skills were much more important contributors to positive social preference for African American children than for White children. In a diverse sample of African American (26%), Latino (38%), and White (36%) children and adolescents, ethnicity was found to moderate the relationship between aggression and peer status. Both physical and relational aggression were associated with low status for African American and White children, but neither type of aggression predicted status for Latino children (Kaplan et al., 1999).

The situation may be different when the distribution of the ethnic groups is not equal—that is, when one ethnic group is in the minority. This occurred in the study by Coie et al. (1982), in which African American children were enrolled in predominantly White classrooms. When these African American children were nominated as leaders, they were more likely to be classified as controversial. When the White children were leaders, they were typically of popular status. In the study of popular boys by Rodkin and colleagues (Rodkin et al., 2000), African American boys were more likely to be part of the "tough" popular subgroup, especially if they were in classrooms in which White children were the majority. Thus, the link between aggression and popularity may be stronger for African American children when they are in a more visible position in the social group.

Age

As indicated earlier, an important feature of the Coie et al. (1990) review paper was its focus on the behavioral correlates of sociometric status for children in different age groups. From indirect comparisons between studies, we know that the role of aggression, for example, changes over time. Aggression was a contributor to high peer status for young age groups, probably because it was confounded with a high activity (play) level, which is also associated with high status at this stage in development. Aggression then became increasingly negatively associated with social preference as the age of the targets increased, presumably because aggression becomes less and less common as children grow older and, as a result, less accepted. However, recent evidence by researchers at the Oregon Social Learning Center (Poulin & Dishion, 2002), as well as from some of our own data, indicates that the relationship between aggression and status changes in early adolescence, when aggression and antisocial behavior tend to become less negatively associated with social preference than in earlier age groups. In a longitudinal study of boys, Pope, Bierman, and Mumma (1989) found teacher-rated aggression to predict negative sociometric nominations for third and fourth graders, but not for fifth and sixth graders (or, indeed, for first and second graders). In fact, as discussed above, aggression has actually been found to be moderately related to high peer status during the adolescent years (Mayeux, Bellmore, & Kaplan, 2002; Rodkin et al., 2000; Rose et al., 2001). Although age has not consistently been found to play a moderating role between behavior and status (e.g., Kaplan et al., 1999), more direct comparison studies such as the one by Pope et al. (1989) are needed, and changes with age also need to be examined for behaviors other than aggression.

Social Context

The social context is also an important moderator of the status–behavior link. Several aspects of group context have been found to have moderating effects. The social norms of the group in which a child is interacting have a significant influence on how that child's behavior will be interpreted and responded to. In a playgroup study involving seven- and nine-year-old boys, group variables were found to affect both the likelihood of occurrence of dyadic aggression and the type of reaction that aggression received by the rest of the group (DeRosier, Cillessen, Coie, & Dodge, 1994). More specifically, groups characterized by higher levels of physical activity, overall aversive behavior, and competition experienced more dyadic aggression among its members. The group was more likely to notice dyadic aggression or become physically or verbally involved if the boys involved in the aggressive act had played well together before the aggression occurred. Furthermore, if the group as a whole was characterized by playful competition, the dyadic aggression was discouraged; for groups in which aversive behavior was frequent, the aggression was actually encouraged. Although DeRosier et al. did not measure sociometric status in their study, its implications for the role of context in the status–behavior link are significant. These findings suggest that among groups of boys who discourage antisocial behavior, aggressive boys may be less accepted because of their deviance from the group norm. Among highly aggressive groups, boys who are not willing to display aggressive behavior may face similar problems.

In a similar study of boys placed in unfamiliar playgroups, individual solitary and aggressive behavior that deviated from the group's normative level was associated with lower peer acceptance among the rest of the playgroup (Boivin, Dodge, & Coie, 1995). This kind of "deviancy from group norms" effect has been termed the *person—group similarity model* by some researchers (Stormshak et al., 1999), and considerable empirical evidence is emerging to support the theory. Stormshak et al., for example, found that classroom levels of aggression and withdrawal moderated the effect of individual levels of these behaviors on sociometric status for a large sample of first graders. The more a child's individual level of aggression or withdrawal differed from the overall classroom level, the more likely the child was to experience rejection. As a result, children's aggressive or withdrawn behavior could work either in their favor or against them, depending on the classroom to which they were assigned. The classroom context has been found to affect the experience of victimization in a similar way in early adolescence. Cillessen and Nukulkij (2002) found that classroom levels of aggression moderated the relationship between several behavioral and psychosocial variables and victimization. For example, being victimized in a high-aggression classroom was associated with more negative outcomes (e.g., social isolation, sadness) than being victimized in low-aggression classrooms. In low-aggression classrooms, victimization was associated with high individual levels of aggression, providing further support for the person–group similarity model. Moreover, poor student–classroom fit actually worsened the effects of the victimization experience: Children who deviated from the class norm were lonelier, more anxious and withdrawn, and less sociable with their peers.

The importance of the context probably goes beyond the demonstration of the effects of specific social contextual variables. Both theoretically and empirically, the social context is central in much of the work presented here and elsewhere, whether it is at the level of dyadic peer relations, the peer system at large, family relations, or the neighborhood. An important research agenda is to determine which aspects of the social context are most strongly influential on social behavior. In the same way that cross-cultural psychologists refer to "unpacking the culture" as part of understanding the impact of the cultural context on child socialization, perhaps researchers need to "unpack" the immediate social context to understand the influence of peers, family, and neighborhood on children's social competence. Coie's work on the impact of social contextual factors on social status and peer group behavior has made an important contribution to this agenda.

Causality

The final issue addressed in this chapter concerns the causal relationship between sociometric status and social behavior. In their observational study, Coie and Kupersmidt (1983) determined that behavior influences status. Coie et al. (1992, 1995) demonstrated that status, specifically peer rejection, has long-term negative effects on later outcomes. Are there also short-term effects of sociometric status on social behavior? The answer to this question has implications for our view on the developmental importance of peer relationships. The short-term effects of peer relationships in children's behavior may demonstrate important developmental functions of peer interaction in the social lives of children. To phrase it differently, we are interested in determining whether sociometric status has any causal effects on children's immediate social behavior in addition to being a consequence of their behavior in the peer group. Evidence from the Coie and Kupersmidt (1983) and Dodge (1983) studies indicated the causal effects of behavior on status but did not address the reciprocal effects.

Cillessen et al. (2003) addressed the reciprocal influence between social status and social behavior in a short-term field study. They measured status and behavior, using various sources of information, at three points during the fourth-grade school year with a highly consistent sample of children. Causal modeling analyses with a continuous measure of peer status (social preference) demonstrated the causal effects of peer group behavior on peer status. Consistent with the results from observational studies, the results from this field study demonstrated that aggression and anxious–withdrawn behavior lead to low social preference. It is interesting that the results also demonstrated the reverse effects of social preference on behavior. Low social preference leads to increased aggression for girls, but not for boys, and to increased anxious–withdrawn behavior for both girls and boys. Thus, the concurrent association between sociometric status and social behavior should not be conceived as unidirectional, but rather as a reciprocal relationship.

It is often assumed that rejected status is an outcome resulting from children's aggressive or withdrawn behaviors in the peer group, despite evidence that rejected status can also influence behavior (e.g., Coie et al., 1992). In a recent longitudinal study of rejected boys, Haselager et al. (2002) provided further evidence to support this causal mechanism. They identified four subtypes of rejected kindergarten and first-grade boys and examined their behavioral and sociometric trajectories across a five-year period. As would be expected, changes in social behavior tended to be associated with changes in peer status. It is interesting, though, that the authors found changes in sociometric status either preceded or co-occurred with changes in behavior; behavioral changes never preceded changes in status. Taken together, these studies collectively suggest that sociometric status can function as both a predictor and an outcome of social behavior; to assume that it must be "either–or" is too simplistic. It should be emphasized, however, that the typical quasi-experimental nature of these designs does not permit strict causal conclusions, although strong suggestions of causality are implied by the advanced statistical methods that were used.

Conclusion

In conclusion, although the concurrent relationship between sociometric status and social behavior may seem old news at first, we hope we have demonstrated that a great number of exciting questions are related to this issue. Some of these questions have been answered over the past two decades in John Coie's research program. It is our agenda to address and resolve these questions further in the years to come.

References

Asher, S. R., & Coie, J. D. (1990). *Peer rejection in childhood*. New York: Cambridge University Press.

Bagwell, C. L., Andreassi, C. L., & Keeley, S. J. (2001, April). *The friendship of aggressive boys: Relationship quality and conflict management*. Paper presented at the biennial meeting of the Society for Research in Child Development, Minneapolis, MN.

Bierman, K. L., Smoot, D. L., & Aumiller, K. (1993). Characteristics of aggressive-rejected, aggressive (nonrejected), and rejected (nonaggressive) boys. *Child Development, 64,* 139–151.

Boivin, M., Dodge, K. A., & Coie, J. D. (1995). Individual-group behavioral similarity and peer status in experimental playgroups of boys: The social misfit revisited. *Journal of Personality and Social Psychology, 69,* 269–279.

Cillessen, A. H. N. (1994, July). *The role of ethnicity in the behavioral basis of children's sociometric status evaluations*. Paper presented at the biennial meeting of the International Society for the Study of Behavioral Development, Amsterdam, The Netherlands.

Cillessen, A. H. N. (1999, April). *The effects of repeated measures of peer status on the prediction of later adjustment*. Paper presented at the biennial meeting of the Society for Research in Child Development, Albuquerque, NM.

Cillessen, A. H. N., Bryan, A., & Mayeux, L. (2003). *Causal architecture of peer status, aggression, and anxious-withdrawn behavior: A short-term field study*. Unpublished manuscript, University of Connecticut.

Cillessen, A. H. N., Bukowski, W. M., & Haselager, G. J. T. (2000). Stability of sociometric categories. In A. H. N. Cillessen & W. M. Bukowski (Eds.), *New directions for child and adolescent development: Vol. 88. Recent advances in the measurement of acceptance and rejection in the peer system* (pp. 75–93). San Francisco: Jossey-Bass.

Cillessen, A. H. N., & Nukulkij, P. (2002, April). *Contextual factors moderate the effects of peer victimization in early adolescence*. Paper presented at the biennial meeting of the Society for Research on Adolescence, New Orleans, LA.

Cillessen, A. H. N., Terry, R., Coie, J. D., & Lochman, J. E. (1992, April). *Accuracy of teacher-identification of children's sociometric status positions*. Paper presented at the biennial Conference on Human Development, Atlanta, GA.

Cillessen, A. H. N., van IJzendoorn, H. W., van Lieshout, C. F. M., & Hartup, W. W. (1992). Heterogeneity among peer rejected boys: Subtypes and stabilities. *Child Development, 63,* 893–905.

Coie, J. D. (1990). Toward a theory of peer rejection. In S. R. Asher & J. D. Coie (Eds.), *Peer rejection in childhood* (pp. 365–401). New York: Cambridge University Press.

Coie, J. D., & Cillessen, A. H. N. (1993). Peer rejection: Origins and effects on children's development. *Current Directions in Psychological Science, 2*, 89–92.

Coie, J. D., & Dodge, K. A. (1983). Continuities and changes in children's social status: A five-year longitudinal study. *Merrill-Palmer Quarterly, 29*, 261–282.

Coie, J. D., & Dodge, K. A. (1988). Multiple sources of data on social behavior and social status in the school: A cross-age comparison. *Child Development, 59*, 815–829.

Coie, J. D., & Dodge, K. A. (1998). Aggression and antisocial behavior. In W. Damon (Series Ed.) & N. Eisenberg (Vol. Ed.), *Handbook of child psychology: Vol. 3. Social, emotional, and personality development* (5th ed., pp. 780–840). New York: Wiley.

Coie, J. D., Dodge, K. A., & Coppotelli, H. (1982). Dimensions and types of social status: A cross-age perspective. *Developmental Psychology, 18*, 557–569.

Coie, J. D., Dodge, K. A., & Kupersmidt, J. B. (1990). Peer group behavior and social status. In S. R. Asher & J. D. Coie (Eds.), *Peer rejection in childhood* (pp. 17–59). New York: Cambridge University Press.

Coie, J. D., & Kupersmidt, J. B. (1983). A behavioral analysis of emerging social status in boys' groups. *Child Development, 54*, 1400–1416.

Coie, J. D., Lochman, J. E., Terry, R., & Hyman, C. (1992). Predicting early adolescent disorder from childhood aggression and peer rejection. *Journal of Consulting and Clinical Psychology, 60*, 783–792.

Coie, J. D., Terry, R., Lenox, K. F., Lochman, J. E., & Hyman, C. (1995). Childhood peer rejection and aggression as predictors of stable patterns of adolescent disorder. *Development and Psychopathology, 7*, 697–713.

Crick, N. R. (1995). Relational aggression: The role of intent attributions, feelings of distress, and provocation type. *Development and Psychopathology, 7*, 313–321.

Crick, N. R., & Grotpeter, J. K. (1995). Relational aggression, gender, and social-psychological adjustment. *Child Development, 66*, 710–722.

DeRosier, M. E., Cillessen, A. H. N., Coie, J. D., & Dodge, K. A. (1994). Group context and children's aggressive behavior. *Child Development, 65*, 1068–1079.

DeRosier, M. E., Kupersmidt, J. B., & Patterson, C. J. (1994). Children's academic and behavioral adjustment as a function of the chronicity and proximity of peer rejection. *Child Development, 65*, 1799–1813.

Dodge, K. A. (1983). Behavioral antecedents of peer social status. *Child Development, 54*, 1386–1399.

French, D. C. (1988). Heterogeneity of peer-rejected boys: Aggressive and nonaggressive subtypes. *Child Development, 59*, 976–985.

French, D. C. (1990). Heterogeneity of peer-rejected girls. *Child Development, 61*, 2028–2031.

Gorman, A. H., Kim, J., & Schimmelbusch, A. (2001). The attributes adolescents associate with peer popularity and teacher preference. *Journal of School Psychology, 2,* 143–165.

Hartup, W. W. (1983). Peer relations. In P. H. Mussen (Series Ed.) & E. M. Hetherington (Vol. Ed.), *Handbook of child psychology: Vol. 4. Socialization, personality, and social development* (pp. 103–196). New York: Wiley.

Hartup, W. W., Cillessen, A. H. N., Haselager, G. J. T., Scholte, R. H. J., & van Lieshout, C. F. M. (2002). *Heterogeneity among popular boys: Subtypes and developmental trajectories.* Unpublished manuscript, University of Minnesota, Minneapolis.

Haselager, G. J. T., Cillessen, A. H. N., Hartup, W. W., van Lieshout, C. F. M., & Riksen-Walraven, J. M. A. (2002). Heterogeneity among peer rejected boys across middle childhood: Developmental pathways of social behavior. *Developmental Psychology, 38*, 446–456.

Hubbard, J. A. (2001). Emotion expression processes in children's peer interaction: The role of peer rejection, aggression, and gender. *Child Development, 72*, 1426–1438.

Kaplan, A. M., Cillessen, A. H. N., & LaFontana, K. M. (1999, April). *Effects of gender, ethnicity, and age on the relationship between social behavior and social status.* Paper presented at the annual meeting of the Eastern Psychological Association, Providence, RI.

Koch, H. L. (1933). Popularity in preschool children: Some related factors and a technique for its measurement. *Child Development, 4*, 164–175.

LaFontana, K. M., & Cillessen, A. H. N. (1998). The nature of children's stereotypes of popularity. *Social Development, 7*, 301–320.

LaFontana, K. M., & Cillessen, A. H. N. (1999). Children's interpersonal perceptions as a function of sociometric and peer-perceived popularity. *Journal of Genetic Psychology, 160,* 225–242.

LaFontana, K. M., & Cillessen, A. H. N. (2002). Children's perceptions of popular and unpopular peers: A multi-method assessment. *Developmental Psychology, 38,* 635–647.

Maccoby, E. E., & Jacklin, C. N. (1974). *The psychology of gender differences.* Stanford, CA: Stanford University Press.

Mayeux, L., Bellmore, A. D., & Kaplan, A. M. (2002, April). *Stability and correlates of perceived popularity in adolescence.* Paper presented at the biennial meeting of the Society for Research in Adolescence, New Orleans, LA.

Newcomb, A. F., & Bukowski, W. M. (1983). Social impact and social preference as determinants of children's peer group status. *Developmental Psychology, 19,* 856–867.

Newcomb, A. F., Bukowski, W. M., & Pattee, L. (1993). Children's peer relations: A meta-analytic review of popular, rejected, neglected, controversial, and average sociometric status. *Psychological Bulletin, 113,* 99–128.

Parkhurst, J. T., & Hopmeyer, A. (1998). Sociometric popularity and peer-perceived popularity: Two distinct dimensions of peer status. *Journal of Early Adolescence, 18,* 125–144.

Pope, A. W., Bierman, K. L., & Mumma, G. H. (1989). Relations between hyperactive and aggressive behaviors and peer relations at three elementary grade levels. *Journal of Abnormal Child Psychology, 17,* 253–267.

Poulin, F., & Dishion, T. J. (2002). *Methodological issues in the use of sociometric assessment with middle school youth.* Manuscript submitted for publication.

Prinstein, M. J., & Cillessen, A. H. N. (2003). Forms and functions of adolescent peer aggression associated with high levels of peer status. *Merrill-Palmer Quarterly, 49,* 310–342.

Putallaz, M. (1983). Predicting children's sociometric status from their behavior. *Child Development, 54,* 1417–1426.

Rodkin, P. C., Farmer, T. W., Pearl, R., & Van Acker, R. (2000). Heterogeneity of popular boys: Antisocial and prosocial configurations. *Developmental Psychology, 36,* 14–24.

Rose, A., Lockerd, E., & Swenson, L. (2001, April). *Prosocial behavior, overt aggression, and relational aggression among sociometrically popular and perceived popular children.* Paper presented at the biennial meeting of the Society for Research in Child Development, Minneapolis, MN.

Sandstrom, M. J., Cillessen, A. H. N., & Eisenhower, A. (2003). Children's appraisal of peer rejection experiences: Impact on social and emotional adjustment. *Social Development, 12,* 530–550.

Stormshak, E. A., Bierman, K. L., Bruschi, C., Dodge, K. A., Coie, J. D., & the Conduct Problems Prevention Research Group. (1999). The relation between behavior problems and peer preference in different classroom contexts. *Child Development, 70,* 169–182.

Sullivan, H. S. (1953). *The interpersonal theory of psychiatry.* New York: Norton.

Terry, R. (2000). Recent advances in measurement theory and the use of sociometric techniques. In A. H. N. Cillessen & W. M. Bukowski (Eds.), *New directions for child and adolescent development: Vol. 88. Recent advances in the measurement of acceptance and rejection in the peer system* (pp. 27–53). San Francisco: Jossey-Bass.

Terry, R., & Coie, J. D. (1991). A comparison of methods for defining sociometric status among children. *Developmental Psychology, 27,* 867–881.

Thompson, B. (2001). Significance, effect sizes, stepwise methods, and other issues: Strong arguments move the field. *Journal of Experimental Education, 70,* 80–93.

Underwood, M. K., & Bjornstad, G. J. (2001). Children's emotional experience of peer provocation: The relation between observed behavior and self-reports of emotions, expressions, and social goals. *International Journal of Behavioral Development, 25,* 320–330.

Underwood, M. K., Galen, B. R., & Paquette, J. A. (2001). Top ten challenges for understanding gender and aggression in children: Why can't we all just get along? *Social Development, 10,* 248–266.

Wilkinson, L., & APA Task Force on Statistical Inference. (1999). Statistical methods in psychology journals: Guidelines and explanations. *American Psychologist, 54,* 594–604.

Zakriski, A. L., & Coie, J. D. (1996). A comparison of aggressive-rejected and nonaggressive-rejected children's interpretation of self-directed and other-directed rejection. *Child Development, 67,* 1048–1070.

2

Gender and Peer Relations: Are the Two Gender Cultures Really All That Different?

Marion K. Underwood

Gender and children's peer relationships are intimately intertwined. Beginning in the third year of life, children strongly prefer to interact with peers of their own gender (Serbin, Moller, Gulko, Powlishta, & Colbourne, 1994). During the elementary school years, children continue to play mostly in same-gender groups, especially at school (Maccoby & Jacklin, 1987). In the past decade, gender scholars have proposed that because boys and girls interact mostly in same-gender groups that differ on many important dimensions, boys and girls grow up in separate gender cultures (see Maccoby, 1990, 1998; Thorne, 1986; Thorne & Luria, 1986, for compelling accounts of this perspective, referred to hereafter as Two Cultures Theory). As children move into preadolescence, they continue to value feeling included in their same-gender peer groups but become more interested in exploring the world of the other gender by engaging in *borderwork* (Sroufe, Bennett, Englund, Urban, & Shulman, 1993). Borderwork is brief but affectively intense interactions with members of the other gender that are charged with qualities of heterosexual romantic scripts, such as chasing and invasion, rituals of pollution, and teasing (Thorne & Luria, 1986).

Although gender researchers have long understood that gender heavily influences most if not all aspects of children's peer relationships, peer relations researchers have been more reluctant to study gender systematically. Many of the pioneering studies of peer relations were conducted with samples of only boys (e.g., Coie & Kupersmidt, 1983; Dodge, 1983; Putallaz, 1983). Although early peer relations researchers rarely stated their reasons for focusing exclusively on boys, several explanations seem possible. First, during the 1970s and 1980s, the explosion of research on children's peer relations was at least in part stimulated by evidence that peer problems in childhood predicted later negative outcomes, especially delinquency and antisocial behavior (Kohlberg, LaCrosse, & Ricks, 1972). Because aggression and delinquency have higher base rates in males (Coie & Dodge, 1998), perhaps it was a sensible choice to begin the careful examination of children's peer relation with samples of boys. Another straightforward reason for the focus on boys initially may have been limited resources. Many of the groundbreaking studies mentioned earlier involve observational methods and detailed coding, and testing for the effects of gender would have required doubling the size of the sample, which may not have been feasible. In recent years, the science of peer relations has become sophisticated enough that complex designs are needed to answer important questions even for one gender, and studying both is sometimes not practical (e.g., Coie et al., 1999). It may also be the case that the early focus on boys was due to the overall tendency for psychologists to study boys' development either because it was assumed that gender differences were not important, or because boys' development seemed more clear and straightforward (Freud, 1914/1961). Feminist scholars have gone so far as to argue that developmental psychology is largely based on theories and research on boys, and that girls' development is ". . .a world psychologists have found hard to trace, a territory where violence is rare and relationships remain safe" (Gilligan, 1982, p. 62).

Whatever the reasons, the historical lack of attention by peer relations researchers to the influence of gender seems to have set an unfortunate precedent that continues in the field today. Although recently investigators have begun to include girls in most peer relations research, the evidence for gender differences is mixed, and theories of gender development have only rarely been invoked to guide questions about the role of gender in children's peer groups. Even after almost three decades of numerous studies of children's peer relations, contemporary large-scale reviews still conclude that the role of gender is unclear and that future research is needed. In their meta-analysis of correlates of peer status, Newcomb, Bukowski, and Pattee (1993) did not test for gender differences and explained this limitation by writing ". . . researchers who have conducted two-dimensional sociometric studies either have failed to find gender differences or have used designs that include only boys as subjects" (p. 124). In a meta-analytic review of differences between children's friendship and nonfriendship relations, Newcomb and Bagwell (1995) similarly argued that gender "is not often a focus of research that examines differences between friends and non-friends" (p. 343). Although a respectable proportion of the studies of long-term outcomes associated with childhood peer problems have included girls in the samples, the only comprehensive review of the relation between childhood peer relations and later outcomes barely mentions gender (Parker & Asher, 1987). In the recent *Handbook of Child Psychology* chapter on peer relations, systematic discussion of gender is relegated to a single paragraph near the end of the chapter, which notes ". . . not much is known about the possibility that the peer culture can play different functions for boys and girls" (Rubin, Bukowski, & Parker, 1998, p. 682).

This lack of systematic attention to gender by peer relations researchers stands in stark contrast to the scholarship of investigators primarily interested in gender. (Here it is important to acknowledge that to make a distinction between gender researchers and peer relations researchers is at least in part artificial. However, as I argue in this chapter, these groups of investigators have been led by at least slightly different goals that may have influenced their methods and findings.) Two Cultures Theory postulates that "when boys and girls are engaged in social play, they congregate primarily with others of their own sex during the preschool and middle childhood years, and that different childhood 'cultures' prevail in these sex-segregated groups" (Maccoby, 1998, p. 1). Gender experts have argued that gender segregation and the different qualities of girls' and boys' peer groups contribute to the strengthening of potentially harmful gender stereotypes and lay the groundwork for difficulties in later other-gender relationships (Leaper, 1994; Maccoby, 1998). Maccoby (1990) argued that psychologists have been mistaken in claiming that parents are primarily responsible for the development of the Two Cultures phenomenon writing as follows:

> I would place most of the emphasis on the peer group as the setting in which children first discover the compatibility of same-sex others, in which boys first discover the requirements of maintaining one's status in the male hierarchy, and in which the gender of one's partners becomes supremely important." (p. 519).

How can Two Cultures Theory be reconciled with the lack of enthusiasm for investigating the role of gender among peer relations researchers? In this chapter I attempt to address this question by briefly reviewing the major tenets of Two Cultures Theory, then considering the extent to which recent research on peer relations supports these theoretical claims. Then, the chapter discusses possible reasons why gender and peer relations researchers seem to have reached different conclusions, and how peer relations researchers might test Two Cultures Theory more directly. To illustrate how this might be possible, I present two specific examples—research on gender differences in intimacy and research on relational aggression—in some detail. Last, the chapter proposes future directions both for peer relations research and for refining Two Cultures Theory.

Comprehensive reviews of gender and peer relations for multiple developmental periods are beyond the scope of this chapter. Therefore, this chapter relies on previous comprehensive reviews whenever possible, highlights mostly recent research, and addresses gender and peer relations for a single developmental period, middle childhood. As another note of clarification, because the term "sex" has sometimes been associated with viewing differences between boys and girls as primarily biological in origin (Leaper, 1991), this chapter instead uses the term *gender*.

Two Cultures Theory

Although its earliest origins are somewhat difficult to trace, Two Cultures Theory appears to have arisen in the 1980s from the work of researchers investigating children's discourse (Maltz & Borker, 1982), ethnographers observing children at elementary schools (e.g., Thorne, 1986; Thorne & Luria, 1986), and developmental psychologists observing young children's playmate choices in the lab and at schools (Maccoby & Jacklin, 1987). The basic argument of Two Cultures Theory is "The distinctive play styles of the two sexes manifest themselves in the distinctive cultures that develop within boys' and girls' groups as the children grow older" (Maccoby, 1998, p. 78).

Because a detailed presentation of a framework as elaborate as Two Cultures Theory cannot be included here, the following summary relies heavily on Maccoby's (1998) clear and authoritative review. According to Two Cultures Theory, boys' and girls' peer groups in middle childhood can be contrasted on several broad dimensions: play styles and activity preferences, discourse, group strength and power, and friendships (Maccoby, 1998).

Overall, boys' peer groups seem to focus more on issues of dominance and the maintenance of social status. Boys engage in higher rates of rough-and-tumble play and physical aggression than do girls (Coie & Dodge, 1998; Smith & Boulton, 1990). Boys seem more concerned with who is tougher than whom, with establishing and maintaining dominance (Maccoby, 1998). Boys' groups form dominance hierarchies fairly quickly that become quite stable (Pettit, Bakshi, Dodge, & Coie, 1990). Boys engage in more competitive activities than do girls, and much of boys' competitive activity takes place in groups (Crombie & DesJardins, 1993). Boys are more interested in games and stories about fighting and adventure, they participate more in organized sports, and overall, boys' interactions seem more closely tied to joint activities.

Although girls' and boys' discourse is similar in many important ways, there are some gender differences although the magnitude of these is not always large. Boys also seem to talk with each other more directly and forcefully than do girls, they are more likely to focus on themselves and to ignore the concerns of others, and they are more likely to assert their own positions in conflict situations (see Maccoby, 1998; Maltz & Borker, 1982, for reviews of gender differences in children's social discourse). Boys engage in more daring, chiding, challenging talk than girls, encouraging each other to take risks. Boys also engage in more "dirty" talk, conversation laden with sexual innuendo, than do girls (Thorne & Luria, 1986).

Although boys and girls report similarly strong same-gender preferences (Serbin, Powlishta, & Gulko, 1993), boys' groups seem more likely to exclude girls than vice versa. As Maccoby so aptly put it, "Boys . . . seem to play mainly to a male audience" (p. 52). Boys tend to scorn other boys who engage in feminine activities (Feiring & Lewis, 1987) and to reinforce each other's masculine behaviors. Boys' groups tend to be more inattentive and disconnected from adults. More than girls, boys' groups tend to take great glee from group violations of rules (Thorne & Luria, 1986).

Although boys do form reciprocal friendships, they are also concerned with the relationships with their larger, more structured male groups (Benenson, Apostoleris, & Parnass, 1997). Boys' friendships are thought to be characterized by less intimacy and self-disclosure, and more focused on mutual participation in activities (Maccoby, 1998).

In contrast, girls' interactions overall emphasize relationships more than activities, and dyadic friendships rather than large groups. Girls' interactions feature less rough-and-tumble play and physical aggression. (Although, as I discuss at length later in the chapter, some less direct forms of aggression may actually be more common among girls than boys.) Across cultures, girls seem less concerned with toughness and relative status in dominance hierarchies (Whiting & Edwards, 1988). Girls spend far less time than boys playing competitive games, and more time engaged in turn-taking activities (Crombie & DesJardins, 1993). Girls tend to choose friends more on the basis of compatibility and are more likely to gather simply for the pleasure of social contact. It is interesting that girls' activity preferences seem broader than boys'; girls are more interested in activities that are stereotypically masculine than boys are interested in more feminine pursuits (Bussey & Bandura, 1992).

In their social discourse, girls take turns talking more easily than boys and more often refer to what someone else has said (see Maltz & Borker, 1982, for a review). Girls tend to avoid conflict by acceding to another's desires. When conflicts arise, girls are more likely than boys to show their anger indirectly, to compromise, and to attempt to clarify the thoughts and wishes of the other person (Miller, Danaher, & Forbes, 1986). Girls report preferring to refrain from shouting and instead to assert their agendas more politely (Crick & Ladd, 1990). Whereas boys encourage each other to take risks and derive intense pleasure from risqué talk about sex, girls are more likely to discuss close relationships and themes of romance (Thorne & Luria, 1986).

The boundaries of girls' social groups appear to be less rigid than those for boys' groups in two important ways. First, girls are less likely to chastise other girls for engaging in masculine activities than boys are to sanction other boys for behaviors more typical of girls. Second, girls' groups are more attentive to and oriented toward the world of adults than are boys' groups. Girls' groups also seem to engage in less clandestine rule-breaking than boys' groups (Thorne & Luria, 1986).

Whereas boys seem to interact in dyads as well as larger, more structured groups, girls' interactions seem primarily focused on dyadic friendships (Maccoby, 1998). Some have argued that girls' groups are composed of interlocking, sometimes highly unstable dyads. Girls' friendships are thought to be more intimate than boys'; girls self-disclose more, touch each other more, seem to be more concerned about who is best friends with whom. Girls' friendships appear to be more closed and exclusive than boys' (see Daniels-Beirness, 1989, for a review).

In addition to emphasizing contrasting qualities of girls' and boys' groups, Two Cultures Theory also argues that these differences have important developmental consequences. One is that because gender segregation is so dramatic, girls and boys lack opportunities to interact with and recognize variance among the members of the other-gender group, which might contribute to the strengthening of harmful and limiting gender stereotypes (see Leaper, 1994, for a thoughtful discussion). Another important developmental consequence of separate gender cultures is that boys and girls might develop sufficiently different goals and values that make successful other-gender interactions less likely (see Maccoby, 1998, for a detailed analysis of the consequences of Two Cultures Theory for heterosexual relations, other-gender relations in the workplace, and parenting). Clearly, the claims of Two Cultures Theory are not insignificant, and the stakes in testing and elaborating this theory are not small.

Peer Relations Research and Two Cultures Theory

Given that Two Cultures Theory emphasizes contrasting qualities of boys' and girls' peer groups, how does research on the more traditional peer relations constructs fit with the theoretical claims outlined above? An exhaustive review of the sprawling field of peer relations is prevented by space constraints (see Rubin et al., 1998, for a thorough discussion). The following overview highlights research on three peer relations variables: friendships, social networks, peer status, and also the developmental outcomes associated with childhood peer relations. As stated earlier, in contrast to Two Worlds Theory, the most recent major reviews of the peer relations literatures tied to each of these constructs do not emphasize the role of gender or the salience of gender differences. What do classic and more contemporary studies suggest about the fit between Two Cultures Theory and research on children's peer relations?

Children's Friendships

Whereas Two Cultures Theory suggests that girls are more concerned with close relationships and that their friendships are more intimate and exclusive than boys', peer relations research suggests that gender differences are more complex. Time sampling studies suggest that although girls and boys do not differ in time spent with same-gender companions, girls spend more time thinking about same-gender peers than do boys (Richards, Crowe, Larson, & Swarr, 1998), and girls spend more time socializing whereas boys spend more time playing video games (Huston, Wright, Marquis, & Green, 1999).

In a thoughtful review of qualities of friendships in early adolescence, Berndt (1982) urged caution in concluding that girls' and boys' friendships differ in dramatic ways, and more contemporary research suggests that this warning is still well taken. When children are asked to name classmates as friends, there are usually not gender differences in number of friends listed (Berndt, 1982; Rose & Asher, 1999). Gender differences seem to be more apparent in investigations of children's ideas about friends or responses to hypothetical vignettes than in studies of particular friendships. When asked to describe friends, girls are more likely than boys to mention intimate interactions and self-disclosure (see Buhrmester & Prager, 1995, for a review), and girls report worrying more about friends' loyalty and rejection (Berndt, 1981). In responding to hypothetical vignettes about conflicts with friends, girls endorse relationship-maintenance goals more than do boys, and boys advocate instrumental and revenge goals more than do girls (Rose & Asher, 1999). However, when preadolescents are asked to report intimate self-disclosure and close knowledge of a particular best friend, no gender differences are found (Sharabany, Gershoni, & Hofman, 1981). Similarly, when fifth graders are asked to rate the intimacy of their same-gender friendships, no gender differences emerge (although sixth-grade girls rate their friendships as more intimate than do sixth-grade boys; Zarbatany, McDougall, & Hymel, 2000).

Researchers have more recently proposed that gender differences in intimacy may be confounded with social context; perhaps girls prefer to spend more time in activities and contexts in which intimacy is likely. If girls and boys are observed in the same social contexts, many of the gender differences in children's discourse become smaller and boys' and girls' conversations appear more similar than different (Leaper, 1994; Leaper, Tenenbaum, & Schaffer,

1999). Also, studying gender differences in intimacy only in the context of dyadic relationships may exaggerate gender differences, because the dyadic context elicits more intimacy and closeness than any other type of interaction. In an observational study of triads of third, fourth, and fifth graders, Lansford and Parker (1999) found that girls' triads engaged in more intimacy and information exchange, but there were no gender differences for other variables such as individual versus collective orientation, exuberance, hierarchical structure and leadership imbalance, responsiveness, and contention and conflict. In a study to be discussed in more detail below that directly tested Two Cultures Theory, the intimacy of same-gender friendships was related to participating in communal activities, which supports the suggestion that gender differences in friendship relations may be closely tied to activities and to particular social contexts (Zarbatany et al., 2000).

Recent peer relations research also casts doubt on the claim that girls' friendships are more exclusive than boys' (see Daniels-Beirness, 1989, for a review of some of the evidence for this argument). Girls and boys do not differ on preferences for dyadic versus triadic interactions (Lansford & Parker, 1999). In another laboratory study of triads in which a "guest" child attempted to join two "host" children of either the same or the opposite gender, host girls were more attentive to guests than boys, and girls' dyads were easier to join than boys' dyads were (Borja-Alvarez, Zarbatany, & Pepper, 1991). In a study in which dyads of host friends had the opportunity to choose between admitting a third child or winning a larger prize, girls were more likely than boys to allow the "guest" to join the interaction than were boys (Zarbatany, Van Brunschot, Meadows, & Pepper, 1996).

Although this brief discussion of gender differences in friendships is by no means a comprehensive review, contemporary peer relations research does not support the Two Worlds Theory claim that girls' friendships are more intimate and exclusive than boys' friendships. Overall, gender differences on friendship variables are stronger for questionnaire studies and less dramatic for observational investigations.

Children's Social Networks

Another central tenet of Two Cultures Theory is that girls' and boys' social networks differ in size and structure. Boys' networks are reputed to be larger and more hierarchically organized, whereas girls' networks are described as smaller and more horizontal in structure (see Daniels-Bierness, 1989; Maccoby, 1998, for reviews of this perspective). Some proponents of Two Cultures Theory also claim that boys' networks exert more influence over members to engage in deviance and rule breaking (Thorne & Luria, 1986).

Contemporary peer relations research does not support either of these claims. Using elegant Social Cognitive Map procedures that take into account multiple perspectives of peer group members and avoid many of the biases of self-reports, Cairns and Cairns (1994) have repeatedly found that girls' and boys' social networks do not differ in size. In another study with similar methods to identify peer cliques for a large sample of preadolescents, there were no gender differences in the size of peer cliques and girls and boys were equally likely to be central members of their respective cliques (Bagwell, Coie, Terry, & Lochman, 2000).

Several contemporary studies of peer group influence do not suggest strong gender differences in peer group socialization. Gender accounts for little of the variance in peer influence on the adjustment to junior high school (Berndt, Hawkins, & Jiao, 1999), children's school engagement (Sage & Kinderman, 1999), alcohol consumption (Pilgrim, Luo, & Urberg, 1999; Schulenberg et al., 1999), and cigarette smoking (Rose, Chassin Presson, & Sherman, 1999). However, Hartup (1999) urged caution in concluding that gender does not affect peer influence because so few investigations have considered both the gender of the child being socialized and the gender of the person or group doing the socialization.

Peer Status

Although Two Cultures Theory does not explicitly propose gender differences in the correlates of children's peer status, these differences seem worth examining for two reasons. First, if the two gender cultures really are so different, it stands to reason that different characteristics and behaviors might be associated with status among girls and boys. Second, peer status is a variable that has been of enormous interest to peer relations researchers, especially since the early 1980s when Coie, Dodge, and Coppotelli (1982) proposed their widely used, two-dimensional classification system.

Overall, most studies of peer status either do not include both genders or find few gender differences (Newcomb et al., 1993). It is interesting that the original Coie et al. (1982) study did include girls as well as boys and found that boys were more likely than girls to be classified as rejected. Boys were more often nominated by peers as "fights" and "seeks help"; girls were nominated more as "shy" and "cooperates"; and there were no gender differences in being nominated for "disrupts" and "leader."

Some research on peer status suggests that correlates of peer status might be associated with peer status to different degrees for boys and girls. For example, Coie and Dodge (1983) found that whereas peer nominations for "starts fights" and "leader" were strongly predictive of peer status for boys, the relationships between these items were less strong for girls. Across studies, physical aggression is a strong correlate of peer rejection for boys, but findings for girls are inconsistent (Coie & Dodge, 1998). For a sample of elementary school girls, peer nominations for aggression did not discriminate between rejected and nonrejected girls (French, 1990). Perhaps because so few girls fight, other behaviors might be more determining of their peer status. But, when rejection and aggression are treated as continuous variables, aggression is more strongly related to peer rejection for girls ($r = 0.73$) than for boys ($r = 0.37$; Lancelotta & Vaughn, 1989). Perhaps children are more likely to be perceived as deviant when they engage in gender nonnormative behaviors, such as physical aggression for girls (Crick, 1997), which at least partially supports the claim of Two Worlds Theory that the different cultures have different values and may sanction different behaviors.

Another important claim of Two Worlds Theory is that children strongly prefer to play with peers of the same gender, and this argument is well-supported by peer relations research on children's sociometric choices. Across many different studies, children nominate more same-gender peers for more positive items, and more other-gender peers for negative items (see Daniels-Bierness, 1989, for a detailed discussion of this phenomenon).

Long-Term Outcomes Associated With Childhood Peer Relations

If there is one point on which Two World Theorists and peer relations researchers agree, it is that children's peer relations have important consequences for future adjustment. Maccoby (1998) argued that gender segregation in childhood contributes to adult difficulties in other-gender relationships, with romantic partners, work colleagues, and coparents. A wealth of evidence suggests that childhood peer problems contribute to school dropout and criminality (Parker & Asher, 1987). Whether the developmental outcomes associated with childhood peer problems differ for boys and girls has been explored in only a few studies. Most previous research has been limited by investigation of outcomes that have higher base rates in males, such as violence, delinquency, school dropout, and substance abuse (Kupersmidt, Coie, & Dodge, 1990; Parker & Asher, 1987). It is not surprising that the predictive relationships between peer problems and outcomes with higher base rates for males are stronger for girls than boys (Kupersmidt et al., 1990). When outcomes more relevant to girls are examined, such as adolescent motherhood, peer variables are predictive for girls (Miller-Johnson et al., 1999; Underwood, Kupersmidt, & Coie, 1996). As more longitudinal data are collected with both girls and boys and as samples mature, it will be important for researchers to explore further how childhood peer problems predict later psychosocial adjustment similarly and differently for girls and boys. To move beyond predicting only severe maladjustment, it could be useful for peer relations researchers to be guided by Two Worlds Theory as to the types of challenges boys and girls might face as they come together in adult relationships.

Overall, peer relations research has not provided resounding support for Two Cultures Theory. As noted by Lansford and Parker (1999), some describe the differences between girls' and boys' friendships to be "so sweeping as to be almost irreconcilable" (p. 90), but peer relations researchers find gender differences in friendships, networks, and peer status to be much less dramatic.

Possible Reasons for the Disparate Conclusions of Gender and Peer Relations Researchers

Why do peer relations researchers and Two Cultures Theory proponents reach such different conclusions about gender and peer relations? One possible explanation is that peer relations and gender scholars have relied on different methods. Two Cultures Theory proponents often cite ethnographic research in support of their claims. Although ethnographies are useful for descriptive purposes and for hypothesis generation, they are less helpful for testing specific claims about the size, composition, and developmental functions of children's peer groups because they rely on less-than-systematic observations of only the most visible children. Another possible reason is that these different methods lead investigators to observe children's behaviors in different social contexts. Ethnographers quite reasonably observe children in naturalistic settings, often during free play when children are far from adults and have more control over their interactions. Peer relations researchers more often observe gender differences in controlled laboratory situations, or in classrooms where adults are present. Thorne (1986) has convincingly argued that other-gender interactions among children are much more relaxed and comfortable when they are involved in a compelling activity, they are not responsible for who is in the group, the group is composed on the basis of something other than gender, and the setting is less public. Playgrounds and classrooms differ on almost all of these dimensions, and these factors may affect the type of behavior seen with and across children's gender groups.

Another reason that peer relations and gender scholars make quite different claims about gender is that for both groups of researchers, the methods used are often confounded with the age group of the children studied, but in different ways. In support of Two Worlds Theory, gender scholars tend to cite mostly laboratory studies with preschool- and early school-age children (see Maccoby, 1998, for examples), and ethnographic studies of children in the later elementary (Thorne & Luria, 1986) and middle school years (Eder, Evans, & Parker, 1995). Peer relations researchers rely more on sociometric and questionnaire methods, especially with older children, and when they do observational studies, these are usually conducted in controlled laboratory settings or in classrooms. Given these vast differences in choices of methods to study different age groups, it is hardly surprising that findings and conclusions do not converge more.

As mentioned earlier, another prominent reason why peer relations researchers and gender scholars have reached such different conclusions is that for these two groups, choices about research design and methods have been led by different questions. For many gender scholars, quite naturally the focus of primary questions is on understanding gender. Peer relations researchers begin by posing questions about the peer group, and in many studies, gender is included as an additional, or even bothersome, variable.

Examples of Peer Relations Research
That Tests Two Cultures Theory

Although peer relations researchers seem fond of citing Two Worlds Theory in discussions sections when they encounter gender differences, expected or not, the design and conceptualization of peer relations research are rarely guided by this theoretical approach. There are, however, some notable exceptions to this point, two of which are discussed here: recent research on intimacy and on relational aggression.

Intimacy

As noted earlier, although Two Cultures Theory strongly suggests that girls' friendships are more close and intimate, research on gender differences in the intimacy of children's friendships has yielded conflicting findings. In a recent study, Zarbatany et al. (2000) designed a study to test a specific claim of Two Worlds Theory: that individual differences in friendship intimacy are related to participation in girls' and boys' peer cultures. The study assessed two dimensions of peer culture: the gender composition of the peer network and the extent to which children participated in agentic and communal activities with peers. If Two Cultures Theory is correct, girls would report greater friendship intimacy, boys with girls in their friendship networks would report greater intimacy with other boys, and friendship intimacy for both genders would be related to participation in more communal and fewer agentic activities.

The results supported some central tenets of Two Worlds Theory, but also suggested some ways in which the theory requires revision. As noted earlier, the expected gender difference in best friend intimacy emerged for sixth but not fifth graders. As hypothesized, boys who had girls included in their friendship networks reported greater intimacy with their same-gender best friends and the converse was not true for girls. Also as expected, participating in communal activities was related to greater same-gender friend intimacy. However, although Two Worlds Theory would predict that girls would participate in mostly communal activities and most of boys' activities would be agentic, this research found considerable overlap in the activities reported by girls and boys. Also, peer intimacy was reported to occur outside of the expected agentic contexts, and some agentic activities seemed to foster both agentic and communal goals, especially team sports for boys. Last, the peer culture variables were more strongly related to girls' friendship intimacy than to boys', suggesting that other dimensions may need to be considered to understand intimacy among young males.

Relational Aggression

Investigators have recently suggested that girls' aggression takes more subtle and indirect forms than physical fighting among boys, and that girls hurt each other by engaging in relational aggression: behavior designed to hurt someone else by harming their friendships or their social status (see Crick et al., 1999, for a thorough discussion of research to date on relational aggression). Although Two Cultures Theory is rarely explicitly invoked, much of the theory of relational aggression rests on the argument that when boys and girls want to hurt one another, they do so in the manner that damages what is most valued by their same-gender groups. The idea that boys' and girls' groups have different values that determine their social behavior is entirely consistent with Two Cultures Theory. Boys are assumed to value toughness and dominance, thus physical aggression is a powerful way for one boy to hurt another. Girls are characterized as valuing close friendships and intimacy; therefore, a potent way for one girl to hurt another is to damage her social relationships. When the expected gender difference is found for relational aggression (i.e., that girls are more relationally aggressive than boys), this variation on Two Cultures Theory is often invoked as an explanation.

As important as it is to examine more subtle forms of aggression among both boys and girls, the specific claims of Two Cultures Theory for relational aggression have rarely been tested directly and are not supported by conflicting findings regarding gender differences. Although it would be conceptually convenient to divide forms of aggression into the "girl" variety that damages relationships and the "boy" type that inflicts physical harm, this is likely not possible because most aggressive behaviors hurt in more than one way and serve multiple goals, and most studies find high correlations between physical and relational aggression (Underwood, Galen, & Paquette, 2001). The claim that relational aggression arises from the values of the girls' gender culture is also weakened by the fact that gender differences in relational aggression are inconsistent. Some studies find that girls are more relationally aggressive than boys are (see Crick et al., 1999), some investigations show no gender differences (e.g., Rys & Bear, 1997), and other research shows that boys are higher on relational aggression than girls are (Henington, Hughes, Cavell, & Thompson, 1998). Although the claims of Two Cultures Theory with respect to relational aggression have only been partially supported, the theory has guided an enormously useful body of research that has helped scholars acknowledge that girls and perhaps also boys can be mean in less physical but no less lethal ways.

Future Directions: Moving Beyond "Conceptual Dead Ends"

These two examples suggest that when peer relations researchers apply our methods to testing Two Cultures Theory, both the theory and our frameworks for understanding peer relations may be enhanced in fruitful ways. Two Cultures Theory suggests specific questions to be tested by peer relations researchers that might help us move beyond simply always including boys and girls and trying to explain gender differences ad hoc when they emerge. The sophisticated methods developed by peer relations researchers to measure specific characteristics of the peer group at multiple levels may be extremely useful tools for testing some of the claims of Two Cultures Theory.

As discussed in the previous section, there is already evidence that peer relations researchers are beginning to be guided by the claims of Two Cultures Theory. In addition, the claims of Two Cultures Theory are beginning to be qualified, interestingly, by one of its early proponents. On the basis of some of her more recent ethnographic work and on her reading of the peer relations literature, Thorne (1993) has challenged the central claims of Two Cultures Theory in the following important ways. Two Cultures Theory does not acknowledge the fluctuating significance of gender in ongoing social interaction and does not explain why some other-gender interactions are relaxed and comfortable. Two Cultures Theory tends to ignore the variation within gender groups and instead emphasizes between-groups differences, in "static and exaggerated dualities" (Thorne, 1993, p. 91). Two Cultures Theory tends to assume that the genders are separate and different, rather than attending to the role of gender in specific social contexts. Perhaps in part because the methods used by ethnographers tend to focus more on the dominant, highly visible children and less on those who are more quiet and more marginalized, Two Worlds Theory has largely failed to acknowledge that children can be masculine and feminine in a variety of ways.

Thorne (1993) concluded that Two Cultures Theory is contradicted by so much of the evidence that the theory has become a "conceptual dead end," but this conclusion seems premature. Thorne argued that "A more complex understanding of the dynamics of gender, of tensions and contradictions, and of the hopeful moments that lie within present arrangements, can broaden our sense of the possible" (p. 173). With our well-validated methods for measuring various qualities of children's peer groups, peer relations researchers can help test some of the compelling claims of Two Worlds Theory, to try to find out exactly where the tensions and contradictions are and where the theory needs to be refined. Two Cultures Theory can guide our questions in conceptually meaningful ways, so that we end up with more than just an assortment of seemingly unrelated gender differences.

To test the claims of Two Cultures Theory using peer relations methods, researchers could take several practical steps. It would be enormously helpful to study contexts that are meaningful for both genders: for example, observing children in smaller close spaces as well as when they are playing games on large areas of playgrounds. It is critically important to use multiple methods. Much of peer relations research has relied on peer nominations and question-naires and much of Two Cultures Theory has relied on less-than-systematic observations. It would be enormously fruitful to make use of new technologies that allow both more careful and less obtrusive observation in naturalistic settings, such as remote observational recording (see Pepler & Craig, 1995, for a discussion of this promising method). Researchers should also be mindful of how their own gender stereotypes might unwittingly bias how they study children's peer relations. It is usually difficult to be blind to gender in research; however, researchers can use multiple methods and coders blind to hypotheses whenever possible to guard against bias. We also need to consider such seem-ingly mundane details as the possible effects of gender of the researchers, perhaps by having research assistants of both genders administer question-naires or run play sessions or code data to test for gender effects. Researchers could benefit from collaborating with other-gender colleagues to guard against bias, which will of course require that we ensure that researchers of both genders continue to contribute to this research area by mentoring both men and women.

Most important, peer relations researchers can benefit by treating the claims of Two Cultures Theory as a beginning point, as a set of fascinating possibilities to be tested, rather than as the end of the story or an explanation to be summoned only when gender differences reveal themselves. By designing research specifically to test the claims of Two Cultures Theory, we open up the theory to empirical debate and help move our field beyond political correct-ness and conceptual dead ends. In a broader culture enamored of the belief that women and men are so different as to have originated from different planets, peer relations researchers need to stake our claim in the debate about gender. Unless we seriously consider gender as we design our research, the debate will continue without us, and we may unwittingly contribute to harmful gender stereotypes that likely underestimate boys as well as girls.

References

Bagwell, C. L., Coie, J. D., Terry, R. A., & Lochman, J. E. (2000). Peer clique participation and social status in preadolescence. *Merrill-Palmer Quarterly, 46*(2), 280–305.

Benenson, J. F., Apostoleris, N. H., & Parnass, J. (1997). Age and sex differences in dyadic and group interaction. *Developmental Psychology, 33*, 538–543.

Berndt, T. J. (1981). Relations between social cognition, nonsocial cognition, and social behavior: The case of friendship. In J. H. Flavell & L. D. Ross (Eds.), *Social cognitive development: Frontiers and possible futures* (pp. 176–199). Cambridge, England: Cambridge University Press.

Berndt, T. J. (1982). The features and effects of friendship in early adolescence. *Child Development, 53*, 1447–1460.

Berndt, T. J., Hawkins, J. A., & Jiao, Z. (1999). Influences of friends and friendships on adjustment to junior high school. *Merrill-Palmer Quarterly, 45*(1), 13–41.

Borja-Alvarez, T., Zarbatany, L., & Pepper, S. (1991). Contributions of male and female guests and host to peer group entry. *Child Development, 62*, 1079–1090.

Buhrmester, D. P., and Prager, K. (1995). Patterns and functions of self-disclosure during childhood and adolescence. In K. K. Rotenberg (Ed.), *Disclosure processes in children and adolescents* (pp. 10–56). New York: Cambridge University Press.

Bussey, K., & Bandura, A. (1992). Self-regulatory mechanisms governing gender development. *Child Development, 63*, 1236–1250.

Cairns, R. B., & Cairns, B. D. (1994). *Lifelines and risks: Pathways of youth in our time.* New York: Cambridge University Press.

Coie, J. D., Cillessen, A. H. N., Dodge, K. A., Hubbard, J. A., Schwartz, D., Lemerise, E. A., & Bateman, H. (1999). It takes two to fight: A test of relational factors and a method for assessing aggressive dyads. *Developmental Psychology, 35*, 1179–1188.

Coie, J. D., & Dodge, K. A. (1983). Continuities and changes in children's social status: A five-year longitudinal study. *Merrill-Palmer Quarterly, 29*(3), 261–282.

Coie, J. D., & Dodge, K. A. (1998). Aggression and antisocial behavior. In N. Eisenberg (Ed.), *Handbook of child psychology* (pp. 779–862). New York: Wiley.

Coie, J. D., Dodge, K. A., & Coppotelli, H. (1982). Dimensions and types of social status. *Developmental Psychology, 18*, 557–570.

Coie, J. D., & Kupersmidt, J. B. (1983). A behavioral analysis of emerging social status in boys' groups. *Child Development, 54*, 1400–1416.

Crick, N. R. (1997). Engagement in gender normative versus gender nonnormative forms of aggression: Links to social-psychological adjustment. *Developmental Psychology, 33*, 610–617.

Crick, N. R., & Ladd, G. (1990). Children's perceptions of the outcomes of social strategies: Do the ends justify being mean? *Developmental Psychology, 26*, 612–626.

Crick, N. R., Wellman, N. E., Casas, J. F., O'Brien, M. A., Nelson, D. A., Grotpeter, J. K., & Markon, K. (1999). Childhood aggression and gender: A new look at an old problem. In D. Bernstein (Ed.), *Nebraska Symposium on Motivation* (pp. 75–140). Lincoln: University of Nebraska Press.

Crombie, G., & DesJardins, M. (1993, April). *Predictors of gender: The relative importance of children's play, games, and personality characteristics.* Paper presented at the biennial meeting of the Society for Research in Child Development, New Orleans, LA.

Daniels-Beirness, T. (1989). Measuring peer status in boys and girls: A problem of apples and oranges? In B. H. Schneider, G. Attilli, J. Nader, & R. P. Weissberg (Eds.), *Social competence in developmental perspective* (pp. 107–120). Dordrecht, The Netherlands: Kluwer Academic.

Dodge, K. A. (1983). Behavioral antecedents of peer social status. *Child Development, 54*, 1386–1399.

Eder, D., Evans, C., & Parker, S. (1995). *School talk: Gender and adolescent culture*. New Brunswick, NJ: Rutgers University Press.

Feiring, C., & Lewis, M. (1987). The child's social network: Sex differences from three to six years. *Sex Roles, 17*, 621–636.

French, D. C. (1990). Heterogeneity of peer-rejected girls. *Child Development, 61*, 2028–2031.

Freud, S. (1961). On narcissism: An introduction. In J. Strachey (Trans. and Ed.), *The standard edition of the complete psychological works of Sigmund Freud*. London: Hogarth Press. (Original work published 1914)

Gilligan, C. (1982). *In a different voice*. Cambridge, MA: Harvard University Press.

Hartup, W. W. (1999). Constraints on peer socialization: Let me count the ways. *Merrill-Palmer Quarterly, 45*(1), 172–183.

Henington, C., Hughes, J. N., Cavell, T. A., & Thompson, B. (1998). The role of relational aggression in identifying boys and girls. *Journal of School Psychology, 36*(4), 457–477.

Huston, A. C., Wright, J. C., Marquis, J., & Green, S. B. (1999). How young children spend their time: Television and other activities. *Developmental Psychology, 35*, 912–925.

Kohlberg, L., LaCrosse, I., & Ricks, D. (1972). The predictability of adult mental health from childhood behavior. In B. B. Wolman (Ed.), *Manual of child psychopathology* (pp. 1217–1284). New York: McGraw-Hill.

Kupersmidt, J. B., Coie, J. D., & Dodge, K. A. (1990). The role of peer relationships in the development of disorder. In S. R. Asher & J. D. Coie (Eds.), *Peer rejection in childhood* (pp. 274–308). New York: Cambridge University Press.

Lancelotta, G. X., & Vaughn, S. (1989). Relation between types of aggression and sociometric status: Peer and teacher perceptions. *Journal of Educational Psychology, 81*, 86–90.

Lansford, J. E., & Parker, J. G. (1999). Children's interactions in triads: Behavioral profiles and effects of gender and patterns of friendship among members. *Developmental Psychology, 35*, 80–93.

Leaper, C. (1991). Influence and involvement in children's discourse: Age, gender, and partner effects. *Child Development, 62*, 797–811.

Leaper, C. (1994). Exploring the consequences of gender segregation on social relationships. In C. Leaper (Ed.), *New directions for child development: Vol. 65. Childhood gender segregation: Causes and consequences* (pp. 67–86). San Francisco: Jossey-Bass.

Leaper, C., Tenenbaum, H. R., & Schaffer, T. G. (1999). Communication patterns of African American girls and boys from low-income, urban backgrounds. *Child Development, 70*, 1489–1503.

Maccoby, E. E. (1990). Gender and relationships: A developmental account. *American Psychologist, 45*, 513–520.

Maccoby, E. E. (1998). *The two sexes: Growing up apart, coming together*. Cambridge, MA: Harvard University Press.

Maccoby, E. E., & Jacklin, C. N. (1987). Gender segregation in childhood. In H. Reese (Ed.), *Advances in child behavior and development* (pp. 239–287). New York: Academic Press.

Maltz, D. N., & Borker, R. A. (1982). A cultural approach to male-female miscommunication. In J. J. Gumperz (Ed.), *Language and social identity* (pp. 195–216). New York: Cambridge University Press.

Miller, P. M., Danaher, D. L., & Forbes, D. (1986). Sex-related strategies for coping with interpersonal conflict in children ages 5 to 7. *Development Psychology, 22*, 543–548.

Miller-Johnson, S., Winn, D. M., Coie, J. D., Maumary-Gremaud, A., Hyman, C., Terry, R., & Lochman, J. (1999). Motherhood during the teen years: A developmental perspective on risk factors for childbearing. *Development and Psychopathology, 11*(1), 85–100.

Newcomb, A. F., & Bagwell, C. L. (1995). Children's friendship relations: A meta-analytic review. *Psychological Bulletin, 117*, 306–347.

Newcomb, A. F., Bukowski, W. M., & Pattee, L. (1993). Children's peer relations: A meta-analytic review of popular, rejected, neglected, controversial, and average status. *Psychological Bulletin, 113*, 99–128.

Parker, J. G., & Asher, S. R. (1987). Peer relations and later personal adjustment: Are low accepted children at risk? *Psychological Bulletin, 102*, 357–389.

Pepler, D. J., & Craig, W. M. (1995). A peek behind the fence: Naturalistic observations of aggressive children with remote audiovisual recording. *Developmental Psychology, 31*, 357–389.

Pettit, G. S., Bakshi, A., Dodge, K. A., & Coie, J. D. (1990). The emergence of social dominance in young boys' play groups: Developmental differences and behavioral correlates. *Developmental Psychology, 26,* 1017–1025.

Pilgrim, C., Luo, Q., & Urberg, K. A. (1999). Influence of peers, parents, and individual characteristics on adolescent drug use in two cultures. *Merrill-Palmer Quarterly, 45*(1), 85–107.

Putallaz, M. (1983). Predicting children's sociometric status from their behavior. *Child Development, 54,* 1417–1426.

Richards, M. H., Crowe, P. A., Larson, R., & Swarr, A. (1998). Developmental patterns and gender differences in the experience of peer companionship during adolescence. *Child Development, 69*(1), 154–163.

Rose, A. J., & Asher, S. R. (1999). Children's goals and strategies in response to conflicts within a friendship. *Developmental Psychology, 35,* 69–79.

Rose, J. S., Chassin, L., Presson, C. C., & Sherman, S. J. (1999). Peer influences on adolescent cigarette smoking: A prospective sibling analysis. *Merrill-Palmer Quarterly, 45*(1), 62–84.

Rubin, K. H., Bukowski, W., & Parker, J. G. (1998). Peer interactions, relationships, and groups. In N. Eisenberg (Ed.), *Handbook of child psychology* (pp. 619–700). New York: Wiley.

Rys, G. S., & Bear, G. G. (1997). Relational aggression and peer relations: Gender and developmental issues. *Merrill-Palmer Quarterly, 43*(21), 87–106.

Sage, N. A., & Kinderman, T. A. (1999). Peer networks, behavior contingencies, and children's engagement in the classroom. *Merrill-Palmer Quarterly, 45*(1), 143–171.

Schulenberg, J., Maggs, J. L., Dielman, T. E., Leech, S. L., Kloska, D. D., Shope, J. T., & Laetz, V. B. (1999). On peer influences to get drunk: A panel study of young adolescents. *Merrill-Palmer Quarterly, 45*(1), 108–141.

Serbin, L. A., Moller, L. C., Gulko, J., Powlishta, K. K., & Colbourne, K. A. (1994). The emergence of gender segregation in toddler playgroups. In C. Leaper (Ed.), *New directions for child development: Vol. 65. Childhood gender segregation: Causes and consequences* (pp. 7–18). San Francisco: Jossey-Bass.

Serbin, L. A., Powlishta, K. K., & Gulko, J. (1993). The development of sex typing in middle childhood. *Monographs of the Society for Research in Child Development, 58*(2, Serial No. 232), 1–75.

Sharabany, R., Gershoni, R., & Hofman, J. E. (1981). Girlfriend, boyfriend: Age and sex differences in intimate friendship. *Developmental Psychology, 17,* 800–808.

Smith, P. K., & Boulton, M. (1990). Rough and tumble play, aggression, and dominance: Perception and behavior in children's encounters. *Human Development, 33*(4–5), 271–282.

Sroufe, L. A., Bennett, C., Englund, M., Urban, J., & Shulman, S. (1993). The significance of gender boundaries in preadolescence: Contemporary correlates and antecedents of boundary violation and maintenance. *Child Development, 64,* 455–466.

Thorne, B. (1986). Girls and boys together but mostly apart: Gender arrangements in elementary schools. In W. W. Hartup & Z. Rubin (Eds.), *Relationships and development* (pp. 167–184). Hillsdale, NJ: Erlbaum.

Thorne, B. (1993). *Gender play: Girls and boys in school.* New Brunswick, NJ: Rutgers University Press.

Thorne, B., & Luria, Z. (1986). Sexuality and gender in children's daily worlds. *Social Problems, 33,* 176–190.

Underwood, M. K., Galen, B. R., & Paquette, J. A. (2001). Top ten challenges for understanding aggression and gender: Why can't we all just get along? *Social Development, 10,* 428–266.

Underwood, M. K., Kupersmidt, J. B., & Coie, J. D. (1996). Childhood peer sociometric status and aggression as predictors of adolescent childbearing. *Journal of Research on Adolescence, 6*(2), 201–223.

Whiting, B. B., & Edwards, C. P. (1988). *Children of different worlds: The formation of social behavior.* Cambridge, MA: Harvard University Press.

Zarbatany, L., McDougall, P., & Hymel, S. (2000). Gender-differentiated experience in the peer culture: Links to intimacy in preadolescence. *Social Development, 9*(1), 62–9.

Zarbatany, L., Van Brunschot, M., Meadows, K., & Pepper, S. (1996). Effects of friendship and gender on peer group entry. *Child Development, 67,* 2287–2300.

3

Friendships, Peer Networks, and Antisocial Behavior

Catherine L. Bagwell

The assumption that children's relationships with their peers and friends contribute to their social and emotional development is easily accepted by most contemporary child development researchers (Parker, Rubin, Price, & De-Rosier, 1995; Rubin, Bukowski, & Parker, 1998). Indeed, much of the current research on peer relations focuses on the identification of specific functions of children's relationships with peers, individual differences in peer experiences and their association with current and future adjustment, and the unique influence of different types of peer relations on children's development. Research on these questions typically proceeds from the perspective that children who successfully form friendships and are well-liked in the peer group follow developmental trajectories leading to positive adjustment. In contrast, children who fail in these areas of social competence with peers, either by failing to establish close friendships or by being rejected in the larger peer group, are expected to experience a myriad of maladaptive outcomes. We are now learning, however, that peer relations are not unidimensional and that some of the friendships children successfully establish may in fact serve as risk factors for particular adjustment difficulties. The purpose of the current chapter is to examine this hypothesis by considering the potential contributions of children's friendships to the development and maintenance of aggressive and anti-social behavior.

The Developmental Significance of Friendship

Since the time of Aristotle, philosophers, sociologists, and psychologists have elucidated the contributions of friendship to healthy adaptation across the life span. The empirical literature on children's friendships, however, reveals a bias toward considering the positive qualities and developmental contributions of this relationship. In contrast, the related literature on children's status within the peer group has attended to the maladaptive properties of poor peer relations, namely peer rejection (Coie & Dodge, 1983; Coie, Terry, Lenox, Lochman, & Hyman, 1995; Kupersmidt, Coie, & Dodge, 1990; Parker & Asher,

1987). The current state of our knowledge about friendship relations permits us to move beyond descriptions of children's interactions with their friends and conceptions of their friendships and to focus on the developmental significance of this relationship and the processes through which friendship relations may move a child along particular developmental trajectories, including toward delinquency and antisocial behavior.

Two assumptions are essential in supporting the hypothesis that friendships play a unique role in the antisocial activity of children and adolescents. First, clear distinctions must be drawn between children's experience with friends and their more general peer relations and position in the larger peer group structure. These aspects of children's social relations with peers are conceptually and qualitatively different experiences, and they are identified in methodologically distinct ways as well (Bukowski & Hoza, 1989; Rubin et al., 1998).

Friendships represent strong affective ties between two individuals who view themselves as equals. Mutual affection, reciprocity, and commitment to the other are quintessential elements of a dyadic friendship (Hartup, 1993). The concept of reciprocity or mutuality is what distinguishes friendship from mere interpersonal attraction. Friendships serve at least three functions (Hartup, 1992). First, they are contexts for the acquisition of social and emotional skills and competencies (Hartup, 1992; Newcomb & Bagwell, 1995). Second, friends are emotional and cognitive resources for one another, providing support and validation of self-worth (Furman & Robbins, 1985; Parker et al., 1995; Sullivan, 1953). Finally, friendships may serve as precursors to future relationships in adolescence and adulthood (Furman, 1999; Hartup, 1996; Hartup & Sancilio, 1986).

In contrast, popularity or acceptance by the peer group is a unilateral concept that describes how members of the peer group feel about an individual child with regard to liking and disliking (Bukowski & Hoza, 1989). The tie between popularity and friendship is their association with liking. Specifically, liking is the acceptance dimension of peer status, and mutual liking is a condition of friendship. Being popular does not guarantee that a child will have a friend, yet a well-liked child has many more opportunities for friendship than does a disliked child (Bukowski, Pizzamiglio, Newcomb, & Hoza, 1996). Because popularity and friendship have at least some distinct emotional and behavioral correlates, it is reasonable to assume that the developmental implications of social status in the peer group and of having close friendships would also differ (Bukowski & Hoza, 1989; Furman & Robbins, 1985; Newcomb & Bagwell, 1996).

Some limited but convincing empirical evidence supports the assumption that friendship and peer acceptance contribute uniquely to positive social and emotional adjustment. For example, both having more mutual friends and low peer rejection are independently related to more positive self-concept and academic adjustment (Vandell & Hembree, 1994) and to less loneliness (Parker & Asher, 1993). In addition, over the long term, having friends and peer rejection are related to different domains of adult adjustment. In a follow-up study from preadolescence to adulthood, not having a close friend in preadolescence was associated with symptoms of depression and lower self-competence in adulthood. In contrast, peer rejection was uniquely associated with low aspirations and school performance and less involvement in community activities in adulthood (Bagwell, Newcomb, & Bukowski, 1998; Bagwell, Schmidt, Newcomb, & Bukowski, 2001).

The second important assumption in considering friendships as determinants of aggressive and antisocial behavior is the recognition that friendships are not solely positive experiences. Only recently have investigators begun to consider potentially negative features of friendship (Berndt, 1992; Hartup, 1996, Newcomb & Bagwell, 1996). Hartup (1996) contends that friendships may contain both risk and protective factors, and thus a romanticized view of this special type of peer relationship inaccurately portrays friendship's contributions to long-term adjustment. Clearly, the processes through which some friendships might contribute to children's antisocial behavior represent risk factors that warrant careful empirical attention.

This chapter examines the role of friendship in the development and maintenance of aggression and antisocial behavior by reviewing the literature addressing four questions:

1. What are the characteristics, features, and quality of aggressive and antisocial children's friendships?
2. What processes within friends' interactions might contribute to escalations in antisocial behavior?
3. What is the role of larger friendship networks in antisocial and aggressive behavior?
4. How do prevention and intervention efforts contribute to our understanding of the links between friendship and antisocial behavior?

Features and Quality of Aggressive and Antisocial Children's Friendships

To specify the role of friendships in the development and maintenance of antisocial behavior, researchers need to examine the features and characteristics of the mutual friendships of aggressive children. Although some theorists assert that antisocial children and adolescents are socially isolated and are unable to form the intense affective bond that characterizes a close friendship, a social learning perspective suggests that friendships between antisocial youth provide a critical training ground for delinquent and antisocial behavior (e.g., Coie & Dodge, 1998; Dishion, French, & Patterson, 1995; Patterson, Reid, & Dishion, 1992). The number of existing empirical studies comparing the friendships of antisocial and nonantisocial children and adolescents is small, yet a clear conclusion is that many aggressive and antisocial children have friends, and their disruptive characteristics do not automatically banish them from involvement in friendship networks or prohibit them from forming mutual friendships. As such, several important questions can be answered through this line of research: Do friendships between antisocial children have different features than friendships between nonantisocial children? Does the broader social context of these friendships differ? Are these friendships of lower quality than other children's relationships? Answers to these descriptive questions may then provide a foundation for understanding the specific processes involved in promoting antisocial behavior in the context of friendship relations.

Positive and Negative Features and Friendship Quality

In a series of studies, Dishion and his colleagues investigated the features and characteristics of friendships between early adolescent boys participating in the Oregon Youth Study (OYS). Although microsocial coding of the rates of positive and negative engagement was not related to the friends' antisocial behavior, observer ratings of social skills and noxious behavior were associated with the level of antisocial behavior of the dyad. Boys in the most antisocial dyads showed significant reciprocity in their negative coercive behavior such that when one friend exhibited negative behavior, the other friend was likely to respond in the same way (Dishion, Andrews, & Crosby, 1995).

There is some evidence to suggest that antisocial friends also show deficits in positive behavior in their interactions, including less positive affect and social competence (Panella & Henggeler, 1986). These findings on social competence are particularly important in light of the context that friendships provide for the development of social skills and social competencies. Some aspect of the relationship between antisocial boys and their friends may hinder this friendship function, or perhaps, antisocial boys who are already deficient in social skills are not able to encourage the development of such skills in their friends.

The relative amount of positive and negative features in a friendship defines its quality (Berndt, 1996). Measures of friendship quality include features such as instrumental help, support and security, intimacy and affection, companionship, and conflict (Bukowski, Hoza, & Boivin, 1994; Parker & Asher, 1993). There is some debate as to whether these features are truly distinct aspects of a friendship or whether friendship quality is more efficiently described simply in terms of a positive and a negative dimension (Berndt, 1996). Conclusions about the importance of having friends are usually confounded with friendship quality because having friends is assumed to mean having supportive, high-quality friendships (Hartup, 1996), yet quality is an important dimension of friendship in its own right. First, it is high-quality friendships that theorists such as Sullivan (1953) determined to be necessary for promoting positive well-being—validating self-worth, learning skills of collaboration, becoming sensitive to another's needs. Second, quality of the relationship may be correlated with the degree of influence the friends have on one another's behavior, although the evidence for this hypothesis is inconsistent (Berndt, 1999).

In addition to studies of the features of aggressive and antisocial children's relationships with their friends, a handful of studies have examined the quality of the relationship between aggressive children and their friends. Among adolescents in the OYS, antisocial boys and their friends rated their friendship more negatively than did nonantisocial boys (Poulin, Dishion, & Haas, 1999). However, there was no difference between antisocial and nonantisocial friends in their perception of a positive dimension in their friendship. Perhaps more important, the antisocial friends did not have a shared perspective on their relationship. In fact, the perceptions of the positive and negative dimensions of antisocial boys' friendships were not at all associated with their friend's view of the quality of the same relationship.

In our own work, we invited aggressive and nonaggressive preadolescent boys (mean age = 10 years, 6 months) to participate with their best friend in individual interviews about their relationship and in several play tasks. On the basis of both friends' reports, aggressive and nonaggressive boys did not differ significantly in the quality of their friendship in the domains of companionship, closeness, help, security, or conflict (Bagwell, Andreassi, & Keeley, 2001). Similar to the older boys in the Poulin et al. (1999) study, aggressive friends did not often agree in their perceptions of their friendship (rs range from –0.11 on security to 0.40 on closeness), but neither did nonaggressive friends (rs range from 0.01 on closeness to 0.51 on conflict). Despite the lack of differences in the quality of the friendships of aggressive and nonaggressive boys from their own reports, interviewers rated aggressive boys' friendships as much lower in quality based on the boys' open-ended descriptions of their relationship in a semistructured interview (e.g., what they do together, what they like most and least about their friendship, what makes their friendship special).

What might account for the limited differences in quality based on the children's perceptions but the large differences according to observers? It is possible that aggressive children do not perceive their friendships as inadequate or lower in quality or that they perceive similar benefits from different features of their friendships. An alternative hypothesis is that aggressive children experience a positive illusory bias in their interpretation and evaluation of their friendship. Such a bias has been shown for children with attention-deficit/hyperactivity disorder when evaluating their self-competence (Hoza, Pelham, Dobbs, Owens, & Pillow, 2002), and we know that aggressive children have trouble accurately encoding and interpreting cues in social interaction (Coie & Dodge, 1998; Crick & Dodge, 1994). This bias is particularly apparent for aggressive children who are also rejected by the peer group. They tend to overestimate their social competence and misjudge peers' negative evaluations of them in self-protective ways (Asher, Zellis, Parker, & Bruene, 1991; Dishion, 1990; Hymel, Bowker, & Woody, 1993; Zakriski & Coie, 1996).

Contextual Features of Friendship

In addition to the quality of the friendship, there are basic contextual dimensions of friendships that show even more pronounced differences between aggressive and nonaggressive children's relationships. The origin of the relationship has implications for the types of activities friends do together and where they engage in these activities. Antisocial adolescents in the OYS tended to meet their close friends outside of school and reside in the same neighborhood. They were less satisfied with their relationship and had relationships of shorter duration that generally ended in an unfriendly manner when compared with the friendships of less antisocial boys (Dishion, Andrews, & Crosby, 1995).

Our own findings with our preadolescent sample support the assumption that the context in which the relationship begins and is maintained might have implications for the influence friends have on one another. Over one third of the aggressive boys in our study had best friends who did not attend school with them, and over half of the aggressive friends lived within walking distance of one another (Bagwell et al., 2001). At least in part because of the tendency for aggressive friends to spend more time with their best friend outside of the school setting, the degree of unsupervised time the friends spent together was significantly greater than for nonaggressive friends. Most of the time aggressive boys spent together occurred in neighborhood and community settings outside of close adult monitoring and supervision.

A comparison of friendships lasting longer than two years with those lasting less than two years showed that aggressive boys had known their friends for a longer period of time than had nonaggressive boys (Bagwell et al., 2001). This finding is at least in part due to the fact that more nonaggressive friendships were school based. In our fourth- and fifth-grade sample, class assignments changed from year to year, but neighborhood friendships were more stable. In adolescence, however, when most schools no longer have self-contained classrooms, school friendships may be more stable as well.

Taken together, these findings suggest that the friendships of antisocial boys are compromised, yet whether this is due to the lack of positive features or the presence of more negative features is unclear. Furthermore, it is possible that children who experience negative features in their friendships may not be gaining as much from the positive aspects that are present in their relationships. Assessments of friendship quality are also complicated by the question of whose opinion is more important—the friends themselves or an outside observer. In other words, if the boys themselves are satisfied, is that all that matters? These results also highlight the importance of investigating the social context of children's relationships. Bronfenbrenner (1989) proposes a process–person–context model that incorporates an analysis of developmental mechanisms and outcomes as a function of both characteristics of the individual and characteristics of the context in which development occurs. Questions about the contributions of children's friendships to antisocial and delinquent behavior should be addressed at this level of analysis. In particular, studying variations in relationships in multiple contexts (i.e., both different friendships across context such as school-based friendships versus neighborhood-based friendships and the same relationship across multiple contexts such as home, school, community) is expected to provide a more complete understanding of the processes through which relationships with friends promote adaptive and maladaptive adjustment.

Interactions Between Friends and Their Influence on Antisocial Behavior

In specifying the role of deviant friends in the development of aggressive and antisocial behavior, there are at least two extreme hypotheses. On the one hand, associating with deviant peers is a necessary part of the pathway leading to delinquent behavior (e.g., Elliott, Huizinga, & Ageton, 1985; Simons, Wu, Conger, & Lorenz, 1994). In this view, the influence of deviant friends causes children to engage in antisocial behavior. On the other hand, it is the stability of disruptive and antisocial behavior over time that explains delinquent behavior in adolescence. The individual characteristics and behaviors that give rise to delinquency incidentally lead to the observed associations among deviant friends. Thus, an outgrowth of early disruptive behavior is that deviant friends are attracted to one another because of similarities in behavior, but this association plays no causal role in the development of further delinquency (e.g., Gottfredson & Hirschi, 1990). An intermediate position suggests that deviant friends moderate rather than mediate the link between early disruptive behavior and later delinquent and antisocial behavior (e.g., Dishion, French, & Patterson, 1995). Thus, having deviant friends is not an essential step in the trajectory to delinquency for children at risk for adolescent antisocial behavior resulting from individual characteristics and other risk factors. However, the association with deviant friends amplifies this path from early disruptive behavior to later delinquency.

In a series of studies, Tremblay and his colleagues have examined these models with a large longitudinal sample of boys. Best friends' aggressiveness was associated with target boys' aggressiveness from ages 10 to 12, but it had no association with target boys' covert or overt delinquent behavior the following year once the target boys' early disruptive behavior (age 6) was taken into account (Tremblay, Masse, Vitaro, & Dobkin, 1995). Similar findings emerged for substance abuse (Dobkin, Tremblay, Masse, & Vitaro, 1995), supporting the *selection* aspect of behavioral similarity. Specifically, substance-abusing boys tended to seek out similar friends once their substance-abusing behaviors were developed.

However, important distinctions were found for the role of deviant friends in subgroups of boys. When the level of the boys' disruptiveness was included as a grouping variable, the later delinquency of the most disruptive boys was indeed not related to their friends' characteristics (Vitaro, Tremblay, Kerr, Pagani, & Bukowski, 1997). The same pattern was true for conforming boys as well. Moderately disruptive boys, in contrast, had levels of delinquency in early adolescence that were similar to the highly disruptive boys *if* they had aggressive, disruptive friends. It was in this group of moderately disruptive boys that the influence of deviant friends was most pronounced. These findings suggest further nuances to the model that contends that the role of deviant friends is to facilitate the emergence of early disruptive behavior (i.e., individual characteristics) into later delinquent and antisocial behavior.

Reinforcement in Friendship Selection and Socialization

A second line of research focuses more specifically on the properties of interactions between aggressive and antisocial friends with the goal of identifying specific processes within their interactions that account for their influence on one another's behavior. Understanding the nature of antisocial children's friendships requires beginning at the start of the relationship and examining the processes involved in friendship formation. The adult social psychology literature on interpersonal attraction contains several theories of how friendships are formed. Although comparable theories and empirical studies of children's friendship initiation are limited (with the notable exception of Gottman's [1983] monograph on how children become friends), the basic underlying processes are expected to be similar. One of these processes is reinforcement.

Reinforcement theories are based on learning theory and explain interpersonal attraction and friendship formation by the principle that people like those who reward them (Perlman & Fehr, 1986). Similarity in personal attitudes, attributes, and experiences is a reinforcing agent (Lott & Lott, 1974). Many of the earliest friendship studies examined similarity of children's attitudes, behaviors, and beliefs, and children who are friends are indeed more similar on a myriad of factors including sociodemographic characteristics (e.g., age, sex, and race), attitudes (e.g., educational goals and attitudes, activity preferences), and behaviors (e.g., drug and substance abuse, prosocial behavior; Hartup, 1983). Interpersonal similarity is present even before children meet their future friends, and the stability of the friendship may be related to the degree of similarity between the partners (Newcomb, Bukowski, & Bagwell, 1999). Similarity in antisocial behavior is apparent among friends according to self-reports, arrest records, and police contacts (Dishion, Andrews, & Crosby, 1995; Dishion, Capaldi, Spracklen, & Li, 1995). Brownfield and Thompson (1991) reported that over 90% of adolescent males whose best friend had at least one contact with police had committed at least two delinquent acts. In contrast, only two thirds of boys whose best friend had never been in police custody committed more than two delinquent acts.

The *shopping* model incorporates the process of homophily (i.e., attraction to others similar to the self) to explain relationship development (Dishion, Patterson, & Griesler, 1994; Patterson, Littman, & Bricker, 1967). In the shopping model, children pursue relationships with those who provide high levels of reinforcement. Establishing common ground through concordances in attitudes and behaviors is a key component of "hitting it off" with another child (Gottman, 1983). In the case of children with antisocial tendencies, rule-breaking is often the common-ground activity that promotes friendship development (Dishion et al., 1994). When reinforcement for rule-breaking is found, children's shopping is a success and the foundations of a relationship are established.

Reinforcement serves at least two important functions in the friendships of antisocial children. First, as described above, children are attracted to others like themselves, and the affirmation of the other's characteristics associated with this similarity is reinforcing. Second, once a friendship is formed, the interaction-based process of socialization helps explain the emergence of greater similarity over time. Dishion et al. (1994) refer to this socialization within friendships of antisocial children as trait confluence, and through this process, characteristics of two friends merge into a dyadic trait. Thus, values established within friendships represent gradual shifts in each friend's behavior toward a central behavior. Within the context of antisocial children's friendships, the induction of similarity is viewed as deviancy training. Reinforcement is one process through which this socialization occurs.

According to reinforcement theories of delinquent behavior, deviant peers are expected to provide a high degree of reinforcement for antisocial behavior and very little positive reinforcement for prosocial behavior (Elliott et al., 1985; Jessor & Jessor, 1977). Furthermore, peer reinforcement is believed to have a more influential effect on an adolescent's behavior than adult reinforcement because the reinforcement schedule is denser and because adolescents spend more time with peers than with adults (Dishion, Spracklen, Andrews, & Patterson, 1996). In addition to shaping antisocial behavior, friends may reinforce maladaptive styles of interaction. For example, Berndt (1996) found that self-reported troublesome behavior increased for children in friendships that had high levels of conflict. Similarly, Kupersmidt, Burchinal, and Patterson (1995) found that children's likelihood of being delinquent increased as the level of conflict with their best friend increased over time. Thus, friendships may provide a context for the reinforcement of coercive and conflictual modes of interacting with others.

Processes Within Friends' Interactions

In additional reports of the interactions between the OYS boys and their friends, Dishion et al. (1996) coded the content of the boys' conversations. Rule-breaking conversations were highly correlated with the boys' antisocial behavior, and normative talk was more frequent in nonantisocial dyads. Furthermore, dyads in which both friends had arrest records responded with the reinforcing affective response of laughter only to rule-breaking talk. Normative talk was not reinforced by these dyads. Overall, laughter engendered more rule-breaking talk in antisocial dyads and more normative talk in nonantisocial dyads. Positive reinforcement in the form of positive affective exchange seems to be one process through which the friendship experience may foster and promote antisocial talk.

These findings invite the question of whether friends' positive affect provides as powerful reinforcement for antisocial *behavior* as it does for antisocial *talk*. Further analyses of the same interaction task revealed that the probability of moving from abstinence to using tobacco, alcohol, or marijuana was much greater for adolescents whose best friend reinforced only rule-breaking talk than for those whose best friend reinforced only normative talk (Dishion, Capaldi, et al., 1995). Likewise, the dyads in which rule-breaking talk was reinforced showed escalations in self-reported delinquent behavior two years later, even after controlling for initial levels of delinquency (Dishion et al., 1996).

In our own study of interactions between aggressive and nonaggressive preadolescent friends, boys played together in a setting designed to provide opportunities for rule-breaking behavior, including using an answer key to cheat on a word puzzle, directly disobeying instructions not to play with toys in the room, and taking candy from a shelf the boys were told not to touch (Bagwell & Coie, 1999). Thus, the findings do not depend on the inference that what friends talk about they later do. Instead, aggressive dyads were not only more likely to engage in rule-breaking talk than nonaggressive dyads but also more likely to provide specific verbal and nonverbal enticements for rule-breaking behavior and to engage in those behaviors when presented with opportunities for rule violations. These forms of social influence—direct enticement for rule-breaking behavior, including failing to prohibit such behaviors and providing social reinforcement for rule violations—characterized the ongoing moment-to-moment interactions of aggressive boys and their best friends.

In addition, the conversations the boys had were coded on the basis of an adapted version of Dishion et al.'s (1996) coding scheme. In addition to coding verbal activity as rule-breaking, normative, or laughter, a category for *temptation talk* was added. Temptation talk included exploration of potential rule violations, such as discussions about whether and how they could use the answer key to cheat on the word puzzle task before actually cheating. It is interesting that aggressive and nonaggressive dyads engaged in the same amount of temptation talk in their discussions. However, sequential analyses revealed that what followed temptation talk varied according to the aggression status of the friends. Specifically, aggressive dyads escalated from explorations of potential rule violations to actually engaging in those behaviors, whereas nonaggressive dyads tended to return to normative conversation following episodes of temptation talk (Bagwell & Coie, 1999).

Temptation talk serves as a way for boys to explore their thoughts and ideas about rule-breaking behaviors with their friend. This type of exploration is a salient process within friendships during middle childhood and early adolescence. It enables children to get feedback on their ideas and helps them mutually negotiate and figure out norms of the friendship as well as of the larger peer group. For aggressive boys, then, antisocial behavior may become an accepted norm within their friendships. It is important to note that the observed pattern of social influence was present in the interactions of 10-year-old boys and their friends. Thus, these processes are at work prior to adolescence, the developmental period on which most research in peer influence and deviant peer associations has focused.

When researchers consider differences in the features and quality of friendships between aggressive and nonaggressive children and how aspects of their interactions influence deviant behavior, we are considering only one specific relationship. However, most children have several close friends and even more than one best friend (Hartup, 1993). These particular friendship relationships are embedded within a larger network of friends. Not all relationships within this network are defined by reciprocal ties, yet these friendship networks or peer cliques are interaction-based groups of children who hang around together.

At the intersection of investigations on dyads of friends and peer cliques lies Giordano, Cernkovich, and Pugh's (1986) interview study of adolescent offenders. The adolescents were asked about the group of friends they "hang around with"; thus, the unit of analysis was determined by each individual adolescent. On various measures of friendship qualities and features, the five groups of adolescents were quite similar in positive relationship qualities. High-frequency major offenders reported more self-disclosure with their friends than nonoffenders, but the intrinsic rewards of trust and caring and identity support did not differ among the groups of adolescents. Furthermore, the level of contact and stability of the relationships did not differ among delinquents and nondelinquents. Several negative friendship features did clearly distinguish between adolescents with various levels of delinquent offending. The greatest imbalance and the most conflict were reported in the most delinquent friendships. Perhaps the most telling distinction between the delinquent groups was in their susceptibility to peer influence. The most delinquent group reported the greatest likelihood both to pressure their friends to behave in certain ways and to be influenced by them. Similarly, in a comparison of residents of a delinquent shelter and nondelinquent high-school students, there were no differences between the groups in adolescents' report of attachment to their friends or intimacy in their relationships; however, delinquent adolescents described significantly greater conflict and ridicule in their friendships than did nondelinquents (Claes & Simard, 1992).

Although most children and adolescents are involved in peer cliques, a specific type of friendship network—the deviant peer clique—is of considerable concern to school officials, parents, and clinicians alike. Numerous studies support the conclusion that associations with a deviant peer group have a pervasive influence on the development of minor delinquency as well as more severe offending and substance abuse. Furthermore, deviant peer group associations predict subsequent delinquency even after controlling for prior levels of delinquency (Elliott et al., 1985; Patterson, Capaldi, & Bank, 1991). Associations with deviant friends are also linked to the *onset* of problem behaviors (Keenan, Loeber, Zhang, Stouthamer-Loeber, & Van Kammen, 1995). Over five successive six-month intervals begun with one cohort of fourth graders and one cohort of seventh graders, onset of three types of antisocial behavior, including overt (e.g., attacked someone with a weapon), covert (e.g., sold drugs, stole something), and authority conflict (e.g., skipped school), was assessed. Concurrent relations between boys' antisocial behavior and their friends' behavior were high across all types of problem behavior. Although the predictive associations were weaker than the concurrent associations, boys whose friends displayed antisocial behavior were more likely to experience an onset of that type of behavior in the next six months than were boys with nonantisocial friends (Keenan et al., 1995).

Identifying Specific Peer Networks

Although these studies establish a strong association between affiliations with deviant friends and the maintenance and onset of antisocial behavior, the measures of peer associations are based on reports of friends' behavior by target children or on social reputations of friends. A better measure of associations with deviant peers would take into account the actual peer cliques to which children belong as well as the behavior of those fellow group members instead of their reputation only. Cairns and his colleagues devised a methodology to address some of these concerns. They asked peer informants to identify the clique structure for their school class or grade (see Cairns, Cairns, Neckerman, Gest, & Gariepy, 1988). With this method of identifying cliques, it was found that seventh-grade students who would drop out of school before completing eleventh grade tended to belong to friendship networks with peers who would also drop out of school early (Cairns, Cairns, & Neckerman, 1989).

Coie and his colleagues developed a similar method, except all adolescents who participated in the assessment were informants about the clique structure (see Bagwell, Coie, Terry, & Lochman, 2000; Coie, Terry, & Christopoulos, 1991). In this way, the clique structure is defined by a consensus of group members about which peers actually belong to that friendship network. A measure of the centrality of students' membership in cliques composed of deviant peers was used to assess deviant peer associations. In eighth grade, adolescents who were more central members of deviant friendship groups engaged in greater antisocial behavior even when levels of prior problem behavior were controlled (Terry & Coie, 1993). Using this same method of identifying cliques, we found that friendship cliques varied greatly in the degree to which they were composed of troublemaking children in fourth and fifth grades (Bagwell et al., 2000). Furthermore, children's centrality of membership in deviant friendship networks varied substantially for these late-elementary-school-age children, suggesting that the influence of deviant friendship groups needs to be examined prior to adolescence.

These studies highlight the importance of teasing apart developmental and contextual considerations in the influence of deviant peer groups. In the Terry and Coie (1993) study, the relation between deviant friendship group involvement and disruptive behavior was not found in sixth grade as it was in eighth grade. Although this difference may represent a developmental phenomenon, evidence of the presence of deviant peer networks earlier than sixth grade (Bagwell et al., 2000; Cairns et al., 1988) suggests it may reflect the constraints of the social context. Specifically, the sixth-grade students (unlike those in eighth grade) had just entered a new school, and stable peer cliques may not yet have been established. Thus, the influence of fellow clique members may not be as strong as when deviant peer groups have had more time to become firmly established.

Deviant Peer Networks and Two Paths to Delinquency

The negative influences of a deviant peer group are viewed as a primary contributor to the increased diversity in antisocial behavior in adolescence. Current developmental theories on the etiology of delinquency and antisocial behavior suggest that there are two groups of antisocial children—the early starters or life-course persistent group and the late starters or adolescence-limited group (Moffitt, 1993; Patterson, DeBaryshe, & Ramsey, 1989). The early starters experience neuropsychological difficulties (e.g., impulsivity and inattention), coercive early family interactions, and deficits in social skills and cognitive processes that lead to the development of antisocial behavior. As these children enter school, their skills deficits, coercive styles of interaction, and limited resources are somewhat more ingrained, and their pattern of antisocial behavior continues and diversifies.

In contrast, the late-starter or adolescence-limited group helps account for the great increase in observed rates of antisocial behavior in adolescence. Late starters appear to experiment with delinquent behavior during adolescence when these behaviors are more prevalent and normative. The antisocial behavior of the adolescence-limited group is expected to desist as adolescents move into early adulthood when societal expectations and privileges match biological maturity (Moffitt, 1993).

The deviant friendship network is expected to play an important role in promoting the antisocial behavior of both the early- and late-starter groups. The late starters are less likely to have peer relationship problems in childhood than the early starters and thus are likely to be more involved in peer groups— including those that might support and encourage antisocial behavior. In an analysis of the age at first police contact among a high-risk sample of adolescents, those who were neither rejected nor aggressive in third grade were divided into two groups based on whether or not they were members of a deviant peer clique in eighth grade (Coie, Terry, Miller-Johnson, & Lochman, 1995). Those who were involved in a deviant peer group had characteristics of the late-starter group. They had only a few arrests before the age of 12 and then increasing numbers of first arrests through the middle of their 15th year by which time approximately 30% had been in contact with the police. In contrast, those who were not involved in a deviant clique showed few arrests across the entire time period, and by age 18, only approximately 17% had come into contact with the police. Thus, involvement with deviant peers may be an important determinant of the onset of deviant behavior in adolescence.

Early starters, however, often have difficulty with peers and, by default, have limited opportunities for association with conventional peers who may reject them. Thus, they are likely to associate with others who are themselves deviant. The hypothesized causal influences on early starters' delinquency and antisocial behavior are not the association with deviant peers per se, but their ingrained pattern of antisocial behavior. Nevertheless, the deviant peer group often serves as a training ground for the escalation of early starters' antisocial tendencies and behaviors into more serious criminal and delinquent offenses. Simons et al. (1994) found support for these two pathways to delinquency for male adolescents. For early starters, a pattern of oppositional behavior predicted affiliation with deviant peers which, in turn, predicted involvement with the criminal justice system. Deviant peer affiliations mediated the association between behavioral orientation and police contact for these early starters. Thus, having an oppositional, aggressive orientation and belonging to a deviant friendship network led to early involvement with police for delinquent behavior. For late starters, affiliation with deviant peers predicted involvement with the criminal justice system; however, an oppositional/defiant behavioral orientation was not associated with either police contact or association with deviant peers. Regardless of the personal characteristics of the adolescents, involvement with deviant peers led to police contact for late starters. For both groups, deviant peer involvement was clearly associated with an increase in police contact although the position of this variable in the pathways to delinquency differed for early and late starters.

What is missing from the literature on deviant friendship networks, however, is a careful analysis of what characteristics make children vulnerable to participation in these groups, how deviant peer cliques are formed, and whether there are any positive outcomes of participation in these friendship networks even though they are deviant. Several studies have investigated the first of these questions, and these have primarily focused on links between peer group status, parenting practices, and involvement with deviant peers.

For example, in a pioneering descriptive analysis, Thrasher (1932) indicated that adolescent gangs often form from childhood playgroups, highlighting the relation between peer association in early and middle childhood and adolescent deviant peer cliques. Dishion, Patterson, Stoolmiller, and Skinner (1991) outlined a temporal relation between peer rejection and later association in deviant peer networks. Children who are rejected by the peer group are more likely to be involved in a deviant friendship network in adolescence. However, in two concurrent investigations of deviant peer involvement as a function of rejection and aggression, Coie and colleagues found that the nonrejected/aggressive children were most involved in deviant peer cliques. This finding was observed in both a mixed-race sample of students in suburban fourth-grade classes (Bagwell et al., 2000) and a sample of predominantly urban African American middle-school students (Coie et al., 1991). Although children who were both rejected and aggressive were more involved in deviant cliques than nonaggressive children, the nonrejected-aggressive group may be more involved with peers overall (including deviant peers) precisely because they are not rejected.

What Can Intervention and Prevention Efforts Tell Us?

Most of the research on the role of friends in the development, maintenance, and escalation of antisocial behavior is firmly embedded within the perspectives of developmental psychology and developmental psychopathology. Nevertheless, recent studies from an applied, clinical perspective have further informed our understanding of the crucial influence friends and friendship networks have on many children and adolescents. First, the prevention of increased externalizing problems for children already showing disruptive behavior may be possible by reducing children's associations with deviant friends. Vitaro and Tremblay (1994) found that a prevention program incorporating parent training, social skills training, and cognitive problem-solving skills training for 8- and 9-year-old boys resulted in decreased aggression and covert antisocial behavior (as compared with control boys) at age 12. At age 12, the friends of boys in the intervention group were less disruptive than were the friends of boys in the control group. This finding suggests that promoting boys' selection of and association with nondeviant friends was one mechanism through which the prevention program exerted positive effects.

Furthermore, the level of the boys' disruptiveness following intervention determined the degree to which associating with less aggressive friends mediated the effect of participating in the prevention program on the development of conduct disorder (CD; Vitaro, Brendgen, Pagani, Tremblay, & McDuff, 1999). Specifically, friends' aggressiveness was not associated with later CD for boys whose disruptiveness was below the mean after the intervention. However, for boys who remained highly disruptive after the prevention program, the risk of developing CD was decreased for those who associated with less deviant friends. Thus, reductions in both disruptive behavior *and* associations with deviant friends may be important goals for prevention programs.

Second, one of the most common strategies for implementing clinical interventions for antisocial behavior with children and adolescents is group skills training. The research reviewed in this chapter suggests that encouraging associations among at-risk children and adolescents who are already engaging in delinquent behavior might serve to escalate precisely those behaviors that clinicians are trying to reduce by creating a deviant peer group. Dishion and his colleagues reported just such a phenomenon in several intervention studies with adolescents (Dishion & Andrews, 1995; Dishion, McCord, & Poulin, 1999).

In an intervention grounded firmly in developmental theory, high-risk adolescents were randomly assigned to one of four intervention conditions: (a) youth cognitive–behavioral skills training groups, (b) parenting skills training groups, (c) both parent and youth groups, and (d) an attention placebo condition. It was hypothesized that the parent and youth training combination would be most effective and indeed, this condition resulted in reductions in negative family interactions. The unexpected long-term findings showed that tobacco use and reports of externalizing behavior by teachers were significantly higher for youth in the youth skills training groups compared with the control groups (Dishion & Andrews, 1995). These iatrogenic effects for tobacco use and teacher-reported delinquency persisted over a three-year follow-up period (Dishion et al., 1999).

In group intervention settings, it is expected that children may provide reinforcement for deviant behavior by laughing and giving attention to those who talk about antisocial activities, resulting in increased motivation to engage in delinquency (Dishion et al., 1999). Reinforcement for one another's antisocial behavior, even if occurring during the course of therapy, is a powerful process. In addition, if interventions serve to introduce high-risk children and adolescents to one another and to promote friendships among them, they may continue contact with one another outside the intervention group sessions.

Future Directions

A substantial body of empirical literature now supports the assumptions that friendships are developmentally significant, that friendships have both positive and negative features, that the nature of these relationships is determined by the characteristics of the two friends as well as their shared experiences, and that friendships function as a critical social context for development. Following directly from these assumptions, the research reviewed in the current chapter has helped address the seeming contradiction that aggressive children are rejected by the larger peer group, yet having deviant friends is associated with escalations in delinquent and antisocial behavior. The field is ripe for more process-oriented research to further specify the role deviant friends play in an individual's antisocial behavior and potential mediators or moderators of that link. The search for moderator variables has begun. For example, Vitaro, Brendgen, and Tremblay (2000) found that childhood disruptiveness, attachment to parents, and attitudes about delinquency moderated the association between deviancy of an adolescent's best friend and his later delinquent behavior. As this research progresses, at least three methodological and conceptual issues are important to consider.

First, we need to continue to use multiple methods of assessment, to assess multiple dimensions of peer relations, and to avoid inflated correlations of friends' behavior due to shared method variance. As is clear from the research reviewed in this chapter, observations of friends' behavior in controlled laboratory settings can identify specific processes, such as deviancy training, that account for friends' influence on one another's deviant behavior. Investigations of these processes should be combined with further clarification of the way in which the subjective experience of deviant friendships determines their effect on development. To date, there are inconsistent findings with regard to the relative lack of positive versus negative features in aggressive and antisocial children's relationships, the degree to which children and adolescents perceive their friendships as low in quality, whether the expected positive outcomes of close friendships are present for antisocial children, and how the dimensions of having versus not having friends, the quality of the relationship, and the characteristics of the friend work together in determining the effect of the relationship on emotional and behavioral functioning. Studies that include separate assessments of children's own behavior (through self-report, teacher-report, parent-report, peer-report, or police records) and their friends' behavior will address the problem of overestimating friends' similarity.

Second, the studies reviewed above differ substantially in their definition of friends. Some rely on mutual friendship nominations, and others ask children about their friends without ever naming a specific peer. Some include only in-school relationships, and others include friends from both within and outside of school. Some take into account only a child's closest or best friend, and others assess a broader network of friends. Although these differences may seem minor, they have the potential to give very different pictures of the role of deviant friends for some children. For example, aggressive children are likely to spend most of their time with peers outside of school rather than inside school; thus, limiting assessments to school-based friendships may miss the friends who are actually most influential in a child's social network. Aggressive children are expected to have a limited number of peers with whom to form friendships because they are rejected by conventional peers. Thus, their best friend may be a friend of convenience or may be their only friend, whereas better-accepted peers may have multiple reciprocal friendships, and the influence of any one friend may be less potent. Children are expected to differ in the degree to which their friendship network is composed of many, some, or only a few deviant friends relative to the number of conventional peers with whom they associate. In addition, unilateral friends, or those peers with whom children want to be friends, may exert an important influence on their behavior in an effort to be liked by that peer.

Third, just as much of the early research on peer relations and friendships in general began with samples of boys, the research on aggressive children's friends and the influence of deviant friends has often ignored girls. This omission is likely due to at least two factors. First, given the national concern about levels of serious antisocial behavior in male adolescents, it is important to begin examining processes in childhood that may result in these maladaptive behavior patterns with boys. Second, gender differences in aggressive children's friendships are expected. For example, girls have been reported to engage in relational aggression more than boys (e.g., Crick & Grotpeter, 1995; Grotpeter & Crick, 1996). This type of aggression includes attempts to damage others' peer relationships, and girls who are relationally aggressive report that this behavior frequently occurs within their close friendships (Grotpeter & Crick, 1996). Thus, relational aggression may be one process through which girls may foster one another's aggressive and antisocial behavior. However, these processes may not be as apparent in the observational, self-report, and peer-report assessment methods used to date.

Regarding the conclusions drawn about the contributions of friendships to the development and maintenance of antisocial behavior, two assumptions must be emphasized. First, the majority of friendships are positive, healthy relationships that provide an advantageous context for the emergence of social and emotional competencies leading to adaptive adjustment. No relationship is devoid of negative features and qualities; nevertheless, in examining how friendships contribute to antisocial behavior, we must recognize that excessively problematic friendships are not the norm. Second, friendships are not assumed to frequently transform a prosocial, well-adjusted child into an antisocial, troubled youth. However, friendships have the potential to promote the maintenance and regulation of existing antisocial tendencies and even to foster the development and expression of more severe antisocial responding to the external world.

Continued efforts from researchers in developmental psychopathology and prevention science will help further clarify which children are most susceptible to the negative influences of friends, which friendships are most likely to provide that negative influence, and whether and how to intervene effectively to promote the positive benefits of friendships and to assuage their negative effects. Further empirical studies are needed to address the question of what is the differential risk associated with antisocial children having or not having a close friend. Are friendships necessary relationships that provide the only context for the emergence of particular social and emotional competencies, or is the potential for increased antisocial behavior so great that some youth would be better off not establishing close friendships at all? Both of these positions are extreme, and the appropriate answer likely rests somewhere in between. Nevertheless, these questions represent a critical future direction for understanding the contributions of friendships to the development and maintenance of antisocial behavior.

References

Asher, S. R., Zellis, K. M., Parker, J. G., & Bruene, C. M. (1991, April). *Self-referral for peer relations problems among aggressive and withdrawn low-accepted children*. Paper presented at the biennial meeting of the Society for Research in Child Development, Seattle, WA.

Bagwell, C. L., Andreassi, C. L., & Keeley, S. J. (2001, April). *The friendships of aggressive boys: Relationship quality and conflict management*. Poster presented at the biennial meeting of the Society for Research in Child Development, Minneapolis, MN.

Bagwell, C. L., & Coie, J. D. (1999, April). Social influence in the friendship relations of aggressive boys. In J. D. Coie (Chair), *A closer look at deviant peer influences on delinquent activity.* Symposium conducted at the biennial meeting of the Society for Research in Child Development, Albuquerque, NM.

Bagwell, C. L., Coie, J. D., Terry, R. A., & Lochman, J. E. (2000). Peer clique participation in middle childhood: Associations with sociometric status and gender. *Merrill-Palmer Quarterly, 46,* 280–305.

Bagwell, C. L., Newcomb, A. F., & Bukowski, W. M. (1998). Preadolescent friendship and peer rejection as predictors of adult adjustment. *Child Development, 69,* 140–153.

Bagwell, C. L., Schmidt, M. E., Newcomb, A. F., & Bukowski, W. M. (2001). Friendship and peer rejection as predictors of adult adjustment. In D. W. Nangle & C. A. Erdley (Eds.), *New directions for child and adolescent development: Vol. 91. The role of friendship in psychological adjustment* (pp. 25–49). San Francisco: Jossey-Bass.

Berndt, T. J. (1992). Friendship and friends' influence in adolescence. *Current Directions in Psychological Science, 1,* 156–159.

Berndt, T. J. (1996). Exploring the effects of friendship quality on social development. In W. M. Bukowski, A. F. Newcomb, & W. W. Hartup (Eds.), *The company they keep: Friendships in childhood and adolescence* (pp. 346–365). New York: Cambridge University Press.

Berndt, T. J. (1999). Friends' influence on children's adjustment to school. In W. A. Collins & B. Laursen (Eds.), *The Minnesota Symposia on Child Psychology: Vol. 30. Relationships as developmental contexts* (pp. 85–107). Mahwah, NJ: Erlbaum.

Bronfenbrenner, U. (1989). Ecological systems theory. In R. Vasta (Ed.), *Annals of child development: Vol. 6. Six theories of child development: Revised formulations and current issues* (pp. 187–249). Greenwich, CT: JAI Press.

Brownfield, D., & Thompson, K. (1991). Attachment to peers and delinquent behaviour. *Canadian Journal of Criminology, 33,* 45–60.

Bukowski, W. M., & Hoza, B. (1989). Popularity and friendship: Issues in theory, measurement, and outcome. In T. Berndt & G. Ladd (Eds.), *Peer relationships in child development* (pp. 15–45). New York: Wiley.

Bukowski, W. M., Hoza, B., & Boivin, M. (1994). Measuring friendship quality during pre- and early adolescence: The development and psychometric properties of the friendship qualities scale. *Journal of Social and Personal Relationships, 11,* 471–484.

Bukowski, W. M., Pizzamiglio, M. T., Newcomb, A. F., & Hoza, B. (1996). Popularity as an affordance for friendship: The link between group and dyadic experience. *Social Development, 5,* 189–202.

Cairns, R. B., Cairns, B. D., & Neckerman, H. J. (1989). Early school drop-out: Configurations and determinants. *Child Development, 60,* 1437–1452.

Cairns, R. B., Cairns, B. D., Neckerman, H. J., Gest, S. D., & Gariepy, J. L. (1988). Social networks and aggressive behavior: Peer support or peer rejection? *Developmental Psychology, 24,* 815–823.

Claes, M., & Simard, R. (1992). Friendship characteristics of delinquent adolescents. *International Journal of Adolescence and Youth, 3,* 287–301.

Coie, J. D., & Dodge, K. A. (1983). Continuities and changes in children's social status: A five year longitudinal study. *Merrill-Palmer Quarterly, 29,* 261–281.

Coie, J. D., & Dodge, K. A. (1998). Aggression and antisocial behavior. In W. Damon (Series Ed.) & N. Eisenberg (Vol. Ed.), *Handbook of child psychology: Vol. 3. Social, emotional, and personality development* (pp. 779–862). New York: Wiley.

Coie, J. D., Terry, R., & Christopoulos, C. (1991, April). *Social networks as mediators of the relation between peer status, social behavior and adolescent adjustment.* Paper presented at the biennial meeting of the Society for Research in Child Development, Seattle, WA.

Coie, J. D., Terry, R., Lenox, K., Lochman, J., & Hyman, C. (1995). Childhood peer rejection and aggression as predictors of stable patterns of adolescent disorder. *Development and Psychopathology, 7,* 697–713.

Coie, J. D., Terry, R., Miller-Johnson, S., Lochman, J. (1995). *Longitudinal effects of deviant peer groups on criminal offending in late adolescence.* Unpublished manuscript. Duke University, Durham, NC.

Crick, N. R., & Dodge, K. A. (1994). A review and reformulation of social information-processing mechanisms in children's social adjustment. *Psychological Bulletin, 115,* 74–101.

Crick, N. R., & Grotpeter, J. K. (1995). Relational aggression, gender, and social-psychological adjustment. *Child Development, 55,* 710–722.

Dishion, T. J. (1990). The peer context of troublesome child and adolescent behavior. In P. E. Leone (Ed.), *Understanding troubled and troubling youth* (pp. 128–153). Newbury Park, CA: Sage.

Dishion, T. J., & Andrews, D. W. (1995). Preventing escalation in problem behaviors with high-risk young adolescents: Immediate and 1-year outcomes. *Journal of Consulting and Clinical Psychology, 63,* 538–548.

Dishion, T. J., Andrews, D. W., & Crosby, L. (1995). Antisocial boys and their friends in early adolescence: Relationship characteristics, quality, and interactional process. *Child Development, 66,* 139–151.

Dishion, T. J., Capaldi, D., Spracklen, K. M., & Li, F. (1995). Peer ecology of male adolescent drug use. *Development and Psychopathology, 7,* 803–824.

Dishion, T. J., French, D. C., & Patterson, G. R. (1995). The development and ecology of antisocial behavior. In D. Cicchetti & D. J. Cohen (Eds.), *Developmental psychopathology: Vol. 2. Risk, disorder, and adaptation* (pp. 421–471). New York: Wiley.

Dishion, T. J., McCord, J., & Poulin, F. (1999). When interventions harm: Peer groups and problem behavior. *American Psychologist, 54,* 755–764.

Dishion, T. J., Patterson, G. R., & Griesler, P. C. (1994). Peer adaptations in the development of antisocial behavior: A confluence model. In L. R. Huesmann (Ed.), *Aggressive behavior: Current perspectives* (pp. 61–95). New York: Plenum Press.

Dishion, T. J., Patterson, G. R., Stoolmiller, M., & Skinner, M. L. (1991). Family, school, and behavioral antecedents to early adolescent involvement with antisocial peers. *Developmental Psychology, 27,* 172–180.

Dishion, T. J., Spracklen, K. M., Andrews, D. W., & Patterson, G. R. (1996). Deviancy training in male adolescent friendships. *Behavior Therapy, 27,* 373–390.

Dobkin, P. L., Tremblay, R. E., Masse, L. C., & Vitaro, F. (1995). Individual and peer characteristics in predicting boys' early onset of substance abuse: A seven-year longitudinal study. *Child Development, 66,* 1198–1214.

Elliott, D. S., Huizinga, D., & Ageton, S. S. (1985). *Explaining delinquency and drug use.* Beverly Hills, CA: Sage.

Furman, W. (1999). Friends and lovers: The role of peer relationships in adolescent romantic relationships. In W. A. Collins & B. Laursen (Eds.), *The Minnesota Symposia on Child Psychology: Vol. 30. Relationships as developmental contexts* (pp. 133–154). Mahwah, NJ: Erlbaum.

Furman, W., & Robbins, P. (1985). What's the point? Issues in the selection of treatment objectives. In B. H. Schneider, K. H. Rubin, & J. E. Ledingham (Eds.), *Children's peer relations: Issues in assessment and intervention* (pp. 41–54). New York: Springer-Verlag.

Giordano, P. C., Cernkovich, S. A., & Pugh, M. D. (1986). Friendships and delinquency. *American Journal of Sociology, 91,* 1170–1202.

Gottfredson, M. R., & Hirschi, T. (1990). *A general theory of crime.* Stanford, CA: Stanford University Press.

Gottman, J. M. (1983). How children become friends. *Monographs of the Society for Research in Child Development, 48*(3, Serial No. 201).

Grotpeter, J. K., & Crick, N. R. (1996). Relational aggression, overt aggression, and friendship. *Child Development, 67,* 2328–2338.

Hartup, W. W. (1983). Peer relations. In P. H. Mussen (Series Ed.) & E. M. Hetherington (Vol. Ed.), *Handbook of child psychology: Vol. 4. Socialization, personality, and social development* (pp. 103–198). New York: Wiley.

Hartup, W. W. (1992). Friendships and their developmental significance. In H. McGurk (Ed.), *Childhood social development: Contemporary perspective* (pp. 175–205). London: Erlbaum.

Hartup, W. W. (1993). Adolescents and their friends. In B. Laursen (Ed.), *Close friendships in adolescence* (pp. 3–22). San Francisco: Jossey-Bass.

Hartup, W. W. (1996). The company they keep: Friendships and their developmental significance. *Child Development, 67,* 1–13.

Hartup, W. W., & Sancilio, M. F. (1986). Children's friendships. In E. Schopler & G. B. Mesibov (Eds.), *Social behavior in autism* (pp. 61–79). New York: Plenum Press.

Hoza, B., Pelham, W. E., Jr., Dobbs, J., Owens, J. S., & Pillow, D. R. (2002). Do boys with attention-deficit/hyperactivity disorder have positive illusory self-concepts? *Journal of Abnormal Child Psychology, 111,* 268–278.

Hymel, S., Bowker, A., & Woody, E. (1993). Aggressive versus withdrawn unpopular children: Variations in peer and self-perceptions in multiple domains. *Child Development, 64,* 879–896.

Jessor, R., & Jessor, S. L. (1977). *Problem behavior and psychosocial development.* New York: Academic Press.

Keenan, K., Loeber, R., Zhang, Q., Stouthamer-Loeber, M., & Van Kammen, W. B. (1995). The influence of deviant peers on the development of boys' disruptive and delinquent behavior: A temporal analysis. *Development and Psychopathology, 7,* 715–726.

Kupersmidt, J. B., Burchinal, M., & Patterson, C. J. (1995). Developmental patterns of childhood peer relations as predictors of externalizing behavior problems. *Development and Psychopathology, 7,* 825–843.

Kupersmidt, J. B., Coie, J. D., & Dodge, K. A. (1990). The role of poor peer relationships in the development of disorder. In S. R. Asher & J. D. Coie (Eds.), *Peer rejection in childhood* (pp. 274–305). New York: Cambridge University Press.

Lott, B. E., & Lott, A. J. (1974). The role of reward in the formation of positive interpersonal attitudes. In T. L. Huston (Ed), *Foundations of interpersonal attraction* (pp. 171–192). New York: Academic Press.

Moffitt, T. E. (1993). Adolescence-limited and life-course persistent antisocial behavior: A developmental taxonomy. *Psychological Review, 100,* 674–701.

Newcomb, A. F., & Bagwell, C. L. (1995). Children's friendship relations: A meta-analytic review. *Psychological Bulletin, 117,* 306–347.

Newcomb, A. F., & Bagwell, C. L. (1996). The developmental significance of children's friendship relations. In W. M. Bukowski, A. F. Newcomb, & W. W. Hartup (Eds.), *The company they keep: Friendships in childhood and adolescence* (pp. 289–321). New York: Cambridge University Press.

Newcomb, A. F., Bukowski, W. M., & Bagwell, C. L. (1999). Knowing the sounds: Friendship as a developmental context. In W. A. Collins & B. Laursen (Eds.), *The Minnesota Symposia on Child Psychology: Vol. 30. Relationships as developmental contexts* (pp. 63–84). Mahwah, NJ: Erlbaum.

Panella, D., & Henggeler, S. W. (1986). Peer interactions of conduct-disordered, anxious-withdrawn, and well-adjusted black adolescents. *Journal of Abnormal Child Psychology, 14,* 1–11.

Parker, J. G., & Asher, S. R. (1987). Peer relations and later personal adjustment: Are low-accepted children at risk? *Psychological Bulletin, 102,* 357–389.

Parker, J. G., & Asher, S. R. (1993). Friendship and friendship quality in middle childhood: Links with peer group acceptance and feelings of loneliness and social dissatisfaction. *Developmental Psychology, 29,* 611–621.

Parker, J. G., Rubin, K. H., Price, J. M., & DeRosier, M. E. (1995). Peer relationships, child development, and adjustment. In D. Cicchetti & D. J. Cohen (Eds.), *Developmental psychopathology: Vol. 2. Risk, disorder, and adaptation* (pp. 96–161). New York: Wiley.

Patterson, G. R., Capaldi, D. M., & Bank, L. (1991). An early starter model for predicting delinquency. In D. J. Pepler & K. H. Rubin (Eds.), *The development and treatment of childhood aggression* (pp. 139–168). Hillsdale, NJ: Lawrence Erlbaum.

Patterson, G. R., DeBaryshe, B. D., & Ramsey, E. (1989). A developmental perspective on antisocial behavior. *American Psychologist, 44,* 329–335.

Patterson, G. R., Littman, R. A., & Bricker, W. (1967). Assertive behavior in children: A step toward a theory of aggression. *Monographs of the Society for Research in Child Development, 32*(5, Serial No. 113).

Patterson, G. R., Reid, J. B., & Dishion, T. J. (1992). *A social interactional approach: Vol. 4. Antisocial boys.* Eugene, OR: Castalia.

Perlman, D., & Fehr, B. (1986). Theories of friendship: The analysis of interpersonal attraction. In V. J. Derlaga & B. A. Winstead (Eds.), *Friendship and social interaction* (pp. 9–40). New York: Springer-Verlag.

Poulin, F., Dishion, T. J., & Haas, E. (1999). The peer influence paradox: Friendship quality and deviancy training within male adolescent friendships. *Merrill-Palmer Quarterly, 45,* 42–61.

Rubin, K. H., Bukowski, W. M., & Parker, J. G. (1998). Peer interactions, relationships, and groups. In W. Damon (Series Ed.) & N. Eisenberg (Vol. Ed.), *Handbook of child psychology: Vol. 3. Social, emotional, and personality development* (pp. 619–700). New York: Wiley.

Simons, R. L., Wu, C., Conger, R. D., & Lorenz, F. O. (1994). Two routes to delinquency: Differences between early and late starters in the impact of parenting and deviant peers. *Criminology, 32,* 247–276.

Sullivan, H. S. (1953). *The interpersonal theory of psychiatry.* New York: Norton.

Terry, R., & Coie, J. D. (1993, November). *Changing social networks and its impact on juvenile delinquency.* Paper presented at the annual meeting of the American Society for Criminology, Phoenix, AZ.

Thrasher, F. M. (1932). *The gang.* Chicago: University of Chicago Press.

Tremblay, R. E., Masse, L. C., Vitaro, F., & Dobkin, P. L. (1995). The impact of friends' deviant behavior on early onset of delinquency: Longitudinal data from 6 to 13 years of age. *Development and Psychopathology, 7,* 649–667.

Vandell, D. L., & Hembree, S. E. (1994). Peer social status and friendship: Independent contributors to children's social and academic adjustment. *Merrill-Palmer Quarterly, 40,* 461–477.

Vitaro, F., Brendgen, M., Pagani, L., Tremblay, R. E., & McDuff, P. (1999). Disruptive behavior, peer association, and conduct disorder: Testing the developmental links through early intervention. *Development and Psychopathology, 11,* 287–304.

Vitaro, F., Brendgen, M., & Tremblay, R. E. (2000). Influence of deviant friends on delinquency: Searching for moderator variables. *Journal of Abnormal Child Psychology, 28,* 313–325.

Vitaro, F., & Tremblay, R. E. (1994). Impact of a prevention program on aggressive children's friendships and social adjustment. *Journal of Abnormal Child Psychology, 22,* 457–475.

Vitaro, F., Tremblay, R. E., Kerr, M., Pagani, L., & Bukowski, W. M. (1997). Disruptiveness, friends' characteristics, and delinquency in early adolescence: A test of two competing models of development. *Child Development, 68,* 676–689.

Zakriski, A. L., & Coie, J. D. (1996). A comparison of aggressive-rejected and nonaggressive-rejected children's interpretations of self-directed and other-directed rejection. *Child Development, 67,* 1048–1070.

Part II

Social–Cognitive and Emotional Processes

4

Social Information Processing and Children's Social Adjustment

Mary E. Gifford-Smith and David L. Rabiner

Children differ from one another in many ways. One difference that is especially important to children's long-term adjustment is the ability to maintain harmonious relationships with peers. Some children are consistently cooperative with peers, are widely liked, and establish enduring friendships. Others are often aggressive toward peers and have few, if any, friends. Still other children withdraw from peers or may be frequently victimized. What factors contribute to these divergent patterns of social adjustment among children and how can children experiencing important difficulties in their relations with peers be helped?

One particularly influential approach for understanding these issues has been the study of children's social cognition—that is, the ways that children think about their relations with others and the processes through which such thinking occurs (Shantz, 1975). The premise underlying this approach is that "... social cognitions are the mechanisms leading to social behaviors that, in turn, are the bases of social adjustment evaluations by others" (Crick & Dodge, 1994, p. 74). This deceptively simple premise has spawned numerous investigations that have greatly increased our understanding of the variability in children's social adjustment.

Multiple aspects of social cognition that contribute to children's adjustment have been identified (e.g., encoding cues, interpreting cues, generating potential responses) and researchers have developed comprehensive models integrating these different social information processing (SIP) components. Although several models have been proposed (Huesmann, 1988, 1998; Rubin & Krasnor, 1986), the most influential has been that of Dodge and his colleagues (Crick & Dodge, 1994; Dodge, 1986), and a brief discussion of this work is thus an appropriate place to begin this review.

Dodge's Original SIP Model

Dodge's original SIP model of children's social competence describes the sequence of mental steps that children are hypothesized to go through when

responding to a specific social stimulus. In this model, the encoding and interpretation of a social stimulus (e.g., being bumped in the lunch line by a peer)
lead to a mental search of possible responses. These responses are evaluated
and the child then chooses to enact the response judged to be most favorable.
These processes are assumed to occur in real time and to be outside of conscious
awareness. Although some influence of later stages on earlier ones is posited
(e.g., how children represent the cues they encode feeds back to influence
subsequent encoding), the process is depicted in a largely linear manner and
reflects the sequential manner in which SIP was suggested to occur. In addition,
any influence of the child's prior experience (i.e., database) or biologically determined capabilities on SIP is presumed to occur at the initial SIP step and to
exert no direct influence on subsequent processing activities.

Crick and Dodge's Revised SIP Model

In 1994, Crick and Dodge published an important revision of Dodge's original
model. Their revised SIP model is presented in Figure 4.1. Although a detailed
discussion of the reformulated model is beyond the scope of this review (see
Crick & Dodge for a discussion), several critical differences from the original
model are important to highlight. The most dramatic difference is that the
revised model is decidedly nonlinear in nature; this is depicted in the multiple
feedback loops and cyclical structure of the revised model. The non-linear
nature of the revised model reflects the assumption that although the processing of a particular stimulus is sequential (i.e., the arrows around the outer
circle), individuals are engaged in multiple SIP activities at one time. Thus,
as new cues are being encoded, prior cues are being interpreted and acted
upon. This revision captures the complexities inherent in most social situations.

In the revised model a clearer distinction is also made between children's
online information processing—that is, the steps listed along the outer circle
in Figure 4.1—and the *database* (also referred to as *latent mental structures*)
represented by the inner circle. The bidirectional arrows linking online processing steps and the database reflect the emphasis on the interplay between
online processing and latent mental structures (e.g., representations of others
influence one's goals for social relationships, which, in turn, contribute to
experiences that may alter one's representations of others). This change provides a clearer basis for hypothesizing about the reciprocal influences between
social experience and SIP.

A third important change to the original SIP model is that an entirely new
step—that is, the clarification of goals—is included. Dodge's original model
contained no explicit discussion of how motivational factors—that is, children's
social goals—might influence the responses children consider, select, and enact.
Although a review of research linking children's selection of goals to social
adjustment is beyond the scope of this chapter (see Erdley & Asher, 1999, for
a comprehensive review), there is now considerable evidence linking children's
social goals to their social outcomes. Thus, the inclusion of social goals in the
revised SIP model represents an important modification.

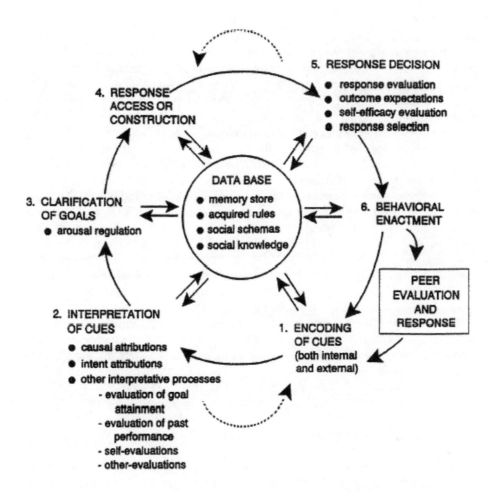

Figure 4.1. A reformulated social information-processing model of children's social adjustment.

Challenges to the Field Highlighted by Crick and Dodge

In addition to describing their revised SIP model, Crick and Dodge (1994) identified a number of important issues for subsequent investigation. Among the areas they identified were (a) studies of the impact that prior experience has on current SIP and social adjustment; (b) studies that examine how children's social cognitions may change as a function of their social experience; (c) examinations of how children's SIP is influenced by their emotional state; (d) investigations of the role that development plays in children's SIP; (e) research that examines whether/how gender modifies the relationship between SIP and social adjustment; and (f) studies in which SIP is examined in relation to adjustment difficulties other than aggression.

In this review, we focus on recent work addressing these challenges to the field. Thus, our goal is to review the progress in relation to these core issues rather than to provide an exhaustive summary of all SIP research published since Crick and Dodge's review. As a result, we exclude numerous studies focusing on specific SIP steps. These studies are important to the overall evaluation of the SIP model, but are beyond the scope of this chapter.

Issue 1: How does prior experience influence current SIP and social adjustment? In their revised SIP model, Crick and Dodge propose a theory for how prior experience is carried forward to influence children's current SIP and social adjustment. They argue that experience leads to the formation of latent mental structures that are carried forward and constitute the database a child brings to new situations. This database, in turn, influences the online processing of social cues, which impacts behavior and social adjustment.

The database, or latent mental structures, are regarded as cognitive heuristics or schemata—variously defined as memory structures, scripts, core beliefs, or patterns of thinking—which organize and translate information in an efficient and meaningful manner (Crick & Dodge, 1994; Huesmann, 1998; Lochman and Lenhart, 1995). Crick and Dodge suggest that these scripts develop in response to a child's social experience and then influence—and are influenced by—each step of SIP. Representations of others as hostile, for example, may lead a child to selectively attend to aggressive cues, to interpret others' intent as hostile, or to generate social goals for dominance or revenge. Similarly, beliefs about the appropriateness or legitimacy of aggression may influence the types of responses a child considers and enacts during peer conflict. Thus, these representations and beliefs are believed to exert an indirect influence on social behavior, an effect that is mediated by SIP patterns.

Linkages Between Latent Mental Structures and SIP

Several studies have examined the link between children's representations of significant others (e.g., parents, peers) and their SIP. Researchers have operationalized children's mental representations of others in various ways, including attachment status classifications, responses to projective instruments, and more direct, self-report measures of children's feelings about their significant relationships. There is growing evidence that children who view others as hostile or rejecting are more likely to interpret ambiguous social information in an aggressive manner.

Cassidy, Kirsh, Scolton, and Parke (1996) have examined links between parental attachment and hostile attributional biases across a range of developmental periods. In all but the youngest age group (i.e., preschoolers), children classified as insecurely attached or who reported experiencing parental rejection were more likely to make hostile attributions in response to hypothetical, ambiguous provocation. Similarly, Burks, Laird, Dodge, Pettit, and Bates (1999) reported that a tendency to view significant others in hostile terms was associated with biased processing as measured by hostile attributional tendencies and aggressive response generation. Finally, in a more direct empirical test of the hypothesis that negative schemas are related to interpretative biases, Graham and Hudley (1994) demonstrated that priming the perception that others' negative actions are intentional can lead to hostile attributional biases in nonaggressive children.

Another increasingly studied form of latent social knowledge is children's beliefs about the appropriateness and legitimacy of aggression. These beliefs are typically assessed with a short questionnaire that taps both general beliefs about using aggression (e.g., "in general, it's OK to use violence") and beliefs about the legitimacy of retaliation in particular circumstances (e.g., "it's OK to hit a boy if he says something bad first") (NOBAGS; Huesmann & Guerra, 1997; Guerra, Huesmann, & Hanish, 1994). Zelli, Dodge, Lochman, Laird, and the Conduct Problems Prevention Research Group (CPPRG; 1999) examined longitudinal relations among children's normative beliefs about aggression and three components of SIP: hostile intent attributions, aggressive response access, and evaluation of aggressive solutions. Whereas children's aggression beliefs and measures of processing were moderately related across years, confirmatory factor analyses supported the validity of distinguishing between these constructs. In addition, third graders who believed that aggression is a legitimate behavioral alternative were more likely to engage in deviant processing in fourth and fifth grade. The converse relationship—linking early processing biases to later aggression beliefs—was also significant but did not hold as strongly. Erdley and Asher (1998) also examined differences in aggressive response evaluation among children who varied in beliefs about the legitimacy of aggression. In their study, fourth- and fifth-grade children with strong beliefs in the appropriateness of aggression were more likely to evaluate aggressive solutions positively and to evaluate prosocial and withdrawal strategies negatively.

Results from these studies suggest that latent knowledge structures are related to SIP patterns in important ways. Specifically, social knowledge reflecting an expectation that others are threatening or rejecting, and beliefs in the legitimacy of aggression, predict a tendency to interpret and respond to hypothetical provocation in an aggressive manner. Additional work to delineate the nature of these relations (e.g., directionality) and enhance understanding of other forms of social knowledge that impacts SIP (e.g., beliefs about oneself) is needed.

Linkages Between Latent Mental Structures and Maladjustment

Another focus of work examining latent social knowledge has been the link between cognitive schemas and children's adjustment. In general, results support the conclusion that a hostile world view, as manifested in negative representations of significant others as well as beliefs supporting aggression, is related to negative social outcomes for children. For example, negative representations of parents/family have been shown to relate to higher teacher ratings of externalizing behavior problems (Burks et al., 1999), teacher ratings of poor social status (Rudolph, Hammen, & Burge, 1995), and observer ratings of low peer competence in laboratory-based tasks (Rudolph et al., 1995). Positive representations of parents, on the other hand, appear related to high status among peers (Rabiner, Keane, & MacKinnon-Lewis, 1993). Similar patterns have been noted for children's negative representations of peers; that is, children who display a tendency to view unfamiliar peers as hostile or unfriendly are more likely to be rated as aggressive by teachers (MacKinnon-Lewis, Rabiner, & Starnes, 1999) and peers (Burks, Dodge, Price, & Laird, 1999). Finally, children with negative representations of familiar peers are more likely to experience rejection or low social status (MacKinnon-Lewis et al., 1999; Rudolph et al., 1995) and to be rated as less socially competent by independent observers (Rudolph et al., 1995).

Children's normative beliefs about aggression also have an impact on social adjustment. Beliefs about the legitimacy of aggression have been linked to aggressive behavior, whether measured by peer nominations (Erdley & Asher, 1998; Guerra et al., 1994; Guerra, Huesmann, Tolan, VanAcker, & Eron, 1995; Huesmann & Guerra, 1997), teacher ratings (Dodge, Lochman, Harnish, Bates, & Pettit, 1997; Huesmann & Guerra, 1997), or self-report (Guerra et al., 1994). This relationship spans cultural groups (Guerra et al., 1994), is particularly strong for beliefs about the appropriateness of retaliatory aggression (Zelli et al., 1999), and grows stronger with age as beliefs about aggression become more stable (Huesmann & Guerra, 1997).

Is the Relationship Between Latent Mental Structures and Social Adjustment Mediated by SIP?

Although findings reviewed above support the general conclusion that children's latent mental structures are related to online SIP and to social adjustment, they do not address Crick and Dodge's (1994) specific hypothesis that the relationship between latent mental structures and social adjustment is mediated by SIP patterns. To date, there have been only two direct examinations of this mediational hypothesis. Lenhart and Rabiner (1995) reported that adolescents' social problem-solving skills—specifically, the degree to which the solutions they provided to hypothetical social conflicts integrated the needs of both parties—mediated the relationship between their representations of parents and their observed behavioral competence with peers. When teacher ratings of adolescents' behavior were used as the dependent variable, however, support for the mediational model was not found. In a more recent study in which the latent mental structure examined was beliefs about aggression rather than representations of others, Zelli et al. (1999) found support for the contention that the effect of normative beliefs about aggression on social adjustment is mediated by biased processing. In this study, a model in which the impact of retaliatory aggression beliefs on aggressive behavior was mediated by three information processing steps (i.e., hostile attributions, response access, and response evaluation, considered simultaneously) provided a significantly better fit for the data than did a direct effects model. In fact, nearly 50% of the effect of retaliation beliefs on aggressive behavior was accounted for by deviant SIP. Findings from these two studies thus provide preliminary support for the hypothesis that representations of others and social knowledge structures affect social behavior through their influence on online SIP.

Results from another recent study, however, suggest that the relationships among latent mental structures, SIP, and behavior are less clear. Burks et al. (1999) examined the relative contributions of hostile representations of others and biased processing on aggression. When representations and processing variables were entered simultaneously, only the path between representations and aggression remained significant. Furthermore, the significant relations between SIP and aggression were all accounted for by children's representations of others, directly contradicting the mediational hypothesis proposed by Crick and Dodge.

In summary, since Crick and Dodge's review, hypothesized linkages between social experience, latent mental structures, online processing, and social behavior and adjustment have been examined in several studies. Research in this area remains rather limited, however, and the theory that Crick and Dodge propose in which latent mental structures develop in response to social experience, and then influence subsequent social experience via the impact of these structures on online information processing, has not yet been adequately tested. Large-scale longitudinal studies utilizing sophisticated techniques such as structural equation modeling will be necessary to fully test these hypotheses.

Issue 2: Does children's SIP change in response to their social experience? Because early SIP models were developed with the goal of understanding the origin of social maladjustment, most prior research has generally examined the premise that biased processing leads to maladaptive social behavior. In their 1994 review, Crick and Dodge underscored the virtual absence of work examining the counterhypothesis—that social maladjustment (e.g., chronic peer rejection; conflictual, aggressive peer interactions) may influence the development and maintenance of biased social cognitions. Although longitudinal studies of the relation between information processing and aggression are becoming more common, studies designed to explore reciprocal effects among these phenomena are still limited.

In a series of longitudinal studies, Dodge et al. (2001) have begun exploring the contribution of social maladjustment to the development of SIP deficits. These authors examined relationships among peer social preference, SIP, and childhood aggression in a sample of 259 children over a three-year period. They found that early rejection by peers predicted deviant SIP two years later. These results remained significant even after controlling for early SIP patterns— that is, low social preference in kindergarten predicted a decrease in social cognitive competence over time. In addition, SIP in grade 2 mediated the relationship between early peer preference and later aggressive behavior. These findings were replicated in a longitudinal study of 585 children, followed from kindergarten to third grade. In this sample, kindergarten social preference predicted both grade 2 response generation and grade 3 aggression scores. Similarly, response generation mediated the impact of early peer experience on the development of aggression. Dodge and colleagues suggest that these findings support a model in which early social cognitive biases or deficits lead to peer rejection. The experience of early peer rejection, either by confirming biased processing patterns or by limiting a child's ability to obtain needed social experience, leads to stronger cognitive biases, which contribute, in turn, to maladaptive behavior such as aggression.

The impact of social experience on the development of SIP patterns has been examined in only one additional study. Egan, Monson, and Perry (1998) examined short-term longitudinal relations among several aspects of response evaluation (e.g., self-efficacy for aggression, expectations that aggression would be rewarded, and response selection) and peer nominations for aggression and victimization in a sample of 189 third through seventh graders. Boys who experienced high levels of victimization in the fall showed a decrease in the expectation that aggression would yield tangible rewards in the spring. These findings suggest that, perhaps as a result of their inability to successfully defend themselves, victimized children change their beliefs about the utility of aggression for obtaining their social goals. Although early levels of aggression did not predict any SIP changes, biased processing early in the school year predicted increased aggression over time only among children who were already fairly aggressive. On the basis of these results, the authors suggest that SIP influences the development of aggression only when processing patterns are supported by children's social experiences.

Several studies have examined reciprocal effects between social maladjustment and negatively biased social knowledge structures. Huesmann and Guerra (1997) examined longitudinal changes in normative beliefs about aggression and peer-nominated aggressive behavior in three cohorts of elementary school children. Among the younger cohort (first and second graders), children who exhibited high levels of aggression at one time were likely to develop cognitions supporting the use of aggression. In contrast, early beliefs in the legitimacy of aggression did not predict subsequent aggression. For the older cohort (fourth graders), the opposite was true—later normative beliefs were best predicted by early normative beliefs and not by early aggression. The authors concluded that early aggression influences the formation of beliefs about aggression, but that such beliefs stabilize relatively early in development and are then less influenced by subsequent experiences with aggression.

Early social maladjustment has also been shown to influence the development of negative representations of peers. MacKinnon-Lewis et al. (1999) found strong evidence for reciprocal relations between social adjustment and children's cognitive representations of their peers among young school-age boys. In this two-year longitudinal study, beliefs about familiar and unfamiliar peers were associated with differential social outcomes. Specifically, boys who held negative feelings about known peers at the beginning of the school year were less likely to be accepted by peers six months later. In turn, low peer acceptance was predictive of ongoing negative beliefs about familiar peers. These findings remained significant even after controlling for the stability of beliefs and earlier social preference. An identical pattern of reciprocal relations emerged between children's feelings about unfamiliar peers and peer-nominated aggressive behavior. In other words, negative representations of unfamiliar peers predicted later aggression, which subsequently predicted negative beliefs about unfamiliar peers. Taken together, these results suggest that boys' beliefs about peers influence their future peer experiences and that these experiences, in turn, refine or alter their original beliefs. These results support the hypothesis that SIP and social adjustment impact each other in a reciprocal fashion over time.

Issue 3: How is SIP influenced by children's emotional state? Although Crick and Dodge (1994) do not explicitly integrate emotion into their revised SIP model, they hypothesized that emotion influences SIP in important ways. In addition to serving as an internal cue to be encoded and interpreted, affective state is posited to influence how situations are interpreted and to prime the retrieval of particular behavioral responses. Furthermore, because goal clarification is thought to be influenced by affect regulation, emotions are hypothesized to "enhance or inhibit a child's motivation to formulate or pursue particular goals" (p. 81). Similar hypotheses were proposed by Huesmann (1998), whose model of SIP explicitly posits a role for emotion at each processing stage. By way of example, Huesmann suggests that negative affect interpreted as anger may predispose a child to attend to and misinterpret hostile cues, facilitate the retrieval of aggressive solutions, and cue normative beliefs about the appropriateness of aggression. Finally, both Huesmann and Crick and Dodge (1994) hypothesize that the relation between emotion and cognition is reciprocal.

Several studies have utilized affect induction techniques to explore the influence of different emotional states on information processing. Cates and Shontz (1996) examined the hostile attributional biases and response tendencies of aggressive and nonaggressive boys under normal testing conditions and under time pressure. Time pressure resulted in higher arousal for both groups, but aggressive boys reported more hostile attributions only when under time pressure. For both groups, time pressure resulted in a higher number and broader range of solutions and a higher proportion of aggressive responses. Similarly, Bodenhausen, Sheppard, and Kramer (1994) found that asking college students to recall a sad or angry episode prior to completing a social perception task influenced the judgments that subjects made about the behavior of hypothetical peers in ambiguous situations. Specifically, students in the angry affect condition were more likely than sad and neutral subjects to make negative judgments on the basis of stereotypic information. Finally, Dorsch and Keane (1994) manipulated children's arousal level prior to administering a SIP task by exposing them to one of four contexts: competition with success; competition with failure; cooperation with success; and cooperation with failure. Hostile attributional biases were significantly more likely after the experience of failure but the generation of aggressive solutions was not directly affected by context.

Results of research reviewed in this section suggest that, as hypothesized, negative emotion plays a significant role in the processing of social information, specifically in preemptive processing and the priming of hostile attributions.

Issue 4: What role does development play in the relationship between SIP and social adjustment? Crick and Dodge (1994) noted that very little conceptual and empirical work has been aimed at exploring developmental change in SIP, a situation that continues to constrain our understanding of the links between SIP and adjustment. In general, research examining SIP has not been well integrated with general theories of cognitive developmental change or with empirical work assessing the development of related social cognitive abilities (e.g., perspective taking, theory of mind), making it difficult to formulate specific, detailed hypotheses about changes in SIP skills over time. Results from existing cross-sectional and short-term longitudinal studies suggest that important age-related change exists in children's SIP skills. Children appear to become more efficient and accurate in their encoding of social information with age, are less likely to make biased attributions, and generate a greater number of competent responses to peer conflict (Crick & Dodge, 1996; Dodge & Price, 1994; Gronau & Waas, 1997).

Developmental changes in the link between social cognitions and social adjustment have also been noted. For example, Huesmann and Guerra (1997) found that children's normative beliefs about the appropriateness of aggression undergo important developmental change during the early elementary school years. In general, as children grow older they increasingly endorse beliefs supporting aggression, with the most dramatic change occurring between first and second grade. Prior to this shift, normative beliefs do not predict concurrent or future aggressive behavior. However, once these beliefs become reasonably stable, normative beliefs supporting aggression become related to aggressive behavior. Similarly, Dodge and Price (1994) examined relations between SIP and socially competent behavior among first through third graders. Older children consistently displayed more competent processing than their younger counterparts and age differences were also found in the magnitude of the relation between processing patterns and social competence. The relevance of specific processing patterns to social adjustment also seemed to change with age.

Empirical support for age-related changes in the association between particular SIP abilities and social adjustment underscores the importance of theoretical and conceptual work addressing developmental changes in SIP. Clearly articulated hypotheses regarding the link between information processing and adjustment are necessary to guide empirical work in this area. In addition, longitudinal research spanning broader developmental periods is necessary to determine the relative salience of discrete SIP steps to adjustment over time.

Issue 5: Does gender moderate the relation between SIP and social adjustment? Despite robust findings indicating that boys and girls approach and manage their social relationships and interpersonal behavior very differently (see Maccoby, 1988 for review), empirical work exploring potential social cognitive correlates of these differences has been limited. Several researchers have hypothesized that gender differences in SIP underlie the social behavioral differences observed between boys and girls. In general, empirical work supports these hypotheses. Girls have been shown to make fewer encoding errors and to engage in less preemptive processing than boys (Gronau & Waas, 1997; Harrist, Zaia, Bates, Dodge, & Pettit, 1997), to endorse relationship maintenance goals over instrumental concerns (Rose & Asher, 1998), and to more strongly endorse accommodation and compromise strategies in response to conflict (Hopmeyer & Asher, 1997; Rose & Asher, 1998). Conversely, boys are more likely to positively endorse aggressive strategies (Dorsch & Keane, 1994; Erdley & Asher, 1998; Hopmeyer & Asher, 1997), to negatively evaluate prosocial and passive responses to peer conflict (Chung & Asher, 1996), to select goals reflecting concerns with dominance and control (Chung & Asher, 1996; Rose & Asher, 1998), and to report beliefs about the legitimacy of aggression (Guerra et al., 1994; Souweidane & Huesmann, 1999). Gender differences in the tendency to display hostile attributional biases (Dorsch & Keane, 1994; Gronau & Waas, 1997; Harrist et al., 1997) or in the number of solutions generated to social dilemmas (Harrist et al., 1997) have not been reported.

Because SIP patterns differ for boys and girls, researchers have hypothe-sized that the relation between SIP and social adjustment may differ for boys and girls as well. This hypothesis has received only limited support. While girls are less likely than boys to demonstrate SIP deficits associated with aggressive behavior, such deficits seem related in similar ways for boys and girls (Gronau & Waas, 1997; Hopmeyer & Asher, 1997; Rose & Asher, 1998). That is, for girls and boys, the tendency to endorse antisocial goals, to positively evaluate aggressive and hostile response strategies, and to believe in the legiti-macy of aggression are positively related to aggressive behavior. However, the relation between these deficits and maladjustment is often weaker for girls (Erdley & Asher 1999; Guerra et al., 1995; Huesmann & Guerra, 1997).

Crick (1995) suggested that the weaker link between SIP deficits and maladjustment in girls stems from two basic limitations of past research: (a) failure to consider the forms of aggression that are most common for girls and (b) failure to evaluate SIP deficits in contexts that are relevant and chal-lenging for aggressive girls. To address these limitations, Crick and colleagues (Crick, 1995; Crick & Werner, 1998; and Nelson & Crick, 1999) initiated a series of studies examining the social cognitive correlates of relational aggression, a form of aggression more salient for girls than boys. Relational aggression is characterized by attempts to hurt or harm others by damaging/threatening to damage the peer relationships of others through such behaviors as gossip, ostracism, and threats to withdraw friendship. Because girls are more likely than boys to engage in relational aggression (Crick & Grotpeter, 1995; but see chap. 2, this volume, for a more detailed discussion of these issues), Crick (1995) has argued that contexts involving relational provocation may be particularly important for exploring SIP patterns of aggressive girls. In a study examining this hypothesis, Crick (1995) found that for boys and girls, children character-ized as relationally aggressive demonstrated hostile attributional biases in response to relational but not instrumental provocation. Physically aggressive children, in contrast, made biased attributions in instrumental conflicts only. In addition, girls were more likely than boys to report feelings of distress in response to relational provocation. Crick and Werner (1998) examined response decision biases in similar contexts. Girls were more likely than boys to positively evaluate relational aggression but only in the context of relational provocation. Boys were more likely to endorse overt aggression than girls, regardless of provocation type. Finally, children engaging in *gender atypical* aggression (i.e., overtly aggressive girls and relationally aggressive boys) demonstrated process-ing biases that are even more deviant than those of children who demonstrate excessive but gender normative aggression.

On the basis of the research summarized in this section, several important conclusions can be drawn. First, boys and girls do demonstrate different pat-terns of SIP that reflect their differing social orientations. Second, to some extent, gender moderates the relation between SIP and overt aggression in that the link between SIP deficits and physical aggression, while apparent for both genders, is stronger for boys. Finally, attention to the types of aggression that are salient to boys and girls suggests that SIP may also mediate the relation between gender and aggression—that is, boys and girls may engage in different levels of overt and relational aggression, in part because of different patterns of SIP. Additional studies with analytical techniques such as structural equation modeling are necessary to test this hypothesis more rigorously.

Issue 6: Can the SIP model be generalized to other forms of social adjustment besides aggression? Although Crick and Dodge's model of SIP was originally conceived as a model for explaining the relation between processing deficits and social maladjustment generally, empirical work aimed at exploring this relation has focused almost exclusively on aggression. Peer rejection, as an index of maladjustment, has also received some attention but appears to be linked to SIP largely through its strong relation with aggressive behavior. Recent work has begun to address the question of generalizability more directly by extending the model to other forms of social adjustment. In general, deficits and biases in SIP appear to be a common characteristic of children with a variety of social adjustment difficulties. However, the nature of these deficits varies considerably and provides important insight into the development/ maintenance of these different disorders.

Internalizing Behavior: Social Withdrawal, Depression, and Anxiety

Several studies have been initiated with the aim of assessing the generalizability of the SIP model to internalizing difficulties including social withdrawal (Chung & Asher, 1996; Harrist et al., 1997; Hopmeyer & Asher, 1997; Stewart & Rubin, 1995), depression (Baker, Milich, & Manolis, 1996; Dodge, 1993), and anxiety (Daleiden & Vasey, 1997). There is growing evidence that children with these forms of social maladjustment share several common processing difficulties, including poor encoding and recall of social cues, attributional biases, and a predisposition to generate and select passive, avoidant responses to social conflict. In addition to these common characteristics, processing patterns specific to the different types of internalizing difficulties have begun to emerge as well (Harrist et al., 1997).

SIP and Withdrawn Behavior

Like aggression, social withdrawal among children is typically identified through the use of peer nomination inventories or teacher ratings, or both. Relative to their nonwithdrawn peers, withdrawn children are less accurate in their encoding of relevant social information (Harrist et al., 1977) and demonstrate a general tendency to perceive intent inaccurately across a variety of situations (Waldman, 1996). It is interesting that this effect seems to be limited to withdrawn children who are further characterized by attentional deficits and impulsive behavior. There is no evidence to date to suggest that withdrawn children demonstrate hostile attributional biases. In fact, there is some suggestion that withdrawn children, particularly those characterized by low sociability and passivity, may *under*attribute hostility in the face of provocation (Harrist et al., 1997).

By far, the majority of studies examining the SIP patterns of withdrawn children have focused on withdrawn children's ability to generate and evaluate responses to social dilemmas. Across studies varying in methodology (e.g., live observations versus responses to hypothetical vignettes), withdrawn children have consistently been shown to generate fewer problem-solving, verbally assertive, and aggressive solutions and significantly more indirect, passive, and avoidant behavioral responses to social dilemmas than their nonwithdrawn peers (Chung & Asher, 1996; Hopmeyer & Asher, 1997; Stewart & Rubin, 1995). In addition, withdrawn children are more likely than their nonwithdrawn counterparts to evaluate passive, withdrawn strategies positively and less likely to hold strong beliefs about the legitimacy of aggression (Erdley & Asher, 1998). Finally, behavioral observations of withdrawn children in naturalistic settings suggest that these children are more likely to experience failure when attempting to initiate social interaction or resolve conflicts and are less likely to persist after initial failure experiences (Stewart & Rubin, 1995).

SIP in Relation to Childhood Depression

To date, research on the SIP patterns of depressed children has been rather limited. Quiggle, Garber, Panak, & Dodge (1992) reported that depressed children demonstrated a hostile attributional bias similar to children who are aggressive. Unlike aggressive children, however, depressed children were also less likely than comparison children to suggest assertive responses to interpersonal problems and they expected assertive responses would lead to more negative and fewer positive responses. In these ways, their SIP patterns were similar to what has been reported for children who are withdrawn and impulsive.

Depressed children selectively attend to negative events and information (particularly when related to the self) (Dodge, 1993), negatively evaluate themselves and others (Baker et al., 1996), report less efficacy for assertive and competent responses, and demonstrate hopelessness about future outcomes (Dodge, 1993). Finally, depressed children and children who are both socially neglected and lonely make stable, internal attributions for social failure and fail to take credit for their social successes (Crick & Ladd, 1993; Dodge, 1993). The conclusion that emerges from these studies is that information processing patterns of depressed children are distinguished most clearly by negative self-evaluations and hopelessness about their ability to effectively manage their social environments.

SIP in Relation to Childhood Anxiety

Anxious children have been found to demonstrate characteristic deficits at multiple stages of SIP. Relative to normal controls, anxious children have been shown to selectively attend to threatening cues (Daleiden & Vasey, 1997), to view ambiguous situations as threatening (Daleiden & Vasey, 1997), to attribute hostile intent in benign situations (Bell-Dolan, 1995), and to choose behavioral responses to conflict characterized by avoidance and distraction (Barrett,

Rapee, Dadds, & Ryan, 1996). Similar to their depressed counterparts, anxious children are also more likely to display internal, stable attributions for failure (Daleiden & Vasey, 1997), to expect negative outcomes, and to doubt their ability to cope successfully with threatening situations (Chorpita, Albano, & Barlow, 1996).

These studies suggest that children who experience internalizing difficulties share a number of common information processing deficits, particularly in their tendency to respond to social dilemmas in passive, avoidant ways. Behavior-specific processing patterns also exist. For example, depressed children are characterized by biases that reflect both a negative view of the self and a perceived inability to effect change in their social environments, whereas anxious children selectively attend to and seek to reduce or avoid anxiety-provoking stimuli. Thus, the links between SIP and internalizing behavior problems reviewed here provide evidence for the generalizability and utility of Crick and Dodge's model for understanding and discriminating among forms of social maladjustment beyond aggression.

SIP in Relation to Proactive and Reactive Aggression

Crick and Dodge's model can also be extended to allow for a more detailed examination of the links between processing deficits and specific subtypes or profiles of aggression. For example, recent theoretical and empirical work has emphasized the importance of distinguishing between children who display predominantly reactive or retaliatory aggression (i.e., angry aggression in the face of perceived threat) and those who display proactive aggression (i.e., non-angry aggression aimed at obtaining instrumental or relational goals), as the correlates and outcomes of these forms of aggression appear to be somewhat distinct (Dodge & Coie, 1987). Several theorists (Crick & Dodge, 1996; Dodge et al., 1997) suggest that the SIP patterns of proactively and reactively aggressive children may differ in (at least) two important ways. First, because reactive aggression is motivated by perceived threat, reactively aggressive children may be more likely than their proactively and nonaggressive peers to demonstrate processing biases in the early stages of information processing (e.g., selective attention to hostile cues, hostile attributional biases). Second, because proactive aggression is motivated by desire to obtain specific outcomes and less tied to angry affect, proactively aggressive children should be more likely to demonstrate biases in the latter stages of processing (e.g., goal setting, response evaluation). Although only a few studies have been conducted to date exploring social cognitive correlates of reactive and proactive aggression, available evidence is generally consistent with these hypotheses. Dodge and colleagues (1997) looked at processing differences among proactively and reactively aggressive children in two studies, one involving a large sample of elementary school children and a second involving a smaller sample of psychiatrically impaired and chronically violent boys. In both studies, reactively aggressive children demonstrated significantly more encoding errors (i.e., fewer relevant responses) than their proactively aggressive and nonaggressive peers. The evidence linking reactive aggression and hostile attributional biases is more equivocal. In the three studies to date examining this question (all with samples of elementary school children), reactive aggression and hostile attributional biases were marginally related in one study (Schwartz et al., 1998) and unrelated in another (Dodge et al., 1997). In the remaining study (Crick & Dodge, 1996), reactively aggressive children were more likely than their nonaggressive peers to demonstrate hostile attributions but did not differ from their proactively aggressive peers on this dimension.

More consistent support has been found for the hypothesis that proactively aggressive children demonstrate specific biases in the latter stages of information processing compared with their reactively aggressive peers. In particular, proactively aggressive children were more likely than their reactive counterparts to anticipate positive outcomes for aggression (Crick & Dodge, 1996; Dodge et al., 1997; Schwartz et al., 1998), to report greater self-efficacy for enacting aggressive solutions (Crick & Dodge, 1996; Dodge et al., 1997), and to choose instrumental rather than relational goals (Crick & Dodge, 1996).

The relation between social cognition and proactive and reactive aggression has been further clarified by recent work that emphasizes the importance of the dyadic context in which aggression occurs. In addition to attending to an individual's general or global social cognitions (e.g., "others are out to get me" or "aggression is effective"), these authors suggest that specific cognitions about one's social partner (e.g., "he's out to get me" or "he always gives in when I threaten him") influence the frequency and type of aggression that occurs. To address these issues, recent studies have attempted to predict the frequency of reactive and proactive aggression within familiar dyads by examining the relative contributions of actor effects (e.g., general predisposition toward aggression, global social cognitions about aggression), partner effects (e.g., tendency to be victimized by others, how one is perceived by others), and relationship effects (e.g., characteristics of a given dyad, such as relationship history, that are independent of actor and partner effects). Coie et al., (1999) examined the frequency of dyadic reactive and proactive aggression in 11 playgroups of school-age boys, in which members were familiar with each other, as well as each child's social cognitions about the other members of the group. Results suggested that relationship factors accounted for more of the systematic variance in reactive aggression between male peers than did either actor or partner effects. Furthermore, boys in dyads characterized by mutual aggression were more likely than boys in randomly selected dyads to attribute hostile intentions to their partners. The opposite was true for expectations regarding the efficacy of aggression; that is, boys in randomly selected dyads were more likely to expect aggression to be effective than were boys from mutually aggressive dyads. These results suggest that the increased frequency of reactive aggression in mutually aggressive dyads may stem from shared hostility and distrust between familiar partners or conversely, that a long history of mutual aggression leads boys to form specific hostile attributions about each other that, in turn, impact their ongoing interactions.

Using the same sample, Hubbard, Dodge, Cillessen, Coie, and Schwartz (2001) extended Coie et. al.'s findings by demonstrating that hostile attributions at the dyadic level predicted dyadic reactive aggression—that is, the frequency of reactive aggression within a particular dyad was predicted by the actor's hostile attributions about his partner. It is important to note that the relation between dyadic hostile attributions and dyadic reactive aggression held, even after controlling for the influence of several factors including the actor's tendency to engage in reactive aggression across partners, the actor's tendency to make hostile attributions across partners, the partner's tendency to be victimized across partners, and the groups' perception of the partner's hostility. Proactive aggression, on the other hand, appears to be less of a dyadic phenomenon. Boys engage in proactive aggression more as a function of partner effects, choosing to aggress against those peers with a history of submissive behavior within the larger peer group. Taken together, these results suggest that specific types of aggressive behavior are predicted by different steps of the SIP model (e.g., hostile attributions versus outcome expectancies) as well as the level at which such processing takes place (e.g., global versus dyadic social cognitions).

SIP and Socially Competent Children

Socially competent children can be reliably distinguished from both their average and less competent peers on the basis of their SIP patterns. Prosocial or well-accepted children have been shown to be more accurate in their encoding of social cues (Dodge & Price, 1994), less likely to attribute hostile intent (Dodge & Price, 1994), and more likely to perceive benign intent in response to both relational and instrumental provocation (Nelson & Crick, 1999). Perhaps because of their stronger tendency to perceive benign intent, prosocial children also report feeling less distressed by peer conflict (Nelson & Crick, 1999). In addition, prosocial children are more likely than their average and less competent peers to endorse relational goals over instrumental ones (Nelson & Crick, 1999) and less likely to endorse revenge goals (Rose & Asher, 1998). Prosocial children are also more likely to generate and positively evaluate prosocial, problem-solving strategies (Chung & Asher, 1996; Dodge & Price, 1994; Erdley & Asher, 1998; Hopmeyer & Asher, 1997; Nelson & Crick, 1999) and less likely to endorse aggressive, hostile strategies (Chung & Asher, 1996; Erdley & Asher, 1998; Nelson & Crick, 1999; Rose & Asher, 1998). Across studies then, prosocial children demonstrate a clear pattern of SIP that reflects a priority for maintaining harmonious relationships with peers.

The studies reviewed in this section provide ample evidence for the generalizability of Crick and Dodge's model of SIP to adjustment patterns beyond aggression. In addition to increasing our understanding of the different social cognitive correlates of global forms of social adjustment (e.g., aggression, internalizing difficulties, socially competent behavior), a SIP perspective provides important insight into subtypes of these behavioral categories as well (e.g., between depression and anxiety; proactive and reactive aggression). In other words, the model provides a general template for understanding the relation between SIP and social adjustment, and this template has proven useful in identifying specific information processing patterns that seem to be associated with different types of adjustment difficulties.

In fact, different stages of the information processing model appear to be salient for different disorders. For example, whereas both anxious and aggressive children are likely to overperceive hostile intent in the face of ambiguous provocation, the nature of their response to this threat has been shown to be quite different. Anxious children are more likely to utilize avoidant responses while aggressive children are motivated to retaliate or reestablish their dominant status through violent behavior. As evident in the results reviewed above, important differences in the causal attributional tendencies in children with these two types of adjustment difficulties as well as likely differences in their social goals and affective states combine to produce these very different responses. Future work is needed to hone and test these emergent hypotheses. Empirical work examining links between affect and processing across children displaying different forms of social adjustment may prove to be particularly fruitful.

General Conclusions and Future Directions

Despite the promising advances reviewed in this chapter, many of the issues outlined above remain unresolved and require additional theoretical and empirical attention. Understanding the emergence of SIP patterns within the context of normal development, gaining a clearer understanding of how social cognition interacts with emotional regulation to produce negative social outcomes, and understanding how patterns of conscious, reflective processing elicited in response to hypothetical scenarios relate to online, automatic processing in naturally occurring social interactions stand out as areas requiring additional exploration. Addressing these more complex and detailed questions, while difficult, remains critical to advancing our understanding of links between children's ability to reason about and negotiate their social worlds.

References

Baker, M., Milich, R., & Manolis, M. (1996). Peer interactions of dysphoric adolescents. *Journal of Abnormal Child Psychology, 24,* 241–255.

Barrett, P., Rapee, R., Dadds, M., & Ryan, S. (1996). Family enhancement of cognitive style in anxious and aggressive children: Threat bias and the FEAR effect. *Journal of Abnormal Child Psychology, 24,* 187–203.

Bell-Dolan, D. (1995). Social cue interpretation of anxious children. *Journal of Clinical Child Psychology, 24,* 1–10.

Bodenhausen, G., Sheppard, L., & Kramer, G. (1994). Negative affect and social judgment. The differential impact of anger and sadness. *European Journal of Social Psychology, 24,* 45–62.

Burks, V., Dodge, K., Price, J., & Laird, R. (1999). Internal representational models of peers: Implications for the development of problematic behavior. *Developmental Psychology, 35,* 802–810.

Burks, V., Laird, R., Dodge, K., Pettit, G., & Bates, J. (1999). Knowledge structures, social information processing, and children's aggressive behavior. *Social Development, 8,* 220–236.

Cassidy, J., Kirsh, S., Scolton, K., & Parke, R. (1996). Attachment and representations of peer relationships. *Developmental Psychology, 32,* 892–904.

Cates, D., & Shontz, F. (1996). The effects of time pressure on social cognitive problem-solving by aggressive and nonaggressive boys. *Child Study Journal, 26,* 163–191.

Chorpita, B., Albano, A., & Barlow, D. (1996). Cognitive processing in children: Relationship to anxiety and family influences. *Journal of Clinical Child Psychology, 25,* 170–176.

Chung, T., & Asher, S. (1996). Children's goals and strategies in peer conflict situations. *Merrill-Palmer Quarterly, 42,* 125–147.

Coie, J., Cillessen, A., Dodge, K., Hubbard, J., Schwartz, D., Lemerise, E., & Bateman, H. (1999). It takes two to fight: A test of relational factors and a method for assessing aggressive dyads. *Developmental Psychology, 35,* 1179–1188.

Crick, N. (1995). Relational aggression: The role of intent attributions, feelings of distress, and provocation type. *Development and Psychopathology, 7,* 313–322.

Crick, N., & Dodge, K. (1994). A review and reformulation of social information processing mechanisms in children's social adjustment. *Psychological Bulletin, 115,* 74–101.

Crick, N., & Dodge, K. (1996). Social information processing mechanisms in reactive and proactive aggression. *Child Development, 67,* 993–1002.

Crick, N. & Grotpeter, J. (1995). Relational aggression, gender, and social–psychological adjustment. *Child Development, 66,* 710–722.

Crick, N., & Ladd, G. (1993). Children's perceptions of their peer experiences: Attributions, loneliness, social anxiety, and social avoidance. *Developmental Psychology, 29,* 244–254.

Crick, N., & Werner, N. (1998). Response decision processes in relational and overt aggression. *Child Development, 69,* 1630–1639.

Daleiden, E., & Vasey, M. (1997). An information-processing perspective on childhood anxiety. *Clinical Psychology Review, 17,* 407–429.

Dodge, K. (1986). A social information processing model of social competence in children. In M. Perlmutter (Ed.), *The Minnesota Symposia on Child Psychology: Vol. 8. Cognitive perspectives on children's social and behavioral development* (pp. 77–125). Hillsdale, NJ: Erlbaum.

Dodge, K. (1993). Social-cognitive mechanisms in the development of conduct disorder and depression. *Annual Review of Psychology, 44,* 559–584.

Dodge, K., & Coie, J. (1987). Social information processing factors in reactive and proactive aggression in children's peer groups. *Journal of Personality and Social Psychology, 53,* 389–409.

Dodge, K., Lansford, J., Burks, V., Bates, J., Pettit, G., Fontaine, R., & Price, J. (2001). *Peer rejection and social information processing factors in the development of aggressive behavior problems in children.* Manuscript submitted for publication.

Dodge, K., Lochman, J., Harnish, J., Bates, J., & Pettit, G. (1997). Reactive and proactive aggression in school children and psychiatrically impaired chronically assaultive youth. *Journal of Abnormal Psychology, 106,* 37–51.

Dodge, K., & Price, J. (1994). On the relation between social information processing and socially competent behavior in early school-aged children. *Child Development, 65,* 1385–1397.

Dorsch, A., & Keane, S. (1994). Contextual factors in children's social information processing. *Developmental Psychology, 30,* 611–616.

Egan, S., Monson, T., & Perry, D. (1998). Social-cognitive influences on change in aggression over time. *Developmental Psychology, 34,* 996–1006.

Erdley, C., & Asher, S. (1998). Linkages between children's beliefs about the legitimacy of aggression and their behavior. *Social Development, 7,* 321–339.

Erdley, C., & Asher, S. (1999). A social goals perspective on children's social competence. *Journal of Emotional and Behavioral Disorders, 7,* 156–167.

Graham, S. & Hudley, C., (1994). Attributions of aggressive and nonaggressive African-American male early adolescents: A study of construct accessibility. *Developmental Psychology, 30,* 365–373.

Gronau, R., & Waas, G. (1997). Delay of gratification and cue utilization: An examination of children's social information processing. *Merrill-Palmer Quarterly, 43,* 305–322.

Guerra, N., Huesmann, L., & Hanish, L. (1994). The role of normative beliefs in children's social behavior. In N. Eisenberg (Ed.), *Review of personality and social psychology, developmental and social psychology: The interface* (pp. 140–158). London: Sage.

Guerra, N., Huesmann, L., Tolan, P., VanAcker, R., & Eron, L. (1995). Stressful events and individual beliefs as correlates of economic disadvantage and aggression among urban children. *Journal of Consulting and Clinical Psychology, 63,* 518–528.

Harrist, A., Zaia, A., Bates, J., Dodge, K., & Pettit, G. (1997). Subtypes of social withdrawal in early childhood: Sociometric status and social-cognitive differences across four years. *Child Development, 68,* 278–294.

Hopmeyer, A., & Asher, S. (1997). Children's responses to peer conflicts involving a rights infraction. *Merrill-Palmer Quarterly, 43,* 235–254.

Hubbard, J., Dodge, K., Cillessen, A., Coie, J., and Schwartz, D. (2001). The dyadic nature of social information processing in boys' reactive and proactive aggression. *Journal of Personality and Social Psychology, 80,* 268–280.

Huesmann, L. (1988). An information processing model for the development of aggression. *Aggressive Behavior, 14,* 13–24.

Huesmann, L. (1998). The role of social information processing and cognitive schema in the acquisition and maintenance of habitual aggressive behavior. In R. Green & E. Donnerstein (Eds.), *Human aggression: Theories, research, and implications for social policy* (pp. 73–109). San Diego, CA: Academic Press.

Huesmann, L., & Guerra, N. (1997). Children's normative beliefs about aggression and aggressive behavior. *Journal of Personality and Social Psychology, 72,* 408–419.

Lenhart, L., & Rabiner, D. (1995). An integrative approach to the study of social competence in adolescence. *Development & Psychopathology, 7(3),* 543–561.

Lochman, J., & Lenhart, L. (1995). Cognitive behavioral therapy of aggressive children: Effects of schemas. In H. van Bilsen (Ed.), *Behavioral approaches for children and adolescents* (pp. 145–166). New York: Plenum.

Maccoby, E. (1988). Gender as a social category. *Developmental Psychology, 24,* 755–765.

MacKinnon-Lewis, C., Rabiner, D., & Starnes, R. (1999). Predicting boys' social acceptance and aggression: The role of mother–child interactions and boys' beliefs about peers. *Developmental Psychology, 35,* 632–639.

Nelson, D., & Crick, N. (1999). Rose-colored glasses: Examining the social information processing of prosocial young adolescents. *Journal of Early Adolescence, 19,* 17–38.

Quiggle, N., Garber, J., Panak, W., & Dodge, K. (1992). Social information processing in aggressive and depressed children. *Child Development, 63,* 1305–1320.

Rabiner, D., Keane, S., & MacKinnon-Lewis, C. (1993). Children's beliefs about familiar and unfamiliar peers in relation to their sociometric status. *Developmental Psychology, 29,* 236–243.

Rose, A., & Asher, S. (1998). Children's goals and strategies in response to conflicts within a friendship. *Developmental Psychology, 35,* 69–79.

Rubin, K., & Krasnor, L. (1986). Social–cognitive and social behavioral perspectives on problem solving. In M. Perlmutter (Ed.), *The Minnesota Symposia on Child Psychology: Cognitive perspectives on children's social and behavioral develpoment Vol. 18* (pp. 1–68). Hillsdale, NJ: Erlbaum.

Rudolph, K., Hammen, C., & Burge, D. (1995). Cognitive representations of self, family, and peers in school-age children: Links with social competence and sociometric status. *Child Development, 66,* 1385–1402.

Schwartz, D., Dodge, K., Coie, J., Hubbard, J. Cillessen, A., Lemerise, E., & Bateman, H. (1998). Social cognitive and behavioral correlates of aggression and victimization in boy's play groups. *Journal of Abnormal Child Psychology, 26,* 431–440.

Shantz, C. U. (1975). The development of social cognition. In Hetherington, E. (Ed.), *Review of child development research.* Chicago, IL: University of Chicago Press.

Souweidane, V., & Huesmann, L. (1999). The influence of American urban culture on the development of normative beliefs about aggression in Middle-Eastern immigrants. *American Journal of Community Psychology, 27,* 239–254.

Stewart, S., & Rubin, K. (1995). The social problem-solving skills of anxious-withdrawn children. *Development and Psychopathology, 7,* 323–336.

Waldman, I. (1996). Aggressive boys' hostile perceptual and response biases: The role of attention and impulsivity. *Child Development, 67,* 1015–1033.

Zelli, A., Dodge, K., Lochman, J., Laird, R., & the Conduct Problems Prevention Research Group (1999). The distinction between beliefs legitimizing aggression and deviant processing of social cues: Testing measurement validity and the hypothesis that biased processing mediates the effects of beliefs on aggression. *Journal of Personality and Social Psychology, 77,* 150–166.

5

Children's Understanding and Regulation of Emotion in the Context of Their Peer Relations

Julie A. Hubbard and Karen F. Dearing

Over the past decade, researchers have paid increasing attention to the role that emotions play in children's peer interactions. Although research on the behavioral and social cognitive correlates of children's peer relations is extensive, research on emotional correlates has emerged more slowly. A decade ago, the edited volume by Asher and Coie (1990), which reviewed each of the prominent areas of peer relations research, did not include a chapter on emotion.

The slow development of research linking emotion and children's peer relations is surprising, given that children's emotional functioning likely influences the quality of their social interactions. The problems with peers that some children experience may stem in part from difficulties with understanding and regulating emotion. Specifically, misinterpretation of a peer's emotions or dysregulation of one's own experience and expression of emotion can strain any peer interaction. If these patterns of misinterpretation and dysregulation are stable over time, they likely contribute to peer rejection and the display of problematic behaviors.

Two possible reasons for the delayed progress in research linking peer relations and emotional functioning stand out. First, researchers have encountered considerable difficulty measuring emotion-related constructs in children. Second, until recently, the field has lacked a model of emotional functioning to guide the development of ideas and the formulation of hypotheses. The primary aim of this chapter is to review existing research on the emotional correlates of peer relations in the context of a model of emotional functioning, or affective social competence (ASC), recently developed by Halberstadt, Denham, and Dunsmore (2001). Throughout this process, we highlight measurement difficulties and corresponding points in the model where empirical data on the emotional correlates of peer relations are lacking.

We begin by describing Halberstadt et al.'s (2001) ASC model. Next, we integrate this model with the constructs of understanding and regulation of emotion. In the body of the chapter, we review empirical literature linking emotion understanding and emotion regulation with peer relations at each point of the model. Finally, we conclude by summarizing what this literature suggests about the emotional functioning of children with problematic peer relations.

A Model of Affective Social Competence

The ASC model presented by Halberstadt et al. (2001) is unique in that it is not described as a sequential process. As can be seen in Figure 5.1, the model

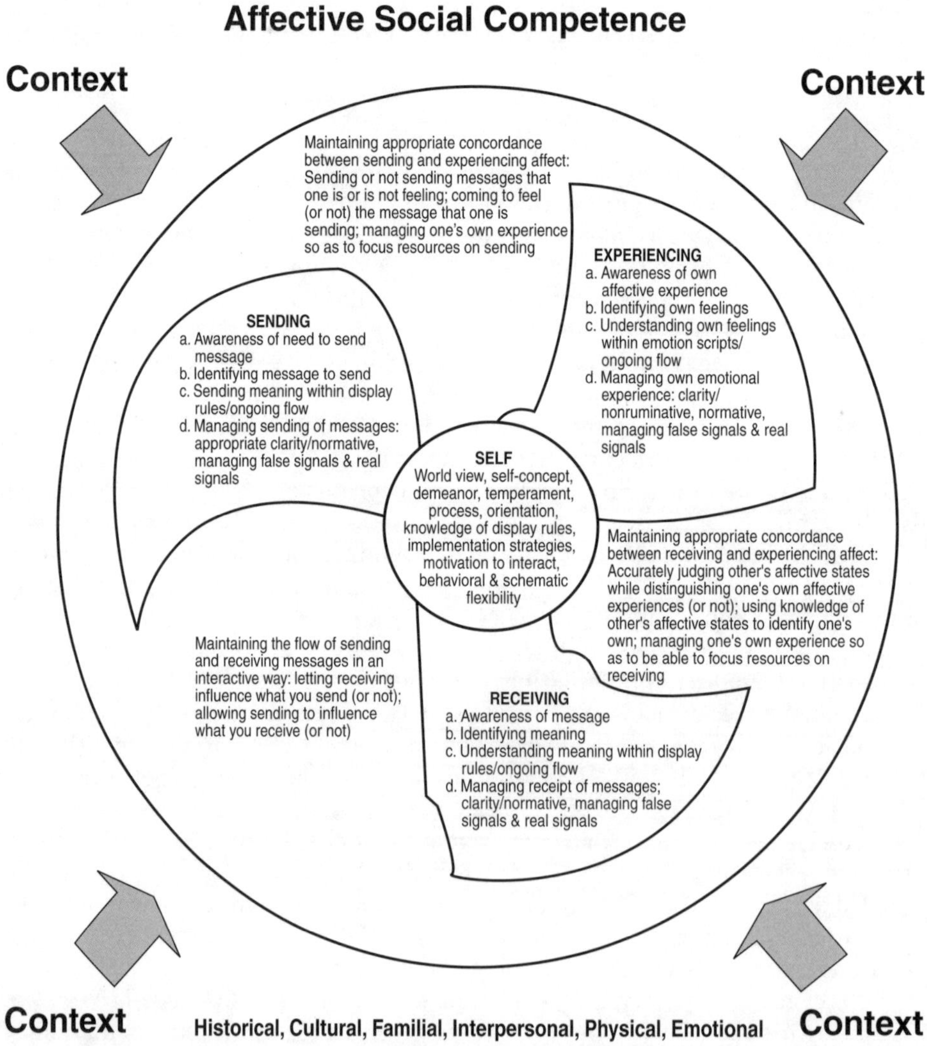

Figure 5.1.   Halberstadt, Denham, and Dunsmore's (2001) model of Affective Social Competence.

is depicted as a pinwheel in order to emphasize that the components of the model are in continuous interaction with one another. The model consists of three components—sending affective messages, receiving affective messages, and experiencing affect—along with a core of skills, dispositional attributes, and schemata that is unique to the self (self-factors). Halberstadt and colleagues lay out each component of the model in considerable detail, describing four processes common to sending, receiving, and experiencing affect. Although these individual processes provide a useful way to think about emotional functioning at a detailed level, our goal is to present a more general discussion of the ways that the three components of sending, receiving, and experiencing affect, plus the self-factors, are specifically linked to children's peer relations.

Integration of the ASC Model With the Distinction Between Understanding and Regulation of Emotion

Although the ASC model is intuitively easy to understand, the components of the model do not map smoothly onto the constructs of emotion understanding and emotion regulation. Historically, researchers have thought of these two constructs as the key elements of emotional functioning and have used this distinction to guide their work. Even though the newly developed model provides a more fine-grained conceptualization of emotional functioning, it is important to integrate this model with the historical breakdown of emotional functioning into understanding and regulation. This integration allows us to place existing research more easily into the framework of the model while at the same time allowing us to identify points in the model where empirical data are lacking. Furthermore, integrating these two approaches affords us an opportunity to examine the construct of emotion regulation more fully. The definition, operationalization, and measurement of emotion regulation have troubled researchers for years, and we believe that the ASC model presents a way to separate the construct of emotion regulation into constituent pieces rather than considering it a single entity.

Theorists and researchers have conceptualized emotion regulation as involving the regulation of both the internal experience of emotion and the external expression of emotion (Eisenberg & Fabes, 1999). For example, Eisenberg and colleagues have distinguished between emotion regulation and emotion-related behavioral regulation, with the first referring to the regulation of the internal experience of emotion and the second referring to the regulation of external expressive behaviors. Internal emotion regulation corresponds largely to the ASC model's experiencing component, while the regulation of the external expression of emotion maps most closely onto the ASC model's sending component. Similarly, researchers have studied understanding of emotion primarily in terms of identifying emotional messages from others, corresponding to the ASC model's receiving component. Finally, several constructs included in the ASC model's self-factors likely influence the regulation of emotion (e.g., temperament), while others may be more related to understanding of emotion (e.g., knowledge of display rules).

Existing Research Linking Understanding and Regulation of Emotion With Peer Relations in the Context of the ASC Model

We begin by presenting research on the connections between understanding of emotion and peer constructs, followed by work on emotion regulation and peer constructs. Within these two sections, we organize literature based on the relevant components of the ASC model. Furthermore, at the level of each component, we divide existing research into two sections: studies relating emotion constructs to social competence and studies relating emotion constructs to problem behaviors. Measures included under the label *Social Competence* include sociometric nominations of liking and disliking; sociometric ratings; and teacher-, parent-, and observer-rated popularity, social skills, socially appropriate behavior, and social competence. Similarly, measures included in *Problem Behaviors* are peer-rated aggression; diagnoses of oppositional-defiant disorder (ODD) and conduct disorder (CD); self-reports of aggression; and teacher- and parent-rated aggressive behavior, disruptive behavior, difficult temperament, conduct problems, externalizing behavior, and problem behavior.

Understanding of Emotion

Research on emotion understanding is plentiful when compared with work on emotion regulation, in part because it is easier to measure. When researchers measure understanding of emotion, children answer straightforward questions that assess their knowledge about things such as identifying emotions and matching situations with appropriate emotions.

Receiving Affective Messages

The primary element of the receiving affective messages component of the ASC model is identifying emotion in others. Research on children's ability to perceive affect in others has been conducted primarily in two areas. First, researchers have measured children's ability to identify emotions in others on the basis of physical cues such as facial expression and tone of voice. Alternatively, children's ability to identify emotions on the basis of situational cues has been assessed through hypothetical vignette methodology involving videotapes, verbal stories, or puppets.

SOCIAL COMPETENCE. A number of researchers have investigated links between social competence and children's ability to identify emotions based on physical or situational cues. At a general level, Vosk, Forehand, and Figueroa (1983) had teachers and peers in third- through fifth-grade classrooms rate children's ability to perceive emotions in others. Children classified as rejected on the basis of peer sociometric nominations and ratings were considered poorer perceivers of emotion in others than children classified as accepted.

More specifically, most of the research on children's ability to identify physical cues of emotions in others has focused on facial expressions. In a study of three- to five-year-old children, Field and Walden (1982) found that the ability to identify facial expressions of emotion was positively related to peer sociometric ratings. Using an older sample of 9- to 12-year-old children, Custrini and Feldman (1989) demonstrated that girls rated as higher in social competence by parents were more accurate in identifying facial expressions of emotion than were girls rated as low in social competence; however, this difference did not hold for boys. In a study by Edwards, Manstead, and MacDonald (1984) involving a similar age group, children classified as high status based on peer ratings of friendliness were more accurate at labeling emotional facial expressions compared with low status children. This same group of researchers found that children classified as rejected and neglected on the basis of peer sociometric nominations were worse at matching faces to emotion labels than were popular children at ages five, six, and nine years. Furthermore, across these time points, rejected children's rate of improvement in their ability to match faces to emotion labels was significantly slower than their peers' rate of improvement (Manstead & Edwards, 1992).

In addition to facial expressions, a few researchers have expanded this work to include other physical cues of emotion. For example, in a large sample of first- to fifth-grade children, Nowicki and Duke (1992, 1994) used facial expressions, tone of voice, gestures, and postures as physical cues of emotions. Children's ability to use all four types of cues to identify emotions in others was related to the number of both liked and disliked nominations received from peers. Likewise, Boyatzis and Satyaprasad (1994) showed that, for four- to five-year-old children, teacher-rated popularity was positively related to the ability to decode emotional gestures in others.

Although the ability to identify emotions in others on the basis of physical cues is clearly a necessary skill, physical cues may not be accurate indices of emotions in others, given that people often dissemble the external display of their internal feelings. Therefore, researchers have also studied children's ability to identify emotions in others on the basis of situational cues and have related this skill to measures of social competence. Specifically, four-year-old children's ability to match emotions to social situations is related to social preference scores based on peer ratings (Denham, McKinley, Couchoud, & Holt, 1990), to social preference scores based on sociometric nominations (Goldman, Corsini, & deUrioste, 1980), to negative nominations from peers (Goldman et al., 1980), and to positive nominations from peers (Rubin & Maioni, 1975). Using a similar age group, Philippot and Feldman (1990) demonstrated that children high in parent rated social skills were better at matching emotions to videotaped scenarios than were children low in social skills.

It is interesting to note that only one study that we know of has used a sample of older children to assess individual differences in the ability to use situational cues to identify emotions in others. In their study of third- through fifth-graders, Vosk et al. (1983) found that those classified as rejected on the basis of peer nominations and ratings made more errors when identifying how a character in a videotaped interaction was feeling than did accepted children. Perhaps researchers have not examined the relation between this ability and social competence as often in older children because it is thought that this is a skill that older children have mastered. However, the findings of Vosk and colleagues suggest that there is still variability in the mastery of this skill in middle childhood which can be explained in part by differences in social competence.

Finally, Cassidy, Parke, Butkovsky, and Braungart (1992) conducted a study in which they combined both physical and situational cues. In a sample of kindergartners and first graders, peer sociometric ratings were positively related to an aggregated variable that encompassed both the ability to identify facial expressions of emotion and the ability to match emotions to social situations.

PROBLEM BEHAVIORS. The literature linking children's problem behaviors to the ability to identify emotions based on physical or situational cues is much more limited than that involving social competence. The only study that we found relating problem behaviors to the ability to identify emotions on the basis of physical cues was conducted by Cook, Greenberg, and Kusche (1994). They asked first- and second-grade children to generate cues for identifying emotions in others and found that parent ratings of disruptive behavior were negatively related to the quality of cues generated. Likewise, Hughes, Dunn, and White (1998) conducted the only study that we know of linking problem behaviors to the ability to match emotions to social situations. Three- to six-year-old children rated by parents and teachers as having difficult temperament and high levels of conduct problems had more difficulty correctly identifying emotions in situations than did a matched sample of normal children.

GAPS IN THE LITERATURE AND FUTURE DIRECTIONS. What stands out is the scarcity of literature linking problem behaviors to skill at perceiving affect in others. Moreover, the relation between problem behaviors and identifying emotion in others needs to be examined in older children. Until more research is conducted in these areas, the role that the ability to receive affective messages plays in the development of children's problem behaviors remains uncertain.

More generally, the type of skills assessed as part of receiving affective messages is limited. Beyond examining knowledge of physical and situational cues of emotion, the field would be expanded by researching other relevant skills, such as the ability to monitor social interaction for the presence of affect in others. In addition, researchers have typically assessed identification skills in laboratory settings with static materials such as photographs. In contrast, identification may be much more challenging within the ongoing flow of social interaction.

Self-Factors Related to Receiving Affective Messages

Two constructs incorporated in the ASC model's self-factors seem closely related to receiving affective messages. First, a child's attributional tendencies may act as a filter when receiving affective messages from others. Children who attribute hostile intent to their peers may be more likely than other children to ascribe a negative valence to the emotional messages that they receive. In addition, a child's knowledge of display rules may influence the meaning that he or she assigns to affective messages. For example, children who more fully understand that the external expression of emotion may not match internal experience will be careful about relying exclusively on physical cues to identify emotions in others.

We are distinguishing knowledge of display rules from use of display rules, because we believe that these two constructs map onto different components of the ASC model. Knowledge of display rules is incorporated into self-factors. This construct involves skills such as understanding that external expression may not match internal experience and being able to generate strategies for emotional dissemblance. In contrast, we believe that use of display rules is most closely related to the actual sending of affective messages. This construct is measured by self-reports or observations of the extent to which children express or dissemble emotion, as well as by children's reports of strategies that they actually used to dissemble their feelings.

SOCIAL COMPETENCE. The one study that we found that explicitly examines the relation between social competence and children's knowledge of display rules was conducted by Jones, Abbey, and Cumberland (1998) and involved a sample of third- and fifth-grade children. Interviewers read hypothetical stories to children and asked them how the character felt inside and looked outside. College students also answered these questions, and children earned points for giving responses similar to those of the college students. Children's ability to generate display rules (to match the responses of college students) was positively related to teacher ratings of social competence and peer ratings.

In contrast, the literature relating attributional tendencies and social competence is much more robust. Crick and Dodge (1994) have thoroughly reviewed this literature; thus, this is the one point at which our review is not intended to be exhaustive. In numerous studies reviewed by Crick and Dodge, the tendency to attribute hostile intent to peers in situations in which the intent of the peer is ambiguous has been negatively related to a variety of different measures of social competence, including both peer and teacher ratings.

PROBLEM BEHAVIORS. Although we know of no studies linking knowledge of display rules to problem behaviors, the literature relating attributional tendencies to problem behaviors is ample and quite consistent. In the same review cited above, Crick and Dodge (1994) summarized a variety of studies showing that the tendency to attribute hostile intent to peers in ambiguous situations is positively related to different measures of problem behaviors, most notably peer nominations for aggression and teacher ratings of externalizing behavior.

GAPS IN THE LITERATURE AND FUTURE DIRECTIONS. Little work has been undertaken linking knowledge of display rules to social competence or problem behaviors. The developmental literature suggests that most children have at least a rudimentary understanding of display rules by the age of two or three. What is less well-known is whether individual differences in social functioning are related to the development of this knowledge.

In addition, other self-factors that have not been studied may act as filters in receiving affective messages and may be related to problematic peer relations. Examples of these self-factors include children's internal working models and aspects of children's self-concept.

Regulation of Emotion

A considerable amount of research has been conducted on a construct that researchers label *Emotion Regulation*. However, there is little agreement on how to define the term. Researchers also differ in their measurement of the construct, in that a wide array of often very different approaches has been used to try to measure emotion regulation. Given how disparate these measurement techniques are, emotion regulation likely consists of several components, rather than being a single entity. Our goal is to use the ASC model as a tool to organize these different methodologies and findings and to present a conceptualization of emotion regulation as consisting of three distinct pieces.

As presented above, three points in the ASC model encompass methodologies thought to measure emotion regulation. First, some researchers have assessed emotion regulation through self-reports of internal feelings or through physiological indices. We believe these methodologies relate to the regulation of the internal experience of emotion, and thus are best included under the Experiencing Affect component of the ASC model. Second, researchers have measured emotion regulation by assessing emotion expression (i.e., observations or self-reports), display rule use (i.e., observations or self-reports of expression), or observed and adult-rated coping. These measurement techniques involve regulating the external expression of emotion and thus fit into the Sending Affective Messages component of the ASC model. Third, researchers have tapped into emotion regulation by measuring children's temperament, self-control, and knowledge of display rules via parent, teacher, and self-report. These measures assess personal qualities and characteristics that affect children's motivation and ability to regulate emotion, and they are best included in the self-factors of the ASC model.

Experiencing Affect

One way that researchers have examined emotion regulation is by assessing aspects of children's internal experience of emotion. Three elements of the experiencing affect component of the ASC model that have been studied in relation to problematic peer relations are the actual experiencing of affect, the ability to identify emotions in oneself, and the use of strategies for managing the internal experience of emotion. Although the actual experiencing of emotion is not equivalent to emotion regulation, the level of emotion experienced is implicitly determined by the regulation of internal feeling states. Similarly, children's ability to identify emotions in oneself is a likely precursor to emotion regulation because efficient regulation often depends on first recognizing the presence and nature of emotion.

Researchers have struggled to validly measure the internal experience of emotion in children. The two methodologies that we believe most successfully assess the actual experiencing of emotion are self-reports of internal feelings and physiological measures of internal states. In terms of physiological measurement, we are limiting our review to those few studies that have linked problematic peer relations (in this case, primarily problem behaviors) to physiological indices in response to emotion-evoking stimuli.

SOCIAL COMPETENCE. We know of no investigations linking children's social competence to physiological indices in response to emotion-evoking stimuli. However, we did find one study that used self-report methodology to relate the actual experiencing of emotion to social competence. In a study of five-year-old children, Eisenberg and Fabes (1995) conducted naturalistic observations and looked for instances of negative emotional display. When such situations were observed, children who witnessed these displays were asked to report how they felt. For girls only, the experience of negative affect in these situations was negatively related to sociometric peer ratings and teacher-rated social skills.

Research relating social competence to identification of emotions in oneself is similarly limited. In the only study we found that assessed this relation, Custrini and Feldman (1989) had 9- to 12-year-old children report how they felt in response to video clips designed to elicit specific emotions. Girls rated as higher in social competence by parents were more likely to report the expected emotion than were girls rated as low in social competence; however, this difference did not hold for boys. Although at least a little research links social competence to the actual experiencing of emotion and to the ability to identify emotions in oneself, as far as we know, no studies to date have investigated the link between social competence and emotion control strategies.

PROBLEM BEHAVIORS. Similar to social competence, only one study that we know of has directly linked problem behaviors to self-reports of the actual experience of emotion. Underwood, Coie, and Herbsman (1992) studied third-, fifth-, and seventh-grade children classified as aggressive or nonaggressive on the basis of peer nominations. When children were shown anger-provoking video vignettes, aggressive children were marginally more likely to report feeling angry and more likely to report feeling angry or sad than were nonaggressive children.

In addition, a small research base has emerged associating problem behaviors with physiological methodologies in emotion-evoking paradigms. El-Sheikh, Ballard, & Cummings (1994) had four-year-old children view two videos of angry interactions between adults. They found that skin conductance reactivity was positively correlated with parent-rated externalizing problems for boys; however, this relation did not hold for girls. Similarly, Zahn-Waxler, Cole, Welsh, and Fox (1995) categorized four- and five-year-old children as low, moderate, or high for disruptive behavior disorders, based on parent and teacher ratings. Skin conductance was measured while children viewed a sad mood induction videotape. Girls classified as high in disruptive behavior disorders had more elevated skin conductance than any other group, male or female.

Finally, in a study of 8- to 11-year-old boys, van Goozen et al. (1998) compared boys diagnosed with oppositional defiant disorder or conduct disorder with normal controls. Children participated in a lengthy frustration and provocation procedure in which they competed against an opponent on a video monitor who continually provoked them. During this procedure, children diagnosed with ODD and CD displayed higher heart rate levels than did controls.

The only study we found linking problem behaviors to the ability to identify emotions in oneself was conducted by Cook et al. (1994). Cook and colleagues asked first- and second-grade children to give examples of times when they felt different emotions and provide cues for how they know that they are experiencing a specific emotion. Parent-rated disruptive behavior was negatively related to children's ability to provide appropriate examples when talking about their own emotional experiences and to the quality of responses for cues used to recognize feelings in themselves.

Similarly, the only study that we found that related problem behaviors to emotion control strategies in particular was conducted by Griffin, Scheier, Botvin, Diaz, and Miller (1999). They asked children to self-report on specific coping skills that they use to control emotion, specifically anger. Sixth graders' report of use of anger control skills was negatively related to their self-report of physical aggression.

GAPS IN THE LITERATURE AND FUTURE DIRECTIONS. The most noticeable gap is the lack of research linking social competence to physiological indices. Because social competence and problem behaviors often relate differentially to various constructs, research is needed that directly investigates associations between social competence and physiological measures. In addition, given the suspect validity of children's self-report, physiological measures are crucial if children's internal experience of emotion is to be measured accurately.

Although a few studies have broached research on individual differences in children's ability to identify emotions in themselves, more research is clearly needed. In the absence of such research, we can draw inferences from the large literature establishing that children with problematic peer relations have difficulty identifying emotions in others.

Research conducted by Griffin and colleagues (Griffin et al., 1999) is the only study we know of to assess directly children's *use* of emotion regulation strategies; more research in this area is clearly needed. In addition, this study highlights the absence of work on children's *knowledge* of such strategies. This work is important because individual differences in children's experience of emotion may result in part from differences in knowledge of strategies about how to regulate the internal experience of emotion. Moreover, such strategies may bear on the ability to regulate the external expression of emotion, the focus of the next portion of the chapter.

Sending Affective Messages

A second way that researchers have studied emotion regulation is by measuring children's external expression of emotion through observations or self-reports, the core of sending affective messages in the ASC model. As with experiencing emotion, others have studied emotion expression without making a connection to emotion regulation. However, emotion regulation is inherently tied to emotion expression, in that the level of emotion expressed depends in part on emotion regulation.

Two other important aspects of sending affective messages have emerged in the literature. The first is the use of display rules to moderate emotion expression, measured through either laboratory observations or self-report methodologies. The second aspect involves the strategies children use to cope with stressful or emotional situations. Coping strategies may be used to regulate both the internal experience and the external expression of emotion. However, given that the methodologies used to measure coping (e.g., observations, adult ratings) can accurately assess only external forms of coping, these studies primarily give us insight into the regulation of the external expression of emotion. Thus, we believe these studies are best placed under Sending Affective Messages.

SOCIAL COMPETENCE. Several studies in our review specifically address emotion expression as it relates to social competence. In a highly cited study, Denham et al. (1990) naturalistically observed four-year-old children in their classrooms. Positive peer ratings were positively related to observed happiness and negatively related to observed anger. With a slightly older sample of second-grade children, Hubbard (2001) observed emotion expression in a laboratory-based, anger-arousing, game-playing paradigm. Children classified as rejected on the basis of sociometric nominations expressed more facial and verbal anger compared with average status children. Rejected children expressed more nonverbal happiness than did average children as well, but only when a turn of the game resulted in a positive outcome for them, suggesting that their positive emotion expression had a gloating quality. Using self-report methodology, Underwood (1997) presented children with hypothetical vignettes designed to evoke six different emotions and asked them to report how much emotion they would express. For 8-, 10-, and 12-year-olds, children classified as rejected on the basis of sociometric nominations were more likely to report that they would express anger more openly than would average children and that they would express disappointment more openly than would popular children.

Fabes and Eisenberg (1992) conducted a study in which they assessed both children's expression of emotion and their coping strategies. Naturalistic observations of four-year-old children revealed that, for boys only, the display of overt anger following physical assault or social rejection was negatively related to teacher-rated social competence and positive peer sociometric ratings. Across both boys and girls, children observed to cope with angry provocations more directly and less aggressively were more likely to be rated by teachers as high on social competence and to receive more positive peer sociometric ratings. For example, more socially competent children were more likely to use active resistance and less likely to use revenge, venting, and adult-seeking forms of coping.

Three other studies by Eisenberg and colleagues have examined children's coping strategies in relation to social competence. Using a similar methodology involving naturalistic observations of children's coping with angry provocations, Eisenberg, Fabes, Nyman, Bernzweig, and Pinuelas (1994) found that, for five-year-old children, sociometric ratings were positively related to the use of verbal objections. Their interpretation is that the use of verbal objections is a more constructive form of coping than other coping strategies measured, such as venting or physical retaliation.

In contrast to observational techniques, two studies by Eisenberg and colleagues measured coping strategies via teacher ratings and examined the relations to social competence. In an initial study, preschoolers' acting out coping was negatively related to teacher- and observer-rated social skills and to peer ratings. Furthermore, for boys only, these same social competence measures were positively related to constructive coping (Eisenberg et al., 1993). In a related study, Eisenberg and colleagues found that low levels of teacher-rated nonconstructive coping and high levels of teacher-rated constructive coping predicted teacher-rated socially appropriate behavior two years later. It is interesting to note that the stronger prediction was for nonconstructive coping (Eisenberg et al., 1995).

PROBLEM BEHAVIORS. As with social competence, researchers have related various measures of problem behaviors to observations of emotion expression. Cole, Zahn-Waxler, Fox, Usher, and Welsh (1996) showed children emotion-arousing videos and coded their facial expressions while viewing the films. On the basis of these observations, children were categorized as inexpressive, modulated expressive, or highly expressive. Both inexpressive and highly expressive children had higher rates of externalizing behavior problems as rated by teachers and parents than did children categorized as modulated expressive. In addition, inexpressive children had higher rates of internalizing symptoms than either of the other groups.

Using a similar methodology, Eisenberg et al. (1996) showed kindergarten through third-grade children a film in which the first half was neutral and the second half was distressing. During both portions of the film, observers coded for distress in children's facial expressions. Increases in facial distress over the course of the film were related to high levels of problem behaviors as reported by teachers and parents.

In contrast to expression, the construct of display rule use is much more difficult to evaluate. We found two studies linking display rule use with problem behaviors, and these studies used quite different methodologies. Underwood et al. (1992) showed seventh-grade children anger-provoking video vignettes and asked children to report on how angry they would feel and how much anger they would express. Using these two measures, Underwood and colleagues identified instances of display rule use when children reported feeling angry but reported not expressing anger. Children classified as aggressive on the basis of peer nominations used display rules less than nonaggressive children did.

In a second study of display rule use, Cole, Zahn-Waxler, and Smith (1994) placed preschoolers in a paradigm in which they received a disappointing gift. Observers coded children's emotion expression as they unwrapped the gift in one of two conditions: one where an experimenter was present and the other where the child was alone. In addition, they collected parent and teacher ratings of disruptive behavior and conduct disorder symptomatology and classified children as high-risk or low-risk. Both high-risk and low-risk boys expressed negative emotion when they were alone. However, the low-risk boys expressed significantly less negative emotion when the experimenter was present, while the high-risk boys expressed the same amount of emotion in both conditions. These findings suggest that high-risk boys used display rules less than low-risk boys did, in that they expressed emotion regardless of the presence or absence of the experimenter. In contrast, the pattern was quite different for girls. Both high-risk and low-risk girls showed minimal amounts of negative emotion when the experimenter was present. However, when they were alone, low-risk girls allowed themselves to express more negative emotion, while high-risk girls continued to minimize their emotional display. Similar to boys, these findings suggest that high-risk girls use display rules less than low-risk girls do, although in this case, the lack of display rule use resulted from an overall minimization of emotion expression in both conditions.

Similar to their research about social competence, Eisenberg and colleagues have studied the relation between coping strategies and problem behaviors. Eisenberg et al. (1995) conducted a longitudinal study in which they followed children for two years from preschool–kindergarten to kindergarten–second grade. Concurrently, high levels of parent-rated nonconstructive coping and low levels of parent-rated seeking-support coping were related to parent-rated problems behaviors, for boys only. Longitudinally, high levels of parent-rated aggressive coping, low levels of parent-rated cognitive restructuring coping, and low levels of parent-rated support-seeking coping predicted parent-rated problem behaviors two years later.

Using a longitudinal design in which they followed children from pre-school–kindergarten to third through fifth grade, Eisenberg and colleagues again evaluated coping strategies with teacher ratings. They related these strategies to parent-rated problem behaviors and to an aggregated social functioning variable, which included measures of teacher-rated popularity and social competence, as well as teacher-rated disruptive behavior and aggression. Parent-rated problem behaviors were associated with high levels of destructive coping concurrently. Destructive coping also predicted the aggregated social functioning variable, both concurrently and several years later (Eisenberg, Fabes, et al., 1997).

GAPS IN THE LITERATURE AND FUTURE DIRECTIONS. One obvious gap is the scarcity of research connecting display rule use with social competence. One way to approach this research would be to use methodologies similar to those used when relating use of display rules to problem behaviors, namely observations in laboratory paradigms and the comparison of self-reports of feelings and expressions. Another approach would be to ask children to self-report on the strategies that they use to dissemble the external expression of emotion in either hypothetical or real-life scenarios. This approach would allow researchers to explore how children go about dissembling their emotions when a display rule guides them to alter their expression.

Self-Factors Related to Experiencing Affect and Sending Affective Messages

Several constructs incorporated in the self-factors described in the ASC model may potentially relate to regulating both the internal experience and external expression of emotion. Eisenberg and colleagues have pioneered research in this area; they are the only researchers we know of to study self-factors specifically related to emotion regulation. The constructs that they have studied fall roughly into two categories. On the one hand, they have measured variables related to self-control, such as attentional control, ego control, impulsivity, and inhibition control. Although we do not believe that self-control and emotion regulation are equivalent, they do overlap because self-control is at least one part of emotion regulation. For example, attentional control can be used to regulate the internal experience of emotion, such as when a child distracts him- or herself in order to lower emotional arousal. On the other hand, they have measured characteristics of temperament, such as emotionality, emotional intensity, negative affect, and soothability. Although not directly a part of emotion regulation, temperamental factors can moderate the ability to regulate emotion. A child's temperament may make emotion regulation more or less challenging, in part because children with difficult temperaments may have more negative or more intense emotions to regulate.

SOCIAL COMPETENCE. In a series of studies, Eisenberg and colleagues have assessed relations between social competence and self-factors related to regulating the internal experience (experiencing affect) and the external expression of emotion (sending affective messages). Among preschoolers, Eisenberg et al. (1993) found that teacher-rated emotional intensity was negatively related to teacher- and observer-rated social skills and peer ratings. In addition, for boys only, these two measures of social competence were positively related to attentional control and negatively related to negative affect. In a related longitudinal study, low levels of teacher-rated negative emotionality and high levels of teacher-rated attentional control in preschool predicted teacher-rated socially appropriate behavior two years later (Eisenberg et al., 1995).

Eisenberg, Guthrie et al. (1997) measured two aspects of self-control in kindergarten through third-grade children. Parents and teachers rated children's ego control, and children participated in a paradigm in which their ability to refrain from looking at the solution to a puzzle was assessed. An aggregate of these measures of self-control was positively related to an aggregate of socially appropriate behavior (a combination of teacher-rated social competence and peer nominations for being nice), but only for children high in parent- and teacher-rated negative emotionality.

PROBLEM BEHAVIORS. Eisenberg and colleagues also have measured the links between these temperamental and self-control variables and problem behaviors. In a sample of kindergarten through third-grade children, parent- and teacher-rated problem behaviors were positively related to parent- and teacher-rated emotionality and to an aggregate variable encompassing parent-

and teacher-rated ego resiliency, ego control, attention shifting, and attention focusing. However, the relation between problem behaviors and the self-control aggregate was moderated by emotionality, such that the relation was stronger as emotionality increased (Eisenberg et al., 1996).

In a study with a similar age group, Eisenberg et al. (1995) created aggregated variables measuring aspects of self-control and temperament and related these variables to a concurrent measure of parent-rated problem behaviors. The teacher-rated self-control aggregate consisted of attention shifting, attention focusing, and self-control and was negatively related to problem behaviors. The parent-rated self-control aggregate, composed of attention focusing, impulsivity, self-regulation, and inhibition control, was also negatively related to problem behaviors. A parent-rated aggregate of unregulated negative emotion (anger and frustration, soothability, negative affectivity, negative emotional intensity) was positively related to problem behaviors, as was parent-rated negative emotionality. Longitudinally, for boys only, parent ratings of emotionality collected two years earlier positively predicted parent-rated problem behavior in kindergarten through second grade.

Using a longitudinal design in which they followed children from preschool–kindergarten to third through fifth grade, Eisenberg and colleagues (Eisenberg, Fabes, et al., 1997) related self-control and temperamental variables to parent-rated problem behaviors and to an aggregated social functioning variable, which included measures of teacher-rated popularity and social competence, as well as teacher-rated disruptive behavior and aggression. They created a self-control aggregate composed of parent and teacher reports of attentional control, impulsivity, and inhibition control, and a negative emotionality aggregate composed of teacher and parent reports of negative emotional intensity and negative affect. Concurrently, parent-rated problem behaviors were associated with low levels of the self-control aggregate and high levels of the negative emotionality aggregate. In addition, both the self-control and negative emotionality aggregates predicted the aggregated social functioning variable, concurrently and several years later.

GAPS IN THE LITERATURE AND FUTURE DIRECTIONS. Eisenberg and colleagues have done an admirable job of investigating several self-factors that are pertinent to the process of emotion regulation. They have undertaken work with constructs that are difficult to measure and have managed to balance research efforts across the two domains of social competence and problem behaviors. However, in contrast to their work on social competence, which involves multiple sources of measurement, Eisenberg and colleagues have measured problem behaviors solely through parent ratings. Measuring problem behaviors via teacher or peer ratings as well would strengthen the link between self-factors and problem behaviors. Similarly, work is needed with older populations of children and developmental processes need to be examined.

Furthermore, the ASC model includes other self-factors that may impact emotion regulation and have not been investigated with respect to social competence or problem behaviors. For example, a child's self-concept may influence the emotions that he or she experiences and the emotional message that he or she sends. In addition, a child's motivation to interact with others may affect his or her emotional experience in social situations and may influence his or her emotional expression in these situations.

Summary

For each of the components of the ASC model, emerging research suggests consistent relations between emotional functioning and problematic peer relations. Although in the body of the chapter we have detailed areas where research is absent or scarce, there are several places where enough work has been conducted to allow us to draw tentative conclusions.

We identified two points in the ASC model that correspond most closely to the construct of emotion understanding: receiving affective messages and aspects of self-factors. In terms of the link between problematic peer relations and receiving affective messages, two findings are robust enough for conclusions to be drawn. Children with deficits in social competence have difficulty identifying the physical cues of emotions in others. Similarly, these children have parallel deficits in their ability to use situational cues to identify emotions in others. However, the link between these abilities and problem behaviors has not been well established.

The construct of hostile attributional biases is the only self-factor uniquely related to emotion understanding regarding which a definitive link to problematic peer relations has been made. Both children with social competence deficits and children who exhibit problematic behaviors are more likely than their peers to attribute hostile intent to others in situations where the other's intent is ambiguous. Hostile attributional tendencies may act as a filter when receiving and understanding emotional messages, such that children who attribute hostile intent to their peers may be more likely than other children to ascribe a negative valence to these messages.

We identified three points in the ASC model that correspond most closely to the construct of emotion regulation: experiencing affect, sending affective messages, and aspects of self-factors. In terms of experiencing affect, a single consistent finding has emerged. Children with behavior problems experience higher physiological responses or greater physiological reactivity in response to emotion-evoking situations than do other children. Given that children with behavior problems exhibit elevated physiology when compared with their peers, these children likely either experience higher initial levels of emotion or encounter more difficulty regulating their internal experience of emotion. However, as noted above, the connection between physiology in response to emotion-evoking stimuli and social competence has not been researched.

In terms of sending affective messages, two findings are sufficiently consistent for conclusions to be drawn. First, children with social competence deficits and children who exhibit problematic behaviors express more negative emotions than their peers, indicating that either they experience more negative emotion or they have difficulty regulating the external expression of that emotion. Second, these children are more likely than their peers to engage in nonconstructive forms of coping in social situations.

Finally, two aspects of self-factors are related to emotion regulation and have been consistently tied to problematic peer relations across several studies. First, in terms of temperamental factors, children with deficits in social competence and children who exhibit problem behaviors are likely to be more emotional and more emotionally intense than other children. Although not directly a part of the process of emotion regulation, temperamental factors can moderate the ability to regulate emotion. Children who are more emotional or more emotionally intense may have more difficulty regulating their emotion, in part because these children may have more negative or more intense emotions to regulate. Second, children with deficits in social competence and children who exhibit problem behaviors have some deficiencies in self-control.

The studies reviewed in this chapter reveal that emotional functioning is indeed an integral part of children's social functioning. Although the field is in its infancy, the body of research reviewed here suggests that children with problematic peer relations experience difficulties in understanding and regulating emotion. The ASC model has proven useful in organizing empirical findings across the field and in organizing the disparate methodologies used to assess emotion regulation. In addition, the ASC model can be used to guide future researchers toward a more complete understanding of the role that emotional functioning plays in children's peer interactions.

References

Asher, S. R., & Coie, J. D. (1990). *Peer rejection in childhood*. New York: Cambridge University Press.

Boyatzis, C. J., & Satyaprasad, C. (1994). Children's facial and gestural decoding and encoding: Relations between skills and with popularity. *Journal of Nonverbal Behavior, 18*, 37–55.

Cassidy, J., Parke, R. D., Butkovsky, L., & Braungart, J. M. (1992). Family-peer connections: The roles of emotional expressiveness within the family and children's understanding of emotions. *Child Development, 63*, 603–618.

Cole, P. M., Zahn-Waxler, C., Fox, N. A., Usher, B. A., & Welsh, J. D. (1996). Individual differences in emotion regulation and behavior problems in preschool children. *Journal of Abnormal Psychology, 105*, 518–529.

Cole, P. M., Zahn-Waxler, C., & Smith, K. D. (1994). Expressive control during a disappointment: Variations related to preschoolers' behavior problems. *Developmental Psychology, 30*, 835–846.

Cook, E. T., Greenberg, M. T., & Kusche, C. A. (1994). The relations between emotional understanding, intellectual functioning, and disruptive behavior problems in elementary school aged children. *Journal of Abnormal Child Psychology, 22*, 205–219.

Crick, N. R., & Dodge, K. A. (1994). A review and reformulation of social-information-processing mechanisms in children's social adjustment. *Psychological Bulletin, 115*, 74–101.

Custrini, R. J., & Feldman, R. S. (1989). Children's social competence and nonverbal encoding and decoding of emotions. *Journal of Clinical Child Psychology, 18*, 336–342.

Denham, S. A., McKinley, M., Couchoud, E. A., & Holt, R. (1990). Emotional and behavioral predictors of preschool peer ratings. *Child Development, 61*, 1145–1152.

Edwards, R., Manstead, A. S., & MacDonald, C. J. (1984). The relationship between children's sociometric status and ability to recognize facial expressions of emotion. *European Journal of Social Psychology, 14*, 235–238.

Eisenberg, N., & Fabes, R. A. (1995). The relation of young children's vicarious emotional responding to social competence, regulation, and emotionality. *Cognition and Emotion, 9*, 203–228.

Eisenberg, N., & Fabes, R. A. (1999). Emotion, emotion-related regulation, and quality of socioemotional functioning. In L. Balter & C. S. Tamis-LeMonda (Eds.), *Child psychology: A handbook of contemporary issues*. Philadelphia: Psychology Press/Taylor & Francis.

Eisenberg, N., Fabes, R. A., Bernzweig, J., Karbon, M., Poulin, R., & Hanish, L. (1993). The relations of emotionality and regulation to preschoolers' social skills and sociometric status. *Child Development, 64,* 1418–1438.

Eisenberg, N., Fabes, R. A., Guthrie, I. K., Murphy, B. C., Maszk, P., Holmgren, R., & Suh, K. (1996). The relations of regulation and emotionality to problem behavior in elementary school children. *Development and Psychopathology, 8,* 141–162.

Eisenberg, N., Fabes, R. A., Murphy, B., Maszk, P., Smith, M., & Karbon, M. (1995). The role of emotionality in children's social functioning: A longitudinal study. *Child Development, 66,* 1360–1384.

Eisenberg, N., Fabes, R. A., Nyman, M., Bernzweig, J., & Pinuelas, A. (1994). The relations of emotionality and regulation to children's anger-related reactions. *Child Development, 65,* 109–128.

Eisenberg, N., Fabes, R. A., Shepard, S. A., Murphy, B. C., Guthrie, I. K., Jones, S., Friedman, J., Poulin, R., & Maszk, P. (1997). Contemporaneous and longitudinal prediction of children's social functioning from regulation and emotionality. *Child Development, 68,* 642–664.

Eisenberg, N., Guthrie, I. K., Fabes, R. A., Reiser, M., Murphy, B. C., Holmgren, R., Maszk, P., & Losoya, S. (1997). The relations of regulation and emotionality to resiliency and competent social functioning in elementary school children. *Child Development, 68,* 295–311.

El-Sheikh, M., Ballard, M., & Cummings, E. M. (1994). Individual differences in preschoolers' physiological and verbal responses to videotaped angry interactions. *Journal of Abnormal Child Psychology, 22,* 303–320.

Fabes, R. A., & Eisenberg, N. (1992). Young children's coping with interpersonal anger. *Child Development, 63,* 116–128.

Field, T. M., & Walden, T. A (1982). Production and discrimination of facial expressions by preschool children. *Child Development, 53,* 1299–1311.

Goldman, J. A., Corsini, D. A., & deUrioste, R. (1980). Implications of positive and negative sociometric status for assessing the social competence of young children. *Journal of Applied Developmental Psychology, 1,* 209–220.

Griffin, K. W., Scheier, L. M., Botvin, G. J., Diaz, T., & Miller, N. (1999). Interpersonal aggression in urban minority youth: Mediators of perceived neighborhood, peer, and parental influences. *Journal of Community Psychology, 27,* 281–298.

Halberstadt, A. G., Denham, S. A., & Dunsmore, J. C. (2001). Affective social competence. *Social Development, 10,* 79–119.

Hubbard, J. A. (2001). Emotion expression processes in children's peer interaction: The role of peer rejection, aggression, and gender. *Child Development, 72,* 1426–1438.

Hughes, C., Dunn, J., & White, A. (1998). Trick or treat? Uneven understanding of mind and emotion and executive dysfunction in "hard-to-manage" preschoolers. *Journal of Child Psychology and Psychiatry and Allied Disciplines, 39,* 981–994.

Jones, D. C., Abbey, B. B., & Cumberland, A. (1998). The development of display rule knowledge: Linkages with family expressiveness and social competence. *Child Development, 69,* 1209–1212.

Manstead, A. S. R., & Edwards, R. (1992). Communicative aspects of children's emotional competence. In K. T. Strongman (Ed.), *International review of studies on emotion, Vol. 2.* (pp. 167–195). New York: John Wiley and Sons.

Nowicki, S., & Duke, M. P. (1992). The association of children's nonverbal decoding abilities with their popularity, locus of control, and academic achievement. *Journal of Genetic Psychology, 153,* 385–393.

Nowicki, S., & Duke, M. P. (1994). Individual differences in the nonverbal communications of affect: The Diagnostic Analysis of Nonverbal Accuracy Scale. *Journal of Nonverbal Behavior, 18,* 9–35.

Philippot, P., & Feldman, R. S. (1990). Age and social competence in preschoolers' decoding of facial expression. *British Journal of Social Psychology, 29,* 43–54.

Rubin, K. H., & Maioni, T. L. (1975). Play preference and its relationship to egocentrism, popularity, and classification skills in preschoolers. *Merrill-Palmer Quarterly, 21,* 171–179.

Underwood, M. K. (1997). Peer social status and children's understanding of the expression and control of positive and negative emotions. *Merrill-Palmer Quarterly, 43,* 610–634.

Underwood, M. K., Coie, J. D., & Herbsman, C. R. (1992). Display rules for anger and aggression in school-aged children. *Child Development, 63,* 366–380.

van Goozen, S. H. M., Matthys, W., Cohen-Kettenis, P. T., Gispen-de Wied, C., Wiegant, V. M., & van Engeland, H. (1998). Salivary cortisol and cardiovascular activity during stress in oppositional-defiant disorder boys and normal controls. *Biological Psychiatry, 43,* 521–539.

Vosk, B. N., Forehand, R., & Figueroa, R. (1983). Perception of emotions by accepted and rejected children. *Journal of Behavioral Assessment, 5,* 151–160.

Zahn-Waxler, C., Cole, P. M., Welsh, J. D., & Fox, N. A. (1995). Psychophysiological correlates of empathy and prosocial behavior in preschool children with behavior problems. *Development and Psychopathology, 7,* 27–48.

6

Understanding the Experience of Peer Rejection

Marlene J. Sandstrom and Audrey L. Zakriski

In their 1990 book, Asher and Coie called attention to the inner experience of peer rejection in their discussion of loneliness and social distress. At the time, the study of children's subjective experiences of their peer rejection represented a fledgling subfield within the broader domain of peer relations, and internal experiences were often overlooked in favor of more objective assessments of children's social adaptation. Hymel and Franke (1985) first articulated the concern that objective ratings were limited in their ability to tell the *whole* story of the rejected child. Asher, Parkhurst, Hymel, and Williams (1990) reemphasized this issue and argued that more objective peer assessments, though useful for many purposes, could not shed light on a child's awareness of his or her status, the importance he or she places on it, or his or her emotional and cognitive responses to it.

Over the past decade, research on children's subjective experiences of peer rejection has proliferated. In addition to further research on loneliness, other indicators of internal distress in response to peer rejection have been examined including social anxiety, depressive symptoms, low self-esteem, and poor self-concept. Issues of causality have been carefully addressed. Also, behavioral, cognitive, and social context mediators of children's subjective experiences of peer rejection have been explored. The present chapter reviews this diverse literature and then employs a transactional model for adaptation to childhood stressors to integrate the various factors that contribute to children's subjective responses to peer rejection. This model allows us to more fully appreciate the experience of peer rejection, as well as to better understand the multiple origins and consequences of childhood peer rejection. It also provides a guiding structure for future research on children's experiences of peer rejection.

Both authors contributed equally to the writing of this chapter and the order of authorship was randomly determined.

The State of the Field in 1990

In 1990, the study of children's internal experiences of peer rejection was still in its early stages. Nevertheless, it was already clear that children's responses to peer rejection, such as loneliness (Asher, Hymel, & Renshaw, 1984) and social anxiety (Hymel & Franke, 1985; La Greca, Dandes, Wick, Shaw, & Stone, 1988), could be reliably and validly assessed, and that these negative emotional responses, along with lowered self-esteem and poor self-concept, were commonly associated with sociometric rejection (e.g., Asher et al., 1984; Boivin & Begin, 1989; Hymel, Franke, & Freigang, 1985). Variability was also noted in the degree to which rejected children felt lonely, sad, anxious, or lacking in self-esteem. Withdrawn-rejected[1] children reported more negative affective responses and self-evaluations than did aggressive-rejected children, and were more likely to identify themselves as candidates for peer-related interventions than were their more aggressive counterparts (Asher, Zelis, Parker, & Bruene, 1991; Boivin & Begin, 1989; Patterson, Kupersmidt, & Griesler, 1990).

In addition to behavioral variables, researchers also began to consider cognitive factors that might explain individual differences in children's subjective responses to peer rejection. Early studies suggested that rejected children's private beliefs about the causes of their social successes and failures differed from those of nonrejected children. Specifically, unpopular children tended to perceive social success as more unstable and externally caused and to perceive social failure as more stable and internally caused (e.g., Ames, Ames, & Garrison, 1977; Sobol & Earn, 1985). Again there appeared to be behavioral subgroup differences, such that aggressive-rejected children were more likely to attribute peer problems to the hostile intentions of others (e.g., Dodge & Frame, 1982). However, the extent to which cognitive and behavioral variables worked together to explain individual differences in children's emotional responses to rejection had not yet been explored.

The Next Decade of Research on Internal Experiences of Peer Rejection

Extensions of Previous Findings

Over the past decade, there have been a number of important replications and extensions of earlier research. First, the scope of negative affect variables has been broadened beyond loneliness and social dissatisfaction to include depressive symptoms (Bell-Dolan, Foster, & Christopher, 1995; Cole & Carpentieri, 1990; Panak & Garber, 1992) and social anxiety (Inderbitzen, Walters, & Bukowski, 1997; La Greca & Stone, 1993). We also have seen

---

[1]Although we have chosen to use the term *withdrawn* in this chapter for the sake of simplicity, there appears to be some heterogeneity within this group of children as well. Some children are best characterized as submissive-withdrawn while others can be characterized as withdrawn but not submissive (Asendorpf, 1991; Rubin & Mills, 1988).

important developmental extensions beyond middle childhood. Associations between peer rejection and loneliness in preschool and kindergarten (e.g., Cassidy & Asher, 1992; Ladd & Coleman, 1997) and in young adolescence (e.g., Sanderson & Siegal, 1995; Sletta, Valas, Skaalvik, & Sobstad, 1996), and with depressive symptoms in high school (e.g., Hecht, Inderbitzen, & Bukowski, 1998), suggest that the relationship between poor peer status and related forms of subjective distress is somewhat stable across development. Also, research replicating the relationship between loneliness and poor peer status in non-classroom domains (Parker & Seal, 1996) has drawn attention to the importance of studying the broader context of peer rejection.

Causal Links

Another advance in the field involves the use of prospective designs to examine the causal links between peer rejection and subjective experiences. Two main causal questions have been addressed. The first involves the nature of the directional relationship between problematic peer experiences and negative affect over time. In a prospective study, Cillessen, Van Lieshout, and Haselager (1992) found strong evidence for a predictive relation between consistent rejection in the early elementary school years and increased loneliness and depression over a four-year interval. Panak and Garber (1992) found that elementary school age children who *increased* in their peer rejection scores relative to their peers were at greatest risk for increased depression. Further, Ladd and Coleman (1997) found that kindergarten peer acceptance predicted significant changes in loneliness over the school year whereas early feelings of loneliness did not predict an increase in peer difficulties over time. Jointly, these studies support the premise that peer rejection plays a causal role in the emergence of depression and loneliness. More research is needed, however, before similar conclusions can be drawn about self-concept, self-esteem, and anxiety.

Given that withdrawn/isolative behavior is associated with internalizing symptoms such as loneliness, depression, and low self-regard, researchers have also addressed the incidental versus causal question of whether peer rejection uniquely adds to the prediction of these problems. Boivin, Poulin, and Vitaro (1994) found a group of withdrawn-rejected children to be more depressed than groups of withdrawn-nonrejected as well as non–withdrawn-rejected children. Similar findings have been reported on a sample of elementary school girls (Bell-Dolan et al., 1995). In both cases causal interpretations are hampered by the concurrent collection of sociometric and depression ratings. Nevertheless, these results are consistent with the notion that internalizing problems are related to the combination of withdrawal and peer rejection rather than withdrawal alone. Stronger support for this premise comes from at least two prospective studies of elementary school children in which peer rejection contributed uniquely to the prediction of later self-reported loneliness, even after controlling for children's initial level of withdrawn behavior (Boivin & Hymel, 1997; Renshaw & Brown, 1993). Taken together, these studies move us beyond early correlational studies and allow us to make certain causal assumptions about the role of rejection in producing negative affect.

Behavioral Characteristics

Over the past decade, research on the heterogeneity in rejected children's subjective experiences progressed from behavioral differentiation to investigations of associated psychological processes as anticipated by Asher et al. (1990). Studies of internalizing outcomes have increasingly focused on withdrawn-rejected children, as these children are thought to be more self-blaming and therefore at greater risk for internalizing negative feelings about the self in social relationships. Consistent with this formulation, withdrawn-rejected children have been found to self-report more social anxiety (Inderbitzen et al., 1997) and a more internalizing cluster of depressive symptoms by their teenage years (Hecht et al., 1998) than do their aggressive counterparts.

In Hecht et al. (1998), withdrawn-rejected children scored high on the low self-esteem and anhedonia subscales of the Children's Depression Inventory, which reflect low self-worth, loneliness, social dissatisfaction, and vegetative symptoms of depression. Aggressive-rejected children, in contrast, scored high on the interpersonal problems scale, which reflects conflict and lack of interest in people, and on the ineffectiveness scale, which reflects global incompetence and school difficulties. Their other-blaming orientation to peer relationships might help shape aggressive-rejected children's perceptions of their social status as well as this manifestation of their depressive symptoms. Although this research did not investigate clinical depression, the findings of depressive symptoms in aggressive-rejected children are important given prior assumptions that aggressive-rejected children are not as distressed by their rejection and are primarily at risk for externalizing problems. Continued attention to types of depressive symptoms in future studies will help clarify the processes by which peer rejection might lead to different depressive outcomes for these two subgroups of children.

From a developmental perspective, researchers have become interested in the emergence and maintenance of internal experience differences, such as differences in loneliness or differences in depressive symptom profiles, between aggressive- and withdrawn-rejected children across time. Middle school withdrawn-rejected children have been found to self-report higher levels of loneliness, more worry about their relations with others, and higher levels of social anxiety compared with average children and aggressive-rejected children (Parkhurst & Asher, 1992). Thus, aggressive-rejected and withdrawn-rejected children seem to show a stable difference in self-reported internalizing distress over the late elementary school period. However, lonely kindergarten children are judged by teachers to be aggressive and disruptive and by their peers to be both shy and aggressive (Cassidy & Asher, 1992). In addition, Williams and Asher (1987) found that aggressive-rejected children were more distressed by their peer difficulties than were average status children in early elementary school. Research demonstrating depressive symptoms in aggressive-rejected high school children (French, Conrad, & Turner, 1995; Hecht et al., 1998) suggests that some forms of internalizing distress may reappear at later points in development. How aggressive-rejected children's subjective distress changes over time is an important topic for future research.

Other recent research suggests that reliance on single behaviors (e.g., withdrawal or aggression) to explain the heterogeneity of rejected children's subjective experiences may be too simplistic. Children who are both aggressive and withdrawn seem to be at heightened risk for peer rejection, more intense social difficulties, and increased risk of later psychopathology (Ledingham & Schwartzman, 1984; Lyons, Serbin, & Marchessault, 1988; Parkhurst & Asher, 1992; Rogosch & Cicchetti, 1994). Research on aggressive versus withdrawn versus aggressive-withdrawn rejected children is quite limited, however, so little is known about differences in their subjective experiences. One study followed aggressive-withdrawn kindergartners through second grade and found that they were consistently more lonely and dissatisfied than their aggressive-only and withdrawn-only counterparts (Ladd & Burgess, 1999).

Although quite a bit of research focuses on how aggressive- and withdrawn-rejected children differ in their subjective responses, far less is known about why these differences exist. One explanation is that these subgroups perceive similar peer experiences quite differently. Withdrawn-rejected children may have more negatively biased perceptions of themselves whereas aggressive-rejected (and perhaps aggressive-withdrawn) children may hold a more positively skewed self-image. Another possibility, however, is that differences in subjective experiences are rooted in actual differences in the way peers treat aggressive-rejected and withdrawn-rejected children. For example, Ladd and Burgess (1999) found that in addition to being more lonely, aggressive-withdrawn rejected children were more friendless and victimized, which suggests that these different social experiences might contribute to the consistent loneliness of this group. Similarly, Milich and Landau (1984; Landau & Milich, 1985) found that whereas both aggressive and aggressive-withdrawn kindergartners received high social rejection scores and experienced frequent negative encounters with peers, aggressive children also experienced offsetting positive nominations and positive peer experiences. Also, Williams and Asher (1987) found withdrawn-rejected children to be more severely rejected than aggressive-rejected children. Cognitive bias has not been examined in conjunction with actual experiences, so the relative contribution of these two potential sources of individual difference in internal experiences of rejection has not been assessed. The potential interplay of behavioral, cognitive, and social context influences on rejection experiences is important and will be explored in later sections of the chapter.

Cognitive Characteristics

ATTRIBUTIONS. In addition to behavioral characteristics, researchers have examined a host of cognitive factors thought to differentiate children who feel bad about their social standing from those who do not. One such cognitive variable is the manner in which children make sense of the causality, stability, and globality of their problems with other children.

In a study of third through fifth graders, Panak and Garber (1992) found that the tendency to make internal, global, and stable attributions for their peer problems contributed to the prediction of rejected children's depressive symptoms one year later. Similarly, Renshaw and Brown (1993) found that children who showed a tendency to attribute rejection experiences to internal-stable factors reported heightened feelings of loneliness. These studies suggest that a depressogenic attributional style (attributing failures to internal, global, stable factors) is associated with negative affect, both concurrently and predictively.

Crick and Ladd (1993) suggest a more complex pattern in which the relationship between attributions for social difficulties and subjective distress (as evidenced by loneliness, social anxiety, and social avoidance) differs as a function of sociometric status. For most nonrejected groups, low social distress was associated with a self-serving attributional style in which children attributed success to themselves and failure to external sources. Conversely, high social distress was associated with a non-self-serving attributional style. However, for rejected children, high social distress was associated with a tendency to blame peers (rather than self) for negative events. In contrast to the previous studies, these results suggest that for rejected children, a tendency to *external-ize* blame for peer difficulties may be particularly maladaptive, leading to high levels of social avoidance.

Thus, whereas some studies suggest that rejected children who internalize blame for peer difficulties are more distressed, others indicate that those who externalize responsibility are at greater risk. How do we make sense of these conflicting conclusions? One likely explanation involves the use of different types of distress measures across studies. A closer examination of Crick and Ladd's (1993) results reveals that rejected children who blame others for their peer difficulties are likely to report greater distress in the form of social avoidance. This particular type of distress, which is more behavioral in nature, may be distinct from the more affective types of distress (loneliness, depression) assessed in other studies.

SELF-PERCEIVED SOCIAL ACCEPTANCE. Another cognitive factor that has been examined as a mediator of children's subjective responses to peer rejection is self-perceived social acceptance. Generally, withdrawn-rejected children tend to be more negative, but accurate, perceivers of their social acceptance than are aggressive-rejected children (Hymel, Bowker, & Woody, 1993). Aggressive-rejected children overestimate their own social acceptance, although they can judge the social status of other children more accurately (Zakriski & Coie, 1996).

Most studies find that aggressive-rejected children more accurately assess their behavioral competence than their social competence (Boivin, Thomassin, & Alain, 1988; Hughes, Cavell, & Grossman, 1997). One proposed explanation is that aggressive children are likely to receive clear feedback about their problematic behavior, especially from teachers, but are less likely to receive such clear feedback about their likability from peers. However, even when they do receive clear rejection feedback in a rigged social manipulation, aggressive-rejected children tend to overestimate how much they are liked compared with others, and do so more than do withdrawn-rejected children (Zakriski & Coie, 1996). Therefore, it seems likely that at least part of aggressive-rejected children's tendency to report less loneliness, depression, and discontent may be related to a self-protective distortion that allows them to miss the message that they are disliked by their peers.

Recent research has raised the possibility that holding positive perceptions of one's social acceptance may provide at least a short-term buffer against certain negative affective responses to peer rejection. Paradis and Vitaro (1999) found that rejected and average status children with positive perceptions of their social acceptance received more votes as favorite playmates from their classmates than average and rejected children who held negative perceptions of their social acceptance. They were also rated higher on aggressiveness–disruptiveness by teachers and lower on social withdrawal. Similarly, Sandstrom and Coie (1999) found that initially rejected boys who mistakenly believed that they were well liked by their peers in the fourth grade were more likely to improve their status by the end of the fifth grade than boys who did not, even after initial level of rejection was controlled for. Thus, evaluating one's relationships favorably, which may be more characteristic of aggressive children, appears to be related to better relationship experiences, at least in the short run.

Of course the nature of this correlation is unclear. Better relationship experiences may be the reason aggressive-rejected perceive their relationships more positively, and may also make it easier for some initially rejected children to improve their social acceptance over the course of a school year. Alternatively, children's positive relationship perceptions may exceed the actual quality of their relationship experiences but provide a self-protective buffer that promotes better relationship experiences in the future. Such a premise is consistent with a growing body of literature suggesting that overly positive self-evaluations and unrealistic optimism are adaptive, particularly in the face of adversity, and are associated with enhanced functioning across a range of mental and physical health outcomes (e.g., Taylor & Brown, 1988). We assume, of course, that a self-protective buffer of this sort could be functional only up to a point, beyond which it would resemble delusional thinking and put a child at risk for inviting even more peer rejection.

Given the significant overlap between low perceived social acceptance and loneliness, and the variability in loneliness among sociometrically rejected children, researchers have begun to question whether previously demonstrated links between sociometric rejection and internalizing symptoms are more directly related to perceived, rather than actual, rejection. For example, Kistner, Balthazor, Risi, and Burton (1999) tested different models (main effect, additive, interactive) of the relationship between fourth- and fifth-grade self-perceived acceptance, peer-nominated acceptance, and eleventh- and twelfth-grade depression. Only perceived acceptance predicted depression, supporting a main effect model. Panak and Garber (1992) similarly found that children's own perceptions of rejection by peers completely mediated the link between actual rejection and subsequent depression.

Taken together, these studies highlight the role of negative perceived social competence in the prediction of depression and suggest that only those rejected children who accurately perceive their poor status are at risk for internalizing problems. However, the relationships among peer status, accuracy of status perceptions, and internalizing outcomes are not entirely straightforward.

Cillessen and Bellmore (1999) found that over all status types, *inaccurate* status perceptions predicted loneliness.

Characteristics of the Social Context

In addition to examining behavioral and cognitive influences, the past decade has seen great advances in our attention to social context as a determinant of children's responses to rejection. There has been a growing awareness that the actual experiences of sociometrically rejected children are varied. Some children may experience rejection in very obvious and painful ways, such as being chronically humiliated, excluded, or physically attacked. For other children, the *lack* of certain positive experiences (not being picked for teams, not being invited to parties, or finding nobody to sit with at lunch) may be far more salient than overt negative experiences. Still other children may experience very few obvious indicators that their classmates dislike them and may actually enjoy positive relationships with a small number of specific peers. Although all of these children may be sociometrically rejected, their everyday peer experiences are diverse. It stands to reason that subjective responses to rejection will vary as a function of actual treatment by peers. We examine two aspects of the social context known to influence children's subjective experience of rejection: friendships and victimization.

FRIENDSHIP. Numerous studies have documented that friendless children are more dissatisfied and lonely than those with at least one mutual friendship (e.g., Bukowski, Hoza, & Boivin, 1993; Parker & Asher, 1993b; Renshaw & Brown, 1993). In addition to presence or absence of friendship, researchers also have examined relationships between dimensions of friendship quality and subjective distress. Parker and Asher (1993a) found that elementary school children with more supportive and less conflicted friendships reported less loneliness than did children with friendships of poorer quality. Using a similar methodology with kindergarten children, Ladd, Kochenderfer, and Coleman (1996) found that higher levels of conflict and disclosure of negative affect were associated with gains in loneliness over a five-month period for boys, but not for girls. Another area of interest has been the extent to which peer group acceptance and dyadic friendships uniquely predict loneliness and subjective distress. Bukowski and Hoza (1989) found that friendship and peer acceptance were differentially associated with specific aspects of subjective distress. Whereas friendship deficits were more closely related to loneliness, poor peer acceptance was more closely related to social isolation. Similarly, at least two prospective studies have demonstrated that both peer group acceptance and friendship make independent contributions to childhood loneliness (Parker & Asher, 1993b; Renshaw & Brown, 1993). These results suggest that poorly accepted children who are able to engage in at least one satisfying friendship are likely to feel less lonely than their friendless counterparts.

Bukowski et al. (1993) found a more complex and mediated relationship among adolescent acceptance, friendship, and loneliness. Results of path analysis suggested that presence and quality of friendship predicted directly to loneliness, whereas the influence of overall group acceptance on loneliness was indirect and mediated by friendship variables. Specifically, highly accepted children were less lonely because they were more likely to participate in high-quality dyadic friendships. Of note, however, is that Bukowski et al. (1993) separated loneliness from children's perceptions of fitting in with their peers and *did* find a direct relationship between peer acceptance and fitting in. Using a somewhat different approach, Ladd, Kochenderfer, and Coleman (1997) examined the relative contributions of friendships, peer group acceptance, and victimization to loneliness among kindergartners. Consistent with the results of Bukowski et al. (1993), number of mutual friends emerged as a unique predictor of children's loneliness during fall and spring of kindergarten whereas contributions made by peer group acceptance were largely redundant with those of friendship and victimization.

These equivocal findings suggest that the relationships among friendship, acceptance, and loneliness operate differently as a function of the peer climate. For sociometrically rejected children who are not openly disliked, dyadic relationships are likely to be a more salient aspect of their everyday peer experiences than are group dynamics. For these children, loneliness may be better predicted by friendship variables than by overall acceptance. The predictive relationship may look different for sociometrically rejected children who are overtly victimized. For these children, the overall tone of their daily peer experiences may be as heavily colored by group dynamics (e.g., being teased, ostracized, or physically attacked) as by the nature of their friendships. In this context, we might expect both friendship and acceptance to uniquely predict to loneliness, as did Williams (1999) who found dissatisfying friendships to be especially predictive of loneliness in the context of victimization. Ladd et al.'s (1997) finding that victimization and friendship, but not rejection, uniquely predict to loneliness is consistent with this hypothesis. If the aversive nature of daily experiences truly mediates the relationship between sociometric rejection and loneliness, controlling for victimization should reduce the magnitude of this relationship. Further investigations of both rejection and victimization are needed to tease apart their independent effects on children's subjective distress.

VICTIMIZATION. Over the past decade, researchers have attempted to map out the interconnections among sociometric rejection (a covert phenomenon in which the peer group privately discloses information about their *attitudes* toward target peers), peer victimization (an overt phenomenon in which members of the peer group *actively behave* in a negative way toward target peers), and distress in order to understand the mechanisms linking sociometric rejection and subjective distress. Perry, Kusel, and Perry (1988) demonstrated that the correlation between rejection and victimization is moderate; for a large subset of children, private peer rejection is publicly manifested in the form of active ridicule, humiliation, physical aggression, and exclusion. However, not all rejected children are victimized.

Studies of peer victims have shown that as is the case for rejected children, victimized children tend to have low self-esteem and feel more lonely, anxious, unhappy, and insecure than do their nonvictimized counterparts (e.g., Boulton & Underwood, 1992; Hodges & Perry, 1996). However, given the overlap between victimization and rejection, it remains unclear whether the distress is attributable to peer sentiment (sociometric rejection), aversive peer behavior (victimization), or some more complex interaction between the two. It is possible that the subjective distress associated with peer rejection is mediated through overt victimization experiences. Rejected children who are not treated aversively by their peers may not be aware that they are disliked, or may not be reminded of it on a daily basis, and therefore not suffer the negative emotional and cognitive consequences that stem from mistreatment.

Boivin and Hymel (1997) found some support for this premise in their sequential modeling of social behavior, peer acceptance, friendship, victimization, and loneliness in 8- to 10-year-old children. The association between social withdrawal and negative self-perceptions (feelings of loneliness and incompetence) was partially mediated by the quality of children's peer experiences (rejection and victimization). So whereas withdrawn children were likely to hold a negative view of self, this was even more the case when they were rejected and victimized by peers. In a second study, Boivin, Hymel, and Bukowski (1995) assessed the interrelationships among social withdrawal, peer rejection, victimization, loneliness, and depressed mood among fourth and fifth graders. Once again, regression analyses demonstrated that the impact of withdrawal on subsequent loneliness was mediated by victimization status. Withdrawn behavior was directly associated with increased victimization, which in turn was associated with increased subjective distress. In addition, self-reported loneliness mediated the depressed mood associated with withdrawal and victimization.

Taken together, these studies represent an important step toward grasping the complex interrelationships among withdrawn behavior, victimization, and subsequent emotional responses. However, not all victims are passive and withdrawn; in fact, a substantial portion of victimized children are perceived as antagonistic and provocative (Perry et al., 1988). What remains unclear is the extent to which victimization experiences influence the subjective responses of these *aggressive* children. Are they similar to those aggressive-rejected children who report very low levels of distress, or do they more closely resemble those victimized children who describe increased levels of internalizing problems? It seems particularly important to learn more about the subjective experiences of these aggressive victims given that they represent the most strongly disliked members of the peer group (Perry et al., 1988).

The Next Frontier

Several broad conclusions about children's subjective experiences of rejection can be drawn from the past decade of research. First, peer rejection is reliably associated with various indices of internal distress (e.g., poor self-esteem, loneliness, depression, and social anxiety) in early and middle childhood, as well as in adolescence. Second, rejection appears to play a causal, rather than merely incidental, role in the emergence of these adjustment difficulties. Third, there appears to be considerable within-group variation in rejected children's subjective experiences, with some of this variability being linked to different cognitive styles and peer group experiences. Although withdrawn-rejected children report more distress than do their aggressive-rejected counterparts, recent studies using multidimensional assessments of internalizing problems provide an important reminder that aggressive-rejected children are not immune to the experience of negative affect.

Despite these advances, important issues remain to be addressed. For example, there is growing research to suggest that certain types of rejection experiences are more salient for girls than for boys (e.g., girls report a greater degree of hurtfulness or distress in response to social exclusion or peer rebuff than do boys; Galen & Underwood, 1997; Paquette & Underwood, 1999). These findings underscore the importance of exploring the interplay among gender, type of rejection experience, and children's subjective response. A second unexplored issue involves the heterogeneity of internalizing outcomes. Although existing research links peer rejection with a host of negative internal experiences, it does not offer a coherent model for discriminating among them. An important task of future studies will be the exploration of more specific linkages among negative peer experiences, self-perceptions of these encounters, and particular types of self-cognitions and negative affects.

Integrating Behavioral, Cognitive, and Social Context Mediators of Rejection Responses

This literature review demonstrates the many advances made in recent research on children's internal experiences of peer rejection. Ultimately, of course, we would like to understand *why* some children are more distressed than others in response to similar rejection experiences, and what role these internal responses play in the relationship between peer rejection and poor psychosocial adjustment. Although we have seen the beginnings of answers to these questions, progress has been hampered by the lack of an integrating model.

In the mid 1990's, John Coie was asked to contribute a chapter to the Handbook of Children's Coping with the task of considering peer rejection from a transactional stress and coping perspective (Sandler, Wolchik, MacKinnon, Ayers, & Rosa, 1997). Although very few peer rejection researchers had explicitly adopted this approach, it fit well with emerging transactional theories and allowed us (Zakriski, Jacobs, & Coie, 1997) to identify some important gaps in our understanding of peer rejection experiences. We now present a more fully developed transactional stress and coping model for adaptation to peer rejection that we believe builds on the important work we have just outlined, provides an integrative theoretical framework, and offers directions for future research.

A transactional model for adaptation to peer rejection appreciates that sociometrically rejected children encounter a variety of events as they interact with their environment and that the interaction of given events with a given child's appraisal of those events provides the basis for internal experiences. These experiences, combined with children's efforts to manage them, drive the adaptation process. This adaptation process continues over time and ultimately results in a broad spectrum of outcomes, ranging from transient rejection and positive adjustment to more chronic rejection and maladjustment.

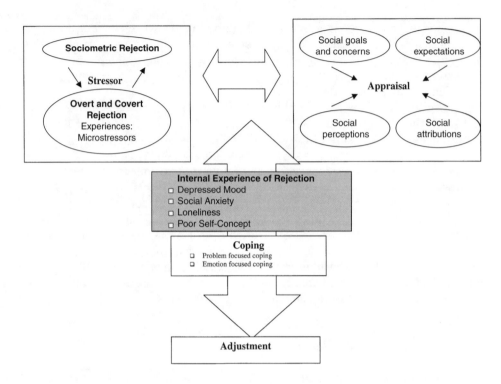

Figure 6.1. A transactional model for adaptation to peer rejection.

Like other integrative theories of peer rejection, this transactional model focuses on person–environment transactions rather than on more stable structures of the personality or environment. Unlike other models, however, this one abandons the assumption that the events associated with sociometric rejection are inherently stressful for all children. It acknowledges that a variety of individual differences, including behavioral subtype, are associated with great diversity in children's appraisal of rejection. Furthermore, it asserts that cognitive and emotional responses of sociometrically rejected children cannot be understood without reference to the broader social context. The overall model presented in Figure 6.1 illustrates the essential links among sociometric rejection, rejection experiences, internal experiences, and outcomes. Each major component of the figure is outlined in the following sections.

REJECTION EXPERIENCES. To truly understand why some sociometrically rejected children feel bad and how their feelings about their rejection might be linked to negative outcomes, we need to closely examine their daily interactions with peers. Rutter (1990) introduced the concept of microstressors, which might be a helpful way to differentiate between sociometric rejection and actual rejection experiences (see Figure 6.1). Rutter explains that a major stressor often sets in motion a series of processes including multiple smaller stressors that impact a child or the child's environment, or both. These processes are proximal to the child and have a more direct impact on development than does the more distal stressor. Sociometric rejection, being only a group summary of private affective evaluations, cannot have a direct impact on a child. The direct impact is passed through multiple smaller stressors that we are only beginning to appreciate. Boivin and Hymel (1997) address the issue of microstressors by pointing to overt victimization and a lack of peer affiliations as the critical aspects of sociometric rejection that mediate the link between peer rejection and loneliness. They also recognize that other factors, such as poor-quality friendships and subtle forms of social disdain, might be important.

The truth is that we really know very little about the everyday events that accompany sociometric peer rejection and exactly how they differ for different rejected children. Asher, Rose, and Gabriel (2001) have begun to document the numerous ways in which peer rejection might be expressed in everyday social interactions. Their observations suggest that rejection is expressed through 32 specific behaviors falling into the following categories: (a) excluding or terminating interactions, (b) denial of access, (c) aggression, (d) dominance, (e) moral disapproval, and (f) involving a third party. These rejection behaviors vary on several dimensions including whether they are blatant or subtle, clear or ambiguous, public or private, quick or extended, or standard or unique, or whether they involve single or multiple forms of rejection.

These specific behaviors have yet to be used to distinguish rejected from nonrejected children, or to explore differences in rejection experiences for aggressive- versus withdrawn-rejected children. We suspect that the range of rejection experiences for sociometrically rejected children will be quite broad, spanning from blatant rejection (e.g., direct statement of disliking) and overt victimization (e.g., hitting, teasing) to tolerance (e.g., picking a disliked child for the team because he or she is a good athlete) and even inadvertent reward (e.g., submitting to a bully without expressing disapproval). We also suspect that the context surrounding any individual rejection event will also vary, and that these contextual differences will be meaningfully related to rejected children's internal experiences. For example, we have seen that having a friend can buffer children from the harmful effects of peer rejection. On the other hand, a chronic lack of positive reinforcement from peers, even in the absence of overtly stressful rejection episodes, is likely to influence the degree to which peer interactions are perceived to be stressful over time.

APPRAISAL OF REJECTION EXPERIENCES. A stress and coping perspective reminds us that the stressfulness of an event cannot be determined solely on the basis of the characteristics of the event, but rather is a joint function of the event and the vulnerability of the child's self-system in relation to that event. Thus in Figure 6.1, we have highlighted the dynamic relationship between rejection experiences and appraisals and their joint relationship with subjective distress. In the appraisal process, the same event can be interpreted differently by two different children because of the children's goals, the importance of those goals, other surrounding social events, generalized beliefs about the world, temperament, behavioral characteristics, and so forth. We have seen individual differences in appraisal of identical rejection events between withdrawn- and aggressive-rejected children (Zakriski & Coie, 1996), but have only begun to understand the self-system vulnerabilities that might cause such a difference.

The existing appraisal research is limited by its neglect of other important aspects of the transactional stress and coping model. For example, very few studies have attempted to match the rejection events that aggressive or with-drawn children are asked to appraise in the laboratory to the kinds of actual rejection events that each type of child is most likely to experience in his or her day-to-day life. With the development of a detailed taxonomy of rejection behaviors, a more careful tailoring of assessment measures may be possible. In addition, it seems important to assess children's appraisal processes in the context of their actual treatment by peers. A rejected child who reports that he or she is liked and receives very little direct evidence to the contrary is living in a different psychological world than a rejected child who reports that he or she is liked despite being victimized routinely by peers. The relationship between reality and appraisal processes may play an important role in explaining individual differences in adaptation.

COPING WITH REJECTION EXPERIENCES. If we are to understand the relationship between subjective experiences and outcomes, we must consider the behavioral and emotional strategies children use to cope with rejection events. This aspect of our model is represented as the link between a child's subjective experience (derived from the events he or she experiences and how he or she appraises them) and the outcomes associated with peer rejection (see Figure 6.1). A number of researchers have examined children's use of problem- and emotion-focused coping in the context of stressful experiences (e.g., Causey & Dubow, 1992; Compas, 1987), and these constructs appear to be well suited to the stressors associated with peer rejection. For example, one rejected child might cope with a peer stressor in ways that are aimed at fixing the problem of being rejected (e.g., choosing different entry strategies next time). A different rejected child might cope in ways that are aimed at taking care of the emotional reaction to the stressor (e.g., reframing: "It's not that she doesn't like me; she is just busy with her other friends").

It remains unclear to what extent behavioral subtypes might interact with type of rejection experience to determine a child's predominant coping strategies. For example, aggressive-rejected children who are not overtly victimized but have few positive interactions with peers may cope via denial that protects them in the short run from loneliness, but creates accumulated interpersonal problems and feelings of ineffectiveness that become troubling into the high school years (Hecht et al., 1998). Conversely, withdrawn-rejected children who are overtly mistreated may adopt a more ruminative strategy that puts them in closer touch with the reality of their social situation but leaves them feeling sad and lonely in the short run and with a poor self-concept and high self-blame over time.

CONCLUSIONS. We believe that a transactional stress and coping model for adaptation to peer rejection puts sociometrically rejected children's internal experiences in their appropriate context. First, this framework offers an emphasis on both the objective and subjective experiences of peer rejection, reminding us that we cannot assume that all sociometrically rejected children are treated in the same way. Instead, more detailed investigations of the everyday social interactions of sociometrically rejected children are needed. Second, the stress and coping perspective embraces individual differences in rejection experiences, appraisal process, and outcomes. What is appraised as stressful for one individual may not be for another, and the specific microstressors associated with different types of rejection experiences may be linked to different outcomes. Finally, a stress and coping model has great potential to inform intervention both at the level of the individual and at the level of the peer group. If we can better understand the processes linking sociometric rejection, self-perceptions, and adjustment, we can more effectively tailor specific interventions for children in need.

References

Ames, R., Ames, C., & Garrison, W. (1977). Children's causal ascriptions for positive and negative interpersonal outcomes. *Psychological Reports, 41,* 595–602.

Asendorpf, J. B. (1991). Development of inhibited children's coping with unfamiliarity. *Child Development, 62,* 1460–1474.

Asher, S. R., Hymel, S., & Renshaw, P. D. (1984). Loneliness in children. *Child Development, 55,* 1456–1464.

Asher, S. R., Parkhurst, J. T., Hymel, S., & Williams G. A. (1990). Peer rejection and loneliness in childhood. In S. R. Asher & J. D. Coie (Eds.), *Peer rejection in childhood* (pp. 253–273). Cambridge: Cambridge University Press.

Asher, S. R., Rose, A. J., & Gabriel, S. W. (2001). Peer rejection in everyday life. In M. Leary (Ed.), *Interpersonal rejection* (pp. 105–142). New York: Oxford.

Asher, S. R., Zelis, K. M., Parker, J. G., & Bruene, C. M. (1991, April). *Self-referral for peer relationship problems among aggressive and withdrawn low-accepted children.* Paper presented at the meeting of the Society for Research in Child Development, Seattle, WA.

Bell-Dolan, D. J., Foster, S. L., & Christopher, J. S. (1995). Girls' peer relations and internalizing problems: Are socially neglected, rejected, and withdrawn girls at risk? *Journal of Clinical Child Psychology, 24,* 463–473.

Boivin, M., & Begin, G. (1989). Peer status and self-perception among early elementary school children: The case of rejected children. *Child Development, 60,* 591–596.

Boivin, M., & Hymel, S. (1997). Peer experiences and social self-perceptions: A sequential model. *Developmental Psychology, 33,* 135–145.

Boivin, M., Hymel, S., & Bukowski, W. (1995). The roles of social withdrawal, peer rejection, and victimization by peers in predicting loneliness and depressed mood in childhood. *Development and Psychopathology, 7,* 765–785.

Boivin, M., Poulin, F., & Vitaro, F. (1994). Depressed mood and peer rejection in childhood. *Development and Psychopathology, 6,* 483–498.

Boivin, M., Thomassin, L., & Alain, M. (1988, July). *Peer rejection and self-perceptions among early elementary school children: Aggressive vs. withdrawn rejectees.* Paper presented at the NATO Advanced Study Institute: Social Competence in Developmental Perspective, Savoie, France.

Boulton, M. J., & Underwood, K. (1992). Bully/victim problems among middle school children. *British Journal of Educational Psychology, 62,* 73–87.

Bukowski, W. M., & Hoza, B. (1989). Popularity and friendship: Issues in theory, measurements, and outcome. In T. Berndt & G. Ladd (Eds.), *Peer relationship in child development: Wiley series on personality processes* (pp. 15–45). Oxford, England: Wiley.

Bukowski, W. M., Hoza, B., & Boivin, M. (1993). Popularity, friendships, and emotional adjustment during early adolescence. In B. Laursen (Ed.), *Close friendships in adolescence* (pp. 23–37). San Francisco: Jossey-Bass.

Cassidy, J., & Asher, S. R. (1992). Loneliness and peer relations in young children. *Child Development, 63,* 350–365.

Causey, D. L., & Dubow, E. F. (1992). Development of a self-report coping measure for elementary school children. *Journal of Clinical Child Psychology, 21,* 47–59.

Cillessen, A. H. N., & Bellmore, A. D. (1999). Accuracy of social self-perceptions and peer competence in middle childhood. *Merrill-Palmer Quarterly, 45,* 650–676.

Cillessen, A. H., Van Lieshout, C. F., & Haselager, G. J. (1992, August). *Children's problems caused by consistent rejection in early elementary school.* Paper presented at the Centennial Convention of the American Psychological Association, Washington, DC.

Cole, D. A., & Carpentieri, S. (1990). Social status and the comorbidity of child depression and conduct disorder. *Journal of Consulting and Clinical Psychology, 58,* 748–757.

Compas, B. E. (1987). Coping with stress during childhood and adolescence. *Psychological Bulletin, 101,* 393–403.

Crick, N. R., & Ladd, G. W. (1993). Children's perceptions of their peer experiences: Attributions, loneliness, social anxiety, and social avoidance. *Developmental Psychology, 29,* 244–254.

Dodge, K. A., & Frame, C. L. (1982). Social cognitive biases and deficits in aggressive boys. *Child Development, 53,* 620–635.

French, D. C., Conrad, J., & Turner, T. M. (1995). Adjustment of antisocial and nonantisocial rejected adolescents. *Development and Psychopathology, 7,* 857–874.

Galen, B. R., & Underwood, M. K. (1997). Developmental investigation of social aggression among children. *Developmental Psychology, 33,* 589–600.

Hecht, D. B., Inderbitzen, H. M., & Bukowski, A. L. (1998). The relationship between peer status and depressive symptoms in children and adolescents. *Journal of Abnormal Child Psychology, 26,* 153–160.

Hodges, E., & Perry, D. (1996). Victims of peer abuse: An overview. *Journal of Emotional and Behavioral Problems, 5,* 23–28.

Hughes, J. N., Cavell, T. A., & Grossman, P. A. (1997). A positive view of self: Risk or protection for aggressive children? *Development and Psychopathology, 9,* 75–94.

Hymel, S., Bowker, A., & Woody, E. (1993). Aggressive versus withdrawn unpopular children: Variations in peer and self-perceptions in multiple domains. *Child Development, 64,* 879–896.

Hymel, S., & Franke, S. (1985). Children's peer relations: Assessing self-perceptions. In B. H. Schneider, K. H. Rubin, & J. E. Ledingham (Eds.), *Children's peer relations: Issues in assessment and intervention* (pp. 75–92). New York: Springer-Verlag.

Hymel, S., Franke, S., & Freigang, R. (1985). Peer relationships and their dysfunction. Considering the child's perspective. *Journal of Social and Clinical Psychology, 3,* 405–415.

Inderbitzen, H. M., Walters, K. S., & Bukowski, A. L. (1997). The role of social anxiety in adolescent peer relations: Differences among sociometric status groups and rejected subgroups. *Journal of Clinical Child Psychology, 26,* 338–348.

Kistner, J., Balthazor, M., Risi, S., & Burton, C. (1999). Predicting dysphoria from actual and perceived peer acceptance in childhood. *Journal of Clinical Child Psychology, 28,* 94–104.

Ladd, G. W., & Burgess, K. (1999). Charting the relationship trajectories of aggressive, withdrawn, and aggressive-withdrawn children during early grade school. *Child Development, 70,* 910–929.

Ladd, G. W., & Coleman, C. C. (1997). Children's classroom peer relationships and early school attitudes: Concurrent and longitudinal associations. *Early Education and Development, 8,* 51–66.

Ladd, G. W., Kochenderfer, B. J., & Coleman, C. C. (1996). Friendship quality as a predictor of young children's early school adjustment. *Child Development, 67,* 1103–1118.

Ladd, G. W., Kochenderfer, B. J., & Coleman, C. C. (1997). Classroom peer acceptance, friendship, and victimization: Distinct relational systems that contribute uniquely to children's school adjustment? *Child Development, 68,* 1181–1197.

La Greca, A. M., Dandes, S. K., Wick, P., Shaw, K., & Stone, W.L. (1988). Development of the Social Anxiety Scale for Children: Reliability and concurrent validity. *Journal of Clinical Child Psychology, 17,* 84–91.

La Greca, A. M., & Stone, W. L. (1993). Social Anxiety Scale for Children–Revised: Factor structure and concurrent validity. *Journal of Clinical Child Psychology, 22*, 17–27.

Landau, S., & Milich, R. (1985). Social status of aggressive and aggressive/withdrawn boys: A replication across age and method. *Journal of Consulting and Clinical Psychology, 53*, 141.

Ledingham, J., & Schartzman, A. E. (1984). A 3-year follow-up of aggressive and withdrawn behavior in childhood: Preliminary findings. *Journal of Abnormal Child Psychology, 12*, 157–168.

Lyons, J., Serbin, L. A., & Marchessault, K. (1988). The social behavior of peer-identified aggressive, withdrawn, and aggressive/withdrawn children. *Journal of Abnormal Child Psychology, 16*, 539–552.

Milich, R. & Landau, S. (1984). A comparison of the social status and social behavior of aggressive and aggressive/withdrawn boys. *Journal of Abnormal Child Psychology, 12*, 277–288.

Panak, W. F., & Garber, J. (1992). Role of aggression, rejection, and attributions in the prediction of depression in children. *Development and Psychopathology, 4*, 145–165.

Paquette, J. A., & Underwood, M. K. (1999). Young adolescents' experiences of peer victimization: Gender differences in accounts of social and physical aggression. *Merrill-Palmer Quarterly, 45*, 233–258.

Paradis, R., & Vitaro, F. (1999). Children rejected by their peers. *Enfance, 51*, 363–377.

Parker, J. G., & Asher, S. R. (1993a). Beyond group acceptance: Friendship adjustment and friendship quality as distinct dimensions of children's peer adjustment. In D. Perlman & W. H. Jones (Eds.), *Advances in personal relationships* (Vol. 4, pp. 261–294). London: Kingsley.

Parker, J. G., & Asher, S. R. (1993b). Friendship and friendship quality in middle childhood: Links with peer group acceptance and feelings of loneliness and social dissatisfaction. *Developmental Psychology, 29*, 611–621.

Parker, J. G., & Seal, J. (1996). Forming, losing, renewing, and replacing friendships: Applying temporal parameters to the assessment of children's friendship experiences. *Child Development, 67*, 2248–2268.

Parkhurst, J. T., & Asher, S. R. (1992). Peer rejection in middle school: Subgroup differences in behavior, loneliness, and interpersonal concerns. *Developmental Psychology, 28*, 231–241.

Patterson, C. J., Kupersmidt, J. B., & Griesler, P. C. (1990). Children's perceptions of self and of relationships with others as a function of sociometric status. *Child Development, 61*, 1335–1349.

Perry, D. G., Kusel, S. J., & Perry, L. L. (1988). Victims of peer rejection. *Developmental Psychology, 24*, 807–814.

Renshaw, P. D., & Brown, P. J. (1993). Loneliness in middle childhood: Concurrent and longitudinal predictors. *Child Development, 64*, 1271–1284.

Rogosch, F. A., & Cicchetti, D. (1994). Illustrating the interface of family and peer relations through the study of child maltreatment. *Social Development, 3*, 291–308.

Rubin, K. H., & Mills, R. S. (1988). The many faces of social isolation. *Journal of Consulting and Clinical Psychology, 56*, 916–924.

Rutter, M. (1990). Psychosocial resilience and protective factors. In J. Rolf, A. D. Masten, D. Cicchetti, K. H. Nuechterlein, & S. Weintraub (Eds.), *Risk and protective factors in the development of psychopathology* (pp. 181–214). New York: Cambridge University Press.

Sanderson, J. A., & Siegal, M. (1995). Loneliness and stable friendship in rejected and nonrejected preschoolers. *Journal of Applied Developmental Psychology, 16*, 555–567.

Sandler, I. N., Wolchik, S. A., MacKinnon, D., Ayers, T. S., & Rosa, M. W. (1997). Developing linkages between theory and intervention in stress and coping processes. In S. A. Wolchik and I. N. Sandler (Eds.), *Handbook of children's coping: Linking theory and intervention* (pp. 3–40). New York: Plenum.

Sandstrom, M. J., & Coie, J. D. (1999). A developmental perspective on peer rejection: Mechanisms of stability and change. *Child Development, 70*, 955–966.

Sletta, O., Valas, H., Skaalvik, E., & Sobstad, F. (1996). Peer relations, loneliness, and self-perceptions in school-aged children. *British Journal of Educational Psychology, 66*, 431–445.

Sobol, M. P., & Earn, B. M. (1985). Assessment of children's attributions for social experiences: Implications for social skills training. In B. H. Schneider, K. H. Rubin, & J. E. Ledingham (Eds.), *Children's peer relations: Issues in assessment and intervention* (pp. 93–110). New York: Springer-Verlag.

Taylor, S. E., & Brown, J. D. (1988). Illusion and well-being: A social psychological perspective on mental health. *Psychological Bulletin, 103,* 193–210.

Williams, G. (1999). *Peer relationship processes and children's loneliness at school.* Unpublished doctoral dissertation, University of Illinois at Urbana-Champaign.

Williams, G. A., & Asher, S. R. (1987, April). *Peer- and self-perceptions of peer rejected children: Issues in classification and subgrouping.* Paper presented at the biennial meeting of the Society for Research in Child Development, Baltimore, MD.

Zakriski, A. L., & Coie, J. D. (1996). A comparison of aggressive-rejected versus nonaggressive-rejected children's interpretations of self-directed and other-directed rejection. *Child Development, 67,* 1048–1070.

Zakriski, A. L., Jacobs, M., & Coie, J. D. (1997). Coping with peer rejection. In S. A. Wolchik and I. N. Sandler (Eds.), *Handbook of children's coping: Linking theory and intervention* (pp. 423–452). New York: Plenum.

7

How Peer Problems Lead to Negative Outcomes: An Integrative Mediational Model

Janis B. Kupersmidt and Melissa E. DeRosier

This chapter reviews new directions for prediction research on peer rejection and subsequent maladjustment, and introduces a mediational model that is designed to integrate several existing literatures about how negative social experiences may impact on children's development into one coherent framework.

As early as the 1970s, psychologists were alerted to the fact that peer relationship problems were related to many forms of maladjustment. Now 30 years later, the insidious, damaging influence of peer rejection (i.e., the active dislike, avoidance, and exclusion of a child by peers) has been repeatedly underscored through decades of research (see recent reviews, McDougall, Hymel, Vaillancourt, & Mercer, 2001; Parker, Rubin, Price, & DeRosier, 1995, as well as Kupersmidt, Coie, & Dodge, 1990; Parker & Asher, 1987). These reviews suggest that when children experience peer relationship problems, they are likely to experience a number of other concurrent behavioral, psychological, and academic problems as well. In the prediction of future adjustment, research supports the influential role of peer problems for numerous negative outcomes, including suicide (e.g., Carney, 2000), drug abuse (e.g., Spooner, 1999), educational underachievement (e.g., Woodward & Fergusson, 2000), delinquent behavior (e.g., Brendgen, Vitaro, & Bukowski, 1998), and depression (e.g., Boivin & Hymel, 1997). For example, peer-rejected children tend to exhibit a higher level of concurrent aggression and are at significantly higher risk for later delinquency than are nonrejected children (see chap. 13, this volume; Coie, Lochman, Terry, & Hyman, 1992; Kupersmidt & Coie, 1990). In addition, the aversive nature of the school environment for a rejected child contributes to school absenteeism, poor school performance, and school dropout (DeRosier, Kupersmidt, & Patterson, 1994; Kupersmidt & Coie, 1990).

Parker and Asher (1987) posed a key research question that mobilized the field to empirically examine whether peer rejection makes an independent, unique contribution to the prediction of negative outcomes (once the effects of negative behavior were accounted for; i.e., the "causal" model) or whether rejection is simply incidental to other problems that the child is experiencing. Over the years since, evidence has been accumulating in support of the causal model. Having peer problems adds to the prediction of negative outcomes even after controlling for prior levels of the problem behavior in question (DeRosier et al., 1994). In fact, peer rejection made a unique contribution to the prediction of both aggressive behavior problems and depressive symptoms five years later (Ialongo, Vaden-Kiernan, & Kellam, 1998).

Methodological Innovations for Improving Prediction

Although peer rejection has been found to be a significant and independent predictor of a range of negative outcomes, a large portion of unexplained variance remains (McDougall et al., 2001). Reported effect sizes predicting adjustment problems three years later range from 5% (internalizing) to 25% (externalizing and academic) explained variance (Coie et al., 1992; DeRosier et al., 1994). Clearly, other factors are influencing prediction besides peer rejection. In an effort to strengthen the prediction of negative outcomes related to peer problems, four methodological approaches have been investigated: (a) those that examine stable rejection, (b) those that examine subgroups of rejected youth, (c) those that examine different definitions of peer problems, and (d) those that examine multifinality.

Stability of Peer Rejection

The first strategy that has been used to improve our predictive models has been to examine the stability of peer rejection. In tests of the effects of the chronicity and proximity of peer rejection on behavioral and academic adjustment, negative outcomes were more likely when peer problems were chronic and severe (DeRosier et al., 1994). For example, chronic peer rejection was associated with significantly heightened levels of aggressive behavior problems in school (DeRosier et al., 1994). Similarly, Laird, Jordan, Dodge, Pettit, and Bates (2001) reported increasing externalizing problems with chronic rejection experiences. Chronic peer rejection has also been associated with greater shy and anxious behavior problems (Burks, Dodge, & Price, 1995; DeRosier et al., 1994). Overall, studies such as these suggest that stable peer rejection improves the prediction of later adjustment problems.

Rejected Subgroups

Despite the clear advantages of utilizing the sociometric classification methodology for determining rejected status, the criteria typically used to classify children into the rejected status group are reasonable but arbitrary (Cillessen & Bukowski, 2000). Traditionally, all children falling within a given status group (i.e., who meet predefined cutoffs for classification) are considered essentially comparable in risk status. Thus, the standard sociometric status grouping ignores within-peer-status-group differences. This realization led to a strategy of examining adjustment related to behavioral subgroups of rejected children (see Boivin, Hymel, & Bukowski, 1995, for review). For example, French (1988) found that approximately 50% of rejected boys were highly aggressive and that the aggressive-rejected subgroup was a greater risk for concurrent behavioral problems than were other subgroups. In contrast, aggression did not differentiate rejected females (French, 1990). Rather, anxious and withdrawn rejected girls exhibited the most deviant adjustment pattern.

More recently, a new algorithm to extend information about a child's sociometric status group classification to include greater within-group sensitivity regarding the strength of classification has been examined (DeRosier & Thomas, 2003). In other words, the strength of a child's classification was measured so that the degree to which a child falls within a given status group was calculated. In this way, children who fall just within the border of a status group can be compared with children who fall more in the mid-range or extreme of a group. Classification strength was found to significantly increase the predictive power of social status for concurrent behavioral adjustment. For example, extremely rejected children were significantly more likely to be seen as bullies and victims by peers compared with borderline rejected children. Children on the borderline of rejected status were not seen as bullies by peers and did not experience high levels of victimization. Thus, classification strength was found to contribute substantially to understanding sociobehavioral adjustment.

Expanding the Definition of Peer Problems

A third strategy used to strengthen the prediction of negative outcomes due to peer rejection has been to examine additional negative peer problems that may contribute to risk predictions. Consideration of other peer problems, beyond peer rejection, may increase the ability to specify the impact of rejection on a given child. For example, the absence of a reciprocated best friend, low group acceptance, and poor friendship quality made separate contributions to the concurrent prediction of loneliness (Parker & Asher, 1993). Also, poor quality friendship was associated with poor school adjustment (Berndt, 1992) as well as anxiety and depression (Goodyer, Wright, & Altham, 1989).

The short- and long-term consequences of antisocial peer affiliations are related to negative outcomes, but these affiliations have not been well investigated for rejected children. Children who are rejected by the normative peer group often find themselves on the outskirts of established social groups (Ladd, Price, & Hart, 1990), which results in restricted social choices. A reduction in the number and quality of interactions with prosocial peers decreases opportunities for skill development, which results in less adaptive socioemotional competencies and less mature friendship relations (see Newcomb & Bagwell, 1996, for review). In addition, rejected-aggressive children are more involved in deviant cliques than are nonaggressive children (Bagwell, Coie, Terry, & Lochman, 2000; Dishion, Patterson, Stoolmiller, & Skinner, 1991). Although social affiliation with an antisocial peer group is a powerful predictor of a range of school problems and antisocial behaviors (Dishion & Loeber, 1985; Elliott, Huizinga, & Ageton, 1985; Patterson & Dishion, 1985), peer rejection was found to be an even stronger predictor of later externalizing problems, and deviant affiliations did not add to the prediction (Laird et al., 2001). More research on the social network characteristics of rejected children is needed, particularly for determining the contribution of antisocial friends to later risk.

In addition to exclusion from positive interactions within the normative peer group, rejected children often experience negative peer interactions, particularly victimization (see Boivin, Hymel, & Hodges, 2001, for review). Victimization and peer rejection appear to reciprocally influence one another with increases in one promoting increases in the other over time (Hodges & Perry, 1999). In addition, victimization appears to moderate the relation between peer rejection and adjustment, which results in more negative adjustment when children experience both peer problems (Boivin et al., 2001). Conversely, presence of a mutual best friendship has been found to buffer the impact of victimization on internalizing and externalizing behavior problems (Hodges, Boivin, Vitaro, & Bukowski, 1999).

The multitude of possible influences of different peer problems on one another and on adjustment is difficult to tease apart. Five indices of problematic peer relations—low peer acceptance, no reciprocated best friend, low perceived social support from the best friend, high conflict with the best friend, and aggressive affiliations—were examined as predictors of aggression and delinquency in adolescence (Kupersmidt, Burchinal, & Patterson, 1995). Multiple peer problems were additively associated with the prediction of each outcome, suggesting that children with many peer problems were at higher risk than children with fewer problems. Peer rejection was the strongest predictor of negative outcomes. Thus, the evaluation of social risk factors requires the assessment of multiple aspects of social functioning with peers.

Multifinality

The final strategy that has helped improve our predictions of negative outcomes from peer rejection has been through studies of multifinality. In other words, the same risk factor, peer rejection in this case, may be associated with multiple negative outcomes or adjustment problems. According to this perspective, the impact of a specific risk factor for a given child will depend upon exposure to other factors, such as additional risk factors, resources, and personal characteristics. Despite consistent findings regarding the fact that negative outcomes are associated with peer rejection, substantial individual differences in the response to peer rejection have been observed. In addition, peer rejection appears to operate as a general stressor rather than a specific precursor to a specific disorder, a pattern consistent with the concept of multifinality. Peer rejection was only modestly predictive of specific negative outcomes such as delinquency, school absenteeism, and school dropout (Kupersmidt & Coie, 1990; Kupersmidt & Patterson, 1991). However, by creating a nonspecific negative outcome variable, the strength of the prediction from peer rejection was improved.

In summary, peer problems are a complex phenomenon in which a variety of factors influence the impact of peer rejection on adjustment. Clearly, the field has advanced greatly in the past 20 years in its understanding of these factors; however, prediction studies that include possible mediators and that test conceptual models are needed.

The First Explanatory Model

John Coie (1990) introduced a groundbreaking conceptual model for understanding the emergence, maintenance, and consequences of peer rejection by building upon a stress and coping conceptual framework. Coie's chapter represented one of the first attempts by a scholar in the peer relations literature to articulate an explanatory model for understanding why and how peer problems might contribute to negative outcomes. By linking peer problems to the coping literature, Coie conceptualized peer rejection as one example of a stressful life experience. Through this lens, the stress and coping literature provided guidance about how stress (in this case, the stress of peer rejection) mediates adjustment. Three mediating mechanisms were introduced in his article: coping skills, social support, and self-esteem. Coie presented evidence for the mediational influence of these three factors in the path between peer rejection and maladjustment. Although many studies have examined pieces of this model, empirical support for the overall model is still lacking and remains an important goal for future research. Other mediators and explanatory processes have been suggested in the literature since this seminal publication (see McDougall et al., 2001; chap. 6, this volume, for reviews); however, they too are lacking a strong empirical base.

An Integrative Mediational Model of
Peer Problems and Maladjustment

In the present chapter, we build upon Coie's conceptual framework by adding more possible mediators of peer experiences on adjustment. In particular, research findings on the relation between social cognition and adjustment are discussed. The Integrative Mediational Model (IMM) describes the processes through which long-term outcomes are influenced by the perception of availability and the utilization of a wide array of resources that serve to increase risk or protection. Figure 7.1 graphically displays the elements included in the IMM. Patterns of negative social experiences, risky or unsupportive contexts, social cognitive deficits, and problematic response styles are each examined as mediational influences on negative outcomes.

Throughout the balance of this chapter, a stark illustration of a particular case study is incorporated into discussion of each of the mediational factors included in the IMM. Although in no way do we suggest that tragic outcomes are typical or even probable as a function of experiencing peer rejection, examination of Evan Ramsey's extreme example may help us conceptualize the full continuum of influences that these mediational factors may have on children

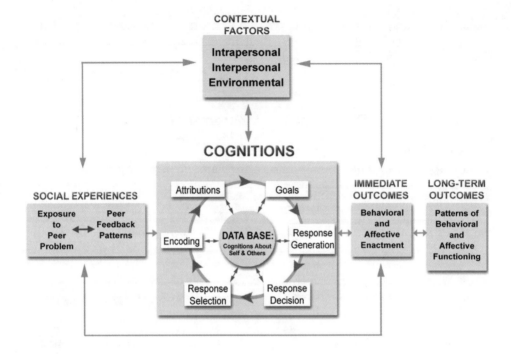

Figure 7.1.   Mediators of negative peer experiences on negative outcomes.

over time. Therefore, elements of Evan's case will be included for illustrative purposes as we discuss each piece of the proposed model.[1]

> In February 1997, Evan Ramsey, then 16 years old, shot and killed the principal of his school and one fellow student in Bethel, Alaska, as well as wounding two other students with a shotgun. Evan is now serving two 100-year sentences in an Alaska prison (Dedman, 2000).

Social Experiences As a Mediator Between Peer Problems and Maladjustment

> Evan Ramsey had experienced chronic and extreme rejection, bullying, and victimization by peers for many years. He was physically and verbally harassed by a number of peers. He was socially isolated, with few friends at school.

The social experiences of rejected children appear to be different from those of more socially accepted children in many ways. Rejected children are more likely to be the victim of direct and relational aggression (DeRosier & Thomas, 2003) and their social approaches are more likely to be rejected by

---

[1]Case history information is also provided through the second author's involvement with the U.S. Secret Service and U.S. Department of Education and their research on school shooters.

peers (Dodge, Coie, & Brakke, 1982). In general, social isolation and exclusion from social activities are consistently related to peer rejection (e.g., Rubin & Mills, 1988). As a consequence of chronic rejection experiences, rejected children become more isolated from and deprived of access to typically developing peers in age-appropriate prosocial activities (DeRosier et al., 1994). Because of this isolation, they are less likely to develop the social competencies that might enable them to integrate into the peer group more effectively. Specifically, they are less likely to receive corrective feedback and observe social norms and practices. In addition to isolation, rejected children receive excessively negative feedback from the normative peer group (Buhs & Ladd, 2001; Dodge et al., 1982). These hypothesized mechanisms associated with social feedback may directly shape and reinforce both immediate and long-term deviant patterns of behavior and extinguish socially skillful behaviors. Both skewed and insufficient feedback from normative peers can be conceptualized as operating on the behavior of the rejected child according to traditional reinforcement theories (e.g., operant conditioning) such that the rejected child may not know how to negotiate the social world, may become developmentally delayed or socially immature, may become socially awkward, or may develop increasingly deviant patterns of affective expression and social behavior over time.

Cognitive Mediators Between Peer Problems and Maladjustment

The reformulated social information processing (SIP) theory provides a theoretical framework for examining cognitions associated with maladjustment (Crick & Dodge, 1994) such that the solving of acute and chronic social problems is influenced by two major cognitive structures and processes. First, long-standing latent structures or cognitions help children to understand their social worlds. These long-standing latent structures are conceptualized as composing the Social Cognitive Data Base. Second, online "in the moment" processing, often referred to as SIP skills, is activated when solving acute social problems, as they are occurring. These two structures interact with one another to influence both acute and long-standing patterns of individual behavioral and affective reactions to the social world. The online processing in the SIP model and its function as a mediator between peer experiences and outcomes are described more fully by Gifford-Smith and Rabiner (chap. 4, this volume).

According to the SIP model, upon contact with a social stimulus, rejected children encode cues or information about the situation and the peers involved. These cues are interpreted and evaluated in terms of the cause, stability, globality, and intent of the peers and the problem. Then, the rejected child decides upon his or her goals and strategies for solving that social problem. Children evaluate the strategies that were generated in terms of their self-efficacy to perform them, likelihood for meeting their goals, and consistency with their values and beliefs. On the basis of this evaluation, they select a specific response(s) for that social stimulus. Prototypic problems in executing any of these cognitive functions can be associated with maladaptive patterns of behavior and affect. For example, selective attention to hostile cues and having hostile attributional biases have been associated with reactive aggression. In other words, frequently perceiving threat and danger in the world has been associated with anger, revenge, and retaliatory aggression toward peers (Dodge, Lochman, Harnish, Bates, & Pettit, 1997). For example, children may have a history of experiences that influences their encoding skills needed to adequately sample and accurately encode information from a specific social event. As Gifford-Smith and Rabiner (chap. 4, this volume) point out, these cognitions have been found to serve as mediators between children's social experiences with peers and their affective and behavioral reactions. Thus, in our case example, although Evan's goals were both self-protective (i.e., wanting the teasing to stop) and affiliative (i.e., wanting to be accepted and respected by his friends), several aspects of his problem-solving skills were deficient. For example, he generated few prosocial solutions to his problems and did not think about the negative outcomes (i.e., victim suffering; incarceration) associated with his chosen solution. Despite the large body of research on the SIP model, less is known about the Data Base that is hypothesized as influencing each step of online processing. In the next section, two components of the Data Base, including cognitions about the self and cognitions about others, are discussed as mediators.

THE SOCIAL COGNITIVE DATA BASE. Repeated exposure to negative social feedback is hypothesized as being associated with problematic cognitions in online processing. It is not clear how this processing in vivo gets codified and generalized across situations and across time to result in a child having chronic maladaptive cognitions. If the Social Cognitive Data Base represents the schemas, scripts, and cognitions that reside in memory and are accessed during specific social interactions to elicit specific behavioral and affective responses, it suggests that we might want to have a deeper understanding of how peer rejection affects it.

COGNITIONS ABOUT THE SELF.

> Evan Ramsey wanted the teasing to stop. His friends told him he was "nothing" if he didn't shoot the gun at people at school.

Despite the fact that there has been a long-standing interest in the meaning or impact of peer rejection on self-perceptions, the field has lacked a unifying theory of how these cognitions may mediate between social experiences and negative outcomes. One theoretical approach that has been suggested by Kupersmidt and colleagues (Kupersmidt, Buchele, Voegler, & Sedikides, 1996; Kupersmidt, Sigda, Sedikides, & Voegler, 1999) involves the application of self-discrepancy theory to explain the role of self-perceptions on the development of negative outcomes. Self-discrepancy theory (Higgins, 1987) provides an excellent framework for understanding social needs as a mediator of the effects of problematic peer relations on maladjustment. According to this theory, self-discrepancies within the representations that are relevant to the social self are associated with negative affect. For example, discrepancies between the actual self and the ideal self are strongly associated with dejection-related emotions such as feeling sad, disappointed, or discouraged (Higgins, Klein, &

Strauman, 1985). The dejection-related emotion most associated with the social domain is loneliness and, in fact, loneliness has been associated with a range of social problems. Consistent with this theory, the lack of best friendships, low peer acceptance, and poor quality friendships, presumably all discrepant from children's ideal social situation, were all associated with loneliness (Parker & Asher, 1993). Likewise, submissive-rejected students report being lonelier than do socially average children (Parkhurst & Asher, 1994). In fact, the number of social self-discrepancies is positively correlated with loneliness, which suggests that the more ways that children's social needs are not met, the lonelier they feel (Kupersmidt et al., 1999).

Behavior change designed to reduce the gap between the ideal and actual social self could be adaptive or maladaptive. For example, a girl who wants to be socially accepted might engage in risky or unhealthy behaviors in the hopes of improving her social status. She may stop attending school in order to avoid continued exposure to the social cues that activate the ideal–actual discrepancy and her accompanying feelings of loneliness or depression. This pattern would be consistent with findings suggesting a significant correlation between depressed affect and school absenteeism (e.g., Kearney, 1993; Young, Brasic, & Kisnadwala, 1990) and in turn, between peer rejection and school absenteeism (Kupersmidt & Coie, 1990). These findings are also consistent with the hypothesis suggested by Coie (1990) that a child who wants to be liked by members of his or her peer group, but who is rejected by them, may avoid peers to avoid further rejection and to decrease exposure to negative behaviors directed at him or her by peers.

In addition to the ideal and actual domains of the self, self-discrepancy theory introduces another relevant self-cognition, the ought self, that is defined as a representation of attributes that ought to be possessed. The ought domain refers to the norms or standards for social development held by each child. Higgins (1987) hypothesized that a discrepancy between the actual self and the ought self would be associated with agitation-related problems such as feeling worried, nervous, or tense. A discrepancy between one's social standards and one's actual social ability or resources might be expected to produce social anxiety. Social anxiety might lead to avoiding volunteering or speaking in class and shyness in everyday social situations with peers. Anxiety-related affect was related to school refusal and school phobia, and children with internalizing disorders had heightened test and performance anxiety (Durlak, 1992). Also, submissive-rejected middle school students reported more concern about the possibility of being rejected or humiliated after lunch and between classes then did average students (Parkhurst & Asher, 1992). Finally, rejected children reported more anxiety in the form of greater concern about peer evaluations than did more accepted peers (La Greca, Dandes, Wick, Shaw, & Stone, 1988).

A third cognitive mechanism was proposed by Ogilvie (1987) who introduced the concept of the undesired self which he proposed as the most dangerous and disowned image of the self. These images are derived from memories of embarrassing experiences, dreaded situations, and unwanted emotions. He argues that a discrepancy between the ideal self and the undesired self may produce a strong negative affective reaction and could be even more motivating than the negative affect produced from other types of self-discrepancies.

A child who has developed an undesired social self, based on previous negative experiences at school, would be strongly motivated to reduce this discrepancy. This situation seems to fit the case of Evan Ramsey, who avoided activating the undesired self (e.g., being called a "nothing" by his peers) by following taunts to shoot peers at school. Thus, these self-discrepancies may provide a framework for understanding individual differences in the affective and behavioral reactions to peer problems.

COGNITIONS ABOUT OTHERS.

> Evan Ramsey believed no one else would help him and that he had to take matters into his own hands.

Negative or hostile cognitions about others, particularly in the form of generalized expectations or schemas, would be expected to yield a particularly powerful influence over both encoding processes and having hostile attributions in specific social situations. In fact, there is some evidence to suggest that viewing others as hostile, unsupportive, or rejecting is associated with the tendency to have a hostile attributional bias (Burks, Laird, Dodge, Pettit, & Bates, 1999; Graham & Hudley, 1993).

Two other latent cognitions in the Social Cognitive Data Base that are relevant to peer rejection experiences are perceptions and standards of relationships with others. Previous research on children's cognitions about their relationships with their parents has examined children's perceptions of "how things are" in the relationship (e.g., Furman & Buhrmester, 1985) and found an association between these cognitions and peer rejection (Patterson, Kupersmidt, & Griesler, 1990). Peer-rejected children reported being less satisfied with their relationship with their father and reported less companionship from their best friend than did other children. Similarly, Evan had the perception that he was isolated and without the benefits of social support or aid from either peers or adults in his environment.

More recently, Matza, Kupersmidt, and Glenn (2001) examined another cognition associated with cognitive representations of others, namely, adolescents' standards of "how something should be" in their parent–child relationship as a function of peer status. There are several ways in which standards may be associated with either immediate or long-term negative outcomes. First, unmet standards are associated with problems in marital interactions (Baucom, Epstein, Rankin, & Burnett, 1996) and may serve as a cognitive reference point for understanding social situations. In other words, children will react to their perceptions, but these perceptions are filtered through their standards. For example, a child who has high standards for loyalty and intimacy in friendships would be likely to have a negative affective or behavioral response to a friend who is seen whispering and talking to another peer in the lunchroom. Second, extreme or overly rigid schema or standards might be problematic for encoding new information or in selecting responses. Consistent with this view, some rejected children use extreme or overly rigid schemata, which can interfere with their ability to process immediate social cues (Crick & Dodge, 1994). Third, a child can have non-normative standards such that the benchmark for evaluating perceptions of relationships may result in unrealistic expectations or goals. One example of a cognition that might be a non-normative standard is that friends should never disagree, when, in fact, having disagreements might be normative during a certain stage of peer relationships or during certain developmental periods. Matza et al. (2001) calculated perception–standard discrepancies to examine unmet standards in the parent–child relationship. The results suggested that rejected adolescents had more unmet standards (i.e., less maternal warmth and less monitoring and supervision) in their relationships with their parents than did more socially accepted peers. No studies were located that examined the relationship between standards or the perception–standards discrepancy for friendship and social or behavioral adjustment; however, one might hypothesize that these types of cognitive distortions associated with peer relationship experiences could negatively contribute to adjustment. Examination of these Data Base cognitions may be a promising line of research in the future.

Contextual Factors

The final component of the proposed model is the context within which the peer experiences occur. A number of contextual factors may mediate the impact of rejection on adjustment by acting as either resources for or additional stressors on the child. Understanding the role of these factors in relation to peer rejection is complicated by the fact that exposure to some contextual factors such as IQ or poverty is uncontrollable by the child, whereas others are selected and strategically implemented or utilized by the child such as seeing a guidance counselor for help or participating in an extracurricular activity. Thus, peer-rejected children may select certain strategies to solve peer problems on the basis of the availability of particular resources needed to execute their desired responses. In other words, less adaptive strategies may be selected because of lack of resources rather than an SIP deficit. Hence, the availability and utilization of contextual factors provide a mediational pathway in addition to social cognitive skills between peer problems and adjustment.

INTRAPERSONAL.

> Evan had few intrapersonal resources. He was a chronically poor student with no particular talents and did not participate in athletic or other prosocial extracurricular activities. His school peers considered him to be physically unattractive and called him names.

A number of intrapersonal factors may function either as resources to help children cope with peer problems or as additional risk factors that diminish coping skills. For example, intelligence is a critical intrapersonal factor and operates as a protective factor against a number of adverse life events (Tiet et al., 2001). Conversely, lower intelligence places children at greater risk for maladjustment as a function of life stressors. Lower IQ has been found to predict later peer problems (Yude & Goodman, 1999) perhaps because of lower social problem-solving skills (Wentzel & Erdley, 1993). Intellectually gifted boys and girls have been found to be significantly less likely to be rejected by peers (Luftig & Nichols, 1990). Similarly, poor academic achievement has been repeatedly associated with peer rejection (Austin & Draper, 1984). Thus, lower intelligence may place children at greater risk for experiencing peer problems as well as hamper their ability to effectively cope with negative experiences, thereby increasing the risk of maladjustment.

A second intrapersonal factor is a child's nonacademic talents or skills. Athletic ability and interest have been associated with lower peer victimization (Boulton & Smith, 1994), greater peer group perceptions of popularity for boys (Lease, Kennedy, & Axelrod, 2002), and greater sociometric popularity in adolescence (Horowitz, 1967). Participation in extracurricular activities, especially highly structured ones such as team sports, has been linked to low levels of antisocial behavior (Mahoney & Stattin, 2000) and higher social status (Franzoi, Davis, & Vasquez-Suson, 1994). In addition, initially rejected children who participated in extracurricular activities were found to show significant improvement in their social status over time (Sandstrom, 1999). Thus, absence of personal talents or skills, and the resulting low level of involvement in prosocial extracurricular activities, may place children at greater risk for experiencing peer problems and decrease prosocial contact with normative peers, thereby increasing the likelihood of maladjustment.

Physical attractiveness may also function as an important intrapersonal factor. Physical attractiveness has been repeatedly associated with higher social preference (e.g., Coie, Dodge, & Coppotelli, 1982) and popular status, particularly for girls (Krantz, 1987; Lease et al., 2002). In fact, peers tend to assume that more attractive children are of higher social status (Johnson & MacEachern, 1985). Attractiveness appears to more directly influence popularity for girls. This relation is less clear for boys for whom athletic ability may play a stronger role in effecting peer popularity (Lease et al., 2002). Research by Cavior and Dokecki (1973) suggests that the mid-range of attractiveness is unrelated to social acceptance and only at the extremes, either very attractive or very unattractive, do we see an impact on liking. However, for both boys and girls, perceived physical attractiveness and satisfaction with appearance are related to self-esteem (Quatman & Watson, 2001). Thus, physical attractiveness may influence peer acceptance as well as impact intrapersonal coping skills through its influence on self-esteem.

Iɴᴛᴇʀᴘᴇʀsoɴᴀʟ.

> Evan's home life had a troubled history. His parents divorced when he was quite young. When he was six, his father was put in prison for a 10-year sentence after holding a publishing editor hostage. His alcoholic mother was neglectful, which resulted in social service involvement and the placement of Evan and his two brothers into foster care when Evan was seven years old. Evan lived in multiple foster homes and, at the time of the shootings, he and his younger brother were in the foster care of the superintendent of the Bethel school region.

A large body of research and theory has explored the family context and its relation to children's peer relationships (see Parke & Ladd, 1992, for review).

Although this literature is too vast to give due diligence here, there are a few key dimensions to mention. The qualities of the parent–child relationship along dimensions such as discord, warmth, and control have been repeatedly found to contribute to social skills and peer relations (e.g., Cassidy, Parke, Butkovsky, & Braungart, 1992). When parents are responsive and available, their children's peer relations are more positive and secure. In contrast, hostile, rejecting, and unresponsive parents have children whose peer relations are less supportive and more conflictual.

In the face of the stress of peer rejection, a positive parent–child relationship may help buffer negative effects by providing the child with interpersonal resources for coping and support. Similarly, a positive sibling relation may help counterbalance negative peer relations. However, an absent or negative parent–child relationship as well as antagonistic sibling relations may place children under additional stress which may, in turn, exacerbate the negative influence of peer rejection on adjustment (Hart, Olsen, Robinson & Mandleco, 1997).

> In an attempt to stop the bullying, Evan asked many people for help through the proper channels including his foster mother, principal, and the dean of students. School officials met with the perpetrators of the bullying, but unfortunately, after a short respite, the bullying resumed at an intensified level. Once again, Evan asked school officials for help and was told to just ignore it. Evan stated in an interview with the U.S. Secret Service that he "figured since the principal and the dean weren't doing anything that was making any impression, that I was gonna have to do something or else I was gonna keep on getting picked on."

Similar to family support, the quality of a child's relationships with other key adults, such as teachers and school counselors, may also play a role in mediating the impact of peer rejection (Howes, 2000). Unfortunately, rejected children tend to perceive their relationship with their teacher to be of lower quality with more conflict and less support than do nonrejected children (DeRosier, 2003). Teachers are also more likely to report that they dislike rejected children more than nonrejected children (DeRosier, 2003). A negative teacher–child relationship may place additional stress on rejected children by decreasing potential social and instrumental support at school and restricting potential resources for coping with the stress of peer rejection. Presence of a positive relationship with a teacher, guidance counselor, or other prosocial adult figure may, conversely, provide support and resources to boost rejected children's coping skills.

> Evan was clearly rejected by the normative peer group and his few remaining social contacts were with peers who encouraged his anger as well as his thoughts and plans of revenge and murder. They told Evan that simply showing up at school with a gun wasn't enough to get the bullies to stop; he had to use it. Evan had not originally planned to kill the principal, but one of his "friends" who hated the principal encouraged Evan to include him. On the day of the shooting, two dozen classmates, one with a video camera to catch the shooting on tape, gathered on the library balcony above

the lobby to watch. When one girl wandered up the stairs, someone told her to get back downstairs because she was "on the list."

As presented earlier, rejected children's social choices are often restricted, which may, over time, contribute to affiliations with others who are social outliers. When these restricted affiliations are with socially immature, unskilled children, then little developmental advancement in social skills may occur (Ladd et al., 1990). Furthermore, when rejected children, particularly aggressive-rejected children, turn to equally or more antisocial peers for companionship, deviance training is likely to occur (Dishion, McCord, & Poulin, 1999). Therefore, in the development of psychopathology, it is important to consider the context of a child's peer affiliations, which may mediate the impact of peer rejection on outcome.

ENVIRONMENTAL.

> Evan's support systems ultimately failed him and he felt betrayed by peers and school officials. He now held the expectation that the victimization would continue unabated. He became extremely depressed, hopeless, and suicidal. He felt that there was no alternative to violence, no other coping strategies left to try, and felt morally justified about taking matters into his own hands.

The final area considered consists of both risky and supportive environmental factors. Poverty represents a powerful environmental stressor largely because of its negative impact on access to resources such as lower access to health care and adequate living circumstances and increased strains (Gersten, 1992). Also, poor children have fewer play companions (Patterson, Vaden, Griesler, & Kupersmidt, 1991) and more problematic behavioral, academic, and social adjustment (Patterson, Vaden, & Kupersmidt, 1991). Poverty has been found to place children at risk for being bullied by peers (Barbarin, 1999). Chronic poverty has a more deleterious effect on children than does intermittent poverty (Bolger, Patterson, Thompson, & Kupersmidt, 1995). In addition, living in a low-income neighborhood is negatively associated with peer rejection as well as aggression and fewer play companions (Kupersmidt, Griesler, DeRosier, Patterson, & Davis, 1995).

Another environmental stressor is living in a single-parent household because these children are more likely to live in poverty (McLanahan & Booth, 1989) and their mothers report greater on-the-job stress (Friedemann & Andrews, 1990). Lower household income for single-parent homes contributes to significantly higher parental stress for single-parent versus dual-parent homes. Children in single-parent homes may be particularly at risk for negative family interactions (Gelles, 1989). Fewer adults in the home also impacts parental supervision of children. With lower supervision, likelihood of affiliations with deviant peers increases (Simons, Johnson, Beaman, Conger, & Whitbeck (1996) and, as a result, risk for delinquency and drug use in single-parent homes is greater (Coughlin & Vuchinich, 1996; Jenkins & Zunguze, 1998).

Race and ethnicity present significant stress through prejudice and discrimination, which results in exposure to a number of related stressors, including employment restrictions, housing restrictions, and interpersonal threats (Williams, 1999). Race has also been shown to influence children peer relations as a function of the racial composition of the peer group at school such that popular African American children were not viewed as leaders when in a racial minority at the school, but were viewed as leaders in schools that were exclusively African American (Coie, Dodge, & Kupersmidt, 1990). Also, being of a racial minority may place students at risk for peer rejection (e.g., Kistner, Metzler, Gatlin, & Risi, 1993).

Each contextual factor—intrapersonal, interpersonal, and environmental—may serve as either a resource for or stressor on the rejected child. The risk of maladjustment as well as the specific path of maladjustment for a given rejected child is likely to be partially mediated by the availability and utilization of contextual resources. Thus, this represents an important direction for future research.

Conclusion

In conclusion, the IMM proposed in this chapter attempts to build on the findings linking peer problems with immediate and long-term adjustment problems. Diverse literatures have been incorporated into this review to examine how children's responses are influenced by a wide array of mediational factors. The social cognitive literature linking social experiences with immediate behavioral and affective responses through SIP has been integrated into the model as well as the context within which social experiences occur. Contextual factors are viewed broadly to include availability of intrapersonal, interpersonal, and environmental contextual factors. Children's perceptions of availability of contextual resources as well as their utilization of those resources may serve to increase risk or protection for outcomes. In effect, patterns of negative social experiences, risky or unsupportive contexts, social cognitive deficits, and problematic behavioral and affective responses may become increasingly rigid, intense, and frequent over time, such that negative long-term outcomes result. The testing of this complex, integrative mediational model remains an important direction for future research and for the development of more comprehensive and refined theories in understanding the role of peer relations in developmental psychopathology. The field will benefit from an integrative approach that attempts to understand not only how each process impacts on outcomes, but also how the processes work together to either promote or deter future negative patterns.

References

Austin, A. M. B., & Draper, D. C. (1984). The relationship among peer acceptance, social impact and academic achievement in middle childhood. *American Educational Research Journal, 21,* 597–604.

Bagwell, C. L., Coie, J. D., Terry, R. A., & Lochman, J. E. (2000). Peer clique participation in middle childhood: Associations with sociometric status and gender. *Merrill-Palmer Quarterly, 46,* 280–305.

Barbarin, O. A. (1999). Social risks and psychological adjustment: A comparison of African American and South American children. *Child Development, 70,* 1348–1359.

Baucom, D. H., Epstein, N., Rankin, L. A., & Burnett, C. K. (1996). Assessing relationship standards: The inventory of specific relationship standards. *Journal of Family Psychology, 10,* 72–88.

Berndt, T. J. (1992). Friendship and friends' influence in adolescence. *Current Directions in Psychological Science, 1,* 156–159.

Boivin, M., & Hymel, S. (1997). Peer experiences and social self-perceptions: A sequential model. *Developmental Psychology, 33,* 135–145.

Boivin, M., Hymel, S., & Bukowski, W. M. (1995). The roles of social withdrawal, peer rejection and victimization by peers in predicting loneliness and depressed mood in childhood. *Development and Psychopathology, 6,* 483–498.

Boivin, M., Hymel, S., & Hodges, E. (2001). Toward a process view of peer rejection and peer harassment. In J. Juvonen & S. Graham (Eds.), *Peer harassment in school* (pp. 265–289). New York: Oxford University Press.

Bolger, K. E., Patterson, C. J., Thompson, W. W., & Kupersmidt, J. B. (1995). Psychosocial adjustment among children experiencing persistent and intermittent family economic hardship. *Child Development, 66,* 1107–1129.

Boulton, M. J., & Smith, P. K. (1994). Bully/victim problems in middle-school children: Stability, self-perceived competence, peer perceptions, and peer acceptance. *British Journal of Developmental Psychology, 12,* 315–329.

Brendgen, M., Vitaro, F., & Bukowski, W. M. (1998). Affiliation with delinquent friends: Contributions of parents, self-esteem, delinquent behavior, and rejection by peers. *Journal of Early Adolescence, 18,* 244–265.

Buhs, E. S., & Ladd, G. W. (2001). Peer rejection as antecedent of young children's school adjustment: An examination of mediating processes. *Developmental Psychology, 37,* 550–560.

Burks, V., Dodge, K. A., & Price, J. M. (1995). Models of internalizing outcomes of early rejection. *Development and Psychopathology, 7,* 683–695.

Burks, V., Laird, R., Dodge, K., Pettit, G., & Bates, J. (1999). Knowledge structures, social information processing, and children's aggressive behavior. *Social Development, 8,* 220–236.

Carney, J. V. (2000). Bullied to death: Perceptions of peer abuse and suicidal behaviour during adolescence. *School Psychology International, 21,* 213–223.

Cassidy, J., Parke, R. D., Butkovsky, L., & Braungart, J. M. (1992). Family-peer connections: The roles of emotional expressiveness within the family and children's understanding of emotions. *Child Development, 63,* 603–618.

Cavior, N., & Dokecki, P. R. (1973). Physical attractiveness, perceived attitude similarity, and academic achievement as contributors to interpersonal attraction among adolescents. *Developmental Psychology, 9,* 44–54.

Cillessen, A. H. N., & Bukowski, W. M. (2000). Developmental processes in peer relations and psychopathology. *Development and Psychopathology, 7,* 587–589.

Coie, J. D. (1990). Toward a theory of peer rejection. In S. R. Asher & J. D. Coie (Eds.), *Peer rejection in childhood* (pp. 365–401). Cambridge, England: Cambridge University Press.

Coie, J. D., Dodge, K. A., & Coppotelli, H. (1982). Dimensions and types of social status: A cross-age perspective. *Developmental Psychology, 18,* 557–570.

Coie, J. D., Dodge, K. A., & Kupersmidt, J. B. (1990). Peer group behavior and social status. In S. R. Asher & J. D. Coie (Eds.), *Peer rejection in childhood* (pp. 17–59). New York: Cambridge University Press.

Coie, J. D., Lochman, J. E., Terry, R., & Hyman, C. (1992). Predicting early adolescent disorder from childhood aggression and peer rejection. *Journal of Consulting and Clinical Psychology, 60,* 783–792.

Coughlin, C., & Vuchinich, S. (1996). Family experience in preadolescence and the development of male delinquency. *Journal of Marriage and the Family, 58,* 491–501.

Crick, N. R., & Dodge, K. A. (1994). A review and reformulation of social-information-processing mechanisms in children's social adjustment. *Psychological Bulletin, 115,* 74–101.

Dedman, B. (2000, October 16). Deadly lessons: School shooters tell why. *Chicago Sun-Times.*

DeRosier, M. E. (2003). *Social status and the quality of the teacher-student relationship.* University of North Carolina at Chapel Hill. Manuscript in preparation.

DeRosier, M. E., Kupersmidt, J. B., & Patterson, J. (1994). Children's academic and behavioral adjustment as a function of the chronicity and proximity of peer rejection. *Child Development, 65,* 1799–1813.

DeRosier, M. E., & Thomas, J. M. (2003). Strengthening sociometric prediction: Scientific advances in the assessment of children's peer relations. *Child Development, 75,* 1379–1392.

Dishion, T. J., & Loeber, R. (1985). Adolescent marijuana and alcohol use: The role of parents and peers revisited. *American Journal of Drug and Alcohol Abuse, 11,* 11–25.

Dishion, T. J., McCord, J., & Poulin, F. (1999). When interventions harm: Peer groups and problem behavior. *American Psychologist, 54,* 755–764.

Dishion, T. J., Patterson, G., Stoolmiller, M., & Skinner, M. L. (1991). Family, school, and behavioral antecedents to early adolescent involvement with antisocial peers. *Developmental Psychology, 27,* 172–180.

Dodge, K. A., Coie, J. D., & Brakke, N. P. (1982). Behavior patterns of socially rejected and neglected preadolescents: The roles of social approach and aggression. *Journal of Abnormal Child Psychology, 10,* 389–409.

Dodge, K. A., Lochman, J., Harnish, J., Bates, J., & Pettit, G. (1997). Reactive and proactive aggression in school children and psychiatrically impaired chronically assaultive youth. *Journal of Abnormal Psychology, 106,* 37–51.

Durlak, J. A. (1992). School problems of children. In C. E. Walker & M. C. Roberts (Eds.), *Handbook of clinical child psychology* (2nd ed.). *Wiley series on personality processes* (pp. 497–510). New York: Wiley.

Elliott, D. S., Huizinga, D., & Ageton, S. S. (1985). *Explaining delinquency and drug use.* Beverly Hills, CA: Sage.

Franzoi, L. S., Davis, M. H., & Vasquez-Suson, K. A. (1994). Two social worlds: Social correlates and stability of adolescent status groups. *Journal of Personality and Social Psychology, 67,* 462–473.

French, D. (1988). Heterogeneity of peer-rejected boys: Aggressive and nonaggressive subtypes. *Child Development, 59,* 976–985.

French, D. (1990). Heterogeneity of peer-rejected girls. *Child Development, 61,* 2028–2031.

Friedemann, M., & Andrews, M. (1990). Family support and child adjustment in single-parent families. *Issues in Comprehensive Pediatric Nursing, 13,* 289–301.

Furman, W., & Buhrmester, D. (1985). Children's perceptions of the personal relationships in their social networks. *Developmental Psychology, 21,* 1016–1024.

Gelles, R. J. (1989). Child abuse and violence in single-parent families: Parent absence and economic deprivation. *American Journal of Orthopsychiatry, 59,* 492–501.

Gersten, J. C. (1992). Families in poverty. In M. E. Procidano and C. B. Fisher (Eds.), *Contemporary families: A handbook for school professionals* (pp. 137–158). New York: Teachers College Press.

Goodyer, I. M., Wright, C., & Altham, P. M. E. (1989). Recent friendships in anxious and depressed school age children. *Psychological Medicine, 19,* 165–174.

Graham, S., & Hudley, C. (1993). An attributional intervention to reduce peer-directed aggression among African-American boys. *Child Development, 64,* 124–138.

Hart, C. H., Olsen, S. F., Robinson, C. C., & Mandleco, B. L. (1997). The development of social and communicative competence in childhood: Review and a model of personal, familial, and extrafamilial processes. In B. R. Burleson & A. W. Kunkel (Eds.), *Communication yearbook 20* (pp. 305–373). West Lafayette, IN: Purdue University.

Higgins, E. T. (1987). Self-discrepancy theory: A theory relating self and affect. *Psychological Review, 94,* 319–340.

Higgins, E. T., Klein, R., & Strauman, T. (1985). Self-concept discrepancy theory: A psychological model for distinguishing among different aspects of depression and anxiety. *Social Cognition, 3,* 51–76.

Hodges, E. V. E., Boivin, M., Vitaro, F., & Bukowski, W. M. (1999). The power of friendship: Protection against an escalating cycle of peer victimization. *Developmental Psychology, 35,* 94–101.

Hodges, E. V. E., & Perry, D. G. (1999). Personal and interpersonal antecedents and consequences of victimization by peers. *Journal of Personality and Social Psychology, 76,* 677–685.

Horowitz, H. (1967). Prediction of adolescent popularity and rejection from achievement and interest tests. *Journal of Educational Psychology, 58,* 170–174.

Howes, C. (2000). Social-emotional classroom climate in child care, child-teacher relationships and children's second grade peer relations. *Social Development, 9,* 191–204.

Ialongo, N. S., Vaden-Kiernan, N., & Kellam, S. (1998). Early peer rejection and aggression: Longitudinal relations with adolescent behavior. *Journal of Developmental and Physical Disabilities, 10,* 199–213.

Jenkins, J. E., & Zunguze, S. T. (1998). The relationship of family structure to adolescent drug use, peer affiliation, and perception of peer acceptance of drug use. *Adolescence, 33,* 811–822.

Johnson, R. W., & MacEachern, A. T. (1985). Attributions of physical attractiveness: Tests of the social deviance and social identity hypotheses. *Journal of Social Psychology, 125,* 221–232.

Kearney, C. A. (1993). Depression and school refusal behavior: A review with comments on classification and treatment. *Journal of School Psychology, 31,* 267–279.

Kistner, J., Metzler, A., Gatlin, D., & Risi, S. (1993). Classroom racial proportions and children's peer relations: Race and gender effects. *Journal of Educational Psychology, 85,* 446–452.

Krantz, M. (1987). Physical attractiveness and popularity: A predictive study. *Psychological Reports, 60,* 723–726.

Kupersmidt, J. B., Buchele, K. S., Voegler, M. E., & Sedikides, C. (1996). Social self-discrepancy: A theory relating peer relations problems and school maladjustment. In J. Juvonen & K. R. Wentzel (Eds.), *Social motivation: Understanding children's school adjustment* (pp. 66–97). New York: Cambridge University Press.

Kupersmidt, J. B., Burchinal, M., & Patterson, C. J. (1995). Developmental patterns of childhood peer relations as predictors of externalizing behavior problems. *Development and Psychopathology, 7,* 825–843.

Kupersmidt, J. B., & Coie, J. D. (1990). Preadolescent peer status, aggression and school adjustment as predictors of externalizing problems in adolescence. *Child Development, 61,* 1350–1362.

Kupersmidt, J. B., Coie, J. D., & Dodge, K. A. (1990). The role of poor peer relationships in the development of disorder. In S. R. Asher & J. D. Coie (Eds.), *Peer rejection in childhood* (pp. 274–305). New York: Cambridge University Press.

Kupersmidt, J. B., Griesler, P. C., DeRosier, M. E., Patterson, C. J., & Davis, P. W. (1995). Childhood aggression and peer relations in the context of family and neighborhood factors. *Child Development, 66,* 360–375.

Kupersmidt, J. B., & Patterson, C. J. (1991). Childhood peer rejection, aggression, withdrawn behavior, and perceived competence as predictors of self-reported behavior problems in preadolescence. *Journal of Abnormal Child Psychology, 19,* 427–449.

Kupersmidt, J. B., Sigda, K. B., Sedikides, C., & Voegler, M. E. (1999). Social self-discrepancy theory and loneliness during childhood and adolescence. In K. R. Rotenberg & S. Hymel (Eds.), *Loneliness in childhood and adolescence* (pp. 263–279). New York: Cambridge University Press.

Ladd, G. W., Price, J. M., & Hart, C. H. (1990). Preschoolers' behavioral orientation and patterns of peer contact: Predictive of peer status? In S. R. Asher & J. D. Coie (Eds.), *Peer rejection in childhood* (pp. 90–115). New York: Cambridge University Press.

La Greca, A. M., Dandes, S. K., Wick, P., Shaw, K., & Stone, W. L. (1988). Development of the Social Anxiety Scale for Children: Reliability and concurrent validity. *Journal of Clinical Child Psychology, 17,* 84–91.

Laird, R. D., Jordan, K. Y., Dodge, K. A., Pettit, G. S., & Bates, J. E. (2001). Peer rejection in childhood, involvement with antisocial peers in early adolescence, and the development of externalizing behavior problems. *Development and Psychopathology, 13,* 337–354.

Lease, A. M., Kennedy, C. A., & Axelrod, J. L. (2002). Children's social constructions of popularity. *Social Development, 11,* 87–109.

Luftig, R. L., & Nichols, M. L. (1990). Assessing the social status of gifted students by their age peers. *Gifted Child Quarterly, 34,* 111–115.

Mahoney, J. L., & Stattin, H. (2000). Leisure activities and adolescent antisocial behavior: The role of structure and social context. *Journal of Adolescence, 23,* 113–127.

Matza, L. S., Kupersmidt, J. B., & Glenn, D. M. (2001). Adolescents' perceptions and standards of their relationships with their parents as a function of sociometric status. *Journal of Research on Adolescence, 11,* 245–272.

McDougall, P., Hymel, S., Vaillancourt, T., & Mercer, L. (2001). The consequences of childhood peer rejection. In M. Leary (Ed.), *Interpersonal rejection* (pp. 213–247). New York: Oxford University Press.

McLanahan, S., & Booth, K. (1989). Mother-only families: Problems, prospects, and politics. *Journal of Marriage & the Family, 51,* 557–580.

Newcomb, A. F., & Bagwell, C. L. (1996). The developmental significance of children's friendship relations. In W. M. Bukowski, A. F. Newcomb, & W. W. Hartup (Eds.), *The company they keep: Friendships in childhood and adolescence* (pp. 289–321). New York: Cambridge University Press.

Ogilvie, D. M. (1987). The undesired self: A neglected variable in personality research. *Journal of Personality and Social Psychology, 52,* 379–385.

Parke, R. D., & Ladd, G. W. (1992). *Family-peer relationships: Modes of linkage.* Hillsdale, NJ: Erlbaum.

Parker J. G., & Asher, S. R. (1987). Peer relations and later personal adjustment: Are low-accepted children at risk? *Psychological Bulletin, 102,* 357–389.

Parker, J. G., & Asher, S.R. (1993). Friendship and friendship quality in middle childhood: Links with peer group acceptance and feelings of loneliness and social dissatisfaction. *Developmental Psychology, 29,* 611–621.

Parker, J. G., Rubin, K. H., Price, J., & DeRosier, M. E. (1995). Peer relationships, child development and adjustment: A developmental psychopathology perspective. In D. Cicchetti & D. Cohen (Eds.), *Developmental psychopathology: Vol. 2. Risk, disorder and adaptation* (pp. 96–161). New York: Wiley.

Parkhurst, J. T., & Asher, S. R. (1992). Peer rejection in middle school: Subgroup differences in behavior, loneliness, and interpersonal concerns. *Developmental Psychology, 28,* 231–241.

Patterson, C. J., Kupersmidt, J. B., & Griesler, P. C. (1990). Perceptions of self and of relationships with others as a function of sociometric status. *Child Development, 61,* 1335–1349.

Patterson, C. J., Vaden, N. A., Griesler, P. C., & Kupersmidt, J. B. (1991). Income level, gender, ethnicity, and household composition as predictors of children's peer companionship outside of school. *Journal of Applied Developmental Psychology, 12,* 447–465.

Patterson, C. J., Vaden, N. A., & Kupersmidt, J. B. (1991). Family background, recent life events, and peer rejection during childhood. *Journal of Personal and Social Relationships, 8,* 347–361.

Patterson, G. R., & Dishion, T. J. (1985). Contributions of families and peers to delinquency. *Criminology, 23,* 63–77.

Quatman, T., & Watson, C. M. (2001). Gender differences in adolescent self-esteem: An exploration of domains. *Journal of Genetic Psychology, 162,* 93–117.

Rubin, K. H., & Mills, R. S. (1988). The many faces of social isolation in childhood. *Journal of Consulting and Clinical Psychology, 56,* 916–924.

Sandstrom, M. J. (1999). A developmental perspective on peer rejection: Mechanisms of stability and change. *Child Development, 70,* 955–966.

Simons, R. L., Johnson, C., Beaman, J., Conger, R. D., & Whitbeck, L. B. (1996). Parents and peer groups as mediators of the effect of community structure on adolescent problem behavior. *American Journal of Community Psychology, 24,* 145–171.

Spooner, C. (1999). Causes and correlates of adolescent drug abuse and implications for treatment. *Drug and Alcohol Review, 18,* 453–475.

Tiet, Q. Q., Bird, H. R., Hoven, C. W., Wu, P., Moore, R., & Davies, M. (2001). Resilience in the face of maternal psychopathology and adverse life events. *Journal of Child and Family Studies, 10,* 347–365.

Wentzel, K. R., & Erdley, C. A. (1993). Strategies for making friends: Relations to social behavior and peer acceptance in early adolescence. *Developmental Psychology, 29,* 819–826.

Williams, D. R. (1999). Race, socioeconomic status, and health: The added effects of racism and discrimination. In N. E. Adler, M. Marmot, B. S. McEwen, & J. Stewart (Eds.), *Socioeconomic status and health in industrial nations: Social, psychological, and biological pathways: Vol. 896. Annals of the New York Academy of Sciences* (pp. 173–188). New York: New York Academy of Sciences.

Woodward, L. J., & Fergusson, D. M. (2000). Childhood peer relationship problems and later risks of educational under-achievement and unemployment. *Journal of Child Psychology and Psychiatry and Allied Disciplines, 41,* 191–201.

Young, J. G., Brasic, J. R., & Kisnadwala, H. (1990). Strategies for research on school refusal and related nonattendance at school. In C. Chiland & J. G. Young (Eds.), *Why children reject school:*

Views from seven countries. The child and his family: Vol. 10. Yearbook of the International Association for Child and Adolescent Psychiatry for Allied Professions (pp. 199–223). New Haven: Yale University Press.

Yude, C., & Goodman, R. (1999). Peer problems of 9- to 11-year-old children with hemiplegia in mainstream schools. Can these be predicted? *Developmental Medicine and Child Neurology, 41,* 4–8.

Part III

Family Influences

8

Parents' Relationships With Their Parents and Peers: Influences on Children's Social Development

Christina L. Grimes, Tovah P. Klein, and Martha Putallaz

It has been well established that the quality of children's peer relationships is influenced by the parenting they experience (Kerns, Contreras, & Neal-Barnett, 2000; Ladd & Le Sieur, 1995). What is less understood are the antecedents of relevant parental behaviors and cognitions—the behavioral, emotional, and cognitive "packages" that adults bring to the parenting role. In his influential review of the determinants of parenting, Belsky (1984) proposed a multiprocess model whereby parents' developmental histories, marital relationships, social networks, and occupational experiences impact parenting (and subsequently, child development) through their influences on parents' personalities and psychological well-being. In line with this model, we focus on two particular aspects of parents' developmental history: their relationships with their parents and peers, both contemporary and as children. Although there is substantial research on the intergenerational transmission of psychopathology and abuse (Dodge, Bates & Pettit, 1990; Rutter & Madge, 1976), the focus here is on issues of normative development. Also, we would be remiss not to underscore the ubiquitous but largely unexplored bidirectional arrow representing child influences or, in this case, child as moderator of influences on parenting. It is highly likely that antecedent influences on parents' behavior are moderated by characteristics of their children. However, no studies have addressed this issue in the context of family-of-origin influences in typical populations.

Finally, a word about methodology. Much of the intergenerational research relies on retrospective recall and current mental representations of early childhood experiences. The veracity of such data and the validity of this methodology continue to be debated (e.g., Rutter, Maughan, Pickles, & Simonoff, 1998). A central question has been whether influences on parenting behavior are derived from actual childhood experiences or from the ways that childhood histories are mentally organized and interpreted in adulthood, or some combination of the two; this question can be answered only by longitudinal investigations. Although the accuracy or reality of parents' memories remains in question,

these retrieved or reconstructed recollections appear to tap meaningful parental perceptions and to have functional utility, both for parents in their daily
interactions with their children and for researchers attempting to understand
intergenerational processes.

This chapter begins with a review of the influences that parents' relationships with their own parents, past and current, have on their parenting and
their children's development, followed by a similar review of the influences of
parents' childhood and contemporary peer relationships.

Parents' Relationships With Their Parents

Influences of Early Parent-Child Relationships: The Intergenerational Transmission of Parenting

> Well, in terms of how I raise my kids, I'm probably my mother reincarnated.
> Well, I mean, not in every way—she was real religious and I would never
> do that to my kids; we don't even go to church. But sometimes, especially
> when I'm not thinking much about what I'm saying or I'm really distracted,
> I'll say something and then stop and go, "Whoa, who said that? Is my mother
> here?" And I just have to laugh, 'cause it's just what she used to say to us
> and we hated it, and here I am saying it to my own kids. . . . She used to
> make each of us feel special, like what we said mattered; she'd even stop
> cooking or whatever and really listen to you, like what you were saying was
> the most important thing in the world to her at that moment, and I try to
> do that with my kids, let them know that I care about what they have to
> say, that I'm there for them no matter how busy I am. (From an interview
> with Linda, age 34, mother of two)

Linda's assessment of how she is and is not like her mother in the way
she parents illustrates many of the issues relevant to studies on the intergenerational transmission of parenting. There are some things she has chosen to do
differently, but there are other qualities she emulates, some consciously, some
apparently in a more automatic unthinking way. Clearly, at least in Linda's
mind, the mothering she has received has had an influence on her parenting.

In the psychological literature, it has long been assumed that parenting
received is related to parenting practiced, but the links are not clear; we are
not carbon copies of our parents nor are we immune from their influence.
Parenting is not a discrete skill or constellation of skills that we learn in
childhood and then call up from memory when the need arises. It involves
behavior in the context of relationships (themselves embedded in other relationships) and is accompanied by values, beliefs, affects, intentions, cognitions,
and unconscious processes. Which of these aspects are most influenced by early
experience? To what extent do parents actively choose to reproduce or react
against the parenting they experienced, or simply forge their own pioneering
path with their spouse and children? Empirical answers to these questions are
few. Even rarer are three-generation studies linking family-of-origin influences
on parenting to children's social development. However, by looking at the
domains that are represented in both the family-peer literature and the litera-

ture on the intergenerational transmission of parenting, we can paint a preliminary picture of influences and processes affecting parenting (and subsequently children's development) in the peer domain (see Putallaz, Costanzo, Grimes, & Sherman, 1998; van IJzendoorn, 1992).

If parenting received is related to parenting practiced, an essential question is how the important linking constructs are carried across the life span by the child-become-adult-parent. Although some childhood influences on later parenting may not find expression until one becomes a parent, it would be unreasonable to assume that they lie dormant and untouched for decades. The intergenerational transmission of parenting thus relies on, or is carried by, intragenerational processes, as illustrated in Elder's well-known analyses of the longitudinal Berkeley Guidance Study initiated in 1928 (Caspi & Elder, 1988; Elder, Caspi, & Downey, 1986). Caspi and Elder found strong correlations among personality, marital, and parenting difficulties within each generation. *Intergenerationally,* unstable personalities (involving explosive behavior and irritability) developed through socialization within family contexts characterized by marital conflict and poor parenting. In a perpetuating cycle, children with unstable personalities then carried this instability into adulthood, leading, *intragenerationally,* to problematic adult relationships, the increased likelihood of conflictual marriages conducive to nonoptimal parenting, and resultant problem behaviors in their children, the next generation. Also demonstrated was the complexity of intergenerational processes. Personality problems in one generation were not linked directly to personality problems in the next. Rather, transmission was more likely to occur if the first generation's personality difficulties led to poor marital quality, a link that developed through such variables as occupational instability for men and the likelihood for women to marry husbands of lower status. The effects of marital difficulties on offspring also appeared to be indirect, operating through poor parenting. Thus although intergenerational processes evidenced clear continuity, pathways were seldom direct and opportunities for discontinuity were many.

With these issues in mind, we turn our attention to intergenerational studies with particular relevance for children's social development, highlighting what is known about the antecedents of parents' behaviors in terms of their relationships with their own parents.

ATTACHMENT AND COGNITIVE MODELS OF RELATIONSHIPS. Securely attached children, compared with those with insecure attachment histories, fare better on a wide range of measures of social competence, ranging from sociability with unfamiliar peers to more synchronous and higher quality friendships (Elicker, Egeland, & Sroufe, 1992; Kerns, 1998). The parental behaviors that have been linked most consistently to children's attachment status are sensitivity and responsiveness, particularly in the case of maternal behavior (De Wolff & van IJzendoorn, 1997). Most investigations of the antecedents or determinants of such parenting behavior have focused on parents' conceptualizations of their early attachments to their own parents, by means of the Adult Attachment Interview (AAI) developed by Main and her colleagues (Main & Goldwyn, 1984; Main, Kaplan, & Cassidy, 1985). The AAI assesses an adult's current state of mind regarding his or her own attachment experiences and results in categories comparable to those obtained for infants in the Strange Situation (the specific adult–infant pairings are autonomous–secure, dismissing–avoidant, preoccupied–resistant, and unresolved–disorganized).

Main and her colleagues compared children's Strange Situation classifications assessed during infancy with parents' AAI classifications assessed when the children were age 6 and found strong evidence for an intergenerational continuity of attachment status, especially for mothers relative to fathers (Main et al., 1985). Their work has generated much interest, and the resulting studies have since replicated the original findings with broader populations and designs (see Hesse, 1999; van IJzendoorn, 1995, for reviews).

Observational data appear to support attachment theory's proposal that such continuity is carried by distinctive parenting styles associated with parental attachment classifications, particularly in terms of the caregiver's ability to read and respond sensitively to attachment-related cues and signals from his or her infant. In comparison to other parents, secure parents have been found to be more sensitive, responsive, and supportive and to provide more structure and help to their children during challenging tasks. Secure mothers are also attuned to a wider range of infant affect, both positive and negative, whereas insecure mothers are attuned to particular affects and ignore others. Insecure parents also use more controlling and confusing styles of interaction (for reviews, see Putallaz et al., 1998; van IJzendoorn, 1992).

The implications of such differences between the parenting of secure parents and that of insecure parents would seem to be that parents are reproducing the parenting they received, a possibility given credence in a recent longitudinal study. In a sample of preterm infants, Beckwith, Cohen, and Hamilton (1999) compared objective ratings of maternal sensitivity in the home during infancy with respondents' AAI categories nearly 17 years later. Young adults who were dismissing with respect to attachment at age 18 had received significantly less responsive maternal care as infants than did the secure or preoccupied groups. Adverse life events reduced the likelihood of secure/autonomous representations and increased the likelihood of preoccupied representations. Other studies, however, describe a group of parents who have developed a balanced, cohesive representation of attachment representations (and are therefore classified as autonomous) in spite of reporting negative attachment relationships in childhood.

These parents (often referred to as *earned* secures) exhibit parenting that is as warm, responsive, and nonintrusive as that of *continuous* secures (Crandell, Fitzgerlad, & Whipple, 1997; Phelps, Belsky, & Crnic, 1998). Children of secure parents interact with their parents in more affectionate and less negative and controlling ways than do children of insecure parents (Cohn, Cowan, Cowan, & Pearson, 1992; Crowell & Feldman, 1988). Other studies using derivatives of the AAI (Cowan, Cohn, Cowan, & Pearson, 1996) and assessments of recalled parental acceptance (Contreras, 2000) have found more competent peer behavior among children whose parents have more positive representations of parenting received. Thus, attachment research provides fairly convincing evidence that representations of early experiences do affect later parenting and child outcomes. However, neither the mechanisms involved nor the content of what is being transmitted during parent–child interactions is clear.

The central premise of attachment theory is that internal working models serve as a mechanism of continuity across relationships. For example, Slade, Belsky, Aber, and Phelps (1999) found continuity between mothers' AAI interviews and their representations of their relationships with their toddlers, which in turn related to their parenting behavior. However, explaining the role of children's working models in intergenerational continuity is more problematic. The construct of an internal working model is open to criticism on many fronts, including its lack of specificity and the lack of agreement about the content of such models. Furthermore, children's attachment behavior is assumed to reflect particular internal representations. However, these representations are often inferred from the very behaviors that supposedly serve as their expression, a tautological argument. Some associations between parents' attachment status and children's attachment behaviors could easily be explained by mechanisms other than internal working models. For example, securely attached children who are warm and affectionate toward parents may merely be imitating their autonomous parents' warm and nurturing behavior.

Operating within more of a social cognitive paradigm, Burks and Parke (1996) have made inroads into addressing the lack of specificity about the components of internal representations. Drawing from the peer literature, they examined mothers' and children's expectations, attributions, and goals in hypothetical mother–peer, mother–child, and child–peer scenarios involving three dilemmas: ambiguous provocation, conflict resolution, and mild rejection. They found clear linkages between mothers' and children's representations, but these linkages were situation specific (i.e., highly dependent on the particular component, type of dilemma, and relationship context [family or peer] involved). This is a promising start in establishing whether cognitive models provide continuity across relationships and across generations; still needed is a clearer understanding of their components, the interactional processes through which they are transmitted, and their expression in actual behavior.

Studies couched in other perspectives, particularly social learning, have also examined parents', and sometimes grandparents', recollections to explore childhood influences on parenting. We turn now to those studies to examine where continuity has been found and to explore other possible mechanisms through which early experiences may have their influence.

GENERAL PARENTING STYLE—WARMTH AND CONTROL. Parents who are observed to engage their children in warm, supportive, agreeable, and moderately directive ways have children who are more popular with peers and who have more positive and harmonious peer interactions. Overcontrolling or negative and critical parent behavior has been related to more abrasive, negative, and aggressive behavior with peers. Mechanisms suggested as providing these links include modeling, teaching of appropriate social behavior through reinforcement and punishment or response evocation, social information processing, and fostering a sense of security and self-confidence which generalizes to peer relationships, similar to the explanations offered by attachment theory (see Putallaz & Heflin, 1990).

Most of the early intergenerational studies in this area involved administering questionnaires to parents and their grown children (often college students) who were not yet parents. Correlations between the two generations were modest at best (van IJzendoorn, 1992). Cross-sectional studies that have relied on the self-reports of two generations of parents (grandmothers' recollective self-reports and their daughters' self-reports of current parenting) have found continuity in both the nurturing and restrictive aspects of parenting (Olsen, Martin, & Halverson, 1999; Vermulst, de Brock, & van Zutphen, 1991), patterns that appear to be mediated by personality factors and marital quality.

A more stringent test of continuity was provided by Cox et al. (1985) who interviewed expectant couples before the birth of their first child and later observed their parenting. Expectant parents' recollections of parenting received in childhood, their current psychological health, and their marital competence were assessed as possible predictors of observed parent–infant interaction three months postpartum. For mothers, childhood recollections were most predictive of their parenting; neither marital competence nor psychological health entered the regression equation. For fathers, only marital competence entered the equation, and even that accounted for only 13% of the variance. Cox et al. suggested that fathers may be more influenced by current relationships and that intergenerational influences on parenting may be stronger for females, a view consistent with others' descriptions of women as the family kin keepers (e.g., Caspi & Elder, 1988; Elder, Downey, & Cross, 1986).

Because fathers are typically less involved than mothers in infant care, another possibility is that intergenerational influences for fathers may become more apparent as their children get older (e.g., Simons, Beaman, Conger, & Wei, 1993; Snarey, 1993). Simons et al. (1993), for example, found that for both mothers and fathers, the more supportive the parenting they received in childhood, the more supportive and nurturing they were with their adolescent children.

SPECIFIC DISCIPLINARY PRACTICES. Generally, power-assertive, restrictive, unpredictable, and harsh disciplinary styles have been associated with children's peer difficulties, specifically higher levels of hostile and aggressive behavior and lower levels of peer acceptance, whereas inductive disciplinary styles have been associated with more prosocial behavior (see Ladd & Le Sieur, 1995; Putallaz & Heflin, 1990). The disciplinary practice that has received the most attention from intergenerational researchers is physical punishment or harsh, punitive discipline. Generally, receiving physical punishment in childhood is correlated with its use in adulthood (Covell, Grusec, & King, 1995; Simons et al., 1993; Simons, Whitbeck, Conger, & Wu, 1991; Stattin, Janson, Klackenburg-Larsson, & Magnusson, 1995). Studies generated from the Iowa Youth and Family Project clearly demonstrate that parents who experienced harsh discipline in childhood were more likely to use similar parenting practices with their own adolescents (Simons et al., 1991, 1993). Findings of intergenerational continuity were qualified by gender and were stronger for mothers than fathers. Grandmothers' harsh parenting was associated with mothers' harsh parenting regardless of their adolescent's gender and with fathers' harsh parenting of sons. Fathers' harsh parenting of daughters, however, was associated with receiving harsh parenting from grandfathers. Simons et al. (1991) postulated that perhaps grandfathers who used harsh parenting practices were also more aggressive with their wives. Thus, fathers' harsh treatment of their daughters could be one result of modeling a generally aggressive style of interaction with women. Simons and his colleagues explored various processes or mediators of transmission, including direct modeling of their harsh childhood experiences, as well as mediation through specific beliefs, parent satisfaction, personality variables (depression and hostility), and transmission of social class characteristics. Across studies, there was evidence for all of these processes, including strong support for direct modeling of harsh discipline, unmediated by other variables assessed (Simons et al., 1991).

Very few studies have specifically examined the antecedents of less power assertive, more inductive styles of parenting. Covell et al. (1995) compared grandmothers' retrospective and mothers' current self-reports of their actual parenting of their three- to five-year old children. Of five disciplinary techniques assessed, only physical punishment (of sons) and material reward (with daughters) were used with similar frequency by both generations. Praise, explanation (inductive discipline), and withdrawal of love were all used less frequently and did not show continuity across generations. Thus, evidence for the influence of early parenting on later disciplinary practices is basically limited to that involving harsh, punitive discipline. From the attachment literature, one could extrapolate that secure parents who are more responsive and supportive would be more likely to use inductive strategies in disciplining their children, whereas insecure parents who are more controlling or avoidant might use more power assertive strategies. Most likely, parents' disciplinary strategies reflect the broader construct of general parenting style, and although disciplinary practices have been linked to children's social cognition and behavior with peers, causal pathways from family-of-origin experiences through particular disciplinary styles to children's social behavior have not yet been examined.

FAMILY CONFLICT AND NEGATIVE AFFECT. Marital conflict has been linked to a number of adjustment difficulties among children. In one of the few studies to examine the full three-generational model including family-of-origin influences, parenting, and children's social behavior with peers, Cowan, Cowan, Schulz, and Heming (1993) reported that parents who recalled growing up in conflictual families reported more marital conflict and more life stressors early in the transition to parenthood. Several years later, their behavior as a couple in the presence of their child was characterized by less warmth and more conflict, and they provided less warmth and less structure in their individual parent–child interactions. All of these variables related to their children's social competence, including a moderate direct correlation between parent recollections assessed prenatally and children's aggressive or shy–withdrawn behavior six years later. Thus parents who recalled being exposed to more conflict when they were young recreated the same conflictual environment for their children, and as in the longitudinal analyses by Caspi and Elder (1988), both individual and marital factors were involved in the continuity across generations.

DEGREE OF FATHERS' INVOLVEMENT. Some fathers who are highly involved in childrearing had fathers who were also highly involved (Sagi, 1982). However, several researchers have also reported a compensatory tendency for men to become more involved in parenting in response to their own fathers' lack of involvement (Barnett & Baruch, 1987; Snarey, 1993). Belsky (1984) suggested that men whose fathers were positively involved in their upbringing are more likely to identify with and model their fathers, whereas men who had noninvolved fathers are more weakly identified with their fathers, less likely to model them, and perhaps more likely to compensate by becoming more involved with their own children.

Snarey's (1993) secondary analysis of longitudinal data on three generations of men from the original Glueck sample collected in the 1940s provides additional insight. Interview data from the fathers as adolescents, archival data from the fathers' family of origin, and current characteristics of the fathers were used to predict the degree of their involvement in their children's social-emotional development (e.g., comforting, spending time together, chaperoning peer activities, giving advice on dating problems). During their children's early years (birth to age 10), fathers' involvement was predicted only by their level of education and their current marital affinity. However, during their children's early adolescence, intergenerational influences appeared. Men who were the most involved in their adolescents' social-emotional development had fathers who were non-nurturant or distant but who were occupationally successful and who worked closely with mothers in creating a warm boyhood home atmosphere.

Snarey (1993) suggested that men's style of fathering was the combined result of modeling the positive aspects of their fathers' parenting and reworking the negative aspects of the father–son relationship they had experienced. The judgments that adult fathers made of their own fathers were usually quite consistent with facts in archival data from their adolescence, but their interpretation and the affect associated with these memories often had changed—that is, men placed their fathers' faults in context or forgave them. This cognitive reassessment of past experiences calls to mind similar findings from the attachment literature, where working models resulting from negative childhood relationships can be reworked over time. In those studies, lack of continuity was often linked to experience with a supportive relationship; likewise, Snarey's more involved fathers were high on marital affinity. Thus the marital relationship is also a likely moderator in understanding why some fathers model or reproduce their own fathers' nonoptimal parenting and others choose to correct their fathers' shortcomings.

Influences of Parent–Child Relationships in Adulthood

Conspicuously absent from discussions about mechanisms or processes linking early parent–child experiences to adult parenting is the continuous development of the parent–child relationship across the life span. Many trajectories relevant to intergenerational influence are possible. A continuing relationship with one's parents into adulthood and subsequent parenthood may provide opportunities for continuity and further reinforcement of early parent–child influences. On the other hand, the parent–child relationship may evolve or dissolve across the life course in ways that lead to a reversal of earlier (usually negative) influences, as seen for example in the reworking of cognitive representations described in attachment studies. However, explanations for these reversals are often exogenous to the parent–child relationship itself (e.g., introspective reflection; involvement in supportive marital relationships). Essentially, not much is known about these longitudinal issues. There is evidence to suggest that warm, emotionally close parent–adolescent relationships are maintained into the adolescent's adulthood (e.g., Rossi & Rossi, 1990), whereas recollections of parental rejection are related to lower quality parent–adult child relationships (e.g., Whitbeck, Hoyt, & Huck, 1993). As with intergenerational effects, this intragenerational stability may be stronger for females (Elder et al., 1986) and may in fact explain why intergenerational influences are more pronounced among women.

For grandmothers and their daughters, coresidence may be, paradoxically, a deterrent to intergenerational continuity. Staples and Warden-Smith (1954) found significant agreement between maternal grandmother–mother pairs on childrearing attitudes, but only for those pairs who lived apart. The authors suggested that coresidence might engender more tension between grandmothers and their daughters, thus highlighting attitude differences or reactivating unresolved conflicts between the two. In a similar vein, mothers who share a residence and childrearing responsibilities with their own mothers may feel a need for greater individuation in order to feel competent in their parenting role. A recent study of African American mothers and grandmothers (Wakschlag, Chase-Lansdale, & Brooks-Gunn, 1996) found that mothers who were observed to be high on individuation (a balance of connectedness and autonomy in their dyadic interactions with the grandmother) exhibited more competent parenting with their preschool children. In addition, Wakschlag et al. found that the grandmother–mother relationship had its strongest influence on mothers' parenting when grandmother and mother lived apart. In short, there is still much to be learned about the development of the parent–child relationship beyond adolescence and about its explanatory power in understanding the mechanisms of intergenerational continuity.

Parents' Relationships With Peers

Influences of Childhood Peer Relationships

> I used to get threatened to be beat up after school. The girls would follow me home, and I would go into the house and they would leave. It was very painful. Do I think that has influenced the way I look at my daughter's social situation? Very much so. I remember a time when Erica was swinging on a swing; she was about two-and-a-half and there was this little girl who wanted to get on the same swing and she ran to Erica and cajoled Erica to get out of the swing, and I thought, "God!" And the girl got into the swing and wouldn't let Erica swing. Erica started to cry, and I said, "Come here, go and get that swing," and I told her to speak her mind and go get that

swing. I definitely remembered all the painful episodes of my childhood at that moment. (From an interview with Sharon, mother of a 10-year-old girl)

Because of the predictive utility of childhood peer status for later adjustment and adult functioning (Coie, 1990; Kupersmidt, Coie, & Dodge, 1990), it seems reasonable to hypothesize a link between childhood peer experiences and later competence in the parent–child relationship, including (maybe even especially) socialization of one's children in the peer domain. It also makes sense that parents' memories and interpretations of these experiences, as in the above example, would affect how they viewed their children's social world and their subsequent management of their children's peer relationships. However, although theory and common sense may predict such influences, surprisingly little attention has been given to this area, and no longitudinal studies have addressed it in typical populations.

Thus we turn again to parents' recollections and cognitive interpretations of their past relationships, in this case with peers. In the first study to specifically address this question, Putallaz, Costanzo, and Smith (1991) reported that mothers' recollections of childhood peer relationships were linked to aspects of their parenting and to their preschoolers' social competence with peers. Examination of these memories and their meanings revealed three distinct profiles. Mothers recalling warm, positive memories of their childhood peer relationships rated themselves as socially competent children, reported being nurturant with their children, and described their children as being socially competent with peers. In contrast, mothers recalling memories of peer rejection rated themselves as socially incompetent children, reported being less nurturant with their children, and viewed their children as the least socially competent. The final group of mothers recalled anxious–lonely memories of childhood peer interactions and, like negative-memory mothers, rated themselves as socially incompetent children. However, the anxious-memory mothers described themselves as nurturant and as more invested in influencing their children's peer relations than the other two groups of mothers. Although anxious-memory mothers rated their children as average in social competence, preschool teachers and objective observers rated their children as the most socially competent, and recently acquainted peers (playmates in a laboratory setting) rated them as most-preferred playmates.

One interpretation offered by Putallaz et al. (1991) was that anxious-memory mothers might have more of an internal locus of control. Unlike negative-memory mothers who attributed their negative childhood experiences to external factors (e.g., unkind peers), anxious-memory mothers attributed their recollected loneliness or social incompetence to their own social anxiety or inadequacy. Their subsequent parenting seemed geared toward creating a sense of self-efficacy in their children that would help them avoid the anxiety or loneliness recalled by parents. Similarly, Cohen and Woody (1991) found more frequent orchestration of children's peer contacts among mothers who recalled being more socially withdrawn in childhood or who considered themselves sociable as adults. Like Putallaz et al., Cohen and Woody suggested that mothers recalling poor childhood peer experiences might be motivated to protect their children from a similar fate. In addition, mothers who were withdrawn in childhood but who became more sociable as adults might view sociability as unstable and malleable, and thus more amenable to their influence.

Putallaz et al. (1991) also suggested that these recollections may reflect particular ways parents had of framing or interpreting social interactions, ways that would differentially influence how they taught their children to view peer relationships. Several follow-up studies utilized parent narrations of videotaped peer interactions involving either their own children (Putallaz, Klein, Costanzo, & Hedges, 1994) or children unknown to them (Klein, 1995). These studies confirmed that mothers' and fathers' interpretive narrations were driven not only by the interactions they witnessed, but also by parents' recollections of their own childhood peer experiences. When both parents and children individually narrated the unknown children's interactions and then described them to each other, mothers' (but not fathers') narrations and interpretive retellings related to their children's (Klein, 1995). Thus, children's interpretations or mental models of the social world may be influenced by the way interactions are interpreted for them by their mothers, interpretations that are related to the affective valence of mothers' own recalled peer experiences.

Recently, Prinstein and LaGreca (1999) found that the kindergarten children who were most well liked by classmates were those with positive-memory mothers. Children of anxious-memory mothers did not fare as well; in fact, their social preference scores were below the mean. Calling on findings from attachment theory that link mothers' anxious attachment and children's poorer social outcomes, Prinstein and LaGreca proposed that mothers' recollections may be a derivative of their internal working models and may be related to their attachment to their children, and subsequently their children's social competence. Although children in the Putallaz et al. study were rated by their preschool teachers, both peer and observer ratings were gathered in a laboratory setting where children played briefly with unfamiliar peers. Children in the Prinstein and LaGreca study were rated by their kindergarten classmates who would likely have access to longer term and more intimate information about agemates that teachers, observers, and recent acquaintances would not. In both studies, this group of anxious-memory mothers was relatively small. A larger sample and studies targeting potential mediators such as attachment, motivations or values, and locus of control are warranted.

What all three studies demonstrate are different peer-related outcomes for children of positive- and rejection-memory mothers. Whether or not mothers' recollections accurately reflect their childhood experiences, their reports or representations of childhood peer experiences are clearly related to their children's social preference (Prinstein & LaGreca, 1999; Putallaz et al., 1991) and to their direct management of their children's peer relationships (Cohen & Woody, 1991; Putallaz et al., 1991). Mothers' childhood peer experiences are also related to their assessments of their children's social competence and behavior (Cohen & Woody, 1991; Klein & Grimes, 1997; Prinstein & LaGreca, 1999; Putallaz et al., 1991). This was not the case for fathers (Klein & Grimes, 1997). Even though fathers appear to have a consistent interpretive framework regarding their early peer experiences and those of children they do not know (Klein, 1995), this framework does not come into play, or is perhaps overridden, when fathers assess their own children's behavior. This overshadowing or disruption of continuity when their own children are involved bolsters the suggestions by intergenerational researchers (e.g., Cox et al., 1985) that fathers are more influenced by the immediacy of current relationships.

Influences of Parents' Present Peer Relationships

Finally, we address the question of how parents' current peer relationships link to their parenting and their children's social outcomes. Multiple pathways of influence are possible, and parents' peer networks may serve a number of functions that have implications for parenting and for children's relationship learning (see Cochran & Niego, 1995). For example, the various forms of social support provided by parents' peers are likely to have a positive impact on parenting. However, for fathers in single-earner families, the higher the percentage of men in their peer networks (and the more female kin in their network), the less involved they were in rearing their six-year-old children. Thus, when fathers had more leeway in their degree of involvement (i.e., their wives did not work), a sizable male peer group seemed to maintain attitudes and activities that actually competed with the fathering role at home (Riley, 1990).

More directly (i.e., not mediated through parenting), parents' relationships with adult peers may affect children's social development by exposing them to a greater number and variety of social partners, including the children of network members. Parent–peer interactions could also serve as a model for children of interpersonal styles and proclivities. For example, Parke and O'Neil (2000) reported that mothers who have less contact with friends have children who are more likely to avoid peer interaction. Also, mothers' skill at initiating peer interactions is related to their children's social skills and status (Prinstein & LaGreca, 1999). Thus, mothers may model for their children both a positive orientation toward relationships and skillful strategies for initiating them. In a similar vein, fathers who report dissatisfaction with their social networks have children who are more aggressive and more disliked (Parke & O'Neil, 2000). Modeling is most likely an incomplete explanation for these links; in fact, some of the correlations between parents' and children's peer behaviors and attitudes may be a byproduct of inherited dispositions, with parents and children having similar temperaments.

The number of friends that parents report is related to the number of their children's regular playmates, maternal ratings of children's social skills, and kindergarten boys' peer-rated social preference (Hormel, Burns, & Goodnow, 1987; Prinstein & LaGreca, 1999). Doyle, Markiewicz, and Hardy (1994) found that mothers with supportive friends had children who experienced closer friendships. In addition, if mothers considered their best friend stimulating and interesting but also felt insecure in that friendship, their children were more likely to have a best friend. Doyle et al. linked this finding to Putallaz et al.'s (1991) study of maternal peer recollections, in which anxious-memory mothers had more socially competent children, which suggests some sort of compensatory parenting by less confident mothers.

The lessons that parents impart to their children about the social world, either directly or through example, and their management of their children's involvement in that world are clearly influenced by the peer interactions that parents have experienced and the interpretive lens that these experiences provide. This body of research is less well developed than the literature on family-of-origin influences. However, it holds at least as much promise for understanding socialization in the peer domain, perhaps even suggesting ancillary targets of intervention for children who are experiencing social difficulties.

Conclusions and Directions for Future Research

It appears that many of the social expectancies and social behaviors that parents develop through their relationships with their parents and peers are transmitted intergenerationally to their children, and that this intergenerational continuity gives rise to life-course continuity in social-behavioral and ideological systems. The mechanisms responsible for these continuities are undoubtedly complex ones, and our current state of knowledge about these mechanisms is somewhat primitive and piecemeal. The preceding review identifies some critical ingredients in the intergenerational mix that seem to provide the enabling materials of transmission. These ingredients include the quality of the emotional and interactional bond between parents and their children, the quality of the parents' lifelong social relationship experiences, the translation of these experiences into schematized forms (like internal working models), the presence of conflict among significant interaction partners in the family context, and the gender of both parent and child. Currently, neither the relative importance of these ingredients nor their media of transmission from parent to child are well mapped. Given the apparent linkages between parents' relationship histories and their children's social development, it is important to specify the *how* and *what* involved in the intergenerational transmission process and to identify the most fruitful avenues for continued research.

Mechanisms

Perhaps the most critical issue to address in this literature is its inconclusiveness about the mechanisms involved in transmission. Attachment research provides results that are consistent with a view that the basis of continuity is the creation of internal working models of relationships early in life. Most important to this conclusion are the findings that adult representations of parental relationships can be predicted from their parents' behavior, can predict their own parenting, and can predict their children's social behavior. From this constellation of research, internal working models appear central to the continuity of social behavior and ideology between parents and children. However, the view of internal working models as the only or even primary mechanism for such continuity appears to ignore the complementarity provided by other potential modes of transmission.

It seems evident, for example, that general parenting style plays a key role in the continuity in social behavior from parents to children. Generally warm and moderately controlling parents appear to raise children who as parents are similarly warm and moderately controlling who, in turn, have children who are socially engaged and socially competent. General parenting style can affect the transfer of social behavior through a plethora of mechanisms including modeling, the creation of personal qualities and abilities in the parented child, and the ongoing development of positive relationships. All of these routes could have as a byproduct the creation of internal working models consistent with attachment theory without those working models being the central operational mechanism.

A second alternative is that parents may directly or indirectly influence the choice and course of their children's nonparental relationships. Through many mechanisms, parents influence the nature of the relationships their children develop with peers, spouses, and even their children. From this perspective, it is the quality of these relationships that directly influences parenting and children's social behavior and social relationships. For example, attachment effects appear to be moderated by the quality of the marital relationship. Further, it appears that the grandmother's relationship with the mother in adulthood has effects on the mothers' parenting. The continuing relationships between mothers and their adult daughters, not just their early relationship histories, are central to these findings.

Moving beyond viewing these varied mechanisms as in competition and instead recognizing the theoretical complementarity they provide may enrich our conceptual understanding of the intergenerational process. It is likely that these modes of transmission work conjointly to influence both the degree and direction of intergenerational transfer of social orientation and social relationships. Internal working models are developed from early relationships and color children's experiences, but so too do many other parental behaviors. Parents may actively construct their children's world to increase the likelihood of positive engagement, or actively cause children to withdraw and focus on nonsocial activities. In this way, early models may be reinforced or modified. Similarly, parents may help children actively construct interpretations of their social world and mechanisms for coping. Thus, children are simultaneously influenced by parent's early interactions, direct intervention into their social world, and active management of their interpretation of that world. Such dynamic interplay between direct parental behavior, parental influence over their children's social experiences, and children's experience with others continues throughout life including in relationships with spouses, friends, and grandchildren.

Several avenues of further research are needed. First, there is a clear need to develop a better elaboration of the form and content of internal working models of relationships. A better articulated understanding of the nature of these models will facilitate evaluation of competing explanations. Second, there needs to be a better understanding of exactly how parents influence their children's social situation or choice of friend or spouse so as to discover how internal working models interplay with more direct intervention. Finally, how mental models are invoked or adapted when experiences, either direct or vicarious, are inconsistent with them needs to be better elucidated. It is essential to understand the processes underlying the reworking of cognitive models.

Gender and Parental Influence

Another intriguing pattern in this review concerns the differences with regard to gender and intergenerational continuity. On the surface, it appears that women are the carriers of social continuity across generations and are most influential in their children's social development, whereas men are most influenced by immediate social circumstances. However, several important nuances reveal themselves. Discipline, especially harsh discipline, reveals intergenerational effects for fathers. Furthermore, fathers' degree of involvement appears to be more important than the direction of their involvement.

Nonparental Relationships

The final set of results requiring greater depth of research concerns the effect of the critical relationships beyond the parent–child dyad on intergenerational continuity. It is clear from this research, for example, that relationships with one's peers and with one's spouse can serve to either mitigate or enhance intergenerational transfer and that parental influence on these relationships is a factor in intergenerational continuity. The relevant research, however, has been largely cross-sectional. The interactive elements of intimate new relationships over time and their connection to parental variables remain unexplored. Research needs to focus on such variables as the evolution of internal working models over the course of new relationships, the nature of conflicts within these relationships and their connection to early parenting, the discourse on relationships within a relationship, and the evolution of social behavior over the course of the relationship, all with the intent of determining how relationships beyond the parent–child dyad serve to enhance or mitigate early parental influence.

The research agenda outlined here, while ambitious, is a necessary next step. Socialization and parent–child interactions develop within a relationship-rich context that extends well beyond that between parent and child. Learning more about the dynamic interplay of parents' relationship histories will further our understanding of the complexities involved in their intergenerational influences on children's social development.

References

Barnett, R. C., & Baruch, G. K. (1987). Determinants of fathers' participation in family work. *Journal of Marriage and the Family, 49,* 29–40.

Beckwith, L., Cohen, S. E., & Hamilton, C. E. (1999). Maternal sensitivity during infancy and subsequent life events relate to attachment representation at early adulthood. *Developmental Psychology, 35,* 693–700.

Belsky, J. (1984). The determinants of parenting: A process model. *Child Development, 55,* 83–96.

Burks, V. S., & Parke, R. D. (1996). Parent and child representations of social relationships: Linkages between families and peers. *Merrill-Palmer Quarterly, 42,* 358–378.

Caspi, A., & Elder, G. H. (1988). Emergent family patterns: The intergenerational construction of problem behavior and relationships. In R. A. Hinde and J. Stevenson-Hinde (Eds.), *Relationships within families: Mutual influences* (pp. 218–240). Oxford: Clarendon.

Cochran, M., & Niego, S. (1995). Parenting and social networks. In M. Bornstein (Ed.), *Handbook of parenting* (Vol. 3, pp. 393–418). Mahwah, NJ: Erlbaum.

Cohen, J. S., & Woody, E. Z. (1991). *Maternal involvement in children's peer relationships: The contribution of mothers' experiences, values, and beliefs*. Paper presented at the biennial meeting of the Society for Research in Child Development, Seattle, WA.

Cohn, D. A., Cowan, P. A., Cowan, C. P., & Pearson, J. (1992). Mothers' and fathers' working models of childhood attachment relationships, parenting styles, and child behavior. *Development and Psychopathology, 4*, 417–431.

Coie, J. D. (1990). Toward a theory of peer rejection. In S. R. Asher & J. D. Coie (Eds.), *Peer rejection in childhood* (pp. 365–401). New York: Cambridge University Press.

Contreras, J. M. (2000). Parents' recall of childhood relationships and sense of love worthiness: Associations with children's socioemotional functioning in middle childhood. *Merrill-Palmer Quarterly, 46*, 491–513.

Covell, K., Grusec, J. E., & King, G. (1995). The intergenerational transmission of maternal discipline and standards of behavior. *Social Development, 4*, 32–43.

Cowan, P. A., Cohn, D. A., Cowan, C. P., & Pearson, J. L. (1996). Parents' attachment histories and children's externalizing and internalizing behaviors: Exploring family systems models of linkage. *Journal of Consulting and Clinical Psychology, 64*, 53–63.

Cowan, P. A., Cowan, C. P., Schulz, M. S., & Heming, G. (1993). Prebirth to preschool family factors in children's adaptation to kindergarten. In R. D. Parke and S. G. Kellam (Eds.), *Exploring family relationships with other social contexts* (pp. 75–114). Hillsdale, NJ: Erlbaum.

Cox, M. J., Owen, M. T., Lewis, J. M., Riedel, C., Scalf-McIver, L., & Suster, A. (1985). Intergenerational influences on the parent-infant relationship in the transition to parenthood. *Journal of Family Issues, 6*, 543–564.

Crandell, L. E., Fitzgerald, H. E., & Whipple, E. E. (1997). Dyadic synchrony in parent-child interactions: A link with maternal representations of attachment relationships. *Infant Mental Health Journal, 18*, 247–264.

Crowell, J. A., & Feldman, S. S. (1988). Mothers' internal models of relationships and children's behavioral and developmental status: A study of mother-child interactions. *Child Development, 59*, 1273–1285.

De Wolff, M. D., & van IJzendoorn, M. H. (1997). Sensitivity and attachment: A meta-analysis on parental antecedents of infant attachment. *Child Development, 68*, 571–591.

Dodge, K. A., Bates, J. E., & Pettit, G. S. (1990). Mechanisms in the cycle of violence. *Science, 250*, 1678–1683.

Doyle, A. B., Markiewicz, D., & Hardy, C. (1994). Mothers' and children's friendships: Intergenerational associations. *Journal of Social and Personal Relationships, 11*, 363–377.

Elder, G. H., Caspi, A., & Downey, G. (1986). Problem behavior and family relationships: Life course and intergenerational themes. In A. M. Sorensen, F. E. Weinart, & L. R. Sherrod (Eds.), *Human development and the life course: Multidisciplinary perspectives*. Hillsdale, NJ: Erlbaum.

Elder, G. H., Downey, G., & Cross, C. E. (1986). Family ties and life chances: Hard times and hard choices in women's lives since the 1930's. In H. Datan, A. L. Greene, & H. W. Reese (Eds.), *Life-span developmental psychology: Intergenerational relations* (pp. 151–183). Hillsdale, NJ: Erlbaum.

Elicker, J., Egeland, M., & Sroufe, L. A. (1992). Predicting peer competence and peer relationships in childhood from early parent-child relationships. In R. D. Parke & G. W. Ladd (Eds.), *Family and peer relationships: Modes of linkage* (pp. 77–106). Hillsdale, NJ: Erlbaum.

Hesse, E. (1999). The adult attachment interview: Historical and current perspectives. In J. Cassidy & P. R. Shaver (Eds.), *Handbook of attachment: Theory, research and clinical applications* (pp. 395–433). New York: Guilford.

Hormel, R., Burns, A., & Goodnow, J. (1987). Parental social networks and child development. *Journal of Social and Personal Relationships, 4*, 159–177.

Kerns, K. A. (1998). Individual differences in friendship quality: Links to child-mother attachment. In W. M. Bukowski, A. F. Newcomb, & W. W. Hartup (Eds.), *The company they keep* (pp. 137–157). New York: Cambridge University Press.

Kerns, K. A., Contreras, J. M., & Neal-Barnett, A. M. (2000). *Family and peers: Linking two social worlds*. Westport, CT: Praeger.

Klein, T. P. (1995). *Parental recollections, social frames and meaning: Pathways of influence on children's peer relationships*. Unpublished doctoral dissertation, Duke University, Durham, NC.

Klein, T. P., & Grimes, C. L. (April, 1997). *Continuities and influences in peer and sibling relationships*. Paper presented at the biennial meeting of the Society for Research in Child Development, Washington, DC.

Kupersmidt, J. B., Coie, J. D., & Dodge, K. A. (1990). The role of poor peer relationships in the development of disorder. In S. R. Asher & J. D. Coie (Eds.), *Peer rejection in childhood* (pp. 274–305). New York: Cambridge University Press.

Ladd, G. W., & Le Sieur, K. D. (1995). Parents and children's peer relationships. In M. H. Bornstein (Ed.), *Handbook of parenting* (Vol. 4, pp. 377–409). Hillside, NJ: Erlbaum.

Main, M., & Goldwyn, R. (1984). Predicting rejection of her infant from mothers' representation of her own experience: Implications for the abused-abusing intergenerational cycle. *Child Abuse and Neglect, 8,* 203–217.

Main, M., Kaplan, N., & Cassidy, J. (1985). Security in infancy, childhood, and adulthood: A move to the level of representation. In I. Bretherton & E. Waters (Eds.), Growing points of attachment theory and research. *Monographs of the Society for Research in Child Development, 50*(1–1, Serial No. 209), 66–106.

Olsen, S. F., Martin, P., & Halverson, C. F. (1999). Personality, marital relationships, and parenting in two generations of mothers. *International Journal of Behavioral Development, 23,* 457–476.

Parke, R. D., & O'Neil, R. (2000). The influence of significant others on learning about relationships: From family to friends. In R. S. L. Mills & S. Duck (Eds.), *The developmental psychology of personal relationships* (pp. 15–48). England: Wiley.

Phelps, J. L., Belsky, J., & Crnic, K. (1998). Earned security, daily stress, and parenting: A comparison of five alternative models. *Development and Psychopathology, 10,* 21–38.

Prinstein, M. J., & LaGreca, A. M. (1999). Links between mothers' and children's social competence and associations with maternal adjustment. *Journal of Clinical Child Psychology, 28,* 197–210.

Putallaz, M., Costanzo, P. R., Grimes, C. L., & Sherman, D. M. (1998). Intergenerational continuities and their influences on children's social development. *Social Development, 7,* 389–427.

Putallaz, M., Costanzo, P. R., & Smith, R. B. (1991). Maternal recollections of childhood peer relationships: Implications for their children's social competence. *Journal of Social and Personal Relationships, 8,* 403–422.

Putallaz, M., & Heflin, A. H. (1990). Parent-child interaction. In S. R. Asher & J. D. Coie (Eds.), *Peer rejection in childhood* (pp. 189–216). Cambridge, UK: Cambridge University Press.

Putallaz, M., Klein, T. P., Costanzo, P. R., & Hedges, L. A. (1994). Relating mothers' social framing to their children's entry competence with peers. *Social Development, 3,* 222–237.

Riley, D. (1990). Network influences on father involvement in childrearing. In M. Cochran, M. Larner, D. Riley, L. Gunnarsson, & C. R. Henderson, *Extending families: The social networks of parents and their children* (pp. 131–153). New York: Cambridge University Press.

Rossi, A. S., & Rossi, P. H. (1990). *Of human bonding: Parent-child relations across the life course*. New York: Aldine De Gruyter.

Rutter, M., & Madge, N. (1976). *Cycles of disadvantage: A review of research*. London: Heinemann.

Rutter, M., Maughan, B., Pickles, A, & Simonoff, E. (1998). Retrospective recall recalled. In R. B. Cairns, L. R. Bergman, & J. Kagan (Eds.), *Methods and models for studying the individual* (pp. 219–242). Thousand Oaks, CA: Sage.

Sagi, A. (1982). Antecedents and consequences of various degrees of paternal involvement in childrearing: The Israeli project. In M. E. Lamb (Ed.), *Nontraditional families: Parenting and child development*. Hillsdale, NJ: Erlbaum.

Simons, R. L., Beaman, J., Conger, R. D., & Wei, C. (1993). Childhood experience, conceptions of parenting, and attitudes of spouse as determinants of parental behavior. *Journal of Marriage and the Family, 55,* 91–106.

Simons, R. L., Whitbeck, L. B., Conger, R. D., & Wu, C. (1991). Intergenerational transmission of harsh parenting. *Developmental Psychology, 27,* 159–171.

Slade, A., Belsky, J., Aber, J. L., & Phelps, J. L. (1999). Mothers' representations of their relationships with their toddlers: Links to adult attachment and observed mothering. *Developmental Psychology, 35,* 611–619.

Snarey, S. (1993). *How fathers care for the next generation: A four decade study*. Cambridge, MA: Harvard University Press.

Staples, R., & Warden-Smith, J. W. (1954). Attitudes of grandmothers and mothers toward child rearing practices. *Child Development, 25,* 90–97.

Stattin, H., Janson, H., Klackenberg-Larsson, I., & Magnusson, D. (1995). Corporal punishment in everyday life: An intergenerational perspective. In J. McCord (Ed.), *Coercion and punishment in long-term perspectives*. New York: Cambridge University Press.

van IJzendoorn, M. H. (1992). Intergenerational transmission of parenting: A review of studies in non-clinical populations. *Developmental Review, 12,* 76–99.

van IJzendoorn, M. H. (1995). Adult attachment representations, parental responsiveness, and infant attachment: A meta-analysis on the predictive validity of the adult attachment interview. *Psychological Bulletin, 117,* 387–403.

Vermulst, A. A., de Brock, A. J. L., & van Zutphen, R. A. H. (1991). Transmission of parenting across generations. In P. K. Smith (Ed.), *The psychology of grandparenthood: An international perspective* (pp. 100–122). Florence, KY: Rutledge.

Wakschlag, L. S., Chase-Lansdale, P. L., & Brooks-Gunn, J. (1996). Not just "ghosts in the nursery": Contemporaneous intergenerational relationships and parenting in young African-American families. *Child Development, 67,* 2131–2147.

Whitbeck, L. B., Hoyt, D. R., & Huck, S. M. (1993). Family relationship history, contemporary parent-grandparent relationship quality, and the grandparent-grandchild relationship. *Journal of Marriage and the Family, 55,* 1025–1035.

9

From Family Relationships to Peer Rejection to Antisocial Behavior in Middle Childhood

Philip A. Cowan and Carolyn Pape Cowan

This chapter is different from most of the others in this volume because it focuses on a single study to illustrate some general theoretical issues about the antecedents and consequences of peer rejection. Our goal in this chapter is to show how the fields of family research and preventive intervention, in which we have been working for the past three decades, may have something to add to the dialogue concerning the developmental sequence of young children's rejection by peers and antisocial behavior, and the causal connections between the two variables.

Peer researchers and family researchers typically draw very different maps of the child's social environment. In studies of peer relationships, children's families appear rarely, if at all (for some exceptions see Dodge, Pettit, & Bates, 1994; Gottman & Katz, 1989; Parke & Ladd, 1992). Yet, family researchers find that there are substantial, significant correlations between the quality of parent–child or marital relationships and the quality of relationship between children or adolescents and their peers in both clinical and nonclinical samples (see Coie & Dodge, 1998; P. A. Cowan, Powell, & Cowan, 1998; Parke & Buriel, 1998, for reviews of recent research). Here we focus specifically on the links among family relationships, peer rejection, social competence, and antisocial behavior in the period from preschool through middle childhood.

Rejection by peers, always a central construct in the peer research field, was featured as a major risk factor for antisocial behavior in childhood and adolescence in a seminal review of peer relationship research (Parker & Asher, 1987) and holds a central position in the title of *Peer Rejection in Childhood* (Asher & Coie, 1990), which has served as a major reference work on the state of peer research. Two important questions are hidden within the correlational data sets obtained by peer and family researchers, with peer rejection playing a central role in each. First, simple correlations do not reveal whether rejection by peers leads to aggression and antisocial behavior or vice versa. Some important new findings shed light on the direction of effects. Miller-Johnson, Coie, Maumary-Gremaud, Bierman, and the Conduct Problems Prevention Research

Group (2002) have recently demonstrated that, over and above the child's aggression in first grade, rejection by first-grade peers predicts development of fourth-grade antisocial behavior. On the basis of these findings, the authors argued that peer rejection is an independent risk factor, not merely a marker or a consequence of aggressive behavior. The question of whether rejection is a *causal* risk factor was left unresolved because of the correlational nature of the study.

Second, it is not clear from the much more limited set of data on family relationships and peer status whether the quality of relationships within the family affects social competence and peer acceptance, or whether children and adolescents who have a difficult time making friends also play a disruptive role in family interactions. We realized that our own intervention study contained data that bear on both questions. In our attempt to evaluate the impact of a couples group intervention on nonclinical families with a first child about to enter elementary school (C. P. Cowan, Cowan, & Heming, in press-a), we assessed families before the children entered kindergarten (prior to the intervention), and again in kindergarten and first and fourth grade. Because our study contained measures of peer rejection, aggression, social competence, and antisocial behavior, we realized that we could attempt to replicate Miller-Johnson et al.'s findings. Furthermore, our study included the evaluation of a preventive intervention for couples *before* their children entered elementary school. If the early intervention for parents produced significant effects on their children's first-grade peer rejection, this would provide support for the hypothesis that family relationships play a causal role in whether children are accepted or rejected by peers. If the experiment-induced changes in peer rejection in early elementary school were associated with lower levels of aggressive and antisocial behavior in subsequent years, we would then be in a stronger position to make claims about peer rejection as a causal risk factor for antisocial behavior in middle childhood.

A Selective Review of the Literature

Peer Rejection and Externalizing Behavior

A summary of studies that span more than two decades of research (Laird, Jordan, Dodge, Pettit, & Bates, 2001) documents consistent correlations between the quality of peer relationships in childhood and indices of adjustment in childhood, adolescence, and adulthood. The authors note that although many dimensions of peer relationships have been assessed, the literature has emphasized both concurrent and predictive links between (a) the experience of rejection by one's childhood peers and (b) the manifestation of externalizing problems, including aggression and antisocial behavior.

Parker and Asher (1987) raised an important question about the theoretical models used to explain the correlations: are children rejected because they are aggressive and potentially antisocial early on, or does peer rejection cause or exacerbate antisocial behavior? Miller-Johnson et al. (2002) point to two longitudinal studies designed to answer this question (Bierman, Smoot, &

Aumiller, 1993; Coie, Lochman, Terry, & Hyman, 1992; Coie, Terry, Lenox, Lochman, & Hyman, 1995). Although results of both studies supported the hypothesis that peer rejection plays an independent or interactive role in predicting externalizing behavior, neither investigation provided information about whether the results hold for peer rejection that occurs before the third grade, the point at which the Coie et al. study began. The Miller-Johnson et al. results following children from first through fourth grades supported the hypothesis that, over and above measures of first-grade aggression, early peer rejection has at least some independent contribution to predicting variations in antisocial behavior in middle childhood. Data from our study allow us to move back a small but important step, to control for children's level of aggression in kindergarten, one year prior to the measurement of peer rejection, to rule out the possibility that ratings of rejection and aggression might be confounded.

Social Skills, Aggression, and Peer Rejection

Aggressive behavior is not the only reason that children reject their peers. There is evidence that rejected children do not have the general social skills and social competence that their nonrejected classmates do (Bierman et al., 1993). Rubin and colleagues (Rubin, Bukowski, & Parker, 1998) place some emphasis on the acquisition of positive social skills as a prerequisite of peer acceptance and, by implication, on less-than-adequate social skills and social competence in children who are rejected.

There are two conceptual and methodological issues in the research on social skills or social competence, rejection, and aggression. First, it is not always clear how to keep these domains distinct. Part of social competence involves dealing with interpersonal problems in a nonaggressive manner that maintains a relationship in the face of disagreement or conflict. Second, an unresolved question that we address below is whether social skills can provide a buffer so that some children avoid turning to aggressive or antisocial behavior despite being rejected.

Family Processes, Aggression, Antisocial Behavior, and Peer Rejection

There is no shortage of evidence that family processes are concurrently correlated with, and also predict, aggression in both childhood (Bates, Pettit, & Dodge, 1995; P. A. Cowan, Cowan, Schulz, & Heming, 1994; Hinshaw, Zupan, Simmel, Nigg, & Melnick, 1997) and adolescence (Conger, Elder, Lorenz, Simons, & Whitbeck, 1994). Most often investigated are variations along the two central dimensions of parenting style: warmth–responsiveness and structure–control (Maccoby & Martin, 1983). Summarizing two decades of research, Coie and Dodge (1998) showed that aggressive children more often have parents who are cold and negative, coercive, inconsistent, punitive, or abusive. The key parenting construct involved in externalizing problems in adolescence appears to be lack of parental monitoring: not knowing the adolescents' whereabouts and not keeping a firm, fair, supervisory eye on their social relationships when they come home (Dishion & McMahon, 1998). Most studies report links between aggressive or antisocial behavior and harsh parenting, but a few show that rejected children tend to have parents who are *either* overly permissive or overly harsh and rejecting (Rubin et al., 1998).

Recent studies of marital conflict and externalizing in children and adolescents are as consistent as results of studies of parenting styles are. Families in which conflict between parents is high, overt, and unresolved are more likely to contain children or adolescents with both externalizing and internalizing problems (Cummings, Davies, & Campbell, 2000). In this body of research, it has not been customary to examine aggression and antisocial behavior as separate subcategories of externalizing behavior, so we do not know whether there are differential paths from marital conflict to these two outcomes. Nor are we aware of specific studies of direct links between marital conflict and peer rejection, although Gottman and Katz (1989) found strong correlations between dysregulation in the marital system and the kind of negative behavior with peers that is generally associated with peer rejection. As in the research on parenting style and children's peer relationships, the direction of marital-to-peer effects remains an unresolved issue. It is reasonable to conclude that when parents provide models of aggression in their relationship as partners (as peers in the marriage), children are less likely to know how to form and maintain noncombative relationships with classmates and other peers. On the other hand, it is also reasonable to assume that an aggressive, antisocial child can contribute to high levels of marital conflict.

In our own study of nonclinical families (P. A. Cowan, Cowan, Ablow, Johnson, & Measelle, in press-b), we found that (a) a couples group intervention offered to parents before their children entered kindergarten had significant positive effects on marital functioning and parenting style, and (b) these effects mediated the impact of the intervention on children's social, academic, and emotional adaptation to kindergarten and first grade. These findings provide support for the hypothesis that there is at least some impact of marital– and parent–child relationship quality on children's subsequent social adaptation. Although there have been a number of attempts to explore mechanisms linking peer rejection, aggression, and antisocial behavior (e.g., Laird et al., 2001), we do not know of any previous attempts to explore links among family processes and all three indices of peer relationship quality as we do in this report.

First, we attempt to replicate Miller-Johnson et al.'s (2002) finding that peer rejection in first grade contributes uniquely to the prediction of children's antisocial behavior in fourth grade, noting one important limitation. For reasons that will become apparent when we describe the study design, our indices of rejection, aggression, and antisocial behavior come not from peer sociometric methods but from teachers' perceptions on a 106-item behavior checklist filled out on all children in the class. We argue that the reliability and validity of our measure may allay at least some concerns about using teachers' ratings rather than children's sociometric choices to describe peer status. Second, we test the hypothesis that a prekindergarten couples group intervention that had positive effects on both marital– and parent–child interaction (C. P. Cowan et al., in press-a) results in the children showing greater social skills, less aggression, and less rejection in kindergarten and first grade, as perceived by their teachers. Third, we provide a speculative attempt to link the two sets of findings to show that (a) family processes play a causal role in peer rejection and, more tentatively, that (b) early peer rejection plays a causal role in antisocial behavior in fourth grade.

A Description of Our Study

Design

The Schoolchildren and Their Families Project began in the spring of 1990 with couples recruited through day care centers, preschools, pediatricians' offices, and public service announcements in the media in northern California. The couples were randomly offered participation in one of two study conditions: (a) a 16-week couples group intervention meeting in the months before their first child entered kindergarten or (b) an opportunity for one consultation each year for three years with the staff couple who interviewed them (a low-dose intervention). Participant couples assigned to a couples group were further subdivided randomly into two variations of the group intervention, one focusing more on marital issues, the other focusing more on parenting issues. In the randomized clinical trial part of the study 80 families were included in the preintervention phase: 55 intervention and 25 consultation controls. Of those, 67 participated at the first-grade follow-up and 65 participated at fourth grade. There were no significant differences in the central variables at pretest between those who continued and those who dropped out of the study.

Participants

The initial 80 families included 46 with a male first child and 34 with a female first child. When their first child was five years old, the average age of the fathers was 37.9 years, the mothers 36.2 years. According to their self-descriptions, 84% of the 200 participants were Caucasian and 16% were divided among three major ethnic groups: 6.7% were African American, 7% were Asian American, and 2.3% were Hispanic.

The couples lived in 27 cities and towns within a 40-mile radius of the university. Their median yearly total family income ($78,000) indicated a relatively affluent sample, with two qualifications: (a) Because the primary sources of recruitment were day care centers and preschools, the study attracted mostly two-job families (71% of mothers were employed at least half-time); and (b) despite the sample's generally high total family income, 22% of the families earned below the median family income of $58,000 for U.S. *dual-worker* families in 1990–1993.

Procedures

In the prekindergarten and preintervention period (PRE), families participated in extensive assessments that included (a) structured interviews, (b) structured observations of marital, parent–child, sibling, and whole-family interaction, all conducted on site in our project playroom, (c) a questionnaire booklet filled out by both parents, and (d) separate observations of the children by project staff, both in our project playroom and at each family's home during the summer. These assessments were repeated during the kindergarten year (POST 1). In the spring and summer after first grade (POST 2), we repeated questionnaires and interviews with the parents and home visits with the children, but not the laboratory observations of the couple, child, or whole family. In our fourth-grade assessment three years later (POST 3), we repeated all of the major modes of assessment from PRE and POST 1.

Measures of Family Interaction

Details of the measures and their psychometric properties can be obtained from P. A. Cowan et al. (in press-b, chap. 2).

(a) Marital interaction observed in a triadic coparenting context. As part of the 2½-hour family visit to our project playroom, mothers and fathers spent 40 minutes together working and playing with their oldest child (the target child) and any younger siblings. The oldest child was presented with a number of challenging tasks and the parents were invited to help as they typically would at home. After the playroom-laboratory visit, two observers filled out global rating scales on eight constructs to describe parents' behavior *toward each other*. Each scale was rated for both highest level of the behavior shown during the interaction (e.g., high warmth) and the typical level shown overall (e.g., moderate warmth). Two factors were identified as characterizing the coparenting relationship, or the quality of the couple's relationship in the presence of the child: negative emotion and conflict.

(b) Parenting style observed in a dyadic context. Parenting style was assessed with observers' ratings of the interaction between mother and child and father and child as each parent–child dyad worked and played together in two separate 40-minute sessions in the project's playroom. Two observers rated each parent's behavior on 17 items. For this study, 12 items were grouped in the following three scales: (1) positive emotion (pleasure, expressiveness, warmth, responsiveness); (2) structure (structure, limit setting, maturity demands, clear communication about the task); and (3) respect for the child's autonomy.

(c) Peer relationships observed by mothers, fathers, and teachers; peer rejection, social skills, and aggression. Our family-based study began when the children were in preschool. By the time the 100 children entered kindergarten, they were attending 92 different schools throughout the San Francisco Bay Area. Because it was not possible for us to obtain peer status measures through sociometric measures in each classroom, we obtained information from their teachers on a newly constructed 106-item behavior checklist (Child Adaptive Behavior Inventory, CABI; P. A. Cowan, et al., 1995). The rationale for developing a new behavior checklist began with the observation that instruments for the assessment of schoolage children tend to focus on either competence or problematic behavior, but not both. For example, in the widely used Child Behavior Check List (CBCL; Achenbach & Edelbrock, 1983), 118 of 138 items describe problem behavior. We chose to begin with a 60-item Adaptive Behavior Inventory (Schaefer & Hunter, 1983) that emphasizes academic and social competence in the classroom. Each item is rated on a 4-point scale, ranging from (1) not at all like this child to (4) very much like this child. To this scale we added 46 items: 16 to assess attributes from sociometric measures of peer status (social isolation, peer rejection, social skills) and 30 to measure problem behaviors, selected from the downward extension of the Quay-Peterson Behavior Problem Checklist (O'Donnel & Van Tuinen, 1979) and from Achenbach and Edelbrock's (1983) CBCL.

We asked teachers to complete the CABI to describe *all children in the class in fall and spring, without revealing which child was in our study*. Because a number of teachers were unable to complete checklists on their entire class, we negotiated with them to describe fewer students, selected randomly by us, with a minimum of six students per classroom. Thus, for the children in the study we obtained a standardization pool ranging from 1,043 to 1,723 in the different assessment periods.

Using an a priori conceptual grouping of items, we created six scales: (1) academic competence, (2) social competence, (3) externalizing aggressive, (4) externalizing hyperactive or inattentive, (5) internalizing depressed, shy or withdrawn, and (6) internalizing somaticizing, all of which have high internal reliabilities (alphas ranging from .88 to .92). We have evidence for the validity of some CABI factors from a study by Katz and Gottman (1993), who reported significant correlations between externalizing and internalizing on CABIs and CBCLs when both were completed by teachers of 7- to 8-year-olds (externalizing $r = .68$, $p < .0001$; internalizing $r = .49$, $p < .001$). Additional evidence from a study of 4-year olds by Wood, Cowan, and Baker (in press) shows relatively high correlations (.6 to .7) between teachers' CABI ratings of externalizing and sociometric measures of peer rejection. The children in our sample appear to be similar to their classmates in mean tendencies *and* distribution of scores, except that they were judged to be slightly more academically competent than their peers.

Reconfiguring the CABI Items for This Study

The challenge in the present study was to take a more detailed look at the CABI items in our study to represent more closely the measures of peer status and the specific peer behaviors in both the Miller-Johnson et al. (2002) study and many other studies of peer relationships. The following scales were created, with normed z-scores derived from the entire samples of children in kindergarten and first and fourth grade.

REJECTION. Four items were chosen from the CABI that described active rejection by peers (other children actively dislike this child and reject him or her from their play, picked on by others, often left out, other children push him or her around). By comparison, the Miller-Johnson et al. (2002) study used a sociometric interview in first and third grades, in which the difference between most liked and least liked choices was standardized within each class-room to control for class size. In that study, children were allowed to nominate boys and girls.

AGGRESSION. Four items described aggressive behavior (gets into fights, hot temper, argues or quarrels, deliberately cruel to other children). The Miller-Johnson (in press) study used peer nominations on one item: "starts fights, says mean things, and hits other kids."

SOCIAL SKILLS. Fourteen items described socially skilled behavior, grouped in four scales (kind, fair, socially perceptive, gets along with others). The Miller-Johnson study used a combination of peer nominations, parent ratings, teacher ratings, and child interviews to assess this construct.

ANTISOCIAL BEHAVIOR. Seven items assessed antisocial behavior that in-cluded lying, stealing, and oppositional defiant behavior (disobeys or breaks rules, takes things that don't belong to him or her, doesn't always tell the truth, punishment doesn't affect his or her behavior, stubborn, uncooperative in group situations with peers, uncooperative in group situations with adults). By comparison, the Miller-Johnson article (2002) used fourth-grade self-reports of delinquency on an instrument named Things That You Have Done.

Despite the small numbers of items in three of the four scales, there was adequate to very high inter-item consistency for all scales at all assessment periods, with alphas ranging from .77 to .94 (median = .88). Furthermore, there was notable consistency over time in all four measures, even though the teachers' reports were separated by as many as four years and each year's ratings were done by different teachers. As children moved from kindergarten to first to fourth grade, attending different classes with different teachers, they showed a significant tendency to stay in the same rank order of rejection, aggression, social skills, and antisocial oppositional behavior. Of 40 correla-tions, 38 were statistically significant. Fall-to-spring correlations (same teachers) ranged from .74 to .82 in first grade, and from .73 to .82 in fourth. Correlations between rejection, aggression, social skills, and antisocial behavior scales in kindergarten spring and fourth-grade fall or spring ranged from .28 to .52. With the exception of rejection scores in the fall of first and fourth grade, correlations between teachers' ratings in first and fourth grade were similar.

Early Rejection As a Predictor of Fourth-Grade Antisocial Behavior

To test the hypothesis that early rejection would predict fourth-grade antisocial behavior, over and above later rejection and early aggression, we performed a hierarchical multiple regression with data from the 65 children whose parents participated in the randomized intervention design and had data for all periods from prekindergarten to fourth grade. Note that the dependent measure of antisocial behavior in fourth grade includes lying, stealing, and defiance of rules, but not aggression. On Step 1, child sex was entered as a covariate. To

Table 9.1. Predictors of Fourth Grade Spring Antisocial Behavior (stealing, disobedient, rule-breaking, oppositional)

| | | Hierarchical Multiple Regression | | |
Variable	R^2	Beta in	Change in R^2	F change
1. Child Sex	.10	−.32	.10	4.68*
2. Kindergarten Spring Aggression	.36	.49	.26	17.35***
3. 4th Fall Rejection by Peers	.52	.46	.16	14.20***
4. 4th Fall Aggression	.67	.70	.15	19.23***
5. 1st Fall Rejection by Peers	.70	.21	.03	4.14*
6. 4th Interaction between 1st Fall Rejection and 4th Social Skills	.78	−.73	.08	13.12***

*p < .05
***p < .001

control for early levels of aggression, we entered aggressive behavior in spring of kindergarten on Step 2. Rather than simply entering early rejection as in the Miller-Johnson et al. paper, we attempted to rule out the potential contribution of concurrent associations among fourth-grade antisocial behavior, rejection, and aggression, so on Steps 3 and 4 we entered rejection by peers and aggressive behavior in fall of fourth grade. The critical test of the hypothesis concerning the role of early rejection occurred at Step 5 when we entered fall first-grade rejection by peers. In addition, to answer the question of whether social skills might buffer the impact of rejection, on Step 6 we added a term representing the interaction between first-grade fall rejection and fourth-grade social skills. Our expectation was that the link between early rejection and later antisocial behavior would not be apparent in the children with higher levels of social skills on entering fourth grade.

In Table 9.1 we can see that, in general, teachers described boys as more aggressive than girls in the fall of the kindergarten year. Aggression in spring of kindergarten contributed substantially to the prediction of antisocial behavior four years later, accounting for 26% of the variance in the dependent variable. Peer rejection and aggression as rated by fourth-grade teachers in the fall each made a substantial contribution to explaining variance in fourth-grade antisocial behavior in spring (16% and 15% as indexed by the R^2 change measure). Taken together, these variables so far accounted for 67% of the variance in children's fourth-grade spring antisocial behavior. Even though rejection and aggression measures were obtained from assessments in fall of fourth grade and antisocial behavior measures were obtained six months later in spring of fourth grade, we recognize that a large proportion of the explained variance in Steps 2 to 4 can be attributed to the fact that the reports come from the same teacher. Nevertheless, we cannot dismiss these high correlations as single-source artifacts. Peer rejection and aggression in fall fourth grade each contributed *uniquely* to the prediction of antisocial behavior in spring of fourth grade. Teachers were not simply casting a halo in their ratings of the children, as revealed in the distinctions they made between peer rejection and aggression.

From the point of view of our main hypothesis, the most important finding in this multiple regression analysis is that, over and above the already high level of predictability of antisocial behavior in fourth grade, a significant amount of additional variance in antisocial behavior (3%, $p < .05$) was accounted for by the children's experience of being rejected in first grade. Given the fact that there were many differences between the Miller-Johnson et al. (2002) study and ours, including the levels of pathology and the different measures of peer rejection in the two samples, it seems noteworthy that we were able to replicate the main features of their results. The findings are consistent with the hypothesis that early experience of rejection by peers sets a child on the path toward rule-breaking, lying, and oppositional behavior in middle school. Coie's chapter in the present volume provides a compelling account of the impact of rejection on self-image, schemas about relationships, and social transactions with escalations of rejection pushing children in the direction of resistance and nonconformity to normal social demands and rules.

The Step 6 interaction between fall first-grade rejection and spring fourth-grade social skills explained an additional 8% of the variance in antisocial behavior. We note that this was the predicted interaction. A more conservative analysis would have entered fourth-grade social skills first as a main effect. When we did this as the sixth step, the main effect accounted for 8% of the variance, with a total of 88% of the variance accounted for overall. This left very little variance to be accounted for by the interaction term, which was no longer statistically significant. Given that this was an exploratory analysis, we proceeded with the analysis of the interaction term as reported in the table.

Dividing the sample by rejection in first grade, we found that in the group of fourth-grade children with fewer social skills, those who had experienced greater rejection three years earlier resorted to more antisocial behavior. By contrast, in the group of children with high fourth-grade social skills, there are virtually no differences attributable to earlier rejection. Here we have a clear example of a buffering effect. Children who have somehow managed to be socially perceptive, kind, and fair and get along with their classmates despite being socially rejected three years earlier showed minimal amounts of antisocial behavior in mid-elementary school.

The Impact of a Couples' Group Intervention on Peer Rejection in First Grade

The results we have reported so far make it clear that there are concurrent and across-time linkages among aggression, peer rejection, social skills, and antisocial behavior in middle childhood, but it is difficult to identify conclusively the engine that drives the system. In an attempt to shed light on this question, we turned to an analysis of family relationship antecedents of peer relationship quality and to the results of a preventive intervention to help clarify whether peer rejection precedes or follows the emergence of aggressive behavior in the early elementary school grades.

A Brief Description of the Interventions

The couples' group interventions in the Schoolchildren and Their Families Project were similar in format, content, and process to those in our earlier study on transition to parenthood (C. P. Cowan & Cowan, 2000). Four participant parent couples and a staff couple who were mental health professionals met weekly for two hours over a period of four months before the couples' first children entered kindergarten. The format was semistructured, combining (a) an open-ended check-in during which couples were encouraged to bring any family issue or problem with (b) an ongoing planned agenda formed collaboratively by participants and leaders. Over the 16 weeks, the staff raised topics for discussion from the six domains of our conceptual model of major aspects of family life: parents' adjustment as individuals, marital relationship quality, parents' working models of relationships in their families of origin, the quality of the parent–child relationships, the quality of the children's sibling relationships, and the balance between life stresses and social supports outside the family (P. A. Cowan et al., 1998). The group leaders helped couples begin to see some of the links among these domains (e.g., how marital conflict might affect their relationship with their child, and how their own experiences as children might affect their parenting practices). What distinguished the focus on marital issues from the focus on parenting issues was the emphasis. When a partner or couple raised a problem, leaders of the maritally focused groups attempted to highlight (a) how the issue was affecting the parents' relationship as a couple and (b) characteristics of their relationship that might affect their ability to solve the problem. By contrast, in the parenting-focused groups, leaders highlighted the implications of the problem for the parents' relationships with their child(ren).

We (P. A. Cowan & Cowan, 2002; C. P. Cowan et al., in press-a) have found that there were significant intervention effects on the couples in the study and that the direct effects were consistent with the orientation of the interventions. Compared with couples in the low-dose consultation condition, couples in the maritally focused groups significantly reduced the marital conflict we observed from before to eight months after the intervention (assessed in our project playroom as they worked and played with their child). Compared with the same controls, couples in the parenting-focused groups showed significantly more effective parenting in dyadic interactions with their child in our playroom. Furthermore, children of parents in the prekindergarten intervention showed significantly positive effects on their tested academic achievement in kindergarten and their externalizing and internalizing behavior in first grade. The question addressed here is whether the interventions made a difference in the children's level of aggression, rejection, or social skills in the early elementary school years.

A Note on the Use of Partial Least Squares Structural Equation Modeling

We have a data set that relies on multiple indicators, both pre- and postintervention, to assess many of the major constructs in the study, with a relatively

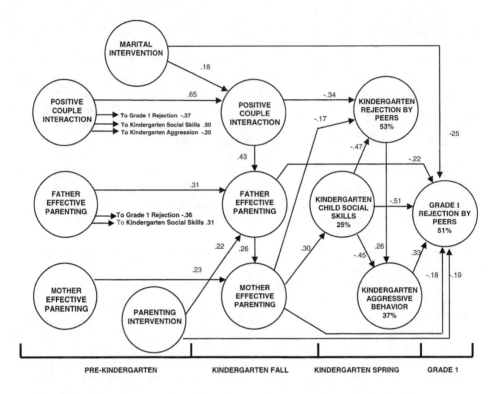

Figure 9.1. Intervention effects on marital interaction, parenting style, and children's peer relationship quality in kindergarten and first grade.

large number of measures relative to the number of subjects. We used structural equation modeling to reduce the data by combining individual measures into latent variables, in a process guided by a priori theoretical constructs. We examined intervention effects using latent variable path analysis with partial least squares (PLS) estimation procedure, or *soft modeling* (Falk & Miller, 1992), specifically because it allows us to explore hypothesized relationships among constructs without imposing certain restrictive statistical and structural assumptions that underlie the widely used LISREL structural modeling programs.

The partial least squares model that we constructed (see Figure 9.1) contained 13 latent variables, with child sex included as a covariate. There were three preintervention observation-based measures of marital and parenting relationships, and the same three postintervention measures one year later, coded by different observers. Two latent variables represented intervention effects. Four outcomes were examined: kindergarten spring measures of social skills, aggression, and peer rejection, and first-grade peer rejection (fall and spring). We described the manifest variables in the method section above. They were entered into the equation in an order dictated for the most part by temporal sequencing (see Figure 9.1).

Model Fit

The root mean square covariance fit index is a statistic in which 0 represents a perfect fit of the model to the data and .20 or higher represents an unacceptable fit (Falk & Miller, 1992). For reasons explained below, we calculated two models, the first including and the second excluding the intervention latent variables. Both models had a fit index of .08, which represents an adequate fit to the data. Furthermore, both models explained statistically significant amounts of variance in kindergarten social skills (25% with the intervention included, 23% with the intervention excluded), rejection (53%, 46%), aggressive behavior (37%, 30%), and first-grade rejection (51%, 33%). In other words, positive couple interaction and effective parenting by mothers and fathers as observed in our laboratory playroom in the prekindergarten year, along with assessments of the same measures in spring of kindergarten year, explained substantial amounts of variance in how teachers viewed children's peer relationships in both kindergarten and first grade.

Intervention Effects on Children

To test for the statistical significance of intervention effects, we ran the model with and without the intervention vectors and tested for the significance of the difference in the nested R^2s. In effect, this constitutes a test of R^2 change— the significance of adding the two intervention vectors to an equation that predicts peer rejection in first grade without the intervention vectors. There were no statistically significant effects of the couples group intervention on kindergarten children's social skills. The impact of the intervention on children's aggressive behavior in kindergarten was marginally significant (F (2,52) = 2.85, $p < .10$). More central to our focus here, the intervention had a small but statistically significant impact on rejection by peers in kindergarten (7% effect size, F (2,52) = 7.43, $p < .05$) and a moderate impact on change in rejection from kindergarten to first grade (18% effect size, F (2,52) = 7.43, $p < .05$).

How do we understand the links between family processes and children's interaction with peers? The latent variable measures of marital and parenting interaction at the beginning of the study before children entered kindergarten were direct predictors of their kindergarten and first-grade peer relationships. Children of parents with positive marital interactions were more likely to have more social skills and less aggression in kindergarten, and less likely to be rejected the next year in first grade. Children of fathers with effective parenting were also more likely to have more social skills in kindergarten and less likely to be rejected in first grade. Mothers' ineffective parenting before their children entered kindergarten did not show direct links with peer outcomes in kindergarten, but as we shall see, ineffective parenting during the kindergarten year was related to children's peer relationships that year.

When couples engaged in warmer interactions with less conflict during kindergarten year than they had shown one year earlier, their children were less likely to be rejected by their peers in kindergarten. Mothers' *change* in effective parenting was linked with children's positive social skills in kindergarten. And, when both mothers and fathers were rated as using more effective parenting styles during kindergarten year than they had one year earlier, their children were less likely to be rejected by their peers the following year in first grade. Children with higher levels of social skills and lower levels of aggressive behavior in kindergarten were less likely to be rejected by their first-grade classmates.

We return to Parker and Asher's (1987) question about the direction of effects between rejection and aggression. Figure 9.1 shows a directional arrow from kindergarten rejection to kindergarten aggression. As these are concurrent measures from the same teacher, it is difficult to determine which comes first. However, a model with the reverse arrow entered shows a path weight of only 0.12. There is no way to test the significance of this difference with PLS models. Furthermore, to our surprise, there were no direct links between rejection in kindergarten and rejection in first grade. A speculative way of interpreting the pattern in Figure 9.1 is that only if children rejected in kindergarten were aggressive, or became aggressive, were they likely to be rejected in first grade. This speculation is supported by our finding that there were significant intervention effects on rejection but not on aggression.

What can we say now about the connections among family processes and children's social skills, aggression, and rejection by peers? Although the language of structural equation modeling is often phrased in causal terms, there is nothing inherent in directional arrows that establishes proof of causality. Structural equation models are still, after all, sets of correlations. Nevertheless, this particular structural model includes significant intervention effects, especially intervention effects on both kindergarten and first-grade rejection. Furthermore, there is a direct link between both marital and parenting interventions before the children entered kindergarten and their subsequent rejection by peers in first grade. When parents participated in either group intervention before their children entered elementary school, their children experienced lower levels of peer rejection in first grade than did children of controls. In addition to these direct effects, there were indirect links stemming from the fact that the interventions affected the quality of both the marital– and parent–child relationship, and *changes* in these relationships were linked with all of our measures of peer relationships in both kindergarten and first grade.

On the basis of the intervention findings, we offer two hypotheses for testing in future research:

1. Marital– and parent–child relationships in the prekindergarten and kindergarten years are causally linked with the development of social skills and aggression in kindergarten children, and these help to determine whether or not the child will be rejected in kindergarten and first grade.
2. Although there is likely to be a reverberating system of influences between aggression and rejection, at least some of the variation in aggression is caused by the experience of rejection rather than the other way around.

Conclusions

Links Between the Fourth-Grade Predictions and the Prekindergarten to First-Grade Intervention Study

In this paper we have presented two parts of a story about rejection and antisocial behavior. First, we found that peer rejection in first grade predicted antisocial behavior in fourth grade, over and above any influences of concurrent rejection and aggression or of earlier aggressive behavior in kindergarten. This finding adds weight to Miller-Johnson's argument that peer rejection is not merely a marker of the child's aggressive behavior. Rejection in first grade is an independent phenomenon and constitutes an independent measure of an early risk for antisocial behavior in mid-elementary school.

We then demonstrated that negative qualities in marital– and parent–child relationships in both prekindergarten and kindergarten are risk factors for low social skills, aggressive behavior, and rejection in the early years of elementary school. Furthermore, we can argue that these family relationship factors are causal risk factors for children in early elementary school because intervention-induced changes in marital and parenting quality resulted in improved family relationships, which, in turn, were associated with more positive peer relationships in the first years of elementary school.

It would have been helpful to establish a direct link between these two stories by entering the fourth-grade outcomes into the model to show intervention effects on fourth-grade antisocial behavior over and above the child's level of aggression and social skills. However, with only 65 subjects, not even the flexibility of PLS allows us to include all of these variables in one model. For now, our final line of argument must remain tentative. Prekindergarten interventions affected both family processes and peer rejection in first grade. Peer rejection in first grade predicted antisocial behavior in fourth grade, over and above measures of the child's kindergarten and fourth-grade aggression and rejection by peers. From the fact that A (intervention) affects B (peer rejection in first grade) and that B was correlated with C (fourth-grade antisocial behavior), we conclude cautiously that family processes play a causal role in antisocial behavior by setting processes in motion that lead young school-age children's peers to reject them. The key question for future research will involve a search to identify the transactions and intrapsychic processes that function as mechanisms linking what happens in the family with what happens at school and other places where peers work out their social relationships.

Caveats

Of course, the results here must be replicated before they can be generalized. Although there was wide variation in the children in this study, in that they did not differ perceptibly from their classmates in externalizing or internalizing behavior, it is important to examine these relationships in both clinical and nonclinical samples, and in samples of children who may not be clinically identified but may be at higher risk by virtue of their rejected status or their level of aggression and social skills.

We have mentioned the fact that our measures of peer rejection are not the gold-standard measures derived from peer nominations or peer ratings. Because each child in the study was in a different classroom in many school districts in different cities, we felt that we had to rely on teachers' descriptions of them. We have some confidence in the teacher ratings, first, because the measures yielded consistent descriptions of the child across a long period of time (kindergarten to fourth grade); second, because they show theoretically relevant links with family processes in this and other studies; and third, because the pattern of results with this measure was very similar to that of Miller-Johnson et al. (2002) with peer nominations. Although the use of teachers' ratings instead of peer sociometric status ratings has been criticized, in fact most studies of peer relationships show sizable correlations between the two (e.g., Coie, Dodge, & Kupersmidt, 1990).

The reader may have noted in Table 9.1 that the first-grade rejection scores added only 3% to the prediction of antisocial behavior and that the interaction of these scores with fourth-grade social skills added only another 6%. These findings should be interpreted in light of the fact that the previous steps in the equation had already accounted for an enormous proportion of the variance (73%). A fairer representation of the connection between first-grade rejection and fourth-grade antisocial behavior may be that the simple correlation between them was .38 over a period of three years. Furthermore, the 6% contribution of the interaction term should be evaluated in light of the fact that it is very difficult to find significant interactions in multiple regression analyses (McClelland & Judd, 1993).

Finally, we acknowledge that we have examined only two domains of family process (marital interaction in a triad and parenting style in the two parent–child dyads). There very well may be other measures and other domains of family life that contribute meaningfully to understanding the quality of the child's peer relationships (e.g., siblings; Bank, Patterson, & Reid, 1996).

The Contribution of Family Research to the Study of Peer Relationships

Findings in the growing peer relationship literature over the past four decades have done much to show that the child's social context plays a central role in our understanding of adaptation, adjustment, and mental health. Nevertheless, in our view this literature has not always done justice to social contexts outside the school and the neighborhoods in which peers form their relationships. The data from the present report provide one of many illustrations that a substantial amount of variation in children's behavior with peers can be accounted for by variations in the quality of family relationships—between their parents and between parents and children—assessed before the child enters elementary school. Furthermore, the longitudinal randomized trial intervention design of this study demonstrated that positive changes in family relationships were causally linked with lower levels of peer rejection in kindergarten and first grade. We do not claim that all of the child's behavior with peers is shaped by family processes, but we are able to conclude that parents *can* have an impact on their child's social life outside the family.

These perhaps not surprising facts have implications for both theories of peer relationships and interventions designed to affect peer relationships and children's adaptation. To take an example of one theoretical issue in the peer literature, we focus on the frequently reported finding that peer status tends to be consistent over time (Cillessen, Bukowski, & Haselager, 2000). This continuity is usually explained by a combination of individual factors (social cognition, social skills) and peer group factors (reputation, group processes) to account for the fact that peer rejection, once established, is difficult to overcome. The fact that the child usually lives in the same family over time and that the family also sets in motion enduring instrumental and emotional supports or barriers to effective interpersonal interaction is acknowledged (Rubin et al., 1998) but rarely investigated empirically.

Finally, the demonstration that a family-based intervention affects peer rejection, and that peer rejection is a precursor of early-onset antisocial behavior, may provide a stimulus to those who wish to design preventive interventions targeted to reducing aggression and antisocial behavior (e.g., McMahon & Slough, 1996). In the Fast Track program, the overall positive impact of family-, classroom-, and individually based interventions has been demonstrated, but we do not yet know the unique contribution of this or other family interventions to the enhancement of peer relationships and the reduction of externalizing or internalizing problems in children and adolescents. It is our hope that this chapter might stimulate peer researchers to redraw their maps with greater attention to the role of the family in shaping and maintaining the quality of the children's relationships with others their own age. We also hope that it might stimulate family researchers and clinicians to redraw their maps with greater attention to children's relationships with peers rather than to individual measures of children's adaptation.

References

Achenbach, T. M., & Edelbrock, C. S. (1983). *Manual for the child behavior checklist*. Burlington, VT: Queen City.

Asher, S. R., & Coie, J. D. (Eds.). (1990). *Peer rejection in childhood*. New York: Cambridge University Press.

Bank, L., Patterson, G. R., & Reid, J. B. (1996). Negative sibling interaction patterns as predictors of later adjustment problems in adolescent and young adult males. In G. H. Brody (Ed.), *Sibling relationships: Their causes and consequences* (pp. 197–229). Stamford, CT: Ablex Publishing Corp.

Bates, J. E., Pettit, G. S., & Dodge, K. A. (1995). Family and child factors in stability and change in children's aggressiveness in elementary school. In J. McCord (Ed.), *Coercion and punishment in long-term perspectives* (pp. 124–138). New York: Cambridge University Press.

Bierman, K. L., Smoot, D. L., & Aumiller, K. (1993). Characteristics of aggressive-rejected, aggressive nonrejected, and rejected (nonaggressive) boys. *Child Development, 64*, 139–151.

Cillessen, A. H. N., Bukowski, W. M., & Haselager, G. J. T. (2000). *Stability of sociometric categories*. San Francisco: Jossey-Bass.

Coie, J. D., & Dodge, K. A. (1998). Aggression and antisocial behavior. In W. Damon (Series Ed.) and N. Eisenberg (Vol. Ed.), *Handbook of child psychology: Vol. 3. Social, emotional, and personality development* (5th ed., pp. 779–862). New York: Wiley.

Coie, J. D., Dodge, K. A., & Kupersmidt, J. B. (1990). Peer group behavior and social status. In S. R. Asher & J. D. Coie (Eds.), *Peer rejection in childhood* (pp. 17–59). New York: Cambridge University Press.

Coie, J. D., Lochman, J. E., Terry, R., & Hyman, C. (1992). Predicting early adolescent disorder from childhood aggression and peer rejection. *Journal of Consulting and Clinical Psychology, 60,* 783–792.

Coie, J. D., Terry, R., Lenox, K., Lochman, J., & Hyman, C. (1995). Childhood peer rejection and aggression as predictors of stable patterns of adolescent disorder. *Development and Psychopathology, 7,* 697–713.

Conger, R. D., Elder, G. H., Jr., Lorenz, F. O., Simons, R. L., & Whitbeck, L. B. (Eds.). (1994). *Families in troubled times: Adapting to change in rural America.* New York: Aldine de Gruyter.

Cowan, C. P., & Cowan, P. A. (2000). *When partners become parents: The big life change for couples.* Mahwah, NJ: Erlbaum.

Cowan, C. P., Cowan, P. A., & Heming, G. (in press-a). Two variations of a preventive intervention for couples: Effects on parents and children during the transition to elementary school. In P. A. Cowan, C. P. Cowan, J. Ablow, V. K. Johnson, & J. Measelle (Eds.), *The family context of parenting in children's adaptation to elementary school.* Mahwah, NJ: Erlbaum.

Cowan, P. A., & Cowan, C. P. (2002). What an intervention design reveals about how parents affect their children's academic achievement and behavior problems. In J. G. Borkowski, S. L. Ramey, & M. Bristol-Power (Eds.), *Parenting and the child's world: Influences on academic, intellectual, and social-emotional development* (pp. 75–97). Mahwah, NJ, and London: Erlbaum.

Cowan, P. A., Cowan, C. P., Ablow, J., Johnson, V. K., & Measelle, J. (in press-b). *The family context of parenting in children's adaptation to elementary school.* Mahwah, NJ: Erlbaum.

Cowan, P. A., Cowan, C. P., & Heming, G. (1995). *Manual for the Child Adaptive Behavior Inventory (CABI).* Unpublished manuscript, University of California at Berkeley.

Cowan, P. A., Cowan, C. P., Schulz, M. S., & Heming, G. (1994). Prebirth to preschool family factors in children's adaptation to kindergarten. In R. D. Parke & S. G. Kellam (Eds.), *Exploring family relationships with other social contexts: Vol. 4. Family research consortium: Advances in family research* (pp. 75–114). Hillsdale, NJ: Erlbaum.

Cowan, P. A., Powell, D., & Cowan, C. P. (1998). Parenting interventions: A family systems perspective. In W. Damon (Ed.), *Handbook of child psychology: Vol. 4. Child psychology in practice.* (5th ed., pp. 3–72). New York: Wiley.

Cummings, E. M., Davies, P. T., & Campbell, S. B. (2000). *Developmental psychopathology and family process: Theory, research, and clinical implications.* New York: Guilford.

Dishion, T. J., & McMahon, R. J. (1998). Parental monitoring and the prevention of child and adolescent problem behavior: A conceptual and empirical formulation. *Clinical Child & Family Psychology Review, 1,* 61–75.

Dodge, K. A., Pettit, G. S., & Bates, J. E. (1994). Socialization mediators of the relation between socioeconomic status and child conduct problems. *Child Development, 65*(2), 649–665.

Falk, R. F., & Miller, N. B. (1992). *A primer for soft modeling.* Akron, OH: University of Akron Press.

Gottman, J. M., & Katz, L. F. (1989). Effects of marital discord on young children's peer interaction and health. *Developmental Psychology, 25,* 373–381.

Hinshaw, S. P., Zupan, B. A., Simmel, C., Nigg, J. T., & Melnick, S. (1997). Peer status in boys with and without attention-deficit hyperactivity disorder: Predictions from overt and covert antisocial behavior, social isolation, and authoritative parenting beliefs. *Child Development, 68,* 880–896.

Katz, L. F., & Gottman, J. M. (1993). Patterns of marital conflict predict children's internalizing and externalizing behaviors. *Developmental Psychology, 29,* 940–950.

Laird, R. D., Jordan, K. Y., Dodge, K. A., Pettit, G. S., & Bates, J. E. (2001). Peer rejection in childhood, involvement with antisocial peers in early adolescence, and the development of externalizing behavior problems. *Development and Psychopathology, 13,* 337–354.

Maccoby, E. E., & Martin, J. A. (1983). Socialization in the context of the family: Parent-child interaction. In P. H. Mussen (Series Ed.) & E. M. Hetherington (Vol. Ed.), *Handbook of child psychology: Vol. 4. Socialization, personality and social development* (4th ed., pp. 1–101). New York: Wiley.

McClelland, G. H., & Judd, C. M. (1993). Statistical difficulties of detecting interactions and moderator effects. *Psychological Bulletin, 114,* 376–390.

McMahon, R. J., & Slough, N. M. (1996). Family-based intervention in the Fast Track Program. In R. D. Peters & R. J. McMahon (Eds.), *Preventing childhood disorders, substance abuse, and delinquency* (pp. 90–110). Thousand Oaks, CA: Sage.

Miller-Johnson, S., Coie, J. D., Maumary-Gremaud, A., Bierman, K., & the Conduct Problems Prevention Research Group (2002). Peer rejection and aggression and early starter models of conduct disorder. *Journal of Abnormal Child Psychology, (30)*3, 217–230.

O'Donnel, J. P., & Van Tuinen, M. V. (1979). Behavior problems of preschool children: Dimensions and congenital correlates. *Journal of Abnormal Child Psychology, 7*, 61–75.

Parke, R. D., & Buriel, R. (1998). Socialization in the family: Ethnic and ecological perspectives. In N. Eisenberg (Ed.), *Handbook of child psychology: Vol. 3. Social, emotional, and personality development* (5th ed., pp. 463–552). New York: Wiley.

Parke, R. D., & Ladd, G. W. (Eds.). (1992). *Family-peer relationships: Modes of linkage*. Hillsdale, NJ: Erlbaum.

Parker, J. G., & Asher, S. R. (1987). Peer relations and later personal adjustment: Are low-accepted children at risk? *Psychological Bulletin, 102*, 357–389.

Rubin, K. H., Bukowski, W., & Parker, J. G. (1998). Peer interactions, relationships, and groups. In N. Eisenberg (Ed.), *Handbook of child psychology: Vol. 3. Social, emotional, and personality development* (5th ed., pp. 619–700). New York: Wiley.

Schaefer, E. S., & Hunter, W. M. (1983, April). *Mother-infant interaction and maternal psychosocial predictors of kindergarten adaptation*. Paper presented at the biennial meeting of the Society for Research in Child Development, Detroit, MI.

Wood, J. J., Cowan, P. A., & Baker, B. L. (in press). Behavior problems and peer rejection in preschool boys and girls. *Journal of Genetic Psychology*.

Part IV _____

Intervention and Prevention

10

The Fast Track Experiment: Translating the Developmental Model Into a Prevention Design

Conduct Problems Prevention Research Group

In this chapter, we overview the Fast Track Program as an illustration of new directions evident in prevention science. In 1993, Coie and colleagues described prevention science as a new research discipline being formed at the interface of a number of professional emphases and disciplines, including psychopathology, criminology, psychiatric epidemiology, human development, and education. Prevention science represents an effort to examine risk factors, change processes, and intervention effects with highly rigorous methodology and thus to provide an empirical basis for the early prevention efforts initiated originally by community psychologists. This focus on prevention science has reenergized mental illness prevention efforts in psychology and related disciplines, making it more likely that the early promise and optimism about prevention can be realized (e.g., Allen, Chinsky, Larcen, Lochman, & Selinger, 1976; Cowen, 1973).

Five principles have been suggested as being important for prevention science (Coie et al., 1993): (a) prevention programs should address fundamental causal processes, (b) prevention programs should address risk factors before they become stabilized, (c) prevention programs should target those children

Members of the Conduct Problems Prevention Research Group include Karen L. Bierman, John D. Coie, Kenneth A. Dodge, E. Michael Foster, Mark T. Greenberg, John E. Lochman, Robert J. McMahon, and Ellen E. Pinderhughes.

This work was supported by National Institute of Mental Health (NIMH) grants R18 MH48043, R18 MH50951, R18 MH50952, and R18 MH50953. The Center for Substance Abuse Prevention and the National Institute on Drug Abuse also have provided support for Fast Track through memoranda of agreement with the NIMH. This work was also supported in part by Department of Education grant S184U30002 and NIMH grants K05MH00797 and K05MH01027.

We are grateful for the close collaboration of the Durham Public Schools, the Metropolitan Nashville Public Schools, the Bellefonte Area Schools, the Tyrone Area Schools, the Mifflin County Schools, the Highline Public Schools, and the Seattle Public Schools. We greatly appreciate the hard work and dedication of the many staff members who implemented the project, collected the evaluation data, and assisted with data management and analyses.

For additional information concerning Fast Track, see http://www.fasttrackproject.org.

who are at high risk for the negative outcome to be prevented, (d) prevention programs should optimally involve coordinated activities in multiple domains, and (e) developmental research has important implications for prevention science.

In the arena of adolescent antisocial behavior, a distinction has been made between two different pathways leading to adolescent delinquency and conduct problems, on the basis of age-related patterns of antisocial behavior (Coie, 1996). Early starters (also described as *life-course persistent*) begin their serious antisocial behavior early in childhood, as early as ages six to eight, and then continue antisocial behavior into adulthood (Moffitt, 1993; Patterson, Reid, & Dishion, 1992). Early starters have been described as being at risk for antisocial behavior because of a combination of biological and family factors, although in some cases family dysfunction may be sufficient to initiate the sequence of escalating aggressive behaviors. Early starters represent approximately 6% of the population (Offord, Boyle, & Racine, 1991). They are likely to engage in a versatile, wide-ranging set of antisocial behaviors, including both overt and covert delinquency (Loeber, 1990; Loeber et al., 1993). In contrast, late starters (also described as *adolescence-limited*) do not begin to exhibit antisocial behavior until early adolescence and usually desist by late adolescence or early adulthood, as they begin to engage in normative roles in the workplace and become involved in stable, intimate romantic relationships. Late starters are less likely to engage in violent crime than early starters. This distinction is consistent with the two subtypes of conduct disorder identified in the *DSM–IV* taxonomic system (American Psychiatric Association, 1994). Within this diagnostic system, oppositional defiant disorder evident in early childhood can evolve into childhood-onset conduct disorder, and then into antisocial personality disorder in adulthood. Childhood-onset conduct disorder is expected to be preceded by physical aggression and poor peer relationships in the elementary-school years. Because of their considerable influence on the rates of serious adolescent antisocial and criminal behavior, prevention programs are particularly needed to target early-starting conduct problem youth. These prevention programs need to be initiated early enough to impact the early stages of the developmental trajectory and need to be designed to influence the multiple causes and the chronic nature of this maladaptive process.

As this chapter explains, each of the five prevention science principles (Coie et al., 1993) is evident in the conceptual framework and intervention delivery plan for Fast Track, a prevention program designed to prevent adolescent problem behaviors and conduct disorder (Conduct Problems Prevention Research Group, 1992). Coie (1996) articulated a developmental model for the prevention of adolescent antisocial behavior, and this model suggests important directions for serious prevention efforts. First, many children at risk for adolescent antisocial behavior can be identified as early as six to seven years of age, on the basis of their display of diverse aggressive, disruptive, and noncompliant behaviors across home and school settings. Second, because high-risk children are likely to progress in a spiral of escalating and more severe behavioral problems over time, early intervention is critical. As the child's behavior spirals down, the child becomes enmeshed in accumulating risk factors, such as peer rejection and academic failure, clearly complicating the ease and effectiveness of intervention. Third, risk cannot be conceived as a static marker, but instead the topography of the risk markers is likely to change with age; more important, early risk factors influence subsequent processes within the child and the family that mediate the child's ultimate antisocial outcomes. These mutable processes can then become the targets for well-conceived prevention programs. Fast Track, in fact, utilized the implications of these developmental patterns to design a prevention program for children. Children with behavior problems evident at home and at school were identified at school entry; intervention began early (in first grade); and the focus of the intervention was adapted progressively from first grade to high school to address developmentally appropriate mediating processes within the child and the child's family and school context.

In the following sections, we explore how research on children's social relationships led to recognition of the behavioral causes and consequences of being rejected by peer groups and to early, partially successful intervention efforts with children with poor peer relationships. On the basis of these early studies and accumulating information about the broad range of mediating factors influencing antisocial behavior, the developmental model that serves as the foundation for Fast Track was articulated. Because it is essential that the developmental model of a preventive intervention map clearly onto the intervention research study's measurement model and onto the intervention model (Coie, 1996), we examine how the Fast Track developmental model was integrated into the corresponding intervention model. The design and procedures for the Fast Track study are outlined, and initial findings of the efficacy of the program are reviewed.

Children's Poor Peer Relationships: Behavioral Correlates and Interventions

Consequences of Peer Rejection

There has been accumulating evidence over the past 20 years that children who have been rejected by their peers during the grade school and preadolescent period have serious negative consequences later (Asher & Coie, 1990). Social rejection has been found to be predictive of a variety of outcomes, including later delinquency, school dropout, and internalizing problems (Coie, Dodge, & Kupersmidt, 1990). In a series of studies with longitudinal designs, social rejection has emerged as a reliable predictor of adolescent and adult criminality, sexual promiscuity and adolescent pregnancy, suicide, schizophrenia, and drug use and alcoholism (McFadyen-Ketchum & Dodge, 1998).

However, because social rejection often covaries with aggressive behavior, it has been unclear whether social rejection is a useful independent indicator of later maladjustment or whether it is essentially a noncausal marker variable for aggression, with aggression responsible for the prediction of later problems (Coie, 1990; Bierman & Wargo, 1995; Coie et al., 1990; McFadyen-Ketchum & Dodge, 1998; Parker & Asher, 1987). A number of longitudinal studies have now documented a causal role for peer rejection along with aggressive behavior.

In a study of African American children who were originally assessed in third grade, Coie, Lochman, Terry, and Hyman (1992) found that both peer rejection *and* aggression were useful predictors of middle-school maladjustment, assessed through parent, teacher, and self ratings. The percentage of children who were maladjusted in middle school doubled for children who, in third grade, had been either rejected and nonaggressive, or aggressive and nonrejected, in comparison with children who had been neither aggressive nor rejected. Even more striking, children who had been both aggressive and rejected had triple the risk rate for later adjustment problems. Thus, it appeared that peer rejection and aggression were additive risk factors for middle-school problems. Similarly, Dodge (1993) found that for both boys and girls, aggressive-rejected kindergarten children had higher rates of third-grade aggression than did other kindergartners, and Bierman and Wargo (1995) found that aggressive-rejected children had more problematic longitudinal outcomes than did aggressive-nonrejected or rejected-nonaggressive children.

This early predictive role for rejection and aggression continues to be apparent even as adolescents develop through the high school years. In general, early childhood aggression appears to predict a wider range of adolescent offending and of involvement in deviant peer groups than does rejection alone (Coie, Terry, Zakriski, & Lochman, 1995; Miller-Johnson, Coie, Maumary-Gremaud, Lochman, & Terry, 1999). However, the combination of aggression and rejection in third grade has predicted serious and nonserious offending through the high school years for boys, and this prediction has been especially evident in predicting felony assault (Miller-Johnson, Coie, et al., 1999). These predictors have less robust capacity to predict adolescent girls' antisocial behavior, although earlier peer rejection does predict adolescent girls' minor assault offenses, and aggression emerges as a primary predictor for girls' juvenile childbearing and arrests (Coie, Terry, Lenox, et al., 1995; Miller-Johnson, Coie, et al., 1999; Miller-Johnson, Winn, et al., 1999). Thus, the picture that emerges is that maladjusted development is not due just to children's deviant behavior or to their social standing with peers; instead, both factors are intertwined and must be considered as risk factors (McFayden-Ketchum & Dodge, 1998) and as factors for identifying children in need of interventions to enhance their social relationships.

Causes and Correlates of Peer Rejection

The child's behavioral and personal characteristics appear to play central roles in the emergence of peer rejection (Coie, 1990). Although some children are rejected by peers because of their physical appearance (Coie, Dodge, & Coppotelli, 1982; Langlois & Stephen, 1981) or, in later childhood, because of their withdrawal from their peer group (Rubin, LeMare, & Lollis, 1990), these factors do not appear to be the most common cause of rejection and, in the case of withdrawal, can be the result of earlier rejection rather than the cause (Coie, 1990). The clearest and most common behavioral pattern that contributes to increasing peer rejection involves aggressive and disruptive behavior (Coie, Dodge, & Kupersmidt, 1990). Longitudinal research conducted by Coie and his colleagues indicated not only that aggressive behavior was a concurrent factor characterizing rejected children, but also that earlier aggression predicted subsequent rejection as well. For this reason, peer rejection has come to be seen as intrinsically, inextricably interwoven with the development of problematic aggressive and disruptive child behaviors. It has become clear that not all types of aggression at all ages are similarly related to rejection. For example, the tendency to escalate the level of aggression after it begins and the failure to stop aggression until the other participant submits are particularly related to peers' rejection of the aggressor (Coie, 1987, 1990).

Once children have become disliked and rejected by their peer group, then certain processes serve to maintain this maladaptive state of peer relations. Being rejected becomes part of the child's identity and often leads to malignant expectations by the child and his or her peer group (Coie, 1990). Rejected children begin to expect that they will not be well received by their peers and hence are often hesitant to initiate entry into peer activities (Coie & Kupersmidt, 1983; Putallaz & Wasserman, 1989). In addition, their rejected status leads to the creation of increasingly toxic social environments around them, as the rejected children's peers have been found to be more aversive with rejected children than with their nonrejected peers (Coie & Kupersmidt, 1983; Dodge, 1983). Because of these expectations and behavioral patterns, children's rejected peer status often becomes stable and ultimately begins to predict later, more severe adolescent adjustment problems (Coie et al., 1992; Lochman & Wayland, 1994).

Social Relations Interventions

Because of the clear implications of children's peer rejection for the development of personal maladjustment, increasing isolation and reliance on deviant peer groups, and increasingly antisocial and problematic outcomes in adolescence, intervention programs have been developed to reduce rejection in the grade school years (Coie & Koeppl, 1990). In the 1970s and the 1980s, the primary focus of these programs was to reduce children's peer isolation. To do so, social skills training programs focused on promoting rejected children's positive play skills, interaction initiation skills, and communication skills. In early studies, social skills training programs were found to improve girls' social preference scores (Gottman, Gonso, & Schuler, 1976), and children became more preferred as playmates by their peers (Gresham & Nagle, 1980; Oden & Asher, 1977), although little change was evident in children's observed interactional behavior in these early efforts. However, augmenting the intervention programs with coaching (direct instruction and modeling, behavioral rehearsal, and performance feedback) produced improvements in some social behaviors as well as changes in peer status (Ladd, 1981; LaGreca & Santogrossi, 1980). In a creative effort to enhance these effects of social skills training and coaching programs, Bierman and Furman (1984) added group experiences in which low-accepted children worked with classmates on cooperative tasks, such as making videotape films of friendly interactions. This program did produce improvements in children's peer acceptance and in positive peer interactions at postintervention, but the improvements in social behavior had faded by the six-week follow-up for the intervention group as a whole.

Although these programs were focused on rejected children in general and on skills designed to promote more frequent positive interactions with peers, they did not primarily address some of the more problematic correlates of peer rejection, such as aggressive and disruptive behaviors. Approximately one-third of socially rejected children are also found to be highly aggressive according to peer ratings, and about one-third are nominated by peers as being highly disruptive (Coie & Koeppl, 1990). Disruptive behaviors typically reduce on-task behavior, inhibiting academic progress as well as disturbing peers. Thus, it became clear that interventions for rejected children should also logically begin to emphasize the aggressive-disruptive behavioral correlates of rejection, and vice versa.

INTERVENTIONS ADDRESSING ACADEMIC DIFFICULTIES. Coie and Krehbiel (1984) examined whether interventions directed at helping rejected children to perform better academically might also influence their social standing. Children who had received tutoring in reading and academic skills demonstrated improvements in reading comprehension and in their social preference scores, at posttest and at a one-year follow-up. These gains were maintained more fully for children who had received tutoring and coaching than for children who had received social skills coaching alone. These important findings indicate that improving children's academic progress and ability to remain on-task in the classroom can also have a positive impact on their social acceptance by their peers.

INTERVENTIONS ADDRESSING AGGRESSIVE BEHAVIOR. Accumulating empirical support has identified several interventions as well-established or promising treatments for children's aggressive, oppositional, and conduct disordered behavior (Brestan & Eyberg, 1998; Kazdin & Weisz, 1998). Most notably, behavioral parent training programs have produced significant reductions in children's and adolescents' aggressive behavior (e.g., Eyberg, Boggs, & Algina, 1995; McMahon & Forehand, 1984; Patterson et al., 1992; Webster-Stratton & Hammond, 1997). Although these parent training programs vary considerably in the specific intervention procedures and activities used in the interventions, they share a common focus on enhancing the parents' abilities to provide social reinforcement for children's positive behavior, to provide clear expectations and directions to their children, and to use discipline methods such as time-out, response cost, privilege removal, contingency contracts, and simple token economies consistently.

Other sets of promising interventions for children's aggressive behavior are more child-focused and involve promoting the development of children's social problem-solving skills and anger management abilities, either with groups of aggressive children (e.g., Feindler, Marriott, & Iwata, 1984; Kazdin, Siegel, & Bass, 1992; Lochman, 1992; Lochman & Wells, 2002) or within classroom settings (Durlak, 1995; Greenberg, Kusche, Cook, & Quamma, 1995). These programs typically have activities that target children's emotional expression and emotional understanding, accurate awareness of others' intentions, anger and emotional regulation, and social problem-solving skills. Interventions that have multiple components targeting both parenting skills and child social-cognitive skills have been found to be particularly effective in reducing children's aggression, especially at follow-up (Kazdin et al., 1992; Lochman & Wells, in press; Vitaro, Brendgen, Pagani, Tremblay, & McDuff, 1999; Webster-Stratton & Hammond, 1997).

INTERVENTIONS ADDRESSING SOCIAL SKILLS AND AGGRESSIVE, DISRUPTIVE BEHAVIOR. Coie and Koeppl (1990) suggested that although social skills training programs had some impact on children's positive interaction skills, social relations programs for rejected children who were also aggressive should include components directed specifically at reducing aggressive behavior as well as promoting positive social skills. Bierman, Miller, and Stabb (1987) had found that aggressive-rejected children who were receiving either social skills coaching or a behavioral intervention displayed reductions in negative behavior at a six-week follow-up, but it was only in the combined social skills and behavioral intervention that children were found to have fewer negative sociometric nominations from nonrejected play partners who were used in the intervention (Bierman et al., 1987). However, even children in the combined condition, who had behavioral improvements and improved status with play partners, did not have improvements in their social status in their classrooms, which suggests that peer perceptions and negative reputations had not caught up with their positive behavior changes.

To further research in this area, Coie and colleagues initiated in the 1980s a longitudinal study of intervention effects with rejected children, some of whom were also aggressive (Lochman, Coie, Underwood, & Terry, 1993). Fifty-two African American fourth-grade aggressive-rejected and nonaggressive-rejected children were randomly assigned to a social relations intervention or to a nonintervention control group. The social relations intervention included both (a) skill training elements designed to promote prosocial behaviors, focusing on skills involved in playing with and maintaining relationships with peers and on skills involved in successfully joining group activities, and (b) cognitive-behavioral elements designed to inhibit reflexive negative responses and stimulate adaptive social problem-solving thinking. Although there were no intervention effects with the nonaggressive-rejected children, aggressive-rejected children who received the intervention demonstrated reductions in teacher-rated aggression, improvements in teacher-rated prosocial behaviors, and improvements in peer-rated social acceptance, in comparison with the aggressive-rejected control group. These positive effects were maintained at a one-year follow-up, although the gains in peer-rated social acceptance had declined. The results did indicate that this broader approach to intervening with both the problem behaviors and prosocial skills could influence children's social status following intervention.

Although promising outcomes on children's aggressive behavior and social relationships were demonstrated in this set of social skills intervention studies, the effects were typically of modest magnitude and dissipated over time. This state of affairs led Coie and his colleagues to begin planning a more comprehensive, multicomponent intervention, known as Fast Track, for children with aggressive-disruptive behaviors and associated social problems. Initial meetings between John Coie, Karen Bierman, and Mark Greenberg led to their joint commitment to seek funding in response to a request for applications from the National Institute of Mental Health (NIMH) to rigorously evaluate interventions designed to prevent conduct disorder. They then sought the involvement of Kenneth Dodge, John Lochman, and Robert McMahon in the investigative team which, with the NIMH funding, developed, implemented, and is evaluating the Fast Track intervention. In more recent years Ellen Pinderhughes has also become an integral member of the investigative team. The Fast Track investigators began by conceptualizing the developmental model that would provide the foundation for the program; they then created measurement models and intervention models that closely mirrored the developmental model.

The Fast Track Developmental Model

Because of the limitations evident in the prior efforts to reduce children's aggressive and disruptive behavior across settings and over time, and to clearly demonstrate preventive effects on serious adolescent antisocial behavior, the Fast Track investigators believed there was a need to examine a broader set of risk and causal factors that can lead to adolescent conduct disorder. Thus, rather than intervening only with children's behavior, or even only with parents' and children's behaviors, intervention should address other academic, peer, school, and neighborhood factors that have been linked to antisocial behavior. The Fast Track intervention is guided by a developmental theory that asserts that multiple influences interact in the development of antisocial behavior (Conduct Problems Prevention Research Group, 1992; Conduct Problems Prevention Research Group, 2000). The effects of early home environment, exacerbated by neighborhood stressors such as poverty and crime, interact during the preschool years with child factors such as impulsivity and irritability to leave high-risk children cognitively, emotionally, and behaviorally unprepared for school. The intervention model is divided into two major phases: the elementary-school and adolescent periods. The elementary-school phase of the prevention program addresses six areas of risk and protective factors derived from the developmental model: parenting, child social problem-solving and emotional coping skills, peer relations, classroom atmosphere and curriculum, academic achievement with a focus on reading, and home–school relations. The adolescent phase emphasizes four domains associated with successful adolescent adjustment: peer affiliation and peer influence, academic orientation and achievement, social cognition and identity development, and parent and family relations.

Preschool and Elementary-School Years

Along with constitutional irritability and impulsivity (Bates, Bayles, Bennett, Ridge, & Brown, 1991; Campbell, Breaux, Ewing, & Szumowski, 1986), environmental and contextual factors during the early preschool and grade school years contribute to children's long-term antisocial development (Coie, 1996; Conduct Problems Prevention Research Group, 1992). At the community level, living in poor, crime-ridden neighborhoods, having relatively few support services and community resources for parents, and having parents who are isolated and disconnected from helpful social supports contribute to children's risk. These community-level factors contribute to parents' experience of high levels of stress. Other sources of parental stress and risk factors for children's development are parents' marginal employment and parent psychopathology, criminality, limited educational attainment, marital conflict, and single parenting (Coie, 1996; Dodge, Bates, & Pettit, 1990; Offord, Alder, & Boyle, 1986).

Contextual difficulties in the child's family and community, often in combination with a child's unusually high level of impulsivity and irritability, set the stage for potentially negative parent–child relations characterized by increasingly coercive interactions between a parent and child. Parents resort to harsh but often inconsistent discipline in response to children's oppositional behaviors, and this variability in parental response contributes to the parents' inadvertent reinforcement of their children's increasing noncompliance (Snyder & Patterson, 1995). In this coercive cycle, both the parents and the child may then increase their rates of aversive behaviors toward each other. Sometimes the child's whining and noncompliance are reinforced when a parent finally gives in; sometimes the parent's escalating harsh, abusive behavior stops the child's behavior, and thus is reinforced (Patterson, 1982). The parents' behavior during these coercive struggles also models the use of aggressive, violent behaviors to dominate others, and the result of these modeling and reinforcement effects is the child's growing reliance on aversive behavior to get what he or she wants.

Coercive parent–child interactions are often accompanied by low rates of positive parental interaction with the child and inadequate parental stimulation and support of the child's developing cognitive skills, social skills, and adaptive emotional regulation capabilities (Cook, Greenberg, & Kusche, 1994; Greenberg, Kusche, & Speltz, 1991). Thus, in addition to relying on highly aversive behaviors to control others, the high-risk child may also enter school poorly prepared for its social and academic demands. The deficits that evolve in children's language abilities because of an impoverished, nonstimulating environment can contribute both to poor reading readiness and to delays in the children's ability to use their cognitive processes to regulate their emotional and behavioral reactions (Coie, 1996; Greenberg et al., 1991). The combination of parents' harsh discipline and uninvolved parent–child interactions, in turn, may impede the development of children's adaptive social-cognitive skills. Children can become hypervigilant to hostile cues and intentions from others and can adopt problem-solving styles that are overly action-oriented and that lack verbally assertive and cooperative strategies (Crick & Dodge, 1994; Dodge, Lochman, Harnish, Bates, & Pettit, 1997; Lochman & Dodge, 1994, 1998). In this developmental model, biologically-based risk factors in the child combine with stressors from the larger community context on the family and with family socialization practices to produce children who enter school poorly prepared for the cognitive, emotional, and social tasks of this important developmental setting.

During the elementary-school years, the negative influence of the contextual risk factors (e.g., poor-quality neighborhoods, poor parenting practices, family pathology, and parental isolation) continues to fuel child aggressive and disruptive behaviors (Greenberg, Lengua, Coie, Pinderhughes, & Conduct Problems Prevention Research Group, 1999). In many cases, the school context becomes an exacerbating rather than a corrective influence. Many high-risk children attend schools with a high density of other unprepared children like themselves (Rutter et al., 1979), which makes effective teaching and school-based preventive interventions difficult (Aber, Jones, Brown, Chaudry, & Samples, 1998; Kellam, Ling, Merisca, Brown, & Ialongo, 1998). As a result, the teachers, like the parents in earlier years, can inadvertently begin to use inconsistent discipline and be verbally harsh and coercive (Coie, 1996). Finally, the parents of high-risk children often have their own history of school problems, and their discomfort in educational settings may lead to a lack of synchrony between home and school. This dysynchrony may be reflected in ineffective and acrimonious communications between parents and teachers, which undermine the child's chance for success (Comer, 1980).

As noted earlier in this chapter, aggressive and disruptive children often become rejected by peers over time (Ladd, Price, & Hart, 1990) and, in turn, become more distrustful of peers (Dodge & Coie, 1987). Their peers begin to stigmatize them and react to them in unusually aggressive ways (Dodge, 1989; Dodge & Coie, 1987). The problematic children's social difficulties are often exacerbated by difficult relationships with their teachers (Coie, 1996). Teachers provide less support to these children, in comparison with their classmates, rather than the increased support they need (Campbell, 1991; Dodge, Coie, & Brakke, 1982). By preadolescence, parental rejection of their problematic children can become more pronounced because of increasingly aversive parent–child interactions and unpleasant confrontations with teachers and other school personnel as a result of the children's school difficulties (Patterson & Bank, 1989; Patterson, DeBaryshe, & Ramsey, 1989). As a result, high-risk children, who have had histories of poor school performance and poor peer relations in elementary school, get ready for their transition to middle school alienated from their most important sources of support and social bonding: family and school (Hawkins & Weiss, 1985).

Middle School and High School Years

Adolescence is marked by changes in both youth characteristics and the contextual influences affecting adjustment. Contextually, youth move from self-contained, single-teacher elementary classrooms to large, fluid middle or junior high schools (Eccles & Midgley, 1990; Eccles, Midgley, & Adler, 1984), which leads to reductions in parent and teacher support and monitoring. Consequently, youth spend more time with and are more influenced by their peers. Four core domains are critical for their successful adaptation: (a) peer affiliation and peer influence, (b) academic achievement and academic orientation,

(c) social cognition and identity development, and (d) parent and family relations.

PEER AFFILIATION AND INFLUENCE. Alienation from conventional sources of social support from parents, teachers, and nondeviant peers can lead high-risk youth to join other adolescents like themselves (Cairns, Cairns, Neckerman, Gest, & Gariepy, 1988; Coie, 1996). Adolescents who associate with deviant peers have a substantially increased risk for adolescent problem behaviors (Aultman, 1980). Keenan, Loeber, Zhang, Stouthamer-Loeber, and Van Kammen (1995) found that, in comparison with boys who did not have best friends who were truant or disobedient, disruptive boys who did have deviant peer associations had three to four times the odds of participating in covert and overt delinquent acts. Adolescents appear to reinforce each others' antisocial beliefs within deviant peer groups (Dishion, Eddy, Haas, & Spracklen, 1997; Dishion, Patterson, & Griesler, 1994).

Deviant peer influences serve both to escalate the seriousness of offending among those youth with a history of delinquency and to instigate initial delinquency among those with more marginal risk profiles (Thornberry, 1987; Vitaro, Tremblay, Kerr, Pagani-Kurtz, & Bukowski, in press). Membership in deviant peer cliques in eighth grade has been found to predict adolescents' rate of police arrests, even for youth who did not fit the early-starting profile (Coie, Terry, Lochman, & Miller-Johnson, 1995).

Whereas girls are at considerably lower risk than boys for overt aggression during elementary school, their risk for becoming involved in early sexual activity, substance use, and covert antisocial activity rises in adolescence, largely because of associations with older antisocial boys (Caspi, Lynam, Moffitt, & Silva, 1993). Girls who enter puberty early and who have learning problems and depressed mood are at elevated risk for associations with deviant boys who, in turn, encourage behaviors such as truancy, substance use, covert delinquency, and sexual activity. For example, girls with this early behavior problem profile are the ones at greatest risk for having babies prior to age 14 (Miller-Johnson et al., 1999).

ACADEMIC ACHIEVEMENT AND ACADEMIC ORIENTATION. Children who have low commitment to school and high rates of school failure are at risk for a range of adolescent problem behaviors (Hawkins, Catalano, & Miller, 1992). Adolescents who dislike school and spend little time on homework are frequently truant, show poor achievement, and have high rates of drug use (Hawkins et al., 1992; Hundleby & Mercer, 1987). Increasing school adaptation by fostering social support in the school setting, promoting positive attitudes toward education, and supporting academic achievement may avoid adolescents' declines in school attachment and self-esteem (Harter, 1986; Hirsch & DuBois, 1991) and reduce negative outcomes such as early initiation of sexual activity (Billy, Landale, Grady, & Zimmerle, 1988; Ohannesian & Crockett, 1993).

SOCIAL COGNITION AND IDENTITY DEVELOPMENT. Adolescents' rates of problem behaviors are heavily influenced by their deviance-prone attitudes and beliefs, such as their low values for school attendance and academic achievement and high toleration of, and values for, deviant behaviors such as stealing and lying (Wills & Filer, 1996). Adolescents who have histories of violence, delinquency, and substance use often lack effective coping skills, demonstrating impulsive behavioral reactivity, poor self-control, weak problem-solving skills, hostile attributional biases, and dominance-oriented social goals (Dodge, Lochman, Harnish, Bates, & Pettit, 1997; Lochman, Wayland, & White, 1993; Wills & Filer, 1996).

As adolescents become increasingly autonomous and as demands for self-discipline increase in schoolwork and other areas, the importance of a positive self-identity increases. Adolescents' *possible selves,* or their images of who they would strive to be, serve to guide adolescents' choices and are important motivators of their behavior (Marcus & Nurias, 1986; Oyserman & Markus, 1993). Among high-risk youth, resilient adolescents are those who develop a positive sense of self, perceive themselves to have internal control over their environment, and have good problem-solving skills and a strong network of relationships with adults (Luthar & Zigler, 1991; Werner, 1986). Indeed, interventions that combine training in social influence resistance with problem solving and decision making have produced reductions in the prevalence of substance use (Botvin, 1986; Hansen, Graham, Wolkenstein, & Lundy, 1988; Pentz et al., 1989). In addition, the availability of a positive adult role model or mentor who is of the same race and gender as the high-risk youth may serve as a protective factor promoting the development of a positive sense of self and supporting effective coping skills (Becker, 1994; Saito & Blyth, 1994).

For some adolescents, especially in certain minority groups, subcultural values and expectations make it difficult to attain certain positive goals, such as achieving school success. Socially marked identities, such as being an African American male, can make adolescents vulnerable to failure because they provide expectations of, and presumed explanations for, failure (Steele & Aronson, 1995). Thus, many African American males may not pursue academic success because of the shared expectation that academic failure is unavoidable and because of their perceptions of their peer groups' resulting lack of positive value for school success.

PARENT AND FAMILY RELATIONS. Poor parenting, involving weak monitoring, ineffective parental control, and low levels of parent support, contributes directly to adolescent deviant behavior (Chassin et al., 1996). Because of the greater mobility of adolescents and their increased needs for personal privacy, parents have less opportunity to monitor their adolescents' activities and their friendships. Research indicates that poor parental monitoring and discipline play a critical role in adolescents' involvement in deviant peer groups and in early- and late-onset delinquency and drug use (Dishion, French, & Patterson, 1995; Dishion & McMahon, 1998; Patterson & Yoerger, 1997).

Strong bonds of attachment to family serve a protective function in youth otherwise at risk for delinquency and substance abuse (Brook, 1993; Johnson & Pandina, 1991). Productive parent-adolescent communication, joint problem solving, and collaborative planning are all indices of supportive family relations in adolescence; interventions focused on promoting communication and conflict resolution skills along with family problem-solving meetings reduce adolescent acting-out behaviors (Henggeler, Schoenwald, & Pickrel, 1995). Effective parental monitoring works both directly through its effects on the adolescents' behavior and indirectly through its effects on the adolescents' involvement in certain peer groups (Fletcher, Darling, & Steinberg, 1995). Promoting positive parent–child relationships, fostering effective parent–adolescent communications, and enhancing parental monitoring and supervision skills may all thus contribute to reductions in adolescent risk for deviant behaviors.

Design for the Fast Track Experiment

This developmental model indicates that the dysfunctional development that is associated with the early-starting pattern of conduct problems is multiply determined and is embedded in transactions among family, peer, school, and neighborhood influences and child characteristics. Hence, prevention efforts must target both the promotion of individual competencies and the promotion of protective contextual supports. Preventive interventions must also be attentive to age-related stressors and the successive issues of risk across important developmental periods (Cicchetti, 1984). Early-starting conduct problems turn into serious and chronic problems because they divert the individual child into a sequence of experiences that intensify risk.

Data from the Rochester study (Thornberry, Huizinga, & Loeber, 1995) suggest that protective factors must be continuously present during the transition from early to late adolescence and not simply in place at a single point in childhood or adolescence. Although the negative impact of early risk factors may be buffered by the provision of protective support services during the grade school years, the risk factors themselves may continue to influence developmental trajectories during adolescence. For example, the high rates of inattention, impulsivity, and cognitive deficits that contribute to the school adjustment problems of many early-starting youth (Moffitt, 1990) may be buffered when protective support is offered during elementary school in the form of academic tutoring and effective teacher management. As the demands for focused attention and independent work completion increase with the transition to middle school, these cognitive risk factors may undermine school adaptation unless continuing support is offered at later grade levels. In addition, developmental research suggests that new risk factors emerge during adolescence that are associated with the escalation of antisocial and related adolescent behavior problems. Elementary-school prevention may improve child readiness to tackle the new challenges of adolescence. However, for high-risk children living in unstable and risky contexts without effective protective supports, the challenges of adolescence may also undermine the gains produced by early preventive efforts. Thus, a successful program for preventing serious antisocial problems requires a long-term intervention commitment.

The significance of the Fast Track Project is that it addresses the three organizing principles for the prevention of serious violent delinquency outlined by Thornberry et al. (1995): it starts early, it is comprehensive, and it is carried out over the long term of development. In Fast Track, high-risk youth were selected at school entry from poor, high-crime neighborhoods. The elementary-school intervention addressed the major risk factors implicated in the initiation of early-starting conduct problems and used an integrated set of developmentally sensitive intervention components to promote competencies in parents (parent training and home visiting), teachers (prevention curriculum and classroom management consultation), and children (social skills training and academic tutoring) and to strengthen bonds of communication between parents and teachers.

The design of the study is a randomized trial with randomization at the level of the school, as children entered first grade. The project contains two levels of preventive intervention (universal; indicated) as well as two types of participants (high risk; all students). Yearly assessments with multiple sources of data for measure constructs are collected. The design permits continuous evaluation of the developmental model, in both tests of mediation of the effects of intervention on the high-risk youth and longer-term modeling of risk-outcomes relationships within the normative sample and the control sample of high-risk youth.

In January 1991, crime records, poverty statistics, and school dropout rates were used to identify 56 high-risk schools in four geographic sites around the country (Durham, NC; Nashville, TN; Seattle, WA; rural central PA). With a multiple-gating procedure for three annual cohorts, all kindergartners were screened for classroom conduct problems by teachers and for home behavior problems by the parents (Lochman & Conduct Problems Prevention Research Group, 1995). Children in the top 10% of risk according to this screening were included in the high-risk group, and their parents were invited to consent to participate in the study ($N = 891$). Schools were then assigned in matched sets either to the intervention or to the control conditions. Analyses of the initial comparability of the intervention and control groups indicated that there were no significant preintervention differences between the groups on demographic and behavioral variables. Analyses of indicated intervention effects with the high-risk group of children thus use this sample of 891 children ($n = 445$ intervention, $n = 446$ control). Analyses of universal intervention effects are conducted with the full populations of the intervention and control schools. The universal intervention continues throughout the elementary-school years. The indicated intervention continues through tenth grade.

To compare improvements made by the intervention group with a normative standard, a representative sample of 387 children was selected from the control schools. Children were stratified to represent the population according to race, sex, and decile of teacher screen scores.

The Fast Track Intervention Model

The Fast Track intervention will be described in its two primary phases: (a) elementary school and (b) transition to middle and high schools, coinciding with the transition to adolescence.

Elementary-School Phase

Corresponding to the developmental risks associated with the early initiation of conduct problems, prevention activities during elementary school targeted the provision of positive behavioral support at school and at home; fostering of the home–school relationship; promotion of parenting skills, child social skills, child social-cognitive skills, and child reading skills; and provision of mentoring for children by a same-sex, same-race community volunteer. Intervention components focused both on building the child's behavioral and cognitive skills and on changing the patterns of interaction with important people in the child's social environment (family, school, and peer) to promote healthy relationships with peers and adults.

The intervention was organized developmentally and included three levels of prevention activities: (a) universal prevention support provided at the school level; (b) standard indicated prevention support services provided to families of children identified as high-risk during the initial kindergarten screening; and (c) additional individualized indicated prevention support provided to high-risk children and families on an as-needed basis (according to criterion-referenced assessments). Prevention support was intensive with massed sessions offered at the important transition into elementary school (grades 1–2). Sustained support was then continued through fifth grade. The content of each of the prevention services was organized developmentally and integrated across components.

At the universal level of prevention, an adaptation of the Promoting Alternative THinking Strategies (PATHS) curriculum (Kusche & Greenberg, 1993) was taught by classroom teachers 2–3 times per week in grades 1 to 5. The PATHS curriculum model synthesizes the domains of self-control, emotional awareness and understanding, peer-related social skills, and social problem solving to increase social and emotional competence (Greenberg & Kusche, 1993). In addition to a person-oriented model that focuses primarily on developmental integration, the intervention model incorporates an eco-behavioral systems orientation (Weissberg, Caplan, & Sivo, 1989), which places primacy on the manner in which the teacher uses the curriculum model. Program impact may be the greatest when teachers generalize support for curriculum-based skills during the day and build a healthy classroom atmosphere that supports the child's skill use and internalization of skills. It is presumed that improvements in social competence can be a function of changes in the child, changes in the ecology, and their interaction. Fast Track staff also consulted with the school principal to bring the philosophy of PATHS to the entire school, resulting in various efforts (on a school-by-school basis) such as placing PATHS posters in school hallways, implementing new school behavior guidelines, and painting problem-solving "stoplights" on school playgrounds.

Classroom teachers were trained in the administration of this curriculum and provided individualized teacher consultation about behavioral management issues. In the early school years, targeted skills were designed to enhance adaptation to the rules and routines of school and to foster the development of positive peer relations. In later years, more advanced topics included decision-making skills, study skills, goal setting, character development, coping with peer pressure, and problem-solving skills.

At the standard indicated level of prevention, two-hour family group meetings were held regularly at local schools. Sessions were held weekly for 22 sessions in grade 1, biweekly for 14 sessions in grade 2, and monthly for 8 sessions each year in grades 3–5. Each session involved separate 60-minute group meetings for parents and social skills training meetings for children. Children then received 30 minutes of tutoring in reading skills, led by a trained paraprofessional and observed by the parent. The last 30 minutes of each session included a parent–child sharing session, in which parents and children participated in joint activities. Parent groups promoted the development of positive family–school relationships (e.g., Burgoyne, Hawkins, & Catalano, 1991) and taught effective communication and discipline skills (including praise and ignoring, clear instructions and rules, and time out) (Forehand & McMahon, 1981; Webster-Stratton, 1989). Child social skills groups focused on friendship and play skills (Bierman et al., 1987; Ladd, 1981; Oden & Asher, 1977) and self-control skills, anger-coping strategies, and interpersonal problem-solving skills (Coie & Koeppl, 1990; Lochman & Conduct Problems Prevention Research Group, 1995; Lochman et al., 1993). Parent–child sharing sessions promoted positive relationships and offered parents an opportunity to practice new parenting skills with staff guidance. As with PATHS, the skill topics addressed in the parent and child groups followed a developmental sequence, with an increasing emphasis over time on communication skills, homework study skills, goal setting, and negotiating parent–child conflicts. (See Bierman, Greenberg, & Conduct Problems Prevention Research Group, 1996; and McMahon, Slough, & Conduct Problems Prevention Research Group, 1996, for extensive descriptions of this phase of intervention.)

Individualized indicated services included academic tutoring, home visiting, and school-based peer pairing to promote friendships. Children and families received a standard level of these services in grade 1. In subsequent years, criterion-referenced assessments were used to adjust the dosage of these three indicated components to match the level of functioning of each family and child. In grade 4, a mentoring program was added, reflecting the growing significance of the child's identity development and the importance of same-gender, same-race positive role models in the identity development process.

Adolescent Phase

The adolescent phase of the intervention plan covered grades 5–10 (Conduct Problems Prevention Research Group, 2000). It began with intensive prevention efforts around the transition into middle school (grades 5–7) that were followed by continuing individualized preventive support through grades 8–10. Because of a growing dispersion of the target sample across schools, it was not possible to serve a substantial segment of the sample with a universal prevention curriculum in adolescence.

Reflecting the developmental characteristics of adolescence, the intervention design differed in some fundamental ways from the design used in the elementary phase. Monthly group sessions involving parents and youth continued during grades 5 and 6. As in the elementary phase, these sessions were held at the school (or other community location), were two hours long, and included separate meetings for parents and youth, along with periods for parent–youth discussion. However, reflecting the protective role of adult supervision and monitoring in adolescence and the corresponding importance of parent–youth communication, group sessions increasingly emphasized joint presentations to parents and youth, along with guided parent–youth discussions. Second, the emerging abstract reasoning capabilities of young adolescents, coupled with their increased independence and mobility, created an opportunity and need to focus on identity development, future goals, and decision making around both vocational and avocational interests and activities. To meet this need, the adolescent phase intervention included identity development workshops for youth in grades 7 and 8, called youth forums. Third, adolescence is marked by several critical developmental changes, including puberty, the initiation of romantic relationships and sexual activity, increasing peer group affiliation, and identity development. Youth differ markedly in the age at which and speed with which pubertal development and these other changes occur, creating heterogeneity that has implications for risk and for preventive intervention. As adolescents become more peer-oriented, deviant peer groups also emerge in early adolescence and can function to support and facilitate antisocial activity (Dishion & Andrews, 1995). Group-based interventions for high-risk adolescents can unwittingly strengthen deviant peer affiliations and thus sabotage prevention effectiveness. Given the need to respond to increasing heterogeneity within the Fast Track adolescent sample, along with the need to avoid supporting deviant affiliations, individualized criterion-referenced services (rather than group sessions) were emphasized in the later grades (grades 7–10).

During the adolescent phase, the standard prevention activities included two kinds of curriculum-based parent and youth groups: (a) groups focused on developmental issues of adolescence, held monthly during grades 5–6 and during the beginning of grade 7, and (b) an additional set of group meetings that comprised a transition support program, timed around the student's transition into middle school or junior high school (grades 5–6 or 6–7, depending on the local school organization). The key goal of the groups was to introduce skills that could delay the onset and reduce the severity of adolescent problems. Topics for parent groups included parental positive involvement and monitoring, communication and conflict resolution skills, and parental support for student achievement. Youth group topics included coping with peer pressure, resistance and refusal skills, advanced problem-solving skills, and goal-setting and decision-making skills. After receiving information about adolescent risks and protective skills during the family sessions, the intervention staff supported candid parent–youth discussions around issues such as middle-school transition adjustment (grades 5–6); romantic relationships and sex education (grades 5–6); alcohol, tobacco, and drug use (grades 6–7); and vocational goal setting (grade 7).

The middle-school transition program was designed to provide additional support to parents and youth during the spring prior to, and the fall following, the youth's transition into middle school. This program included visits to the middle school, discussions with the school counselor, coaching in organizational and study skills, and support from middle-school student mentors. The family sessions of the transition program were directed toward helping youth and parents acquire knowledge about middle school, learn skills of adapting to middle-school life, communicate more effectively around middle-school issues, and build a positive relationship with middle-school counselors and teachers.

A new aspect of the standard intervention in adolescence involved youth forums designed as workshops for groups of 4–8 youth. In grades 7 and 8, eight of these forums, based on Oyserman, Sanchez-Burks, and Harrison's (1996) Future Selves Program, encouraged youth to think about their short- and long-term life goals, to explore different life opportunities and choices, and to explore vocational opportunities, budgeting and life skills, summer employment opportunities, and job interview skills.

In addition to these curriculum-based group programs, individualized prevention supports were offered to some of the high-risk youth on an as-needed basis, according to criterion-based assessments. Given individual growth trajectories and life situations, considerable heterogeneity existed within the high-risk sample in adolescence. Individualized prevention services were designed to strengthen protective factors in areas of particular need for specific youth. The goal was to work toward equalizing the strength of protective factors across high-risk youth, rather than equalizing the amount of intervention delivered to each high-risk youth. Individualized services included (a) academic tutoring, (b) mentoring, (c) support for positive peer-group involvement, (d) home visiting and family problem solving, and (e) liaisons with school and community agencies.

Fast Track Outcomes

The initial analyses of the Fast Track Program have indicated that the program is having significant impact on the proximal outcomes that are assessed in the elementary-school phase of the project. These initial improvements in behavior, social skills, and parenting strategies can lead to some of the high-risk children exiting from the early-starter pathway or to reducing their involvement in the antisocial behaviors they would have otherwise emitted. Our ongoing longitudinal assessments extending now into the adolescent years will allow us to examine these trajectories for intervention and control children in the years ahead. In this section, we will briefly overview some of the indications of the initial impact of the program.

End of First Grade

In two recent publications, the effects of the Fast Track Program on the high-risk children and on the full classrooms at the end of the first grade have been presented (Conduct Problems Prevention Research Group, 1999a, 1999b). In comparison with the high-risk control children, the high-risk intervention children displayed moderate positive improvements in their social, emotional, and academic skills, as they had improved emotion recognition, improved emotion coping, improved abilities to generate competent solutions to social problems, improved word attack skills, and higher language arts grades (Conduct Problems Prevention Research Group, 1999a). In addition, the intervention children displayed improvements in independently observed positive interactions with peers at school and had improved social preference scores on sociometric ratings. These findings about children's functioning indicate that the academic tutoring and social competence components of the program appear to have begun to have meaningful impacts as early as the first-grade year. However, because Fast Track is a comprehensive program, the gains in children's peer relations and social competence, and in their social cognition and reading, are not necessarily due to single components, such as social skills groups or tutoring, but rather to the full integrated intervention program. Thus, the parent groups, through their focus on helping parents to facilitate their children's developmentally appropriate academic and social skills, likely contributed to these outcomes as well.

Fast Track was found to enhance certain aspects of parenting. Following the first year of intervention, parents reported that they would use lower rates of physical punishment in vignettes of difficult parent–child situations, they were observed to interact in warmer, more involved ways during observed parent–child interactions in the home, they were rated by the observers as using more appropriate and consistent discipline, they were more positively involved with their children's schools, they placed more value on encouraging children's learning, and they were very satisfied with the intervention. With regard to children's actual behavior, high-risk intervention children displayed significantly greater behavioral changes during the year according to the parent and teacher ratings, and teachers rated the intervention children as having significantly lower rates of aggressive, oppositional behaviors in the school setting. In addition, the intervention children had lower rates of special education services than did control children, indicating that they were functioning in more adaptive ways academically and behaviorally at school than were the high-risk control children.

Analyses examined whether these effects with the high-risk children were different across the four sites of Fast Track implementation, or between boys versus girls. There were no systematic indications that these variables moderated intervention effects, indicating instead that the intervention was operating in similar ways with children in different geographic settings, and in similar ways for boys and girls.

Because the PATHS program was provided to all children in the intervention schools, not just the high-risk children, and because other program components (e.g., peer pairing) included the lower risk classmates of our target children, we have also examined the universal preventive effects of Fast Track at the end of the first-grade year (Conduct Problems Prevention Research Group, 1999b). Analyses were conducted by removing the high-risk children from the analyses, thus permitting an examination of the effects on the remaining classmates. By means of hierarchical linear modeling (HLM) analyses with 369 classrooms, intervention classrooms were found to have lower peer-rated aggression and lower peer-rated hyperactive-disruptive behaviors than were the control classrooms. Ratings by independent observers in the classrooms indicated that the intervention classrooms had better classroom atmosphere, indicated by students being better able to follow rules, by students being better able to express feelings appropriately, by higher levels of enthusiasm and interest in the classroom, and by the classroom's ability to stay focused and on task. In implementation analyses, teachers' rated skill in teaching the PATHS concepts emerged as a predictor of degree of improvement evident in the observers' codings of the classroom atmosphere, further indicating the role of the program in producing these positive outcome effects. These improvements in general classroom behavior and classroom functioning have important preventive effects for all students and, in particular, increase the likelihood that our intervention effects with the high-risk children will be maintained because of the improved classroom context in which our target children are embedded.

End of Third Grade

Analyses of program outcomes at the end of third grade provide evidence for the continuing positive outcomes from Fast Track (Conduct Problems Prevention Research Group, 2002a). By the end of grade 3, lower teacher ratings of conduct problems, as well as lower weekly use of special education services, indicated that the intervention children, in comparison with the control children, were continuing to display reductions in conduct problem behavior. Parent reports of children's aggressive behavior also tended to decrease in comparison with the control group. However, these parent-rated outcome effects were evident only on the Parent Daily Report, not on psychopathological symptoms assessed by structured interviews. Intervention effects were also evident on some of the social-cognitive mediating processes. Intervention children had improved social problem-solving skills and reductions in their hostile attributional biases. In contrast to the effects noted at the end of the first grade, the intervention effects were no longer evident for emotion-related thinking or for reading achievement. On vignettes about parenting situations, intervention parents reported less use of physical punishment. Thus, the Fast Track results at the end of third grade provide partial validation of the model of early-starting conduct problems and, from an intervention viewpoint, indications of the utility of early preventive interventions in reducing elementary school children's conduct problems (Conduct Problems Prevention Research Group, 2002a).

Predictors of Third-Grade Outcomes

A recent study examined selected child, family, and community baseline characteristics that may have predicted proximal outcomes from the Fast Track intervention (Conduct Problems Prevention Research Group, 2002b), after three years of intervention participation. Modest evidence of prediction of outcome effects was found because none of the baseline variables were found to predict all three outcomes, and different patterns of prediction emerged for different outcomes. Thus, none of the baseline variables systematically predicted poorer outcome within the intervention children for all three outcomes. In these results, outcomes for intervention children in the school setting were somewhat better predicted than was an outcome in the home setting. Among children who had received the Fast Track intervention, larger reductions in teacher-rated aggression and lower levels of special education services by the end of third grade were evident for children who, in kindergarten, had higher levels of cognitive ability, had better reading achievement, and were female. Five other baseline variables predicted one of the two school-related outcomes. Greater reductions in teacher-rated aggressive behavior were evident among Fast Track children who had caretakers who were less depressed at baseline, who came from two-parent families, who came from higher socioeconomic status (SES) families, and who were white. Lower third-grade levels of special education involvement were apparent for Fast Track children who had lower levels of hyperactive behavior in kindergarten. Few interaction effects were evident between intervention status and the predictor variables, although intervention status did influence the relationship between baseline levels of caretaker social support and children's later parent-rated aggression and special-education involvement.

Prevention Science in Practice: Fast Track

At the beginning of this chapter, five principles for prevention science were outlined (Coie et al., 1993). It is useful to return to those principles to see how Fast Track illustrates them. Perhaps most important, Fast Track is an example of how a carefully articulated developmental model that accounts for the change and accumulation of risk factors and of mediating processes throughout the long developmental period starting with children at school entry and continuing through adolescence in high school can inform a complex, multicomponent intervention model. When this principle is met, as in the Fast Track model, then the remaining principles for prevention science can be readily addressed. The Fast Track Program addresses fundamental causal processes that mediate the relation between early risk factors and later antisocial outcomes. By intervening early at the entry to school, Fast Track attempts to address risk factors before they become stabilized and relatively intransigent to intervention. Fast Track, as an indicated preventive intervention, does address high-risk children, who are screened with a multiple-gating procedure with teacher and parent ratings, but, in addition, Fast Track includes a universal preventive focus on all children in the intervention schools. Finally, because the developmental model articulates a range of factors within the child and within the child's context that contribute to children's entry and retention on the developmental trajectory leading to serious adolescent conduct problems, Fast Track has necessarily included coordinated activities in multiple domains that change over the long course of intervention.

Our experience with the Fast Track intervention also has implications for refinements in the developmental model we used. For example, we have become aware of how hard it is to overcome contextual adversity, including children's presence within dangerous, crime-ridden neighborhoods and within impoverished families in which substantial parental psychopathology and substance abuse can be evident before intervention even begins. These broader contextual factors limit the extent to which an intervention addressing child processes and parenting processes can produce substantial change. Qualitative and empirical results from interventions can thus assist in refining the hypothesized development model.

Thus, Fast Track emerges as one exemplar of how prevention science can contribute to children's welfare and public policy. Initial findings from Fast Track analyses indicate that risk and putative causal factors can be influenced even for early-starting conduct problem children, as the children display improvements in behavior and social competence and their parents display productive changes in their interactions with their children. We have begun research that will explore the cost–benefits of Fast Track and will enhance our understanding of the transferability of Fast Track to new settings. Fast Track can have major influences on the future development of prevention science, as the longer term outcomes for Fast Track are assessed and as it becomes clear whether the early observed changes in the high-risk children contribute directly to their avoidance of adolescent problems involving violence, criminal behavior, conduct disorder, school failure, and substance use.

References

Aber, J. L., Jones, S. M., Brown, J. L., Chaudry, N., & Samples, F. (1998). Resolving conflict creatively: Evaluating the developmental effects of a school-based violence prevention program in neighborhood and classroom context. *Development and Psychopathology, 10,* 187–213.

Allen, G. J., Chinsky, J. M., Larcen, S. W., Lochman, J. E., & Selinger, H. V. (1976). *Community psychology and the schools: A behaviorally oriented multilevel preventive approach.* Hillsdale, NJ: Erlbaum.

American Psychiatric Association. (1994). *Diagnostic and statistical manual of mental disorders* (4th ed.). Washington, DC: Author.

Asher, S. R., & Coie, J. D. (1990). *Peer rejection in childhood.* Cambridge, England: Cambridge University Press.

Aultman, M. (1980). Group involvement in delinquent acts: A study of offense type and male-female participation. *Criminal Justice and Behavior, 7,* 185–192.

Bates, J. E., Bayles, K., Bennett, D. S., Ridge, B., & Brown, M. M. (1991). Origins of externalizing behavior problems at eight years of age. In D. J. Pepler & K. H. Rubin (Eds.), *The development and treatment of childhood aggression* (pp. 93–120). Hillsdale, NJ: Erlbaum.

Becker, J. (1994). *Mentoring high-risk kids.* Minneapolis, MN: Johnson Institute.

Bierman, K. L., & Furman, W. (1984). The effect of social skills training and peer involvement on the social adjustment of preadolescents. *Child Development, 55,* 151–162.

Bierman, K. L., Greenberg, M. T., & Conduct Problems Prevention Research Group (1996). Social skills training in the Fast Track program. In R. D. Peters & R. J. McMahon (Eds.), *Preventing childhood disorders, substance abuse, and delinquency* (pp. 65–89). Thousand Oaks, CA: Sage.

Bierman, K. L., Miller, C. L., & Stabb, S. D. (1987). Improving the social behavior and peer acceptance of rejected boys: Effects of social skills training with instructions and prohibitions. *Journal of Consulting and Clinical Psychology, 55,* 194–200.

Bierman, K. L., & Wargo, J. B. (1995). Predicting the longitudinal course associated with aggressive-rejected, aggressive (nonrejected), and rejected (nonaggressive) status. *Development and Psychopathology, 7,* 669–682.

Billy, J. O., Landale, N. S., Grady, W. R., & Zimmerle, D. M. (1988). Effects of sexual activity on adolescent social and psychological development. *Social Psychology Quarterly, 51,* 190–212.

Botvin, G. (1986). Substance abuse prevention efforts: Recent developments and future directions. *Journal of School Health, 56,* 369–374.

Brestan, E. V., & Eyberg, S. M. (1998). Effective psychosocial treatments of conduct-disordered children and adolescents: 29 years, 82 studies, and 5,272 kids. *Journal of Clinical Child Psychology, 27,* 180–189.

Brook, J. E. (1993). Interactional theory: Its utility in explaining drug use behavior among African-American and Puerto Rican youth. In M. R. De La Rosa & J. Recio-Adradoes (Eds.), *Drug use among minority youth: Advances in research and methodology* (Research Monograph No. 130, pp. 79–101). Rockville, MD: National Institute on Drug Abuse.

Burgoyne, K., Hawkins, J. D., & Catalano, R. (1991). *How to help your child succeed in school.* Seattle, WA: Developmental Research and Programs.

Cairns, R. B., Cairns, B. D., Neckerman, H. J., Gest, S. D., & Gariepy, J. L. (1988). Social networks and aggressive behavior: Peer support or peer rejection? *Developmental Psychology, 24,* 815–823.

Campbell, S. B. (1991). Longitudinal studies of active and aggressive preschoolers: Individual differences in early behavior and outcome. In D. Cicchetti & S. L. Toth (Eds.), *Rochester Symposium on Developmental Psychopathology: Vol. 2. Internalizing and externalizing expressions of dysfunction* (pp. 67–90). Hillsdale, NJ: Erlbaum.

Campbell, S. B., Breaux, A. M., Ewing, L. J., & Szumowski, E. K. (1986). Correlates and prediction of hyperactivity and aggression. *Journal of Abnormal Child Psychology, 14,* 217–234.

Caspi, A., Lynam, D., Moffitt, T. E., & Silva, P. (1993). Unraveling girls' delinquency: Biological, dispositional, and contextual contributions to adolescent misbehavior. *Developmental Psychology, 29,* 19–30.

Cicchetti, D. (1984). The emergence of developmental psychopathology. *Child Development, 55,* 1–7.

Coie, J. D. (1987, April). *An analysis of aggression episodes: Age and peer status differences.* Paper presented at the biennial meeting of the Society for Research in Child Development, Baltimore, MD.

Coie, J. D. (1990). Toward a theory of peer rejection. In S. R. Asher & J. D. Coie (Eds.), *Peer rejection in childhood* (pp. 365–401). Cambridge, England: Cambridge University Press.

Coie, J. D. (1996). Prevention of violence and antisocial behavior. In R. DeV. Peters & R. J. McMahon (Eds.), *Preventing childhood disorders, substance abuse, and delinquency* (pp. 1–18). Thousand Oaks, CA: Sage.

Coie, J. D., Dodge, K. A., & Coppotelli, H. (1982). Dimensions and types of social status: A cross-age perspective. *Developmental Psychology, 18,* 557–571.

Coie, J. D., Dodge, K. A., & Kupersmidt, J. B. (1990). Peer group behavior and social status. In S. R. Asher & J. D. Coie (Eds.), *Peer rejection in childhood* (pp. 17–59). Cambridge, England: Cambridge University Press.

Coie, J. D., & Krehbiel, G. (1984). Effects of academic tutoring on the social status of low-achieving, socially rejected children. *Child Development, 55,* 1465–1478.

Coie, J. D., & Koeppl, G. K. (1990). Adapting intervention to the problems of aggressive and disruptive rejected children. In S. R. Asher & J. D. Coie (Eds.), *Social rejection in childhood* (pp. 309–335). Cambridge, England: Cambridge University Press.

Coie, J. D., & Kupersmidt, J. B. (1983). A behavioral analysis of emerging social status in boys' groups. *Child Development, 54,* 1400–1416.

Coie, J. D., Lochman, J. E., Terry, R., & Hyman, C. (1992). Predicting early adolescent disorders from childhood aggression and peer rejection. *Journal of Consulting and Clinical Psychology, 60,* 783–792.

Coie, J. D., Terry, R., Lenox, K., Lochman, J., & Hyman, C. (1995). Childhood peer rejection and aggression as predictors of stable patterns of adolescent disorder. *Development and Psychopathology, 7,* 697–713.

Coie, J. D., Terry, R., Lochman, J. E., & Miller-Johnson, S. (1995). *Longitudinal effects of deviant peer groups on criminal offending in late adolescence.* Paper presented at the annual meeting of the American Society for Criminology, Boston, MA.

Coie, J. D., Terry, R., Zakriski, A., & Lochman, J. E. (1995). Early adolescent social influences on delinquent behavior. In J. McCord (Ed.), *Coercion and punishment in long-term perspectives* (pp. 229–244). New York: Cambridge University Press.

Coie, J. D., Watt, N. F., West, S. G., Hawkins, J. D., Asarnow, J. R., Markman, H. J., et al. (1993). The science of prevention: A conceptual framework and some directions for a national research program. *American Psychologist, 48,* 1013–1022.

Comer, J. P. (1980). *School power.* New York: Free Press.

Conduct Problems Prevention Research Group. (1992). A developmental and clinical model for the prevention of conduct disorders: The Fast Track Program. *Development and Psychopathology, 4,* 505–527.

Conduct Problems Prevention Research Group. (1999a). Initial impact of the Fast Track prevention trial for conduct problems: I. The high-risk sample. *Journal of Consulting and Clinical Psychology, 67,* 631–647.

Conduct Problems Prevention Research Group. (1999b). Initial impact of the Fast Track prevention trial for conduct problems: II. Classroom effects. *Journal of Consulting and Clinical Psychology, 67,* 648–657.

Conduct Problems Prevention Research Group. (2000). Merging universal and indicated prevention programs. *Addictive Behaviors, 25,* 913–927.

Conduct Problems Prevention Research Group. (2002a). An end of third-grade evaluation of the impact of the Fast Track prevention trial with children of high risk for adolescent conduct problems. *Journal of Abnormal Child Psychology, 30,* 19–35.

Conduct Problems Prevention Research Group. (2002b). Predictor variables associated with positive Fast Track outcomes at the end of third grade. *Journal of Abnormal Child Psychology, 30,* 37–52.

Cook, E. T., Greenberg, M. T., & Kusche, C. A. (1994). The relations between emotional understanding, intellectual functioning and disruptive behavior problems in elementary school-aged children. *Journal of Abnormal Child Psychology, 22,* 205–219.

Cowen, E. L. (1973). Social and community interventions. *Annual Review of Psychology, 24,* 423–472.

Dishion, T. J., & Andrews, D. W. (1995). Preventing escalation in problem behaviors with high-risk young adolescents: Immediate and 1-year outcomes. *Journal of Consulting and Clinical Psychology, 63,* 538–548.

Dishion, T. J., Eddy, J. M., Haas, E., Li, F., & Spracklen, K. (1997). *Friendships and violent behavior during adolescence.* Unpublished paper.

Dishion, T. J., French, D. C., & Patterson, G. R. (1995). The development and etiology of antisocial behavior. In D. Cicchetti & D. J. Cohen (Eds.), *Developmental psychopathology* (pp. 421–471). New York: Wiley.

Dishion, T. J., & McMahon, R. J. (1998). Parental monitoring and the prevention of problem behavior: A conceptual and empirical reformulation. In R. S. Ashery (Eds.), *Research meeting on drug abuse prevention through family interventions.* Rockville, MD: National Institute on Drug Abuse.

Dishion, T. J., Patterson, G. R., & Griesler, P. C. (1994). Peer adaptations in the development of antisocial behavior: A confluence model. In L. R. Huesmann (Ed.), *Aggressive behavior: Current perspectives* (pp. 61–95). New York: Plenum.

Dodge, K. A. (1983). Behavioral antecedents of peer social status. *Child Development, 54,* 1386–1399.

Dodge, K. A. (1989). Enhancing social relationships. In E. J. Mash & R. A. Barkley (Eds.), *Behavioral treatment of childhood disorders* (pp. 222–244). New York: Guilford.

Dodge, K. A. (1993). *Social information-processing and peer rejection factors in the development of behavior problems in children.* Paper presented at the biennial meeting of the Society for Research in Child Development, New Orleans, LA.

Dodge, K. A., Bates, J. E., & Pettit, G. S. (1990). Mechanisms in the cycle of violence. *Science, 250,* 1678–1683.

Dodge, K. A., & Coie, J. D. (1987). Social information processing factors in reactive and proactive aggression in children's peer groups. *Journal of Personality and Social Psychology, 53,* 1146–1158.

Dodge, K. A., Coie, J. D., & Brakke, N. P. (1982). Behavioral patterns of socially rejected and neglected preadolescents: The roles of social approach and aggression. *Journal of Abnormal Child Psychology, 18,* 389–409.

Dodge, K. A., Lochman, J. E., Harnish, J. D., Bates, J. E., & Pettit, G. S. (1997). Reactive and proactive aggression in school children and psychiatrically-impaired chronically-assaultive youth. *Journal of Abnormal Psychology, 106,* 37–51.

Durlak, J. (1995). *School-based prevention programs for children and adolescents.* Thousand Oaks, CA: Sage.

Eccles, J. S., & Midgley, C. M. (1990). Changes in academic motivation and self-perception during early adolescence. In R. Montemayor, G. R. Adams, & T. P. Gullotta (Eds.), *From childhood to adolescence.* Newbury Park, CA: Sage.

Eccles, J. S., Midgley, C. M., & Adler, T. (1984). Age-related changes in the school environment: Effects on achievement motivation. In J. P. Nicholls (Ed.), *The development of achievement motivation* (pp. 283–331). Greenwich, CT: JAI.

Eyberg, S. M., Boggs, S. R., & Algina, J. (1995). Parent-child interaction therapy: A psychosocial model for the treatment of young children with conduct problem behavior and their families. *Psychopharmacology Bulletin, 31,* 83–91.

Feindler, E. L., Marriott, S. A., & Iwata, M. (1984). Group anger control training for junior high school delinquents. *Cognitive Therapy and Research, 8,* 299–311.

Fletcher, A. C., Darling, N. E., & Steinberg, L. (1995). Parental monitoring and peer influences on adolescent substance use. In J. McCord (Ed.), *Coercion and punishment in long-term perspectives* (pp. 259–271). New York: Cambridge University Press.

Forehand, R., & McMahon, R. J. (1981). *Helping the noncompliant child: A clinician's guide to parent training.* New York: Guilford.

Gottman, J. M., Gonso, J., & Schuler, P. (1976). Teaching social skills to isolated children. *Journal of Abnormal Child Psychology, 4,* 179–197.

Greenberg, M. T., Kusche, C. A., Cook, E. T., & Quamma, J. P. (1995). Promoting emotional competence in school-aged deaf children: The effects of the PATHS Curriculum. *Development and Psychopathology, 7,* 117–136.

Greenberg, M. T., Kusche, C. A., & Speltz, M. (1991). Emotional regulation, self control, and psychopathology: The role of relationships in early childhood. In D. Cicchetti & S. L. Toth (Eds.), *Rochester Symposium on Developmental Psychopathology: Vol. 2. Internalizing and externalizing expressions of dysfunction* (pp. 21–66). Hillsdale, NJ: Erlbaum.

Greenberg, M. T., Lengua, L. J., Coie, J. D., Pinderhughes, E. E., & Conduct Problems Prevention Research Group. (1999). Predicting developmental outcomes at school entry using a multiple risk model: Four American communities. *Developmental Psychology, 35,* 403–417.

Gresham, F. M., & Nagle, R. J. (1980). Social skills training with children: Responsiveness to modeling and coaching as a function of peer orientation. *Journal of Consulting and Clinical Psychology, 48,* 718–729.

Hansen, W. B., Graham, J. W., Wolkenstein, B., & Lundy, B. Z. (1988). Differential impact of three alcohol prevention curricula on hypothesized mediating variables. *Journal of Drug Education, 18,* 143–153.

Harter, S. (1986). Processes underlying the construction, maintenance, and enhancement of the self-concept in children. In J. Suls & A. G. Greenwald (Eds.), *Psychological perspectives on the self* (Vol. 3, pp. 137–181). Hillsdale, NJ: Erlbaum.

Hawkins, J. D., Catalano, R. F., & Miller, J. Y. (1992). Risk and protective factors for alcohol and other drug problems in adolescence and early adulthood: Implications for substance abuse prevention. *Psychological Bulletin, 112,* 64–105.

Hawkins, J. D., & Weiss, J. G. (1985). The social development model: An integrated approach to delinquency prevention. *Journal of Primary Prevention, 6,* 73–95.

Henggeler, S. W., Schoenwald, S. K., & Pickrel, S. G. (1995). Multisystemic therapy: Bridging the gap between university- and community-based treatment. *Journal of Consulting and Clinical Psychology, 63,* 709–717.

Hirsch, B. J., & DuBois, D. J. (1991). Self-esteem in adolescence: The identification and prediction of contrasting longitudinal trajectories. *Journal of Youth and Adolescence, 20,* 53–72.

Hundleby, J. D., & Mercer, G. W. (1987). Family and friends as social environments and their relationship to young adolescents' use of alcohol, tobacco, and marijuana. *Journal of Clinical Psychology, 44,* 125–134.

Johnson, V., & Pandina, R. J. (1991). Effects of the family environment on adolescent substance abuse, delinquency and coping styles. *American Journal of Drug and Alcohol Abuse, 17,* 71–88.

Kazdin, A. E., Siegel, T. C., & Bass, D. (1992). Cognitive problem-solving skills training and parent management training in the treatment of antisocial behavior in children. *Journal of Consulting and Clinical Psychology, 60,* 733–747.

Kazdin, A. E., & Weisz, J. R. (1998). Identifying and developing empirically supported child and adolescent treatments. *Journal of Consulting and Clinical Psychology, 66,* 19–36.

Keenan, K., Loeber, R., Zhang, Q., Stouthamer-Loeber, M., & Van Kammen, W. B. (1995). The influence of deviant peers on the development of boys' disruptive and delinquent behavior: A temporal analysis. *Development and Psychopathology, 7,* 715–726.

Kellam, S. G., Ling, X., Merisca, R., Brown, C. H., & Ialongo, N. (1998). The effect of the level of aggression in the first grade classroom on the course and malleability of aggressive behavior into middle school. *Development and Psychopathology, 10,* 165–185.

Kusche, C. A., & Greenberg, M. T. (1993). *The PATHS Curriculum.* Seattle, WA: EXCEL.

Ladd, G. W. (1981). Effectiveness of a social learning method for enhancing children's social interaction and peer acceptance. *Child Development, 52,* 171–178.

Ladd, G. W., Price, J. M., & Hart, C. H. (1990). Preschoolers' behavioral orientations and patterns of peer contact: Predictive of peer status? In S. R. Asher & J. D. Coie (Eds.), *Peer rejection in childhood* (pp. 90–115). Cambridge, England: Cambridge University Press.

LaGreca, A. M., & Santogrossi, D. (1980). Social skills training with elementary school students: A behavioral group approach. *Journal of Consulting and Clinical Psychology, 48,* 220–227.

Langlois, J. H., & Stephen, C. W. (1981). Beauty and the beast: The role of physical attractiveness in the development of peer relations and social behavior. In S. Brehm, S. Kassin, & F. Gibbons (Eds.), *Developmental and social psychology* (pp. 152–168). New York: Oxford University Press.

Lochman, J. E. (1992). Cognitive-behavioral intervention with aggressive boys: Three-year follow-up and preventive effects. *Journal of Consulting and Clinical Psychology, 60,* 426–432.

Lochman, J. E., Coie, J. D., Underwood, M., and Terry, R. (1993). Effectiveness of a social relations intervention program for aggressive and nonaggressive rejected children. *Journal of Consulting and Clinical Psychology, 61,* 1053–1058.

Lochman, J. E., and Conduct Problems Prevention Research Group. (1995). Screening of child behavior problems for prevention programs at school entry. *Journal of Consulting and Clinical Psychology, 63,* 549–559.

Lochman, J. E., & Dodge, K. A. (1994). Social-cognitive processes of severely violent, moderately aggressive and nonaggressive boys. *Journal of Consulting and Clinical Psychology, 62,* 366–374.

Lochman, J. E., & Dodge, K. A. (1998). Distorted perception in dyadic interactions of aggressive and nonaggressive boys: Effects of prior expectations, context, and boys' age. *Development and Psychopathology, 10,* 495–512.

Lochman, J. E., & Wayland, K. K. (1994). Longitudinal prediction of negative adolescent outcomes using peer ratings of aggressive and social acceptance. *Journal of the American Academy of Child and Adolescent Psychiatry, 33,* 1026–1035.

Lochman, J. E., Wayland, K. K., & White, K. J. (1993). Social goals: Relationship to adolescent adjustment and to social problem solving. *Journal of Abnormal Child Psychology, 21,* 135–151.

Lochman, J. E., & Wells, K. C. (2002). Contextual social-cognitive mediators and child outcome: A test of the theoretical model in the Coping Power Program. *Development and Psychopathology, 14,* 971–993.

Lochman, J. E., & Wells, K. C. (in press). The Coping Power program for preadolescent aggressive boys and their parents: Outcome effects at the one-year follow-up. *Journal of Consulting and Clinical Psychology.*

Loeber, R. (1990). Development and risk factors of juvenile antisocial behavior and delinquency. *Clinical Psychology Review, 10,* 1–42.

Loeber, R., Wung, P., Keenan, K., Giroux, B., Stouthamer-Loeber, M., Van Kammen, W. B., & Maughan, B. (1993). Developmental pathways in disruptive child behavior. *Development and Psychopathology, 5,* 103–133.

Luthar, S. S., & Ziegler, E. (1991). Vulnerability and competence: A review of research on resilience in childhood. *American Journal of Orthopsychiatry, 61,* 6–22.

Marcus, H., & Nurius, P. (1986). Possible selves. *American Psychologist, 41,* 954–969.

McFadyen-Ketchum, S. A., & Dodge, K. A. (1998). Problems in social relationships. In E. J. Mash & R. A. Barkley (Eds.), *Treatment of childhood disorders* (2nd ed., pp. 338–365). New York: Guilford.

McMahon, R. J., & Forehand, R. (1984). Parent training for the noncompliant child: Treatment outcome, generalization, and adjunctive therapy procedures. In R. F. Dangel & R. A. Polster (Eds.), *Parent training: Foundations of research and practice* (pp. 298–328). New York: Guilford.

McMahon, R. J., Slough, N., & Conduct Problems Prevention Research Group. (1996). Family-based intervention in the Fast Track program. In R. D. Peters & R. J. McMahon (Eds.), *Preventing childhood disorders, substance abuse, and delinquency* (pp. 90–110). Thousand Oaks, CA: Sage.

Miller-Johnson, S., Coie, J., Maumary-Gremaud, A., Lochman, J., & Terry, R. (1999). Relationship between childhood peer rejection and aggression and adolescent delinquency severity and type among African American youth. *Journal of Emotional and Behavioral Disorders, 7,* 137–146.

Miller-Johnson, S., Winn, D., Coie, J., Maumary-Gremaud, A., Hyman, C., Terry, R., & Lochman, J. (1999). Motherhood during the teen years: A developmental perspective on risk factors for child-bearing. *Development and Psychopathology, 11,* 85–100.

Moffitt, T. E. (1990). Juvenile delinquency and attention deficit disorder: Boys' developmental trajectories from age 3 to age 15. *Child Development, 61,* 893–910.

Moffitt, T. E. (1993). Adolescence-limited and life-course-persistent antisocial behavior: A developmental taxonomy. *Psychological Review, 100,* 674–701.

Oden, S., & Asher, S. R. (1977). Coaching children in social skills for friendship making. *Child Development, 48,* 495–506.

Offord, D. R., Alder, R. J., & Boyle, M. H. (1986). Prevalence and socio-demographic correlates of conduct disorder. *American Journal of Social Psychiatry, 6,* 272–278.

Offord, D. R., Boyle, M. H., & Racine, Y. A. (1991). The epidemiology of antisocial behavior in childhood and adolescence. In D. J. Pepler & K. H. Rubin (Eds.), *The development and treatment of childhood aggression* (pp. 31–54). Hillsdale, NJ: Erlbaum.

Ohannesian, C., & Crockett, L. J. (1993). A longitudinal investigation of the relationship between educational investment and adolescent sexual activity. *Journal of Adolescent Research, 8,* 167–182.

Oyserman, D., & Markus, H. (1993). The sociocultural self. In J. Suls (Ed.), *Psychological perspectives on the self* (Vol. 4, pp. 187–220). Hillsdale, NJ: Erlbaum.

Oyserman, D., Sanchez-Burks, J., & Harrison, K. (1996). *Social identity and possible selves in adolescence.* Unpublished manuscript, University of Michigan.

Parker, J. G., & Asher, S. R. (1987). Peer relations and later personal adjustment: Are low-accepted children at risk? *Psychological Bulletin, 102,* 357–389.

Patterson, G. R. (1982). *Coercive family process.* Eugene, OR: Castalia.

Patterson, G. R., & Bank, C. L. (1989). Some amplifying mechanisms for pathological processes in families. In M. R. Gunnary & E. Thelen (Eds.), *The Minnesota Symposia on Child Psychology: Vol. 22. Systems and development* (167–209). Hillsdale, NJ, Erlbaum.

Patterson, G. R., DeBaryshe, B. D., & Ramsey, E. (1989). A developmental perspective on antisocial behavior. *American Psychologist, 44,* 329–335.

Patterson, G. R., Reid, J. B., & Dishion, T. J. (1992). *Antisocial boys.* Eugene, OR: Castalia.

Patterson, G. R., & Yoerger, K. (1997). A developmental model for late-onset delinquency. In D. W. Osgood (Ed.), *Nebraska Symposium on Motivation: Vol. 44. Motivation and delinquency* (pp. 119–177). Lincoln: University of Nebraska Press.

Pentz, M. A., Dwyer, J. H., MacKinnon, D. P., Flay, B. R., Hansen, W. B., Wang, E. Y., & Johnson, C. A. (1989). A multi-community trial for primary prevention of adolescent drug abuse. *Journal of the American Medical Association, 261,* 3259–3266.

Putallaz, M., & Wasserman, A. (1989). Children's naturalistic entry behavior and sociometric status: A developmental perspective. *Developmental Psychology, 25,* 1–9.

Rubin, K. H., LeMare, L. J., & Lollis, S. (1990). Social withdrawal in childhood: Developmental pathways to peer rejection. In S. R. Asher & J. D. Coie (Eds.), *Peer rejection in childhood* (pp. 217–249). Cambridge, England: Cambridge University Press.

Rutter, M., Maughan, B., Mortimore, P., Ouston, J., & Smith, A. (1979). *Fifteen thousand hours: Secondary schools and their effects on children.* Cambridge, MA: Harvard University Press.

Saito, R. N., & Blyth, D. A. (1994). *Understanding mentoring relationships.* Minneapolis, MN: Search Institute.

Snyder, J. J., & Patterson, G. R. (1995). Individual differences in social aggression: A test of a reinforcement model of socialization in the natural environment. *Behavior Therapy, 26,* 371–391.

Steele, C., & Aronson, J. (1995). Stereotype threat and the intellectual test performance of African-Americans. *Journal of Personality and Social Psychology, 69,* 797–811.

Thornberry, T. P. (1987). Toward an interactional theory of delinquency. *Criminology, 25,* 863–891.

Thornberry, T. P., Huizinga, D., & Loeber, R. (1995). The prevention of serious delinquency and violence: Implications from the program of research on the causes and correlates of delinquency. In J. C. Howell, B. Krisberg, J. D. Hawkins, & J. Wilson (Eds.), *Sourcebook on serious violent and chronic juvenile offenders.* Thousand Oaks, CA: Sage.

Vitaro, F., Brengden, M., Pagani, L., Tremblay, R. E., & McDuff, P. (1999). Disruptive behavior, peer association, and conduct disorder: Testing the developmental links through early intervention. *Development and Psychopathology, 11,* 287–304.

Vitaro, F., Tremblay, R. E., Kerr, M., Pagani-Kurtz, L., & Bukowski, W. M. (in press). Disruptiveness, friends' characteristics, and delinquency: A test of two competing models of development. *Child Development.*

Webster-Stratton, C. (1989). *The parents and children series.* Eugene, OR: Castalia.

Webster-Stratton, C., & Hammond, M. (1997). Treating children with early-onset conduct problems: A comparison of child and parent training interventions. *Journal of Consulting and Clinical Psychology, 65,* 93–109.

Weissberg, R. P., Caplan, M. Z., & Sivo, P. J. (1989). A new conceptual framework for establishing school-based social competence promotion programs. In L. A. Bond & B. E. Compas (Eds.), *Primary prevention and promotion in the schools* (pp. 255–296). Newbury Park, CA: Sage.

Werner, E. E. (1986). Resilient offspring of alcoholics: A longitudinal study from birth to age 18. *Journal of Studies on Alcohol, 47,* 34–40.

Wills, T. A., & Filer, M. (1996). Stress-coping model of adolescent substance use. In T. H. Ollendick & R. J. Prinz (Eds.), *Advances in clinical child psychology* (Vol. 18, pp. 91–132). New York: Plenum.

11

If You Can't Beat 'em ... Induce Them to Join You: Peer-Based Interventions During Adolescence

Shari Miller-Johnson and Philip Costanzo

In this chapter, we discuss peer-based interventions to reduce conduct problems and other related problem behaviors of adolescence. In the past decade, our knowledge base has improved dramatically in terms of developmental models to describe the progression of antisocial behavior across the life span (Conduct Problems Prevention Research Group, 1992; Moffitt, 1993; Patterson, Capaldi, & Bank, 1991). Many researchers, including some whose work is included in this volume, have emphasized the importance of considering developmental models and key transition points when designing and implementing prevention programs (Coie et al., 1993; Reid, 1993). One important assumption of this approach is that methods of prevention must change as new risk factors enter the developmental picture over time. During adolescence, associations with deviant peers play an increasingly important role in promoting involvement in problem behaviors (Elliott & Menard, 1996; Thornberry, 1996). The power of peer associations is advancing simultaneously with the transition to middle school, which presents a key shift in terms of changes in individual tasks and responsibilities (Eccles, Lord, & Buchanan, 1996). In addition, entry to middle school exposes youth to a broader social context that may promote and intensify risk-taking behaviors.

Therefore, the design and implementation of peer-based interventions must be informed by research on the transitions in peer relations during adolescence. The goal of this chapter is to review theoretical issues that relate the adolescent shift in peer importance to the deployment of peer-based interventions during adolescence. Specifically, we discuss the impact of peers on the development of antisocial behavior. Doing so requires us to explore the normative status of problem behaviors during adolescence and attitudes relating to risk taking during adolescence, and how involvement in problem behaviors is mediated by processes of social influence and leadership in peer cliques. We then discuss research on the social psychological factors promoting social influence and how these might enable intervention strategies directed at deviant peer groups and their leaders. We end by proposing a model of intervention that is built on the implications of these important theoretical issues.

The Impact of Peers on Antisocial Behavior

The purpose of this chapter is not to provide a detailed review of current theories of the development of antisocial behavior (for these purposes, see Conduct Problems Prevention Research Group, 1992; Moffitt, 1993; Patterson et al., 1991). However, we do want to place our discussion of peer interventions during adolescence in their social-developmental context and highlight the impact of peer factors on delinquency during the teen years. Recent theories delineate two groups that are responsible for the high prevalence of delinquency during adolescence. The first group who is at highest risk for antisocial behavior during adolescence is thought of as comprising *early starters* (Patterson et al., 1991) or *life-course-persistent* youth (Moffitt, 1993). These youth have a chronic pattern of conduct problems that extend as far back as early childhood. Family processes set the stage for coercive exchanges, and families of these children exhibit high levels of stress, instability, parental psychopathology, and punitive or inconsistent discipline.

The antisocial behavior of these early starters begins in childhood, continues into adolescence, and persists into the adult years. By comparison, *late starter* or *adolescent limited* youth do not begin their antisocial behavior until the onset of the teen years, and this group accounts for the increase in antisocial behavior that occurs during adolescence (Patterson & Yoerger, 1997). As compared with the early-starting group, the antisocial behavior of the late-starters tends to decline as they enter young adulthood and begin to settle into more stable work and family patterns. Thus, although the early-starter youth account for the chronic and persistent antisocial behavior, the adolescent limited youth are responsible for the sharp, albeit temporary, increase in delinquency during the teen years.

Both Moffitt (1993) and Patterson and Yoerger (1997) attribute a great deal of importance to the impact of deviant peers on the late starters' delinquent behavior. Moffitt generally places the late starters in a more developmentally normative framework and views the deviant behavior of late starters as related to reinforcement and punishment contingencies emanating from the peer group. She speculates that during adolescence, delinquency becomes associated with power and prestige, and teens become increasingly exposed to peer models for which delinquency has become a desired social asset. Thus, the late-starting delinquents imitate the early-starting delinquents, and this *social mimicry* becomes a statement of independence and autonomy and a way to evidence maturity in the social structure. In this way, the delinquent behavior of the early starters becomes coveted, and early starters enjoy a phase in which their behavior becomes a desired social asset and an asset to be emulated.

Patterson and Yoerger (1997) view the developmental history of late starters as more problematic than does Moffitt, although not as problematic as the group of chronically delinquent early starters. They contend that deviant peer associations are a risk factor for involvement in antisocial behavior for both the early and late starters. However, for late starters, deviant peer influences are thought to be the primary risk factor, whereas for early starters, early family experiences set the stage for later conduct problems. Peer groups are thought to be fertile ground for deviancy training in terms of beliefs, talk, and behaviors. Thus, deviant peers serve a critical role as instigators, coparticipants, and reinforcers of antisocial behavior.

The social acceptance of deviant peer groups in the wider peer culture may also vary across development. Coie, Terry, Zakriski, and Lochman (1995) found striking developmental shifts in associations between social acceptance and aggressive behavior in the Durham, NC, longitudinal study, a prospective investigation of the development of antisocial behavior among a sample of urban, African American boys and girls. In third grade, social preference was negatively associated with aggression. This relationship was no longer significant at sixth grade. By eighth grade, social preference was positively associated with aggression and deviant peer involvement, such that members of deviant peer cliques were more socially preferred in comparison with those from more conventional peer cliques. In addition, members of deviant peer cliques were more likely to be seen as leaders.

Other concurrent studies have found similar associations between social preference or popularity and problem behaviors. In a recent study, Rodkin, Farmer, Pearl, and Van Acker (2000) extended this question to a younger sample of fourth to sixth graders. Using cluster analyses, they found two popular subtypes of fourth- to sixth-grade boys: popular-prosocial boys (*model*) and popular-antisocial boys (*tough*). The tough group described themselves as being aggressive, popular, and physically competent, whereas the model boys described themselves as nonaggressive and academically competent. These tough boys were also viewed by peers and teachers as being popular. Similarly, Luthar and McMahon (1996) investigated correlates of peer reputation in a sample of inner-city teens and found that aggressive behaviors were positively associated with popular status.

These studies inform us that by early adolescence, the social context for youth is changing such that problem behaviors are becoming increasingly accepted. Furthermore, unlike earlier in childhood, this acceptance is now extending beyond the group of high-risk children to the wider peer context. Norms and beliefs surrounding aggressive behavior may also vary as a function of the social context, and different peer processes may operate for youth living in impoverished neighborhoods that are plagued by high crime levels (Coie & Jacobs, 1993; Luthar, 1997). Youth residing in low socioeconomic neighborhoods are surrounded by high levels of interpersonal violence and drug use and may have to use force (or at least appear capable of doing so) to survive socially. In this way, behaviors viewed as deviant by mainstream society may be considered a source of status and maturity, and involvement in risk-taking behaviors may be considered not only somewhat normative, but perhaps even adaptive. Youth in inner cities are often faced with choosing between the values of the local peer community and those of the larger adult society. Winfield (1995) coined the term *oppositional social identity* to describe an adolescent resolution to the tensions between these viewpoints. Thus, the peer social context of teens living in low socioeconomic neighborhoods may be characterized by unique ideologies, role expectations, and behavioral standards that differ substantially from those of more affluent or conventional middle-American communities (Burton, Allison, & Obeidallah, 1995). For youth that reside in high-crime, inner-city neighborhoods, the meaning of "deviant peers" may be less clear, particularly during adolescence. To put it succinctly, behaviors that are considered problematic by mainstream society may actually be associated with status and prestige among the youth of disadvantaged communities.

Therefore, the leaders in less mainstream, deviant peer groups may have undue influence on the peer culture and may be instrumental in perpetuating a climate of tolerance for violence, drug use, and early and risky sexual behavior. It is this less mainstream type of leader who is likely to be in a position of influence both within deviant peer cliques and in the wider peer context, given that the social context of adolescence is marked by increasing acceptance of more deviant behaviors. However, most studies of leadership during adolescence have tended to use a more conventional, socially sanctioned definition of leadership (e.g., Edwards, 1994).

One exception is a recent study by Miller-Johnson, Coie, Maumary-Gremaud, Bierman, and the Conduct Problems Prevention Research Group (2002) in which they examined associations between two patterns of leadership and problem behaviors in a sample of urban, African American seventh graders. The first leadership pattern was composed of youth who were in conventional positions of authority in established groups (e.g., student government, extracurricular activities). The second, unconventional type included youth who did not have formal status as leaders but were natural leaders of informal peer groups and set peer trends in dress, speech, and behavioral norms. The two styles of peer leadership revealed diametrically opposed patterns of association with risky behaviors. Specifically, the conventional leadership style was associated with lower levels of involvement in problem behaviors, and the unconventional style was associated with higher levels of involvement in problem behaviors. Similarly, Luthar and McMahon (1996), in their study of peer reputation among inner-city teens, used cluster analyses and identified two patterns of social influence. The first group was characterized by conventionally valued behavior, such as prosocial behavior and academic achievement, and disruptive and aggressive behaviors and poor school performance characterized the second group. Specifically, 20% of ninth graders were characterized as being both aggressive and popular.

These results suggest the importance of distinctions between groups of influential adolescents and how these patterns may be differentially associated with involvement in risk-taking behaviors. The conventional leader is the type of youth whom adults would typically value as a role model for peers, and this more conventional type of leader is likely to take on roles in group activities that are already established and socially sanctioned by adults. However, the conventional leader may be in less of a position to influence because shifting norms now promote and support involvement in deviant behaviors such as interpersonal violence, substance use, and sexual behavior. The unconventional leader seems to be responsible for creating the shift in peer attitudes and behavior toward greater risk taking that takes place in early adolescence. On the surface, at least, this latter form of peer leader has greater influence on peer orientations that challenge conventional values.

The Miller-Johnson et al. (2002) study also examined associations between the two leadership styles, peer status, and involvement in problem behaviors. Controversial status youth, or those who were both highly liked and highly disliked, exhibited the highest rates of involvement in risky behaviors, and this finding may be relevant to social influence processes and dynamics operating within adolescent peer groups. These youth typically possess many positive and effective social qualities, as well as being disruptive and aggressive (Parkhurst & Asher, 1992). Thus, they have the requisite social skills to influence others and are highly visible within the peer culture, both in childhood and in adolescence. Not surprisingly, they were also found to be among the unconventional leaders in seventh grade and looked upon by peers as those who set trends. In their behaviors, these controversial youth may transmit messages that support involvement in risky behaviors and promote a context that supports aggressive behavior, substance use, and early sexual behavior. In this way, problem behaviors become more accepted among urban middle-school peer groups (Coie et al., 1995; Luthar & McMahon, 1996) and are reinforced in the broader peer culture. The next question to be considered is how best to redirect or reduce the influence of these deviant peer groups and their leaders in order to reduce rates of risk-taking behaviors. In the next section, we provide an approach to this question based on the research and theory on the dynamics of social influence.

The Social Dynamic Antecedents of Interventions in the Problem Behaviors of Youth

From the above brief review, one might infer that at a point in the early adolescent transition, deviant behavior could become a positive mark of independence from authority. Given the individuating struggles of young adolescents (see Costanzo, 1992), such concrete and readily available exemplars of distinction can carry a great deal of weight. Thus, for even the average young adolescent seeking identity affirmation, deviant peer leaders might possess distinctive powers of influence. This may be particularly true in inner-city, minority, and impoverished circumstances in which mainstream values, although imposed by the surrounding society, constantly put youth in a position of negative social comparison. For these reasons, it may well be that the peers who are most willing to take risks and explore non-normative behaviors emerge as particularly suitable clique or group leaders. It may also be the case that the most competent and ambitious members of such youth communities readily employ this alternative route to leadership and social recognition. Indeed, one might speculate that many late starters are derivative of this subset of competent but risk-prone individuals who set trends and occasion the admiration of their peers.

With the increasing complexity of the social dynamics of peer group status in early adolescence, simple authority-directed intervention approaches might fall on not only deaf but also decidedly oppositional ears. Social skills training, disciplinary interventions, values education, and knowledge-based curricular instruction all have their place; however, they are unlikely to make much of a dent in the powerful and identity-promoting structure of adolescent peer groups. To design intervention approaches to reduce the deleterious consequences of risky and destructive youth behaviors, interventions must begin by acknowledging the powerful aspects of the structure of adolescent peer groups. To intervene successfully, practitioners must also neither implicitly nor explicitly oppose the power of deviant peers or the cliques they lead. To use the natural strengths of the developing peer culture, it is quintessentially important for interventionists to understand and deploy the dynamics of the naturally occurring social influence of which deviant peer leadership is a part. Social-psychological scholars have devoted much effort to understanding the structure and processes of social influence, and there is a strong empirical and theoretical base for the construction of a socialization-sensitive and developmentally appropriate model of intervention. However, there has not been much formal cross-talk between the literatures of social psychology and those of developmental psychopathology and child intervention. In this section, we attempt a concise summary and formulation of those primary principles of social influence that have intervention implications for those who work with deviant youth or with the prevention of problematic outcomes.

Two broad and dichotomous dimensions of social influence processes are relevant to the design of effective intervention. First are the intrinsic versus extrinsic pressures from others in the social structure. Extrinsic factors, such as compliance pressure, prestige suggestion, and reward control, and intrinsic components associated with self-persuasion, such as behavior-attitude consistency, self-mediated commitment and choices, and identity-relevant or competence-relevant actions, constitute the two anchor points of this dimension. In a sense, we can be persuaded by powerful or prestigious outside influences, or we can self-persuade on the basis of being induced to manifest new norms through our overt behavior, especially if we perceptually or actually minimize the role of external forces.

From a developmental or socialization-based life course perspective, the most frequently alluded-to path to self-mediated behavior change can be characterized as proceeding from the extrinsic to the intrinsic. In other words, the initial acquisition of new behaviors, beliefs, and attitudes is likely to begin with externally imposed influences but reach its culmination when the individual locates *self* as the intrinsic origin of those attitudes, behaviors, and beliefs. In essence, then, the developmental flow of influence involves a movement from compliance-directed action to a belief in the self-mediation of action. The works of Lepper and his colleagues (Lepper & Greene, 1979) constitute the most prominent empirical exemplars of the necessity for extrinsic sources of influence to be reconstructed as intrinsic prior to persistent shifts in behavior. Kelman's (1961) seminal model of the microgenesis of social influence is perhaps the most articulated exposition of the extrinsic-to-intrinsic path in successful social influence. In his model, the movement from compliance to internalization of attitudes and beliefs is mediated by a middle step of identification with the original external source of influence.

In the peer networks that develop in early adolescence, the source of influence shifts rather dramatically from those in authority (e.g., parents, teachers) to peers, and from peers congruent with authority figures to peers who deviate from authority. In essence, adolescent peers who are most likely to serve as opinion leaders are those who behaviorally illustrate independence from traditional authority norms to vulnerable age-mates who struggle with self-definition. Deviance, aggression, and norm-violation are the most dramatic exemplars of the normative independence of adolescents from sources of adult control. Such normative independence from adults is likely to expedite the transition from the extrinsic influence of deviant peers to the perception of intrinsic behavioral change in the objects of that influence. To the extent that the trend-setting consequences of deviant peers have the impact of enhancing the sense of intrinsic identity of young adolescents in search of self-definition, they will induce compliance. Simultaneously, however, because they oppose the traditional adult-centered norms of behavior, the recipient of this influence sees these attitudes and behavior as intrinsic components of the self. Theoretically then, during the period of early adolescent development, individuals are vulnerable to deviant peer influence partly because it psychologically transforms a following or conforming response into an act of independence. Given our discussion of deviant peer leadership in the first section of this chapter, it is no wonder that trendsetters are generally central members of adolescent peer cliques.

The second broad dimension employed in the social influence literature refers to the *centrality* or *peripherality* of the route to influence (Petty & Cacciopo, 1981). *Central influence routes* are predicated on the provision of logically ordered information that allows the individual recipient of influence to deliberate and engage in behavior consistent with these deliberations (e.g., the effects of drugs on changes on the central nervous system; the association of unprotected sex with the incidences of sexually transmitted diseases). In contrast, *peripheral influence routes* are those that employ tangential informationally irrelevant cues with desirable people or things (e.g., Michael Jordan advocating the consumption of 7 UP® to admiring recipients). Peripheral or heuristic (see Cialdini, 1993) cues operate in automatic fashion, while central cues are the product of deliberative process. In much of the literature on social influence, peripheral cues are described as resulting in a more rapid and immediate effect on attitudes than central cues (see Eagley & Chaiken, 1993). However, the deliberative route and the effortful processing central cues promotes engender more enduring attitude change than does peripherally based processing. Thus, in developmental- or socialization-based contexts, it is important to arrange a sequence of attitude socialization efforts from initial, peripheral influence to subsequent central processing of information-rich sources. However, many conventional approaches to reduce problem behaviors initiate interventions by implicitly demanding central information processing at the outset of influence (e.g., moral education; social knowledge manipulations; presenting illness or danger-related aspects of problem behavior). As most adult intervenors lack the desirability of peripherally potent socializers (such as deviant peers), their influence is muted by their failure to initially capitalize on automatic peripheral processes.

As implied above, during early adolescence, deviant peer leaders gain much of their power and centrality in cliques because they facilitate the transition from extrinsic to intrinsic attributions for behavior and attitude change *and* because they also promote the transformation of the rapid changes evident in peripheral influence to central and effortful forms. As such, they influence actions and beliefs in others that are eventually internalized as parts of one's intrinsic self-identification. The intra-clique identification with the trend-setting leaders is the mediating step in this transition. As such, deviant adolescent trendsetters blur the psychological distinction between conformity and independence in the recipient of their influential messages. As long as one's behavior and normative constructions deviate from those of the mainstream adult community, they are subject to being owned by the clique member as products of one's active choices (i.e., they become self-defining). Consequently adolescents who have a reputation for getting into trouble dominate many peer cliques that are formed during adolescence. In inner-city schools where there may be a higher proportion of adolescents who are aggressive, the social network may be defined by the normative beliefs and behaviors of aggressive adolescents who are willing to challenge adult rules (Coie & Jacobs, 1993).

In short, any model of intervention that expects to decrease the frequency of problem behaviors must (a) extend the treatment focus beyond identified individuals to their embeddedness in powerful group contexts; (b) employ the very potent peer pressures that are naturally emergent in young adolescent peer groups as part of the intervention structure; (c) be cognizant of the fact that conformity to deviant norms will be construed by youth as independence from conventional norms, and therefore become an intrinsic property of the self; (d) deliberately structure the early stages of influence to capitalize on extrinsic forms of influence and peripheral routes for attaining such influence; and (e) employ the more permanence-promoting intrinsic influences implemented through central routes in the later stages. Finally, it must be acknowledged that deviant group leaders and central clique members have a decided power over their peers' behavior and beliefs. As a consequence, if one can successfully intervene with the leaders of these deviant peer groups, one can have a spread of effect to less central but risk-prone clique members.

Implications for Altering High-Risk Behavior Among Adolescents

Our proposed and piloted intervention model builds on the naturally occurring influence of deviant peer groups and centers on the use of peer leaders to influence other teens to reduce involvement in risky behaviors. A number of previous programs have utilized peer leaders as agents of social change (e.g., Kelder et al., 1996; Perry, Williams, Veblen-Mortenson, & Toomey, 1996; Price, Gioci, Penner, & Trautlein, 1993). However, these interventions focused on mainstream types of leaders who exhibit socially acceptable behaviors and are likely to have a limited sphere of influence on the larger peer context. Even if the intent of an intervention is to decrease the frequency of problem behavior in the rank and file of young adolescents, a sizable portion of the initial intervention targets should be selected because they operate as trend-setting, perhaps deviant, leaders.

Our proposed model applied the theories of social influence and resocialization of social identity that were reviewed above. The intervention process flowed from peripheral messages that were communicated by extrinsic sources, to central messages that involved self-persuasion. The influence process involved an initial phase that utilized valued authority figures as external symbols of messages related to the reduction of risk-taking behaviors. This process then shifted to a phase in which peer leaders generated components of messages related to prevention of problem behaviors. Last, peer leaders generated products to be used as influence materials to new audiences. The central assumption of this intervention model was that it is in the act of persuading others that one's commitments to both attitudes and attitude-relevant courses of action are cemented.

We had an opportunity to pilot such an intervention on a small scale.[1] The peer leader intervention was part of a larger school-based intervention and evaluation program to reduce violence, substance use, and early and risky sexual behaviors among middle-school students. Pilot procedures were implemented across four middle schools in a small southeastern city school district characterized by children who were predominantly African American (90%) and of low socioeconomic status.

Sociometric procedures were used to select peer leaders, including designation of both conventional leaders and more deviant, "antiestablishment" peer leaders. In our pilot work, conventional leadership was based on nominations from the item "persons who are leaders and good to have in charge." Unconventional leadership was based on the descriptor "persons whom other kids listen to; these people set the trends for other kids." Ratings from these two leadership items were then averaged to create a composite score. The clique structure within each of the schools was then derived using a q-type factor analytic procedure with oblique rotation on a correlation matrix that indexed the extent to which each pair of students was consistently named as hanging out together (Coie et al., 1995). Participants received factor loading scores for each of the cliques in the school; the factor with the highest loading was designated as the primary clique. Within each of the cliques, the student who received the highest leadership composite score was selected and invited to participate in the peer leader intervention.

There were three phases to the peer leadership intervention. The first was the *peripheral influence attention phase*. Because the group meetings themselves were directed at outcomes generally opposed by these leaders, the first phase was treated as a counterattitudinal intervention. Peer leaders were informed of the *positive* basis for their selection for participation in a group project. In other words, they were told that they were selected to help because

---

[1]As a result of a merger and reorganization in the Durham school system, a majority of students were reassigned to new schools. Therefore, the research design of the project was severely compromised; we were able to pilot the feasibility of the program but were not able to evaluate its effects. As such, this proposal remains an idea of promise.

they were acknowledged by their peers as natural leaders and they were likely to provide the most influential help. Employing *authority stars* as co-conveners of the groups increased the extrinsic value of being a leader and participating in the group. In this way, the power of the extrinsic forces was sufficient to allow for compliance in the face of the counterattitudinal nature of the groups. These authority stars as co-conveners possessed greater power to influence initial peripheral-route change than ordinary adult conveners such as teachers or therapists. In our pilot work, we utilized local college athletes as the authority stars, and these college students had considerable prestige and status among the middle-school students. The college student athletes were simultaneously enrolled in an undergraduate course on child interventions, and their participation in the peer leader groups was part of their course requirements. During this initial phase, the authority stars met with the peer leaders in their groups. Consistent with the theoretical underpinning of the model, peer leaders also received other extrinsic rewards (e.g., food, field trips) for their role as agents of social change.

The second phase of the peer leader intervention was *small group strategy generation*. The task of the group meetings was directed at promoting increasingly *central-route* encounters with norms. To promote increasing centrality of processing, the authority stars asked the students to collaborate on the construction of an influential creative product that would counter a deviant behavior (e.g., drug use, aggression, or unprotected sex). This product could be a group-constructed poster, piece of music, film, or video, for example. In this way, creative products deriving from the efforts of group participants were much more likely to be owned than would material that was more passively received. The goal of the projects was to generate messages that educated and convinced other students to adopt prosocial attitudes and behaviors. In the early phases, the authority stars worked closely with the students in designing and developing the projects, thereby providing additional reinforcement for adoption of prosocial attitudes. Over time, however, their presence became less significant and frequent so that the peer leaders would begin to intrinsically own their projects. In addition, once the creative projects were under way, extrinsic bases for gathering in the group were slowly withdrawn.

The final phase of the peer leadership intervention was *presentation and advocacy*. This final phase of the intervention was critical because it emphasized that the route to attitude and behavior change is through the act of persuading others to adopt beliefs and practices. The intent was to make the constructed antideviance influence product strong enough to convince other peers (throughout the school) to adopt its message. At this time, the work groups presented their messages to the other students, including small presentations to invited groups of peers and larger presentations to the entire student body.

Given the formally imposed change in school structure noted above, we were never adequately able to empirically evaluate the group effects of the intervention efforts described in this section. Our targeted subjects were redistributed among the city–county schools and our groups were thus disbanded and the peers in the cliques to whom the leaders belonged were also dispersed throughout the system. Despite this circumstance, we can report that the peer leader intervention groups approached the tasks with enthusiasm and pride of ownership and consulted central informational materials in constructing their products (e.g., posters, radio scripts, musical performances). Finally, although the initial enthusiasm was largely anchored on the presence of prominent authority stars, it did not dissipate when these stars were slowly withdrawn from the group intervention context. On informal observation, then, the intervention was sufficiently motivating and resulted in self-sustaining, counter-attitudinal, antirisk advocacy behavior among these high-risk adolescents.

We encourage other investigators in more stable school circumstances to initiate these social-psychological-based interventions. Our trial of these procedures indicates that they are feasible, well received, and potentially fruitful. The model we describe above could also be made to fit into the context of health-education classes or other curricular-centered instructional contexts.

Qualifications and Conclusions

We want to mention two caveats in our consideration of peer-based interventions to reduce problem behaviors. The first is that if we are successful in changing the beliefs and attitudes of the group members, the previously endorsed deviant leaders may no longer be perceived as having influence over their peers. In other words, these deviant peer leaders may now be viewed as more conventional peer leaders, which may alter their status within the peer context. In part, whether a peer leader is viewed as more conventional may depend on the stage of leadership of the particular individual. Youth who are in established positions of authority for longer periods of time may be able to deviate more from existing beliefs and attitudes. This pattern is consistent with Hollander's notion of *idiosyncrasy credit,* which suggests that once one receives acknowledgment as a valued group member, he or she is much freer to deviate from established group norms. Because we are advocating the selection of adolescents already sociometrically chosen as central by their peers, we believe that Hollander's principle would clearly apply.

A second concern relates to the potential for creating, in a sense, a *superordinate* group of deviant youth through bringing together deviant peer leaders. This forewarning is related to recent research that has questioned common practices that place high-risk youth together in group interventions and potential iatrogenic effects. Data from some recent studies suggest that group-based interventions may lead to increases in problem behaviors (Dishion & Andrews, 1995; Dishion, McCord, & Poulin, 1999; McCord, 1997; Poulin, Dishion, & Burraston, 2001). The implication of these findings is that placing deviant peers together in a homogeneous group may inadvertently encourage the reinforcement of antisocial attitudes and promote antisocial friendships that may extend outside of the intervention. A number of important unanswered questions remain about group interventions and their potential negative impact on problem behaviors. One possibility is that the group processes that promote and encourage deviant beliefs and friendships are not activated until some critical mass or number of deviant youth is in a group. Therefore, groups that are less homogeneous and contain a mixture of high-risk and non-high-risk youth may be less likely to promote the type of deviant talk and dialogue that supports involvement in problem behaviors. Inclusion of nonreferred youth may also have the effect of promoting prosocial attitudes and behaviors. It is also plausible, however, that deviant peers may negatively influence the nonreferred youth, particularly during adolescence when shifting norms and beliefs may promote rather than impede involvement in risky behaviors. Indeed, despite some of the potential pitfalls of grouping deviant peer leaders in the same intervention context, the balance of power it encourages may allow for equally distributed participation—a long-term goal of such group efforts. Although we do not advocate throwing caution to the wind in constructing deviant intervention groups, we do believe that most of the appropriate cautionary barriers can be traversed if the group is rewarding enough to keep its participants motivated to succeed at joint goals and shared products.

We began this chapter by arguing that the peer-centered normative structure of adolescent social groups must be considered in the construction of developmentally appropriate interventions for high-risk adolescents and the construction of appropriate prevention efforts for all adolescents. No matter how well motivated our authority-directed intervention approaches might be, and no matter how clearly they employ sound therapeutic psychoeducational and informational practices, the mainstream norm-exemplifying nature of the interventions might limit their effectiveness in adolescent subcultures. If the beginnings of influence are characterized by credible compliance pressure (as social psychology's voluminous literature would suggest), peers must be employed in adolescent intervention efforts. Trend-setting peers must clearly be used not only as intervention targets (because of their high-risk profiles) but also as intervention allies. Frequently, mainstream society ignores the impressive competence of deviant peer leaders. However, the kinds of interventions proposed in this chapter acknowledge the positive power of trend-setting peers and endeavor to induce its use toward positive social ends. If we desire initial compliance to low-risk regimens to be transformed into lifelong internalization of values, such acknowledgments are necessary beginnings. For these reasons, we hope this chapter takes at least a small step in encouraging the development of peer-based interventions.

References

Burton, L. M., Allison, K. W., & Obeidallah, D. (1995). Social context and adolescence: Perspectives on development among inner-city African American teens. In L. J. Crockett & A. C. Crouter (Eds.), *Pathways through adolescence* (pp. 119–138). Mahwah, NJ: Erlbaum.

Cialdini, R. B. (1993). *Influence: Science and practice* (3rd ed.). New York: HarperCollins College Publishers.

Coie, J. D., & Jacobs, M. R. (1993). The role of social context in the prevention of conduct disorder. *Development and Psychopathology, 5,* 263–275.

Coie, J. D., Terry, R., Zakriski, A., & Lochman, J. E. (1995). Early adolescent social influences on delinquent behavior. In J. McCord (Ed.), *Coercion and punishment in long-term perspectives* (pp. 229–244). New York: Cambridge University Press.

Coie, J. D., Watt, N. F., West, S. G., Hawkins, J. D., Asarnow, J. R., Markman, H. J., et al. (1993). The science of prevention. A conceptual framework and some directions for a national research program. *American Psychologist, 48,* 1013–1022.

Conduct Problems Prevention Research Group (CPPRG). (1992). A developmental and clinical model for the prevention of conduct disorder: The Fast Track Program. *Development and Psychopathology, 4,* 509–527.

Costanzo, P. R. (1992). External socialization and the development of adaptive individualization and social connection. In D. N. Ruble & P. R. Costanzo (Eds.), *The social psychology of mental health: Basic mechanisms and applications* (pp. 55–80). New York: Guilford.

Dishion, T. J., & Andrews, D. W. (1995). Preventing escalation in problem behavior with high-risk adolescents: Immediate and one-year outcomes. *Journal of Consulting and Clinical Psychology, 63,* 538–548.

Dishion, T. J., McCord, J., & Poulin, F. (1999). When interventions harm: Peer groups and problem behavior. *American-Psychologist, 54,* 755–764.

Eagley, A. & Chaiken, S. (1993). *The psychology of attitudes.* Orlando, FL: Harcourt Brace Jovanovich.

Eccles, J. S., Lord, S., & Buchanan, C. M. (1996). School transitions in early adolescence: What are we doing to our young people? In J. A. Graber (Ed.), *Transitions through adolescence: Interpersonal domains and context* (pp. 251–284). Mahwah, NJ: Lawrence Erlbaum Associates.

Edwards, C. A. (1994). Leadership in groups of school-age girls. *Developmental Psychology, 30,* 920–927.

Elliott, D. S., & Menard, S. (1996). Delinquent friends and delinquent behavior: Temporal and developmental patterns. In J. D. Hawkins (Ed.), *Delinquency and crime: Current theories* (pp. 28–67). New York: Cambridge University Press.

Kelder, S. H., Orpinas, P., McAlister, A., Frankowski, R., Parcel, G. S., & Friday, J. (1996). The Students for Peace project: A comprehensive violence-prevention program for middle school students. *American Journal of Preventive Medicine, 12,* 22–30.

Kelman, H. C. (1961). Processes of opinion change. *Public Opinion Quarterly, 25,* 57–58.

Lepper, M. R., & Greene, D. (1979). *The hidden costs of reward.* Hillsdale, NJ: Erlbaum.

Lepper, M. R., Sethi, S., Dialdin, D. & Drake, M. (1997). Intrinsic and extrinsic motivation: A developmental perspective. In S. S. Luthar & J. A. Burack (Eds.), *Developmental psychopathology: Perspectives on adjustment, risk, and disorder* (pp. 23–50). New York: Cambridge University Press.

Luthar, S. S. (1997). Sociodemographic disadvantage and psychosocial adjustment: Perspectives from developmental psychopathology. In S. S. Luthar, J. A. Burack, D. Cicchetti, & J. R. Weisz (Eds.), *Developmental psychopathology. Perspectives on adjustment, risk, and disorder* (pp. 459–483). New York: Cambridge University Press.

Luthar, S. S., & McMahon, T. J. (1996). Peer reputation among inner-city adolescents: Structure and correlates. *Journal of Research on Adolescence, 6,* 581–603.

McCord, J. (1997, April). *Some unanticipated consequences of summer camps.* Paper presented at the biennial meetings of the Society for Research in Child Development. Washington, DC.

Miller-Johnson, S., Coie, J. D., Maumary-Gremaud, A., Bierman, K., & the Conduct Problems Prevention Research Group. (2002). Peer rejection and aggression and early starter models of conduct disorder. *Journal of Abnormal Child Psychology, 30*(3), 217–230.

Moffitt, T. E. (1993). Adolescence-limited and life-course-persistent antisocial behavior: A developmental taxonomy. *Psychological Review, 100,* 674–701.

Parkhurst, J. T., & Asher, S. R. (1992). Peer rejection in middle school: Subgroup differences in behavior, loneliness, and interpersonal concerns. *Developmental Psychology, 28,* 231–241.

Patterson, G. R., Capaldi, D. M., & Bank, L. (1991). An early starter model for predicting delinquency. In D. J. Pepler & K. H. Rubin (Eds.), *The development and treatment of childhood aggression* (pp. 139–168). Hillsdale, NJ: Lawrence Erlbaum.

Patterson, G. R., & Yoerger, K. (1997). A developmental model for late-onset delinquency. In D. W. Osgood (Ed.), *Nebraska Symposium on Motivation: Vol. 44. Motivation and delinquency* (pp. 119–177). Lincoln: University of Nebraska Press.

Perry, C. L., Williams, C. L., Veblen-Mortenson, S., & Toomey, T. L. (1996). Project Northland: Outcomes of a communitywide alcohol use prevention program during early adolescence. *American Journal of Public Health, 86,* 956–965.

Petty, R. E. & Cacciopo, J. T. (1981). *Attitudes and persuasion: Classic and contemporary approaches.* Iowa: W. C. Brown.

Poulin, F., Dishion, T. J., & Burraston, B. (2001). Long-term effects associated with aggregating high-risk adolescents in preventive interventions. *Applied Developmental Science, 5, 214–224.*

Price, R. H., Gioci, M., Penner, W., & Trautlein, B. (1993). Webs of influence: School and community programs that enhance adolescent health and education. In R. Takanishi (Ed.), *Adolescence in the 1990's. Risk and opportunity* (pp. 29–63). New York: Teachers College Press.

Reid, J. B. (1993). Prevention of conduct disorder before and after school entry: Relating interventions to developmental findings. *Development and Psychopathology, 5,* 243–262.

Rodkin, P. C., Farmer, T. W., Pearl, R., & Van Acker, R. (2000). Heterogeneity of popular boys: Antisocial and prosocial configurations. *Developmental Psychology, 36,* 14–24.

Thornberry, T. P. (1996). Empirical support for interactional theory: A review of literature. In J. D. Hawkins (Ed.), *Cambridge criminology series. Delinquency and crime: Current theories* (pp. 198–235). New York: Cambridge University Press.

Winfield, L. F. (1995). The knowledge base on resilience in African American adolescents. In L. J. Crockett & A. C. Crouter (Eds.), *Pathways through adolescence* (pp. 87–118). Mahwah, NJ: Erlbaum.

12

Research Meets the Real World: Lessons Learned in Three Community Implementations of Fast Track

Donna-Marie C. Winn and
Magaretha G. Hartley Herman

Funding agencies and private foundations continue to promote large, cross-site prevention research on sociopsychological programs that use highly rigorous methodologies. They have funded such expensive prevention research projects over the past decade in recognition that improving the science of prevention necessarily includes a recursive progression from clinical trials to large-scale field trials to community implementation, and relies on close collaboration between multiple disciplines and communities (Coie, Miller-Johnson, & Bagwell, 2000). Ironically, not enough has been done to document whether translation from large-scale field trials to community implementation is even possible or how such a task should be undertaken. Early research indicates that community implementation projects typically had less positive outcomes than did the original large-scale field trials and were difficult to implement (Berman & McLaughlin, 1978; Rappaport, Seidman, & Davidson, 1979). Hence, more careful analysis of what makes dissemination of field trials successful seems warranted. We offer our own experience in dissemination as the focus of this chapter in hopes that the strategies we employed to resolve issues that arose will serve as a warning or a guide for others.

This chapter describes the processes and barriers we encountered in our efforts to form community partnerships while disseminating the preventive intervention field trial called Fast Track. Fast Track is a multisite, 10-year-long, university-based preventive intervention program whose research goal is to test the efficacy of combining seven intervention programs to decrease problem behaviors in youth (Conduct Problems Prevention Research Group, 1992). The intervention programs were selected for the Fast Track field trial because of their prior efficacy or their relevance in addressing issues thought to adversely impact healthy, prosocial child development. The seven programs are home visiting, a socioemotional classroom curriculum entitled Promoting Alternative Thinking Strategies (PATHS), pairing peers to practice social skills, academic tutoring, parenting groups, child socioemotional skill-building

223

groups, and parent–child skill practice and relationship-building groups. The lessons we offer arise from three separate attempts to disseminate the first two or three years of the Fast Track program at one of the four Fast Track sites, and we believe they are broadly useful for dissemination efforts of university-based prevention programs.

The three dissemination projects were located in primarily African American, low-wealth, southern urban communities. In dissemination of Project A, Fast Track researchers were approached by community representatives to help them obtain grant funds to develop and implement a program in a local elementary school that would increase children's success and decrease their misbehaviors. We applied for and received state funding to implement the program and subcontracted a small portion of the grant to other community agencies for related program expenses. All of the program staff were employees of the university, but the staff offices were in a local community center and programs were held in the local school or community center. For Project A, the funding agency mandated an advisory board composed of agency and community representatives but did not delineate the scope and nature of responsibilities for the board. Project A replicated Fast Track (with the omission of the Peer Pairing intervention), worked with first-grade classes in one elementary school, and served approximately 150 children and their families over a three-year period.

Project B partnered with a school district to replicate most of the Fast Track interventions in seven elementary schools, each with its own site-based management team that operated in conjunction with central school system administration. The project implemented all of the Fast Track intervention components except the tutoring program, for which Reading Recovery was substituted. In partnering with Project B, the school administration functioned as the lead agent in writing and receiving grant funds, and we at the university received a subcontract for our supervision, training, consultation, and program evaluation. All program personnel staff were hired by our partner, the school system.

Project C was a partial downward extension of the Fast Track curriculum for preschoolers ages four to five (the tutoring program was omitted; a modified version of the Turtle Curriculum of PATHS for preschoolers was used; curriculum was adapted for parent and child groups; and home visits occurred) and served several hundred children who attended child-care centers. Community representatives approached us, asking that we write a grant for and receive most of the funds for implementing the program and write a small subcontract to the community center to cover office rent and other miscellaneous expenses. As with Project A, project staff members were employees of our university, but their offices and the programs they conducted were in the local community. In all three dissemination efforts, funding was obtained from state or federal agencies, and the university supplied program content, training for the projects, and weekly clinical supervision.

Serrano-Garcia (1990) identified three distinct phases in the process of developing participatory relationships with partners: entry, continuation, and ending. During the entry phase, parties share information, clarify roles and responsibilities, establish decision-making bodies, negotiate the research question and study design, and establish trust. The continuation phase is marked by further expansion of community awareness and understanding about the purpose of the research, delineation of the boundaries of confidentiality for both individuals and the communities themselves, and discussions about the expected use and purpose of data. The ending phase is characterized by data analysis, interpretation and feedback from research participants, goal setting for future action plans, and clarification of the role of the researchers in future collaborations. We have organized the strategies we employed to create and sustain community partnerships in disseminating Fast Track by slightly modifying the Serrano-Garcia categorization of three stages of the partnership process, to meet the particular idiosyncrasies of the dissemination process. For the purposes of this chapter, we have entitled them the initiation, implementation, and conclusion phases of dissemination.

Initiation Phase of the Partnership

Four formidable issues confronted us at the beginning of our attempts to disseminate Fast Track. These were issues of trust, financing, negative attitudes about research, and power to control the project.

Building Trust

The successful establishment of trust during the initial phase of our partnerships evolved differently across the three projects. Members of a grassroots community organization initiated the partnership with us in Projects A and C; in Project B, we approached a local board charged with coordinating youth programs to seek their endorsement of our partnering with the school system. The degree of trust seemed to vary according to who initiated the partnership, either the community partners or us as researchers. The school superintendent was a member of that local board and immediately identified members of her staff to take the lead in applying for the grant.

In Projects A and C, in which the impetus for the dissemination originated with our partners, it eventually became clear why the community representatives requested our assistance. Our partners genuinely wanted to decrease or end altogether the problems of pernicious delinquency and academic failure in their communities. Had we not had a long history of successfully working with children with behavioral issues and a track record in obtaining grant funding, skills central to helping with their concerns, the community likely would not have approached us to partner, as Hatch, Moss, Saran, Presley-Cantrell, and Mallory (1993) suggest. The degree of trust seemed to vary according to who initiated the partnership, either the community partners or us as researchers. When community members initiated the partnerships by coming to us, they tended to hold very positive expectations for the project, acted as liaisons to the rest of the community, invested considerable time volunteering to help the project become a success, and provided otherwise unavailable access and opportunities through their relationships within the community. Community partners spoke at churches, parent–teacher meetings, political action meetings, and public fairs to recruit participants to the program. Several openly shared the benefits that they had received from the programs when recruiting others. Our partners' willingness to recruit others bespoke their individual commitment to making the programs successful. However, this willingness did not preclude the tension that arose from our partners' desire to place service goals ahead of scientific goals, such as program fidelity or from skepticism about or motives for agreeing to partner with them (Debro and Conley, 1993; Pokorny et al., 2004; Rebach, 1991). Initially, we did not thoroughly discuss this tension and our failure to do so eroded a significant amount of the trust that had been established.

Trust, however, needs to be reciprocal, and for us to trust our partners, we researchers needed to evaluate our partners, just as they did us. One dimension we learned to evaluate was the scope and legitimacy of our partners' claim to represent or lead a given constituency. In Project C, representatives who adequately represented all of their constituents approached us. In Projects A and B, our partners' stated span of influence and representation was broad and deep, but their influence eventually proved insufficient to garner comprehensive support for the program's implementation. As Conway, Hu, and Harrington (1997) predicted, we learned that respectful, discreet, and thorough assessment of our partners' ability to accurately represent all of their stated constituents' views is an important step in forming successful partnerships. Our unexamined trust in a project's ability to represent and mobilize its stated constituents proved costly. For example, from Project B we learned that even though a school administration wholeheartedly endorses the adoption of a program, individual teachers who ultimately bear most of the responsibility for implementing changes can still greatly affect the efficacy and impact of the program. We now advocate carefully evaluating the history and likelihood of successful program implementation in each classroom, as well as evaluating the impact on existing policies of changing teaching practices and school procedures (e.g., mandatory teaching times, end-of-course evaluations, suspension and expulsion policies). When partnering with communities, we also learned to pay particular attention to potential program participants who might be underrepresented or misrepresented by the current leadership structure (e.g., recent immigrant populations, age-based or geographic subgroups within communities). During Projects A and C, effective, well-respected new leaders emerged from various sectors of the community, including employees of local human service organizations, members of the clergy, members of civic organizations, grassroots organization leaders, local business leaders, and potential recipients of the programs' services themselves, much as Hatch and colleagues (1993) described.

In Project B, the partnership that we initiated, trust was more difficult to establish. Some partner staff, for example, assumed we had self-aggrandizing motives for participating in the partnerships. Before we even approached this partner, we evaluated our willingness to work with them, assessing interpersonal styles, work practices, and productivity, as well as the social, political, and historical climate of the communities, as Beauvais (1999) suggested. Once we were reasonably certain that our styles were compatible, we approached them. They evaluated us as well; issues of power, parity, and respect loomed large for them. To help establish trust in our willingness to be equal partners, we met at locations convenient to them (school administration offices and local restaurants with readily accessible parking) as well as at our own university-based office. As Pokorny et al. (2004) noted, doing so demonstrated both our willingness to engage and feel comfortable in their environment and our openness for them to see our facilities and offer hospitality to them. When we met, we discussed the pressures and concerns that might alter our partners' ability to participate fully in meetings or complete tasks on time. We routinely shared and inquired about family celebrations or illnesses; community controversies, celebrations, or sorrows; work pressures and grant deadlines; and end-of-semester crunch or summer planning for children on vacation. The careful balance between effective listening and self-disclosure seemed to strengthen mutual trust.

Financing

Our partners held deep concerns about financing the disseminations. Why were our projects so expensive compared with other projects they had undertaken? What kind of benefit would each party derive from undertaking the project? How much of these benefits would each partner receive? We know now that careful negotiation about profitability for all parties should be clearly delineated before agreeing to proceed with the partnership, because perceived inequalities in profitability can give rise to resentment and schisms that render the partnership ineffective. Several of our partners expected to receive details about such things as salaries, personnel qualifications, benefits, and disposition of equipment upon the conclusion of the project. The sometimes-extraordinary cost of partnering with a university (including an overhead rate of 54%, fringe benefit rates for employees, and fees for consultation) was a source of much misunderstanding and contention. In each dissemination project, we successfully persuaded our university to substantially lower its overhead rate, thus cutting the cost of the programs. We learned to accurately estimate the operating expenses of subcontractors, because their tight budgets made it impossible for them to cover unexpected costs.

Partner Attitudes About Research

Another important consideration during the initiation phase is understanding and managing partners' attitudes about research. Several of our partners held very negative attitudes about research and the harm research causes its participants. As other researchers also have experienced, we encountered several community representatives whose disdain for research was due in large measure to their awareness of a Tuskegee research project that used trusted, influential members of the community to injure unsuspecting participants (Debro & Conley, 1993; Hatch et al., 1993; Jones 1981; Thomas & Quinn, 1991). Our partners were adamant that they not become a part of victimizing their own community, but because the interventions we offered had a high degree of face validity (e.g. tutoring, support groups for parents), many of our partners appeared to only modestly scrutinize our program components. Some partners were also concerned about our protocols for selecting only children with multiple problems, or our paying parents to attend parent classes. They felt that others might see children in the program as high risk, or parents might expect to be paid for enhancing their children's skills. Because we felt that these two aspects of our program (selection criteria and providing compensation for participants' time) were essential, we brainstormed creative ways to accomplish the goals of all partners. As a compromise, instead of being given direct cash payments for their attendance, parents were given books for their children, coupons for free services, and other small gifts of appreciation. These payments were given out of respect for participants' willingness to spend their valuable time learning and sharing ways to help their children succeed, much like Delgado (1996) suggested. We enrolled participants whose children displayed significant problems with aggression and noncompliance, but we also enrolled participants who displayed strong motivation to be a part of our program, as the community desired. We learned not to use the word *research* because it held so many negative connotations and used phrases such as "gather evidence/evaluate to see if the program works."

Many of our partners' concerns about research focused on the uses of data. To address their concerns we shared copies of the funding agencies' requirements for evaluation of the programs' effectiveness. We shared our experience of how we had collected similar data in the past, and we offered to add questions they developed to the data collection measures. But we naively assumed that researchers owned the data and that an individual respondent's datum was confidential. So when members of the community in one project wanted to see for themselves what individual respondents wrote about their experiences with the project, we had to explain that we could not compromise on this issue without getting prior written consent from all participants. We never shared individual respondents' data and chose instead to share aggregated data or data with some details modified to preserve anonymity.

Power and Control

It is crucial to anticipate and address issues of power and control among partners (Bond, 1990; Tolan, Baptiste, Madison, & Paikoff, 2002). In Project A, the issue of power and control emerged during the second stage of our partnership, the implementation phase, and it proved to be so time consuming and thorny that we now strongly advocate using preventive strategies for addressing these questions during the initiation phase of the partnership. To address issues of power and control, we held a series of meetings with interested community representatives, to define everyone's roles. Initially, several partners on Project A's advisory board expected to participate in all aspects of personnel decision making (hiring, promotions, salary increases, and terminations) and also expected to use certain sites for the program, even though such expectation would have precluded maintaining the anonymity of participants. Some of the partners also considered it their right to alter the content or intensity of the interventions, to determine eligibility criteria to participate in the program, and to approve the content of written products or presentations, including subsequent grant proposals. These were serious conflicts, and we learned that failure to discuss real and perceived imbalances of power and control can undermine the entire partnership. Our experience also taught us that productive discussions about differences in power can foster increased respect for what other partners bring to the relationship and decrease the likelihood that partners will inadvertently flaunt their own power.

Having just described how issues of trust, financing, negative attitudes about research, and power and control can potentially derail the very early stages of university/community partnerships when disseminating projects, we emphasize the need for early, careful, and deliberate discussions about these topics.

Implementation Phase of the Partnership

Once the initiation phase of planning and preparing for the program is complete, the implementation phase begins. Typically, during this phase a program identifies and serves program participants and collects data for the evaluation. The working relationships established during the initiation phase mature and evolve (Baker, Homan, Schonhoff, & Kreuter, 1999; Butterfoss, Goodman, & Wandersman, 1993) and need ongoing attention. The lessons we learned with our partners about how to successfully negotiate the implementation phase of a dissemination project include creating ways (a) to maintain and strengthen relationships among all partners, (b) to respond to shifting community priorities, (c) to handle shifts in the decision-making processes of partners over time, and (d) to resolve discrepancies between university and funding agency regulations and community expectations.

Relationships

Of vital importance during the implementation phase of any project is the need to maintain and strengthen relationships among all of the partners, leaders, and implementers, because there will be changes. Projects A and C lost a very supportive community leader as a result of his unexpected death. In Project B, we secured consent to apply for funding from six middle-school principals, yet one year later, only one of those six principals remained. And in Project A, changes in board memberships significantly altered the breadth of support for our partnership. These major losses of key personnel with whom we had established trust during the initiation phase taught us not to rely on a narrow band of support for our partnerships. Our projects survived changes in key personnel because experience had taught us the value of seeking allies throughout the community. We took time to meet with direct human service providers (outreach workers from health departments and social service organizations), housing department representatives, recreation providers (Boys & Girls clubs, athletic leagues, parks and recreation programs), religious organizations (heads of houses of worship, youth outreach workers, charitable gift organizations and ministries), educational leaders (administrators and teachers, but also informal leaders within the institutions), owners of businesses (particularly ones revered by the community, e.g., funeral homes, food establishments, and financial institutions), elected community leaders (long-time appointees and newcomers alike), and, most important, potential program participants. Although labor-intensive, activities such as maintaining visibility, attending community meetings, and networking were critical in finding allies and maintaining broad support for the partnerships. Doing this community work had two added benefits: We learned about others' concerns as they arose, before issues became so complex that they were difficult to resolve, and we gave others an opportunity to better understand the program and its purpose. In many instances, the relationships we built with such community members made them self-appointed ambassadors for a program, markedly enhancing the community's participation.

Key personnel changes among our research staff, graduate assistants, and office administrators also occurred and meant that we needed to begin anew in establishing trust between our partners and our new personnel. Respect for and trust in one researcher was not automatically transferred to another researcher, even when the initial researcher took steps to encourage it. In one dissemination project, the principal investigator (PI) and a junior researcher together built a relationship with the partners. When the PI transferred the majority of the day-to-day contact to a capable junior researcher, our partners doubted our commitment to the project and our desire to make it a success. In addition to offering many verbal reassurances in response to our partners' concerns over the PI "abandoning" the project, the junior researcher made herself more visible in the community and increased her interactions with program staff and community members. Over time, the junior researcher proved to be as available and responsive as the PI, and a new equilibrium of trust and respect was achieved.

Shifts in Policies and Priorities

Besides attending to the quality of relationships, a research partner needs to be attuned to shifts in partners' priorities and policies during the implementation phase and negotiate adjustments to the implementation plan. During the 1990s, for example, public schools shifted their placement policy for students with behavioral and emotional disabilities and began to more frequently segregate youth with disruptive behaviors, so that they have only each other as peer models (U.S. Department of Education, 2000; Zhao, 2002). Consequently, it has become more difficult to implement programs such as Fast Track, which are predicated on the benefits to aggressive children of being exposed to positive peers. Another shift in school policy had an adverse impact on our methodology for recruitment of target children, such that while implementing Project B, we needed to alter our recruitment strategy. Our Project B partner also decided to shift program services to an older target population than the one originally agreed upon, which required further adaptations. In Project C, we had to develop services to address a growing immigrant population, a new priority target for our partner. Community and university researcher partnerships may also experience shifts in decision-making processes. As partners develop, they may change their regulations, by-laws, or partnership practices. In Project A, one partner's policy shifted from a priori approvals of grant resubmissions to distribution of draft applications to its constituents for ratification prior to grants being resubmitted. This distribution and feedback process consumed valuable application preparation time and could have had a detrimental impact on the quality of future grant applications, so one partner's suggestion was adopted: Prepare a one-page summary of the program for constituents to review and ratify in concept, before writing a grant application. Because it is not always possible to anticipate policy, priority, or process shifts, it is important to stay alert for such changes and manage them as they arise.

Resolving Discordant Regulations and Expectations

Yet another set of issues that arose during the implementation phase of our partnerships concerned the discrepancies between university regulations and community expectations on such matters as employment access and qualifications, the hiring process, personnel rights, and confidentiality for participants in the projects' programs. For Projects A and C, our partners strongly advocated that many of the positions created by the projects be filled by local residents, but we did not find nearly as many qualified applicants from the community as everyone would have liked, despite our collective posting of job listings throughout the community (at churches, schools, agencies, recreation centers). We were able to honor one community's request to include years of relevant experience as a substitute for a degree for one candidate, but not for others. University policies that give priority to qualified candidates who are being terminated from other university positions were in conflict with partners' desires to select mostly community-nominated candidates for positions created by the projects. We came to value those community residents who worked on the projects; they were industrious, gave their opinions unabashedly, and helped the project to become better, so over time, we began to include in grant proposals the costs of training required by community residents to successfully perform both semiskilled and highly skilled jobs. Such training enhanced their performance as family service workers and administrators, much as Arnold and colleagues described (1999). The credibility of employees who live in the community, have extensive knowledge of the project, and believe in its worth proved crucial in times when others questioned the efficacy and efficiency of a program, so the effort involved in reconciling university regulations with community desires is decidedly worthwhile.

University regulations about personnel issues were often sources of dissension in the partnerships. Our community partners expressed concern about salaries being too high for some positions and too low for others. Some partners wanted to screen applicants and have input on performance appraisals, merit raises, and disciplinary actions. For two projects, we decided to obtain university approval to include community representatives on the official search committee, and they added substantially to the quality of the interview by asking detailed questions about applicants' knowledge of community resources and by probing their strategies for recruiting residents who might demonstrate reluctance to participate.

When community representatives developed negative appraisals of employees' performance (e.g., they thought a particular employee was afraid to visit certain homes or dressed inappropriately), we had to balance university protections of employee rights with our partners' desires to be part of the process. We eventually established a process for incorporating external performance appraisals into employees' university performance review, consulting closely with the university's human resources department. Our failure during the initiation phase of Project C to negotiate and define together the legal limits of the partner's involvement in determining a range of personnel issues (qualifications for positions, writing performance evaluations, defining salary range and increases and procedures for determining those, disciplining and dismissing employees) almost proved fatal. We had assumed that our partners knew that such specific information was confidential within a private university setting, but they did not have that knowledge, and our inclusion of community representatives on the search committees fueled their expectations for complete inclusion in all personnel matters. When we ourselves had to terminate staff whose performances some community members praised, we painstakingly documented our reasons and relied heavily on consultation from university human resources. Because some of the staff members misrepresented the circumstances of their receiving disciplinary actions and university regulations did not allow us to explain the true circumstances to our community partners, the trust that some of our partners had in us was badly eroded. Clarifying all procedures related to employees during the initiation phase is the wiser course.

In each of the three projects, our partners, community leaders, or funding agency requested identifying information on program participants, something university regulations forbid. One local grantor requested, during the middle of a funding cycle, that we provide individual social security numbers for participants and attempted to make our receipt of further funding that year contingent on our providing these numbers. In another instance, community members' discontent with the job performance of several program employees prompted community members to request an independent assessment of participant satisfaction with the program, yet university regulations prohibited us from complying with such a request because doing so would breach program participant confidentiality. So we now routinely discuss during the initiation phase of any new partnership our limitations in releasing personal information or providing community members with access to program participants.

The lessons we learned during the implementation phase of disseminating research projects can be summed up as follows: Although there is no substitute for careful and deliberate initial discussions between partners prior to beginning the programs, partners need to revisit issues of trust and changes in relationships; shifts in partners' priorities, policies, and processes; and discrepancies among partners' regulations for implementing programs.

Conclusion of the Partnership

The last phase of disseminating a project is the conclusion of an active partnership; the program is still being implemented, but all partners are planning for the ending of the project. Four issues arose during the conclusion phase of our three projects that we wish to highlight: (a) the process for review of written documents; (b) the use and misuse of data; (c) the plan for acknowledging program participants and others involved in the projects' successes; and (d) the plan to increase the communities' capacity to conduct similar projects in the future.

Documents Review

As projects conclude, oftentimes in a flurry of activity, it is important to review all the procedures for writing final summaries about the project. Documents written to summarize the outcome of a project serve as a legacy of the project's success and remain memorable in the minds of community representatives. In Project A, we asked our donor agency for an extension of the deadline for the final report so community members could have enough time to thoroughly review the document and provide their input. Of course the documents that we circulated needed to be written in an easily understood format, so we prepared two comparable documents: one for our partners and another for the granting agency. During the conclusion phase of a project it is also important to make final decisions about the process for reviewing any documents written after the conclusion of the project.

Uses of Data

Preliminary decisions should be made during the initial phase of a partnership regarding how university researchers may use the data collected during the project in publications or public presentations. Even so, during the conclusion phase of all three projects we invariably found that concerns arose about the content and tenor of written documents. For Project A, we began the practice of distributing draft reports to the project advisory committee and to the appropriate community governance bodies, so that we could respond to such concerns. We learned, however, that distributing written reports was not without risks. In discussions with our partners we expressed our concern that information contained in written documents could be taken out of context and potentially used to harm either program participants or the community itself, and that misinterpretation of data can occur easily among individuals not trained in data analysis. We offered to assist our partners when they were submitting similar grants in which the results from our partnerships could be used to support their applications. We also strongly encouraged them to use text that we wrote to describe the projects and their results. By so doing, we were able to exempt ourselves from the need to preapprove any of our partners' new documents. If researchers do expect to preapprove or coauthor subsequent writings about the project, this expectation should be explicitly discussed during the initiation phase, because late demands for preapproval can create a very clear hierarchy with researchers in the dominant position, which is a very undesirable outcome.

Acknowledging Success

During the conclusion phase it is also valuable for partners to plan an end to the program by acknowledging participants and those involved in the program's success. We did this in several ways: For Project A, we honored members of the advisory board by arranging a buffet catered by a community resident. For Project C, we held a graduation ceremony to honor the accomplishments of the children who met or exceeded program goals, and we honored families for their excellent participation rates and new successes in advocating for their children's needs. We actively solicited input from our partners and program participants about their perceptions of how ending the project would impact the community. We also implemented our partners' suggestions on ways to minimize the negative impact of the program's ending. For example, supplies and materials purchased by Project B were donated to the local community center, rather than the funding agency or university retaining possession.

To identify the parameters under which future partnerships might occur is another task for the conclusion phase of a project. During our work with partners in Project A, we realized that our next partnership would almost assuredly need to include employment, training, and career growth opportunities for significant numbers of local residents. From our Project C partners we learned that we should include in our grant application the costs of building renovation and maintenance, in order to enable programs to remain community-based beyond the life of the initial project. For both Projects A and C, the community's capacity to be self-sufficient increased over the life of our partnership and, as a result, their needs for programming space increased. Acknowledging and clarifying what we learned from our partnership through a process of creating parameters for future partnerships supported the termination process by leaving open the possibility for future partnerships.

Building Capacity

When programs were successful, our partners sometimes wanted to continue them. Plan carefully during the conclusion phase to ensure the partner's capacity to continue the project beyond the conclusion of the partnership. Providing them with models of grants; helping them identify alternative sources of funding; agreeing not to compete with them for local, more readily accessible funds; talking candidly about the expectations of fiduciary responsibility and accountability required by different granting agencies; and agreeing to review their grant applications before they are submitted are just a few of the activities that we have undertaken to increase the likelihood that partners will be able to continue projects. Efforts such as these ensure that communities will reap the benefits of partnering with universities long after the partnership has ended and will value such partnerships in the future.

Over the decade or so of our partnering with communities, we as university-based researchers have made many mistakes and learned many lessons when attempting to partner with others to deliver community-based prevention programs. The mistakes and lessons learned occurred throughout the lives of the projects. The temporal sequencing of the mistakes we made has been presented to highlight our suggestions about optimal ways to handle issues that may arise. Our experience has taught us that partnerships are dynamic, complex entities; hence it is important to keep careful documentation of how the partners resolve issues, either through meeting minutes that highlight decisions or in the form of a memorandum of understanding with the roles, rights, responsibilities, and timelines for all parties. A summary of issues to be resolved in a memorandum is presented in the appendix.

Transforming the components of Fast Track, a large-scale field trial, into three distinct dissemination projects or community implementations was a challenging process. The active inclusion of community partners required that we shift the kind of authority we typically possess, as others have noted (Dressler, 1994; Israel, Schurman, & Hugentobler, 1992). Concerns about sharing control with our partners, adhering to methodological rigor and fidelity, lack of community resources (economic, personnel, knowledge about research), large time commitments, and local politics and historical schism were all valid, but the dream of a perfect partner has faded to myth. Each partner brought strengths and weaknesses that affected our ability to work together effectively. We offer our experiences in an effort to soften the learning curve as university researchers continue to disseminate large-scale research trials to communities. Power inequalities between partners and differences in mission must be anticipated but can be realigned to strengthen the collaborative effort and improve program outcomes. The process of initiating and maintaining successful relationships among university, agency, and community partners requires that researchers be willing to examine their own and their partners' perspectives as issues arise and decide which parameters of the field trail are essential to maintain and which are modifiable.

Appendix 12.1.
Checklist for Researchers in Dissemination Partnerships

Initiation Phase

Work to build trust among all partners.
>   Establish a respectful and hospitable relationship.
>>   Arrange meetings at times and places convenient for community partners.
>>   Agree on procedures for postponing or changing meetings.
>>   Circulate promptly all minutes, and keep accurate records of amendments.
>>   Create times for partners to share personal or vocational information.
>   Discuss your own motivations for engaging in the project.
>   Be frank regarding how much money you and your colleagues receive.
>   Expect skepticism from partnerships with few monetary resources.
>>   Clarify how grant overhead is used and why personnel fringe rates seem high.
>>   Investigate the possibility of lower overhead rates for this program, or offer other intangibles to offset the high rate.
>>   Openly identify personal or institutional benefits you or the university will derive from the partnership.
Address partners' concerns about any potential harm of the program.
>   Talk together about their personal experiences with harm: What kinds of harmful things do they fear or have they heard of in other research projects?
>   Offer your appraisal of potential harm, and discuss the role of your Institutional Review Board and advisory boards to the project.
>   Decide on strategies to minimize the likelihood of harm.
Identify with your partners what each one brings to the partnership and what each one needs from the other partners.
>   Consider each partner's history in successfully completing similar tasks;
>   Clarify what priority this will be for each partner, and what other projects might take precedence;
>   Evaluate how much influence and trust each partner has established with the project's target audience;
>   Identify whom each partner legitimately represents;
>   Review each partner's history of working together, and successful policies or procedures they established; and
>   Note how partners deal with conflicts.
Clarify each partner's roles and responsibilities in implementing the project.
>   Identify who can change the program content and data to be collected.
>   Identify how the timing of the program could be changed, and by whom.
>   Establish clear procedures regarding hiring personnel.
>>   Determine which partners set pay rates and criteria for employment.
>>   Decide who has input in hiring decisions, who designs the interview questions, and who makes the final hiring decisions.

Consider positions for community residents

Select clear hiring priorities for the project, and clarify any differences from the priorities usually established by the hiring agency.

Describe the personnel rights of the hiring agency.

Establish training needs and procedures.

Identify which partner will provide the training.

Agree on duration and implementation of responsibilities for training.

Establish procedures for interagency coordination.

Clarify partners' expectations regarding coordination meetings.

Identify policies and procedures of partners that could affect the program or staff.

Discuss the burdens on host or partner agencies that the program will impose: personnel time, additional meetings, data collection.

Create a process for incorporating negative feedback on the program or staff.

Identify partners' responsibilities for reporting on the project.

Design a process for writing, reviewing, and amending documents required by the funding agency and local advisory boards, and assign responsibilities to each partner.

Design a process for writing, reviewing, and amending nonessential documents such as press releases and journal articles.

Decide what actions will be taken if a partner deems a document harmful.

Implementation Phase

Maintain and strengthen relationships among the partners.

Retain hospitality and respect as vital elements of the work.

Plan for changes in key partners or program supporters.

Identify other potential allies, meet with them, and solicit their input and support.

Participate in community meetings and events.

Plan for changes in the project staff.

Work to establish trust for each new project member.

Talk with partners about the impact of personnel losses.

Reconcile differences between university and partner financial and personnel policies.

Continue discussions of the hiring process established in the initiation phase.

Review hiring criteria.

Inform partners of significant deviations in hiring, staffing, or compensation of program staff.

Expect shifts in partners' priorities and decision-making processes.

Periodically evaluate the impact on the project of any such shifts.

Encourage partners to give advance notice of shifts and plan together how to minimize any negative impact on the project.

Conclusion Phase

Review documents produced about the project.
> Establish or revise timelines for reviewing documents, as provided for in the review plan created during the Initiation Phase.
> Distribute documents, noting parts omitted because of confidentiality requirements.
> Incorporate partners' suggestions, using established procedures.
> Provide partners with final copies of documents.

Clarify uses of outcomes.
> Review plan established during Initiation Phase for how data will be used.
> Prevent misinterpretations of data by providing partners with written descriptions of outcomes.

Honor program participants.
> Use neighborhood resources (caterers, musicians, venues) to celebrate.
> Invite community dignitaries to events.
> Present plaques, gift certificates, or other expressions of appreciation.

Obtain feedback on the program.
> Conduct meetings to elicit constituent feedback and consider using external consultants.
> Get feedback from partners, program participants, and community organizations.
> Solicit input on disposal of material assets, and seek to leave them in the community.

Increase community capacity to seek future funding.
> Help identify further funding.
> Review or help write future grant proposals.

Arrange for training on grant writing.

References

Arnold, D. H., Ortiz, C., Curry, J. C., Stowe, R. M., Goldstein, N. E., Fisher, P. H., Zeljo, A., & Yershova, K. (1999). Promoting academic success and preventing disruptive behavior disorders through community partnership. *Journal of Community Psychology, 27,* 589–598.

Baker, E. A., Homan, S., Schonhoff, R., & Kreuter, M. (1999). Principles of practice for academic/practice/community research partnerships. *American Journal of Preventive Medicine, 16*(Suppl. 3), 86–93.

Beauvais, F. (1999). Obtaining consent and other ethical issues in the conduct of research in American Indian communities. In M. R. De La Rosa, B. Segal, & R. Lopez (Eds.), *Conducting drug abuse research with minority populations: Advances and issues* (pp. 167–184). New York: The Haworth Press.

Berman, P., & McLaughlin, M. W. (1978). *Federal programs supporting educational change: Vol. 8. Implementing and sustaining innovations* (Contract No. R-1589/8-HEW). Washington, DC: U.S. Office of Education.

Bond, M. A. (1990). Criteria of excellence IV. Collaboration and action: A. Defining the research relationship: Maximizing participation in an unequal world. In P. Tolan, C. Keys, F. Chertok, & L. Jason (Eds.), *Researching community psychology: Issues of theory and methods* (pp. 183–186). Washington, DC: American Psychological Association.

Butterfoss, F. D., Goodman, R. M., & Wandersman, A. (1993). Community coalitions for prevention and health promotion. *Health Education Research, 8,* 315–330.

Coie, J. D., Miller-Johnson, S., & Bagwell, C. (2000). Prevention science. In A. J. Sameroff, M. Lewis, & S. Miller (Eds.), *Handbook of developmental psychopathology* (2nd ed., pp. 93–112). New York: Kluwer Academic/Plenum Publishers.

Conduct Problems Prevention Research Group (CPPRG). (1992). A developmental and clinical model for the prevention of conduct disorders: The Fast Track program. *Development and Psychopathology, 4,* 509–527.

Conway, T., Hu, T., & Harrington, T. (1997). Setting health priorities: Community boards accurately reflect the preferences of the community's residents. *Journal of Community Health, 22,* 57–68.

Debro, J., & Conley, D. J. (1993). School and community politics: Issues, concerns, and implications when conducting research in African-American communities. In M. R. De La Rosa & J. L. Adrados (Eds.), *Drug abuse among minority youth: Advances in research and methodology* (pp. 258–279). Rockville, MD: National Institute on Drug Abuse.

Delgado, M. (1996). Aging research and the Puerto Rican community: The use of an advisory committee of intended respondents. *The Gerontologist, 36,* 406–408.

Dressler, W. W. (1994). Community research: Partnership in black communities. Commentary. *American Journal of Preventive Medicine, 9*(Suppl. 6), 32–34.

Hatch, J., Moss, N., Saran, A., Presley-Cantrell, L., & Mallory, C. (1993). Community research: Partnership in black communities. *American Journal of Preventive Medicine, 9*(Suppl. 6), 27–31.

Israel, B. A., Schurman, S. J., & Hugentobler, M. K. (1992). Conducting action research: Relationships between organization members and researchers. *Journal of Applied Behavioral Science, 28,* 74–101.

Jones, J. H. (1981). *Bad blood.* New York: The Free Press.

Pokorny, S. B., Gaptiste, D. R., Tolan, P. H., Hirsch, B. J., Talbot, B., Ji, P., Paikoff, R. L., & Madison-Boyd, S. (2004). Prevention science: Participatory approaches and community case studies. In L. A. Jason, C. B. Keys, Y. Suarez-Balcazar, R. R. Taylor, M. I. Davis, J. A. Durlak, & D. H. Isenberg (Eds.), *Participatory community research: Theories and methods in action.* Washington, DC: American Psychological Association.

Rappaport, J., Seidman, E., & Davidson, W. S. (1979). Demonstration research and manifest versus true adoption: The natural history of a research project to divert adolescents from the legal system. In R. F. Munoz, L. R. Snowden, & J. G. Kelly (Eds.), *Social and psychological research in community settings* (pp. 101–144). San Francisco: Jossey-Bass.

Rebach, H. (1991). Substance use and black college students. In *Drug abuse research issues at historically black colleges and universities* (pp. 111–146). Tuskegee, AL: Tuskegee Institute, Department of Social Work.

Serrano-Garcia, I. (1990). Implementing research: Putting our values to work. In P. Tolan, C. Keys, F. Chertok, & L. Jason (Eds.), *Researching community psychology: Issues of theory and methods* (pp. 171–182). Washington, DC: American Psychological Association.

Thomas, S. B., & Quinn, S. B. (1991). The Tuskegee Syphilis Study, 1932–72: Implications for HIV education and AIDS risk education programs in the Black community. *American Journal of Public Health, 81,* 1498–1505.

Tolan, P. H., Baptiste, D., Madison, S., & Paikoff, R. (2002, June 15). *Collaborative approaches to prevention science.* Invited address to the Second Chicago Conference on Community Research: Participatory Methods, Chicago, IL.

U.S. Department of Education. (2000). *Twenty-second annual report to congress on the implementation of the Individuals with Disabilities Educational Act.* Washington, DC: Author.

Zhao, Y. (2002, April 24). Students' placement in special education is leveling off. *New York Times,* p. B5.

Part V _____

Conclusion

13

The Impact of Negative Social Experiences on the Development of Antisocial Behavior

John D. Coie

Several recurrent themes run through the chapters of this volume. The most obvious, given the title, is an underlying interest in prevention. The end point for much of the research that is described is to conduct developmental science that has utility for the implementation of prevention activity with high-risk children. This coming together of developmental and prevention science has been taking place with increasingly greater rigor over the past three or four decades, but the roots of this union were present as early as the birth of Head Start in the early 1960s. A second theme in this volume is the specific concern with the impact of negative peer relationships on children's future adjustment. This concern is relatively new for developmental and prevention scientists, although by the mid-1970s a handful of published studies linked childhood peer relational difficulties to future problems of adjustment, the most prominent of which were longitudinal studies by Cowen, Pederson, Babigian, Izzo, and Trost (1973) and Roff, Sells, and Golden (1972). In a highly influential review of research attempting to identify the best childhood risk predictors, Kohlberg, LaCrosse, and Ricks (1972) concluded that the most promising variables were early antisocial behavior and poor childhood peer relations.

This conclusion of Kohlberg et al. (1972) was at odds with the way prevention-oriented researchers thought about risk and protective factors at the time. Interventions aimed at risk factors for children primarily focused on the adult influences on child development. The goal was to improve parenting or educational practice (Felner, Jason, Moritsugu, & Farber, 1983; Sarason, Levine, Goldenberg, Cherlin, & Bennett, 1966). When developmental scientists of the 1960s argued about the relative influence of nature versus nurture in the development of child behavior, particularly disordered behavior, nurture was equated largely with parent influences. Child peer influences were not usually considered as a significant factor. Folk wisdom, of course, recognized the negative influence of bad company and the negative effects of gang membership, and social scientists recognized deviant friendships as important to the emergence of delinquency. Nonetheless, the broader dimension of children's

peer relations was not part of the framework for understanding the development of psychopathology or the planning of prevention programs.

At the time of the Kohlberg et al. (1972) review there was no consistent way
of assessing poor peer relations and, as Parker and Asher (1987) subsequently
pointed out in their classic review of childhood risk factor research, the independent contributions of poor peer relations and the childhood behaviors that led
to poor peer relations had not been evaluated because investigators rarely
included both types of variables in the same longitudinal studies. Much of the
initial research on childhood peer problems by myself and some of the other
contributors to this volume focused on developing reliable measures of peer
social status (Coie, Dodge, & Coppotelli, 1982), identifying behavioral determinants of childhood peer status (Coie, Dodge, Terry, & Wright, 1991; Coie &
Kupersmidt, 1983; Dodge, 1983; Dodge, Coie, & Brakke, 1982; Dodge, Coie,
Pettit, & Price, 1990), and evaluating the stability of peer status across time
(Coie & Dodge, 1983). During this period a growing number of other investigators were addressing similar issues and giving shape to a field of developmental
research that was important on its own, but was invariably justified in terms
of the original hypothesis that poor childhood peer relations was a significant
causal factor in the development of childhood and adolescent adjustment problems. Nonetheless, there was relatively little new longitudinal evidence supporting this hypothesis, particularly research that was designed to separate
the effects of peer rejection from the child characteristics that contributed to
their rejection by peers.

The most compelling variable for consideration as the true risk factor for
which peer rejection might simply be a marker was childhood aggression. From
the time of the Kohlberg et al. (1972) review to the Parker and Asher (1987)
review it had become quite clear that aggression was an important risk factor
in human development, especially in the development of delinquency and antisocial behavior patterns. It had also become clear from many recent observational studies that aggression was a major determinant of rejected social status
(Coie, Dodge, & Kupersmidt, 1990). For this reason Parker and Asher concluded
that the important next question for the peer relations field was to determine
whether childhood peer rejection is, itself, a valid predictor of subsequent
antisocial behavior, or is simply a marker of the child's aggression, which is
the true predictor variable.

Separating Rejection From Aggression Effects

The first longitudinal evidence indicating some support for the independent
contributions of peer rejection and aggression to the prediction of adolescent
adjustment appeared in a follow-up study of the mixed-ethnicity sample of 115
fifth-grade children first studied by Coie et al. (1982). Kupersmidt and Coie
(1990) found that only childhood aggression was predictive of adolescent delinquency, school dropout, and truancy on the entire sample. However, when only
the Caucasian majority (70%) portion of the sample was considered, both peer
rejection and aggression made independent contributions to the prediction of
these indices of poor adjustment in adolescence. In the earlier study of behav-

ioral determinants of peer status, Coie et al. (1982) found evidence of racial prejudice in the determinants of rejected status among the African American minority children. Kupersmidt and Coie argued that peer rejection might not have been effective in predicting adjustment in the African American subsample because of this prejudice in the assignment of status.

Because of these concerns about the effects of racial prejudice invalidating a test of the Parker and Asher question, Coie, Lochman, Terry, and Hyman (1992) pursued this question with a sample of African American children from urban elementary schools serving predominantly African American children. Two purposes were served by this choice of samples. One is that the problem of racial bias in responding to the sociometric questions was eliminated. Second, it permitted a test of the generalizability of the findings obtained earlier in the Caucasian-only analyses to African American youth. Three successive cohorts of third-grade children were administered a classroom sociometric measure including items of social behavior such as aggression and peer status indices of being liked most and liked least. Of the more than 1,500 children on whom these data were collected in third, fourth, and fifth grade, a random, stratified sample were contacted in sixth grade to be part of an adolescent adjustment study. Every other year, beginning in sixth grade and continuing for four years past the point at which most of the sample completed high school, self-report and parent ratings of adjustment were obtained on the 622 youth who agreed to participate in the study. Parents completed the Child Behavior Checklist (Achenbach & Edelbrock, 1983), and youth answered questions from the Child Assessment Schedule (Hodges, 1987) and the delinquency and substance use items from the National Youth Survey (Elliott, Huizinga, & Ageton, 1985). For the first two cohorts, it was possible to obtain teacher ratings on adjustment to the first year of middle school (sixth grade) from each of the multiple teachers who had worked with each child. A record of police contacts during adolescence and the early adult years was obtained from juvenile court records and state criminal files.

The independent effects of peer rejection and aggression as influences on adolescent adjustment in this sample of youth from predominantly low-income African American homes were first examined at the end of sixth grade on the two cohorts for whom teacher ratings, as well as self- and parent report, were available (Coie et al., 1992). Using a one standard deviation cutoff point for determining problematic adjustment on each of the three sources of ratings, the decision was made to categorize an adolescent as having had difficulty in adjusting to the first year of middle school if two of the three sources rated that individual as having problems in adjustment. With this criterion, 62% of youth who had been both socially rejected and aggressive in third grade met the consensus definition of poor adjustment at the end of sixth grade. By contrast, only 18% of the youth who were neither rejected nor aggressive in third grade met that criterion. Of those youth who were aggressive but not rejected in third grade, 40% were rated as poorly adjusted, and 34% of those who were rejected but not aggressive in third grade were rated as poorly adjusted. Significant main effects for both aggression and peer rejection were obtained in the chi-square analysis, indicating that both childhood risk factors were, indeed, independent predictors of adolescent adjustment problems. In addition to providing support for the conclusions of the earlier study by Kupersmidt and Coie (1990), these results extend their generalizability to urban African American youth and support the hypothesis that the rejection variable did not work for the African American children in that study because of the validity problems resulting from their minority status and the racial bias that may have entered into judgments of dislike.

Coie, Terry, Lenox, Lochman, and Hyman (1995) followed up on this initial study of the sample's adjustment in adolescence by comparing growth curves of dysfunctional behavior across three time periods—sixth, eighth, and tenth grade—on the four groups defined by the aggression and rejection variables. Because sixth grade was the initial year of middle school, it was possible that many students might have been exhibiting time-limited adjustment problems because of the stresses of this transition. Separate analyses were conducted for boys and girls and by source of information on adjustment—self-report versus parental report. The impact of earlier childhood rejection as a predictor of later adolescent adjustment appears to increase across the period of adolescence. From sixth to tenth grade, adolescents who had been rejected as children showed increasingly poorer adjustment as they got older. The patterns differed in complexity according to gender and source of reporting, but, overall, the rejected and aggressive subgroup had the most consistently dysfunctional profile. This contrast was most vivid in the case of boys' self-reported antisocial behavior. The rejected, aggressive boys' antisocial behavior increased dramatically from sixth grade to tenth grade whereas the other three groups all had a flat trajectory from sixth grade onward. The self-reported internalizing problems of the rejected, aggressive group also showed this same increasingly problematic trajectory from sixth through tenth grade. The self-reports of girls revealed only a main effect for childhood aggression on antisocial behavior, which was significantly lower than boys, as expected. The adjustment data obtained from parents consistently supported rejection as the primary childhood risk factor for both types of adjustment problems among both boys and girls.

Early- Versus Late-Starting Delinquency

The preceding results demonstrate that aggressive boys who also experience rejection by their elementary school peers are at greater risk for a trajectory of escalating delinquency during their adolescent years than are boys who are aggressive but not rejected by their peers. Similar conclusions were reached in the Oregon Social Learning Center study of 200 boys from Eugene, OR (Patterson, Reid, & Dishion, 1992). Patterson and his colleagues found that early-starting delinquency was preceded by a combination of male aggressiveness, poor parental discipline and monitoring of youth behavior, and peer social rejection. A significant part of the behavioral profile of early-starting delinquency is a greater tendency toward violence. In several recent longitudinal studies of early offending behavior, a disproportionate number of the youth showing a pattern of chronic violent offenses had begun their offending behavior at an early age (Thornberry, Huizinga, & Loeber, 1995). In one sample of

Rochester youth, 39% of the chronic violent group began committing violent acts by age nine. In a second sample of Denver youth, 62% of the chronic violent offending group had started their delinquent careers by this same age. If it is true, then, that a disproportionate number of chronically violent men begin their delinquent careers at an early age, then an important question for prevention theory is whether the same childhood variables that predict early-starting delinquency also predict the identity of youth who are most apt to be chronically violent. Miller-Johnson, Coie, Maumary-Gremaud, Lochman, and Terry (1999) used data from the Durham longitudinal study described earlier to address this question. Youth self-reports of offending behavior for the same period of sixth through tenth grade were broken down by type of offense, and third-grade data on aggressiveness and peer rejection were used to predict types of offending behavior. Childhood aggression was a significant predictor of vandalism, robbery, felony theft, minor assault, and felony assault among males, but not females. Peer rejection was a significant predictor of minor theft and felony assault among males and minor assault among females, and there was a significant interaction effect for aggression and peer rejection for felony assault by males. Thus, there is support for the hypothesis that childhood peer rejection and aggression, in combination, are significant predictors of both chronic adolescent delinquency and the most violent forms of antisocial behavior reported in adolescence.

One additional, and very important, hypothesis of current theories of early-starting delinquency (Moffitt, 1993; Patterson, Capaldi, & Bank, 1991) is that early starters are more likely to persist in their offending behavior into the adult years than are late-starting youth. There is much less evidence available in support of this hypothesis than other aspects of the theory, but two unpublished studies of the Durham longitudinal sample provide some relevant findings. Rabiner, Coie, Miller-Johnson, and Lochman (2001) divided the individuals who had reported a felony assault during at least one of the first four assessment periods—sixth, eighth, tenth, or twelfth grade—into two groups: those who reported committing another felony assault during either of the next two young adult follow-up periods and those who did not. Persistence or desistence of felony assault from adolescence into young adulthood was predicted by logistic regression from gender, peer social status in fifth grade, aggression in fifth grade, and attention-deficit/hyperactivity disorder (ADHD) symptoms that were self-reported in sixth grade. Gender, of course, was a powerful predictor of persistence of violent offending, but preadolescent aggression was not. ADHD symptoms and peer social status were significant predictors as well. Thus, although aggression and peer rejection are important childhood predictors of adolescent violent behavior, only peer rejection continues to predict the persistence of violent behavior into early adulthood. The fact that ADHD emerges as a predictor of persistence in violent behavior is a point worth noting, because it also is relevant to understanding the emergence of early peer rejection among aggressive children.

The second study extending findings from the Durham longitudinal project into the early adult years speaks to the question of whether early starters are more likely to persist in early adult offending behavior than the late starting group, although it does not directly address the issue of violence as predicted

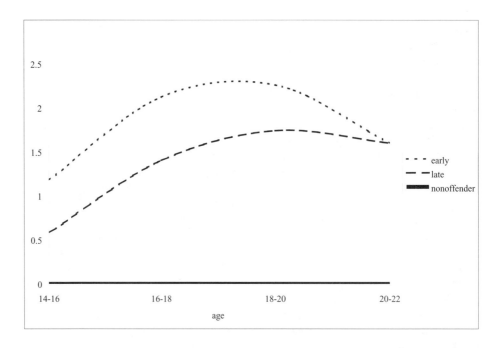

Figure 13.1. A comparison of growth curves on number of arrests for early-starter, late-starter, and nonoffender groups (as defined by police arrests and self-reported delinquency data) across the adolescent and early adult years.

from childhood peer rejection (Coie, Miller-Johnson, Maumary-Gremaud, & Lochman, 2001). The youth in this study were defined as consensus early starters if they had been arrested at least once by the end of grade six and admitted to one index offense (e.g., serious assault or theft) or four or more less serious offenses by the end of grade six. Late starters were identified as those youth who failed to meet either of the early-starter criteria at grade 6 but met both criteria by the end of grade 12. Growth curves extending into the two early adult assessment periods were contrasted for these early- and late-starter groups on both self-reported delinquency and police arrest. In the growth curves of self-reported serious offences, neither the early starters nor the late starters exhibited the U-shaped curves (peaking at age 17 or 18) typically found in FBI statistics of delinquent behavior plotted by age. Instead, both groups showed essentially flat trajectories in self-reported serious offending behavior from sixth grade through four years post–high school. The early starters reported twice the number of serious offenses all across the adolescent period as did the late starters.

The growth curves for police arrest revealed different findings, however. As Figure 13.1 reflects, the early starters did show the expected U-shape curve and were arrested much more often during adolescence than were the late starters. The late starters, however, showed a pattern of increasing arrest across adolescence, as would be expected by the way this group was defined, which leveled off at about the same age that the early starters peaked in their number of arrests. Contrary to the prediction from the theory, however, the late starters did not decrease in the frequency of their arrests across the following four early adult years. As a result, this urban, African American group of late-starting offenders does not appear to be desisting in their offending behavior and has a level of early adult arrest rate at age 22 similar to that of the early-starter group.

What these findings seem to suggest is that once urban, African American youth begin to get into trouble with the law, their risk for continued arrest continues to be quite high, no matter what the age of onset. One obvious explanation for these findings is that in this low-income, urban context the dropout rate tends to be high and reasonable jobs in a conventional setting are not easy to obtain. As a result, many youth turn to illegal ways of getting money, along with the accompanying risks of exposure to violence-inducing circumstances. This fact, coupled with the fact that they have a record for prior arrest, places them at high risk for continued police arrest. Whether or not both groups are equally at risk for continued arrest beyond their early 20s is a question that cannot be resolved by these data. Nonetheless, these results do suggest that social context may play a significant role in determining the generalizability of the early- versus late-starter theory of adolescent delinquency.

Because the findings were so different for self-report and police arrest data, it is not a simple matter to reconcile them. However, if the self-report data are taken at face value, it may mean that lower rates of initial delinquency for the late-starter group disproportionately decrease the probability of their arrest rates in early adolescence, relative to the early-starter group. In other words, there may be a threshold for antisocial activity that must be reached in order for police to make an arrest, and late starters simply fail to reach this threshold until later in adolescence, even though they have been involved in delinquent activity earlier in their lives. On the other end of the adolescent period, by contrast, the early starters may have begun to learn how to continue their level of illegal activity without coming under police scrutiny as often, and have acquired these skills sooner than did the late starters simply because of their greater early experience with the police. This would explain why the trajectories of self-reported delinquency were relatively flat for both early and late starters, but at different levels of elevation, whereas the arrest records show the contrasting curvilinear patterns reflected in Figure 13.1. In any case, the data do suggest that persistence in offending is a serious problem for both groups of youth and indicate that developmental theories of antisocial behavior need to take greater account of the environmental circumstances of development than do present theories of early- and late-starting delinquency.

The results of this second study suggest that although early starters account for more antisocial activity overall than do the late starters, the long-term implications of early-onset delinquency may not be quite as dramatically different from late-onset delinquency as has been inferred from earlier longitudinal studies of delinquency. This change in emphasis may be the consequence of the increased level of illegal drug selling among contemporary urban adolescents and their easier access to automatic weapons. Nonetheless, there is still good reason to see the early-starting group as being at greater risk, particularly if they are more involved in violent activity than are other delinquent adolescents, as our data seem to suggest.

Early Childhood Antecedents of Rejection and Aggression

Bierman, Smoot, and Aumiller (1993) studied a sample of Caucasian boys from rural Pennsylvania, ranging in age from first through fifth grade. Using sociometric data obtained from classroom peers, they divided the boys into four groups on the basis of the rejection and aggression dimensions described earlier. They found, concurrently, that the rejected, aggressive boys were more argumentative, inattentive, and disruptive than other boys, including the nonrejected, aggressive boys, and had poorer social skills. Although both the rejected and nonrejected aggressive boys showed higher levels of aggression than all the other boys, the aggression of the nonrejected boys was typically more goal-directed and instrumental, whereas that of the rejected boys seemed more uncontrolled than their nonrejected counterparts. The implication was that problems associated with ADHD were more characteristic of the rejected, aggressive boys than of the nonrejected, aggressive boys. In a follow-up study, two years later, Bierman and Wargo (1995) found that the rejected, aggressive boys continued to exhibit higher levels of disruptive and aggressive behavior, as well as poorer social skills, than did the nonrejected, aggressive boys.

In a similar attempt to understand the differences between aggressive boys who were rejected by their peers and those who were not rejected, Coie, et al. (1991) observed the two subgroups of aggressive boys in experimentally organized playgroups containing unfamiliar age-mates over five daily sessions. They focused particularly on differences in the way the two subgroups of aggressive boys behaved in episodes involving aggression with other group members. For one thing, the rejected aggressive boys initiated more reactively aggressive episodes, that is, episodes that seemed to be triggered by anger at the target of aggression rather than by instrumental motives (Dodge, Price, Coie, & Christopoulos, 1990). This finding replicated one of the principal findings from the study by Bierman et al. (1993). In addition, rejected, aggressive boys tended to continue aggressive episodes for longer time periods than did the nonrejected, aggressive boys. In part, this is because they seemed more prone to retaliate even when they were the initiators of aggression, something most other boys rarely did. It was as though they had more difficulty ignoring confrontational or assertive behavior by others once they were emotionally engaged by anger. Their fights more often ended with a clear winner or loser (regardless of whether they were themselves the winner or the loser). A secondary consequence of this latter difference, perhaps, is that other boys were less inclined to respond to aggressive overtures by the rejected, aggressive boys because a higher proportion of their aggressive initiations were ignored or met with unresponsive behavior than that of other boys. These findings suggest that there are characteristics of the aggressive behavior of the two subgroups of aggressive boys that lead one group to become rejected by peers and the other not. More broadly, these findings are quite congruent with those of Bierman et al. (1993), namely, that the rejected, aggressive boys seem to be more emotionally reactive and more impulsive and uncontrolled than those who are not rejected.

This potential linkage between the characteristics that go into the diagnosis of ADHD and the behavioral patterns that distinguish rejected, aggressive boys from nonrejected, aggressive boys, stated most clearly by Bierman and her colleagues, finds further support in the results of a summer day camp study of ADHD boys ages 6 to 12. Erhardt and Hinshaw (1994) brought 25 boys who had been diagnosed with ADHD together with 49 previously unfamiliar boys who did not have this diagnosis. As early as the end of the first day of camp, the ADHD boys were overwhelmingly rejected by peers. The sociometric scores for these boys could clearly be related to their behavior, particularly their aggressive behavior. These results suggest that the behaviors that comprise the ADHD syndrome contribute to the peer rejection of some aggressive boys, in addition to their deficits in prosocial behavior.

The fact that aggression can be distinguished from ADHD symptoms, per se, and that ADHD symptoms also predict childhood rejection next raises the question analogous to Parker and Asher's: Does peer rejection play a meaningful role in the development of antisocial behavior once aggression and ADHD-related behaviors are entered into the predictive equation?

The answer to this question, at least in part, comes from longitudinal data from the Fast Track project (Miller-Johnson, Coie, Maumary-Gremaud, Bierman, & Conduct Problems Prevention Research Group, 2001). Data on aggression and symptoms of ADHD were collected toward the end of first grade on children who formed a normative sample of first graders from the schools in which the control group children for this preventive intervention trial were selected, as well as the control group children themselves. A total of 657 children were assessed, of whom 57% were male and 47% were African American and 51% were European American. Sociometric nominations of peer social status and aggression were collected in first through third grade, and measures of early delinquent behavior were collected in fourth grade by means of self-report. The first-grade measures of aggression and ADHD symptoms utilized parent and teacher ratings. Thus, unlike many studies in which these variables have been related longitudinally, the sources of information on the major constructs at the three developmental points were assessed from different sources, eliminating the possibility that the strength of prediction for these variables results simply from the consistency of perceptions within a given data source.

A series of multiple regressions were conducted to test the joint and additive contributions of early risk factors on fourth-grade antisocial behavior. Both aggression and ADHD symptoms in first grade made significant predictions to fourth-grade antisocial behavior, which is what has often been found in other longitudinal studies (Campbell, 2000). When peer social status, as indexed by social preference scores averaged across second and third grade, was entered into the model along with first-grade aggression and ADHD, peer status added marginally to the prediction of fourth-grade antisocial behavior. This latter finding suggests that peer rejection, assessed subsequently to both aggression and ADHD constructs, adds to the prediction of antisocial behavior even when these factors that, themselves, contribute heavily to the development of peer rejection are already included in the predictive equation. Finally, when the indirect effects of first-grade aggression and ADHD on fourth-grade antisocial behavior were tested with second- and third-grade peer status in the model, the effects of aggression on antisocial behavior did not appear to be mediated by peer status, whereas the effects of ADHD were mediated by peer rejection.

It is interesting to note that Cowan and Cowan (see chap. 9, this volume) also report on longitudinal data in which peer rejection in first grade predicted antisocial behavior in fourth grade even when the effects of aggression in kindergarten were controlled, along with concurrent aggression and rejection.

These results suggest two things about peer rejection as a risk factor for later antisocial behavior. Even though peer rejection is itself caused by disruptive behaviors, as measured by the aggression and ADHD constructs, the consequence of being rejected by peers increases the predictability of antisocial behavior. Second, one of the ways the early ADHD symptoms lead to later antisocial behavior, other than through their manifestation in disruptive acts, such as aggression, is that they cause children to be rejected by peers and this rejection, in turn, leads to increased antisocial behavior.

How Does Rejection Add to Antisocial Risk?

In considering the role of childhood peer rejection as a risk factor in antisocial development, two somewhat different questions must be addressed: First, why are rejected, aggressive boys at greater risk than nonrejected, aggressive boys for becoming early-starting delinquents, along with the accompanying risks of greater persistence of delinquency through to young adulthood and greater propensity for violence? Second, what does the experience of peer rejection add to the developmental process by which some youth become early, persistent, and violent offenders?

The first question asks what is different about the two subgroups of aggressive boys and implies that the same characteristics that cause the peer rejection of one subgroup may account for much of the difference in risk between the two groups. In answer to this question, there seem to be three important differences between the two groups of rejected boys and the evidence suggests that these differences were present prior to one group becoming rejected by peers and the other not. The Miller-Johnson et al. 2002 and Bierman et al. (1993) studies indicate three important differences between rejected, aggressive boys and nonrejected, aggressive boys. First, the rejected, aggressive boys are more impulsive and have problems sustaining attention. As a result, they are more likely to be disruptive of ongoing activities in the classroom and in focused group play.

Second, rejected, aggressive boys are more emotionally reactive. They are aroused to anger more easily and probably have more difficulty calming down once aroused. Because of this they are more prone to become angry at peers and attack them verbally and physically. Once engaged in aggressive interactions, they are more apt to want to overcome their opponents and inflict pain on them, feeling that they are justified in doing so. This makes them dangerous companions for peers and may lead peers to avoid them, especially to avoid any potential conflict with them. It is also the most likely reason that peers reach a consensus about them that they are less socially desirable as companions.

Third, rejected children have fewer social skills in making friends and maintaining positive relationships with peers. They have fewer strategies for resolving conflict other than the threat of force and they are less adept at repairing relationships once they are strained. One probable consequence of this is that they are more likely to get into irresolvable conflicts with peers and thus become engaged in more aggressive episodes. Furthermore, they are more likely to hold grudges and develop hostile relations that have the potential for future aggressive interactions. These three characteristics of rejected, aggressive children all serve to explain why they might be more violence prone than their nonrejected counterparts. They also suggest reasons why these children may be more persistently involved in antisocial behavior. Thus, any reasonable analysis of the relation between childhood peer rejection and risk for long-term antisocial behavior must recognize that peer rejection does serve as a marker for preexisting behavioral tendencies that can account for increased risk by themselves. This is what Rudolph and Asher (2000) refer to as the *incidental* model of the relation between peer rejection and the development of psychopathology.

The longitudinal data that have been reviewed in this chapter, on the other hand, do suggest that it is not simply the characteristics that cause some aggressive children to become rejected that account for their greater antisocial risk, but it is the fact that they have been rejected by peers that adds incrementally to their risk for increased antisocial behavior. Why this is true is the answer to our second question. A number of different consequences to being socially rejected by other children could account for increased risk for antisocial behavior. Each of the consequences that we will consider can be understood best in what Sameroff and Chandler (1975) referred to as a transactional model of development. By this is meant the dynamic interplay between children's actions and the responses to those actions by significant people in their environment in continuous sequences that unfold across time. More concretely, in the case of peer rejection, this means that a boy who exhibits both aggressive behavior with classmates and hyperactivity and impulsivity in the classroom will come to be disliked by many of his peers (Coie et al., 1990; Erhardt & Hinshaw, 1994). They may manifest these feelings in a variety of ways, depending on how much they fear his anger and aggression. They will tend to jump to the conclusion that he is responsible for most of the fights he gets into (Dodge, 1980) and inform their teacher to this effect. If they do not fear him, they may provoke him to anger just for the entertainment value of his reactions. Likewise they may pick on him and provoke him to fights with boys that are tougher than he. Unless he is skillful at games, he will be shunned from group play or not so subtly informed that he is a nuisance. As this boy grows older, the exclusionary behavior of peers may become more subtle but more effective, leaving him to find his friends among other peers like himself or among younger children (Bagwell, Coie, Terry, & Lochman, 2000; Ladd, 1983).

Along with this negative treatment by peers will likely come a great deal of negative attention and rebuke by his teacher (Dodge et al., 1982) and, if he has academic difficulty, as many rejected, aggressive children do, he will begin to feel stigmatized as stupid or lazy. As these different social consequences unfold, this rejected boy will react with increasing anger toward peers, with less provocation (Dodge, 1993), thus confirming peers in their judgment of him and leading them to treat him with even greater resentment and prejudice. A similar process of escalating negative expectations and prejudice may also take place with teachers (Kuklinski & Weinstein, 2000). In time, some of these negative opinions of peers and teachers will come to be internalized by the boy and undermine whatever social confidence he has in himself (Hymel & Franke, 1985). At the same time he will begin to think of himself as aggressive and bad, although he may be extremely resistant to acknowledging that to others verbally, acting it out instead. At the same time that this gradually acquired self-image as a bad kid is being consolidated by treatment from peers and adults, the kinds of peer affiliations he is taking on serve to heighten the potential for antisocial acts (Coie & Miller-Johnson, 2001). In these friendships, aggressive boys tend to incite each other to engage in bolder and more exciting delinquent activities, sometimes by humor, sometimes by challenging each other (Dishion, Patterson, & Griesler, 1994). In time, the level and frequency of delinquent behavior reach the point at which police attention is attracted and the boy then is caught up in the juvenile legal system. The preceding hypothetical scenario is supported by a substantial body of peer relations research. Most of this research is concurrent in nature, but more and more longitudinal evidence suggests its accuracy.

There are, therefore, at least three consequences of peer rejection that may increase aggressive children's tendencies toward antisocial behavior. One is that it changes how they think and feel about peers in ways that amplify their suspicions of peers. A second is that it changes how they behave toward peers, often intensifying or exaggerating patterns already in existence, but sometimes also reflecting the sense that they know they do not belong. A third is that it reduces their social options and channels them toward peers whose influence will amplify their own aggressive and unskillful behavior.

Rejection Leads to More Negative Expectations of Peers

Being rejected by peers can lead to changes in the way that these peers are perceived by the rejected child. Whether rejection takes the form of overt bullying and intimidation or more covert acts of exclusion or gossiping, rejected children begin to develop expectations and make attributions of motives of the rejecting peers. Numerous studies detail the various ways that socially rejected children have less adaptive ways of cognitively processing the kinds of social information that are critical to making good social decisions. Crick and Dodge (1994) have an excellent review of this literature, but most of these studies document social cognitive deficits that are assessed at the time that peer social status has already been determined. However, Dodge (Dodge, 1993) has analyzed longitudinal data on changes in social cognitive processes in relation to both peer rejection and changes in aggressive behavior, and he demonstrates some of the negative impact that being rejected by peers can have on the way rejected children view their peers and behave toward them, as a result. He found that peer rejection as early as the kindergarten years was connected to a number of deficits in subsequent social cognitive skills, including the increased tendency to make hostile attributions about peers' intentions to harm them. These acquired social information processing biases mediated the relation between earlier peer rejection and increased aggressive behavior in third grade. Thus, as illustrated in our earlier hypothetical example, a boy who is rejected by peers comes to expect negative treatment from peers and attributes hostile motives to them even when circumstances do not clearly justify these inferences. On the strength of these hostile inferences, this boy is more apt to behave aggressively with peers because he sees himself as justified, even necessitated, in striking out at peers for perceived slights and threats by them.

One important question remains regarding the process by which biased social information processing is acquired: Do these biases operate on both a general and a specific basis? In other words, do children acquire their tendency to make hostile attributions about other children's intentions, for example, only with respect to specific peers of their acquaintance or do they develop more general social expectations on the basis of particular peer experiences? Much of the research reviewed by Crick and Dodge (1994) employs methods that support the idea that these attributions are broadly applied. In a recent observational study of groups of nine-year-old boys who knew each other because they came from the same school classroom, Hubbard, Dodge, Coie, Cillessen, and Schwartz (2001) analyzed the relation between hostile attributions and patterns of aggressive interaction among the boys. They found support for the idea that these biases vary reliably across dyads. Hostile attributions toward a particular peer were related to reactively aggressive acts toward that same peer, even after controlling for the general aggressive behavior of both participants. This same dyadic relation did not hold for proactive aggression, which was related to the characteristics of the aggressor or the victim. In fact, in a separate analysis of dyads identified as being highly involved in mutually aggressive behavior in the school context, this same pattern was quite pronounced. Dyads that school classmates described as starting fights with each other more often than did other boys had heightened hostile expectations of each other, compared with their expectations of each other (Coie et al., 1999).

The importance of the preceding findings regarding the dynamics of dyadic aggression is that they may help explain the phenomenon of heightened rates of homicide and assault among male youth. The majority (84%) of young murder offenders are male, and the victims are predominantly acquaintances (47%) or family members (36%) according to FBI statistics (Snyder, 2001). This suggests that social expectations and patterns of hostile attributions that build up in relations over time may play a significant role in juvenile violence. The fact that rejected, aggressive males show persistently higher tendencies toward hostile attribution biases, as well as other social cognitive deficits related to aggression, fits with their pattern of higher involvement in violent delinquent acts in adolescence and their tendency to persist in violent behavior into the early adult years. As young children, these boys may have had a tendency toward angry outbursts that they had difficulty controlling. This resulted in their being rejected by peers and subjected to the kinds of treatment that exacerbated their tendency to see certain peers as having hostile intentions toward them. Across time the number of peers toward whom they make these attributions increases and heightens the potential for angry outbursts toward acquaintances. Once they reach adolescence and become physically stronger and have greater access to weapons of various kinds, their potential for more serious violence is quite high, relative to other peers.

Rejection Leads to Poorer Social Behavior

The second potential consequence of being rejected by peers is that it changes the way they behave in social situations. The Dodge (1993) study already illustrated the way that being rejected increases the long-term frequency of reactive aggression. Several studies document observable changes in behavior relating to feedback on peer evaluation. In the three different observational studies of previously unacquainted boys playing together in newly formed groups (Coie & Kupersmidt, 1983; Dodge, 1983; Dodge, Coie, et al., 1990), once boys became rejected by other group members they tended to withdraw more from interactions with the other boys.

In another type of observational study, Rabiner and Coie (1989) tested the effects of positive feedback from unfamiliar peers on the behavior of boys who were known to be either popular or rejected in their home school settings. Thus, in the first meeting a rejected third-grade boy (or popular boy) was introduced to two third-grade boys from another school and the three of them were asked questions about things they enjoyed doing and then they played a structured game. In the second meeting, a week later, the rejected boy (or popular boy) was brought back to join the two boys he had met in the previous meeting, but he joined them after the other two had begun a game together. Half the boys were told that the other two boys had liked him and were hoping to get to play with him again. The other half were simply told they were going to join the two boys they met the previous week. The rejected boys who were led to expect a positive reception from the other two boys were, in fact, rated significantly more positively by these two boys in a debriefing after the play session than were rejected boys who did not receive this induction. There was no such effect for the positive expectation induction on the popular boys. In a second study (Rabiner & Coie, 1989), the same result was obtained with rejected girls. In the case of the girls, it was possible for objective observers, blinded to the procedure, to identify the competent behavior that made a difference in the ratings of the other two girls. These results suggest that children who have been rejected by familiar peers enter new peer situations with expectations that lead them to behave less competently in these new situations than they are capable of behaving. Popular children, on the other hand, do not need to be reassured about how other children will receive them and so the induction made no difference to them. Thus one clear consequence of being rejected by peers is that it causes the rejected children to behave less competently. Over time, with familiar peers who have rejected a child, this can result in a spiraling self-fulfilling prophecy in which the rejected child develops negative expectations about the way peers will react and behaves in a way that fulfills both his or her expectations and the expectations of the peers. Given this scenario it would not be surprising for aggressive, rejected children, especially boys, to become increasingly aggressive and disruptive with peers, as a consequence of their rejection.

Rejection Leads to Negative Social Influences

The third consequence of peer rejection that may intensify the antisocial tendencies of aggressive, rejected children is that it channels them into greater contact with similarly aggressive or socially unskillful peers like themselves. Ladd (1983) conducted playground observational studies of early school-age children and found that the rejected children played, primarily, with other lower social status children and with children who were younger than themselves. One consequence of these associations is that rejected children have less opportunity to acquire the kinds of social skills and sense of age-group norms for behavior that would allow them to become a part of the mainstream peer group. When playing with younger children, rejected, aggressive children can continue to get what they want through physical intimidation and not have to learn more sophisticated ways to negotiate with peers and resolve conflicts. Although this may be satisfying to them in the short term, ultimately it places them at a greater adaptive disadvantage relative to their same-age peers (Coie, 1990).

In addition to limiting the development of their social skills by channeling them to younger and less socially skillful peer associations, there is evidence that childhood peer rejection puts children in a position to be subject to greater deviant peer group influence in their preadolescent years. The impact of deviant peer group influences on the crystallization of an antisocial developmental trajectory has been solidly documented. At one point in the investigation of this issue there was some ambiguity about the direction of causality in the heavy correlation between antisocial behavior and deviant peer associations. As Cairns and Cairns (1994) have demonstrated, youth who are already highly aggressive tend to associate with each other, so it is possible to conclude that deviant peer groups form as a result of mutual interests and behavioral similarity, and that group membership is secondary to preexisting antisocial tendencies.

Several recent longitudinal studies indicate that deviant group membership adds incrementally to the antisocial activity of youth who may already be involved in this kind of delinquent behavior. Elliott and Menard (1996) tracked the transitions from several levels of deviant of peer association to self-reported delinquent behavior on youth ages 11 to 17 from the National Youth Survey. They found that the transition from nondelinquent friends to slightly delinquent peer associations typically preceded the transition from no illegal activity to minor delinquent activity. The transition probabilities are even stronger when the shift from nondelinquent peers to delinquent peers precedes the transition from minor delinquency to serious delinquency. In general, acquiring slightly delinquent friends leads to minor offending behaviors which, in turn, lead to more deviant peer associations which then lead to serious antisocial behavior. Conversely, Thornberry, Krohn, Lizotte, and

Chard-Wierschem (1993) found that youth who joined gangs increased the level of their illegal activities while they were gang members, but decreased this activity when they left the gang.

The next question for discussion is whether there is evidence that being rejected as a child makes aggressive youth more susceptible to deviant peer group influence. The evidence is incomplete on this point but an argument can be made in support of this point from data that links peer rejection to member- ship in deviant peer groups and to status within these groups. Bagwell et al. (2000) plotted the peer group structure in 33 fourth-grade classrooms serving an ethnically and economically diverse population. They found that aggression was the strongest predictor of deviant peer group membership, generally, but that nonrejected, aggressive youth were more central to these groups whereas the rejected, aggressive youth were more peripheral group members.

One might conclude from these findings that the nonrejected, aggressive youth would therefore be more susceptible to group pressures because of their more central status. However, it may be more plausible to conclude, given everything else that is known about rejection, that the nonrejected youth are more central to their groups because of their greater leadership qualities and social skills, whereas the rejected youth are more peripheral for the opposite reasons and hence are vulnerable to exclusion or expulsion from their groups. This vulnerability in their group status would make them more susceptible to conformity to group norms and influence rather than less so. Because of this greater susceptibility rejected, aggressive youth may be more apt to try to prove their loyalty by engaging in more risky illegal acts or by accompanying any other group members looking for accomplices. Support for this conclusion comes from Hollander's (1958) concept of *idiosyncrasy credit*. According to Hollander, group leaders may acquire tolerance to deviate from group norms by virtue of their value to the group. It would therefore follow that less important members would have less latitude for not following group norms. In the case of so-called deviant peer groups, in which norms include some expectation of aggression and delinquent behavior, less secure members may be motivated to prove their worth by exhibiting such behavior. It is also the case that, because of their greater emotional reactivity and heightened sensitivity to the potentially hostile motives of others, membership in a group of other youth who are prone to provocation and aggression would make these same rejected, aggressive youth more likely to explode in acts of violence toward fellow group members because the greatest proportion of adolescent male violence is directed toward acquaintances.

Prevention Implications

The design of prevention trials depends on a prior knowledge of the causal factors of the disorder to be prevented (Coie et al., 1993). The science of preven- tion has been conceived of as a cyclical process involving five stages, the first being a study of the epidemiology of the disorder. The second stage entails the identification of risk and protective factors and the synthesis of this knowledge into a model of the development of the disorder (Mrazek & Haggerty, 1994). Fully articulating the development of something like conduct disorder is obviously not something that can be expected to be completed prior to taking the next step of designing a prevention trial. The process of creating and refining a developmental model is ongoing, with major advances in understanding the role of risk and protective factors giving rise to new insights into the design of the next generation of prevention trials.

What, then, are the implications of the research just reviewed for designing conduct disorder prevention trials? What weight should be given to including procedures for addressing peer rejection as a risk factor and how should this be attempted and when? Before addressing these questions it is necessary to place peer rejection, as a risk factor, in a larger context. Clearly, we are not saying that peer rejection is a primary factor in the development of antisocial behavior.

In a discussion of the multiple risk factors implicated by longitudinal research studies, the Fast Track group articulated a combination of child, family, and community variables that seem critical to the development of serious and chronic antisocial behavior (Conduct Problems Prevention Research Group, 1992; chap. 10, this volume). Biologically based child factors that cause deficits in behavioral inhibition and neural processing systems linked to risk taking and emotional reactivity can interact with family environment and parenting practices to produce children who show irritable, aggressive, and inattentive behavior patterns in the first three or four years of life. Community poverty and high levels of neighborhood crime and violence place stressors on the family that exacerbate parenting vulnerabilities, as well as provide models and incentives for aggressive and other antisocial behavior. Children who enter school with these risk factors in their background and without the compensatory skills to get along with other children in a structured situation will soon become highly rejected by their peers and teachers. The developmental sequence that follows this rejection is what has been outlined earlier in this chapter. Thus, if it were possible to intervene effectively with these early child, family, and community risk factors prior to the child's significant entry into peer contexts, the need for attending to peer rejection as a contributing risk factor would be greatly reduced. There are several reasons why this latter circumstance is not very probable in contemporary Western society.

The first of these reasons is that early elementary school or preschool is the first circumstance in which it is possible to identify the children who have the behavior patterns of impulsivity, emotional reactivity, and aggressiveness that make up primary risk. It is only when they have to adjust continually to a peer context across time that these patterns are both visible and significant and, of course, this is when the phenomenon of peer rejection first emerges. In some sense, it is primarily with peers that the signs of antisocial behavior become evident and it is in the interaction with the peer group that an identity as an aggressive or disruptive child begins to form. Our own longitudinal findings suggesting that peer rejection leads to increased aggressive and disruptive behavior, coupled with similar findings by Ladd and his colleagues (1997) connecting academic problems in the early school years to peer rejection, reflect just how quickly adjustment to the peer system becomes important in the life of children.

Second, schools are the first place in which it is possible to conduct community-based screening for risk status, something that is essential to a public health perspective (Coie & Bagwell, 1999). Compulsory education ensures that virtually all children can be assessed for the kinds of early risk-related behavior patterns that make possible an identification of the children who are most likely to become chronically antisocial. There is now good evidence that high-risk children can be screened effectively during the first two years of school by asking teachers to rate their students on disruptive behavior items (Lochman & Conduct Problems Prevention Research Group, 1995).

For all of the preceding reasons, dealing with peer rejection should be seen as an integral part of any comprehensive plan for the early prevention of chronic antisocial behavior. How, then, should peer rejection be dealt with as a risk factor? First of all, the findings of the Miller-Johnson et al. (2002) study suggest that intervening with aggressive behavior and ADHD successfully should reduce peer rejection. Thus, targeting the primary risk factors for chronic antisocial behavior should, theoretically, have a positive effect on peer rejection as a mediating factor, as well. In point of fact, however, virtually all the interventions that have been developed to reduce aggression include components that have also been key elements in programs designed to reduce peer rejection (e.g., social problem solving, positive play skills, conflict resolution skills), as can be seen in a review of such programs by the Conduct Problems Prevention Research Group (see chap. 10, this volume). In the Lochman, Coie, Underwood, and Terry (1993) study, for example, social skills critical to forming and maintaining relationships with peers were taught along with cognitive-behavioral components designed to reduce impulsive and aggressive responding to conflict, frustration, or perceived threat. The thinking was that conflict often emerges out of lack of skill in maintaining play or joining others at play. In other words, aggression is itself reduced by promoting positive social interaction capabilities. Whether this is true for all children who are highly aggressive or just those who are both aggressive and rejected by peers is not possible to determine from the existing intervention literature. In point of fact, the intervention described by Lochman et al. was effective in improving peer relations and reducing aggressive behavior only with children who were both aggressive and rejected by their fourth-grade peers.

Conversely, in thinking about how to intervene with the peer relations aspect of the problems of aggressive children who become rejected by peers, it may be useful to recall that social expectations play a significant role in their peer problems. Hostile attributions regarding the motives of other children play an important role in the reactive aggression of these children, and reactive aggression is harmful to their status among peers in the short term (Coie et al., 1991; Dodge et al., 1990) and may be a critical factor in their greater risk for violence in adolescence (Miller-Johnson et al., 1999). Hudley and Graham (1993) have demonstrated the effectiveness of a relatively brief (12-session) cognitive intervention with aggressive fifth-grade boys. This intervention altered both hostile attributions and behavioral preferences for resolving conflict and led to reduced teacher ratings of aggressiveness. No data were collected on the peer relations of these boys, but it would be interesting to know whether a side benefit to this intervention was improved peer status. An additional piece of this problem of reactive aggression is the problem of excessive emotional reactivity. Less is known about direct approaches to improving emotional reactivity than about the social cognitive aspects of aggression, although the Promoting Alternative THinking Strategies (PATHS) curriculum (Kusche & Greenberg, 1994), which has been modified for use in the Fast Track prevention trial to reduce aggression in classrooms, does strongly emphasize cognitive behavioral training to promote emotional development.

Although social skills and cognitive behavioral interventions have been employed with aggressive and peer-rejected children for at least three decades, it is still the case that research on the significance of social and emotional development to conduct problem behavior has advanced much more effectively than research on the development of programs to prevent deficits in these areas. This is one of the most compelling needs of the early childhood prevention field. Training programs invariably consist of direct tuition on the deficits found in basic research studies without much consideration of the best way to encourage growth in these areas. The experiential dimension of this kind of development is largely undeveloped, and the possibility of using virtual reality techniques for giving children guided practice in controlling emotional and behavioral reactions to challenging peer situations is just one example of new methods that need to be explored.

Peer relations researchers have not typically considered the need to deal with ADHD symptoms when planning interventions to improve children's peer relations. This may be due, in part, to the fact that ADHD concerns have been the provenance of child clinical researchers, whereas social skills training for children has had its greatest use in applied developmental settings, even though the concept of social skills had its origins in the attempt to understand the deficits associated with serious clinical disorders (McFall, 1982). Those researchers who are concerned primarily with the treatment of ADHD have sometimes found that a behavioral intervention package that contains social skills training can be a useful adjunct to stimulant medication in maintaining its effects on reducing ADHD symptoms across time (MTA Cooperative Group, 1999). The question of the utility of stimulant medication for reducing peer relations difficulties has now been examined as part of the more general assessment of the comparison of multimodal treatment packages in the MTA trial. Although the results of this trial did not generally support the large incremental effects of stimulant medication over the behavioral intervention when these behavioral interventions are sustained, there was some evidence that stimulant medication had incremental utility in improving the peer relations of these children who had been diagnosed with ADHD. Children who had the combined package of stimulant medication and behavioral interventions that included social skills training were found to have received fewer less-liked nominations from their peers than children who received only the behavioral intervention package of interventions. On the other hand, adult ratings of peer relations did not support this finding of incremental value for medication. The long-term implications for serious conduct problems still has to be evaluated in this trial, but, despite the equivocalness of these results, there is some value to considering the effectiveness of stimulant medication in comprehensive preventive interventions in which peer rejection is treated as a mediating risk factor in the development of chronic antisocial behavior.

Peer rejection is also closely related to other risk factors. Coie and Krehbiel (1984) found that academic tutoring could be used to improve the peer status of rejected children. Of even greater interest is the finding by Cowan and Cowan (see chap. 9, this volume) that an intervention directed at improving the relationship of parents can have significant positive impact on the children's subsequent peer relations in kindergarten and first grade. The conclusion one should reach from these different studies is that intervening with peer rejection is a multidimensional enterprise involving many aspects of children's competence as well as that of their families.

This multidimensional approach is at the heart of the Fast Track project described in this volume. Peer relations is just one of several important risk factors that were intervened with across the period of elementary school for a large sample of high-risk children. Components of this intervention were designed to have an integrated impact on multiple aspects of the children's skill development in cognitive, emotional, and social functioning, as well as improvements in parenting and family life and in the atmosphere of the classroom. This makes it hard to attribute the success of the intervention to the reduction of any particular risk factor, but as we saw in our earlier discussion of interventions on just two dimensions of child functioning, these effects can be reciprocal and interactive. The success of this intervention in preventing the incidence of serious conduct disorder by a third more children than in the control group, at least up to the end of the third year (Conduct Problems Prevention Research Group, in press), points to the effectiveness of this approach.

Conclusions

Two broad conclusions can be drawn from the research reviewed in this chapter. The first is that there is a reasonable basis for concluding that the experience of being rejected by childhood peers has a pathogenic influence on the development of antisocial behavior among children, boys particularly, who are already at risk for this kind of developmental trajectory because of personal characteristics such as aggressiveness and impulsivity. The second conclusion is that the decades-old debate regarding the significance of environmental versus biological factors in the development of antisocial behavior needs to be replaced with a more detailed search for the way biological factors contribute to behaviors that, themselves, create social events that, in turn, amplify and give more advanced shape to the same behavioral patterns that may have their origins in biological vulnerabilities.

In this chapter, peer rejection has been discussed as a painful social experience rather than as a descriptor of some groups of children, as might be inferred from some of the research literature on peer rejection. It has been denoted as a painful experience to emphasize that rejection is something that happens to some children even if it also appears to be the case that it is a consequence of their own behavior with peers, at least to some extent. Although it might be tempting to debate as to whether some or all children should be considered victims, in the terms that are currently used to draw greater concern for a significant social issue, the more important scientific point is to understand how it is that rejection comes about and what it then has as consequences. The evidence that has been reviewed suggests that this experience of peer rejection leads to a greater wariness and suspicion of peers and their motives. This impairment in social perception results in less effective social functioning and increasingly greater antisocial behavior over time (Coie & Dodge, 1998).

This discussion of the effects of peer rejection on development has implications for the larger issues in developmental science. First, the idea that peer experiences play a central role in development is relatively new to the behavioral sciences, despite the oft-cited references to Harry Stack Sullivan's (1953) Interpersonal Theory on this point. The debate over the effects of nature versus nurture that permeated the discussion of personality development in the 1960s and 1970s focused almost exclusively on the importance of parenting. The fact that there is evidence for the significance of peer rejection on development does not mean that rejection is the predominantly important peer experience to be recognized, any more than it means that the importance of parents' behavior toward children should be discounted in favor of peer influences, as some theorists such as Judith Harris (1995) have suggested. Evidence for the impact of peer rejection has taken a relatively long time to acquire, but it has emerged as a result of systematic efforts to document and understand a meaningful human phenomenon, one that most of us would recognize as figuring in our own childhood experiences if we were to allow ourselves to recall this aspect of our childhoods. Concerns for inclusion and exclusion predominate the middle- and junior-high school years, especially. It is something of a mystery that developmental psychologists failed to explore this phenomenon for so long, except for the fact that as youth enter later adolescence, talking about people one does not like becomes less socially acceptable, something that most peer researchers discover when they attempt to get permission to conduct classroom sociometric assessments. The lesson from this research literature may be for developmentalists to study the effects of specific types of social experience, as these are transacted with individuals whose behavioral tendencies are likely to have a similar impact on their social environment. This point may be relevant to studying the effects of parenting. Specific types of parental behavior will have different effects on different types of children and will be prompted differently by these different types of children.

A second lesson from this peer rejection review may be worth noting. Peer rejection amplifies the preexisting behavioral tendencies of aggressive and impulsive children. One would think that this kind of negative peer response would diminish these tendencies in the way that parental punishment is intended to diminish unacceptable behavior. It is possible that in some cases peer rejection does work in the way that parental punishment is intended, but the evidence suggests that the predominant effect is to amplify it across time. This is one of the sad lessons from observing children in school and other settings. Children often get the opposite of what they need, or less of what they need than children who could manage with less themselves. In this sense, then, biological heritage may have the greatest absolute importance for adaptive and maladaptive individual differences in behavior, as it propels children toward social experiences, with peers and adults, that serve to exaggerate their vulnerabilities and dysfunctional behavior. This point, however, does not diminish the need to understand the significance of these social experiences, because they may provide context for deflecting vulnerable children from long-term problems. This is the great challenge of prevention research: to fly in the face of common societal patterns of response to maladaptive behavior and provide developmentally compensatory experiences and training that encourage more healthy, adaptive functioning on the part of high-risk youth.

References

Achenbach, T. M., & Edelbrock, C. (1983). *Manual for the Child Behavior Checklist and Revised Child Behavior Profile.* Burlington: University of Vermont.

Bagwell, C. L., Coie, J. D., Terry, R. A., & Lochman, J. E. (2000). Peer clique participation and social status in preadolescence. *Merrill-Palmer Quarterly, 45,* 280–305.

Bierman, K. L., Smoot, D. L., & Aumiller, K. (1993). Characteristics of aggressive-rejected, aggressive (nonrejected), and rejected (nonaggressive) boys. *Child Development, 64,* 139–151.

Bierman, K. L., & Wargo, J. B. (1995). Predicting the longitudinal course associated with aggressive-rejected, aggressive (nonrejected), and rejected (nonaggressive) status. *Development and Psychopathology, 7,* 669–682.

Cairns, R. B., & Cairns, B. D. (1994). *Lifelines and risks: Pathways of youth in our time.* New York: Cambridge University Press.

Campbell, S. B. (2000). Attention-deficit/hyperactivity disorder: A developmental view. In A. J. Sameroff, M. Lewis, & S. M. Miller (Eds.), *Handbook of developmental psychopathology* (2nd ed.). New York: Kluwer Academic/Plenum.

Coie J. D. (1990). Toward a theory of peer rejection. In S. R. Asher & J. D. Coie (Eds.), *Peer rejection in childhood* (pp. 365–401). Cambridge, England: Cambridge University Press.

Coie, J. D., & Bagwell, C. L. (1999). School-based social predictors of serious adolescent dysfunction: Implications for prevention. In D. Cicchetti & S. L. Toth (Eds.), *Rochester Symposium on Developmental Psychopathology, Vol. 9: Developmental approaches to prevention and intervention* (pp. 25–55). Rochester, NY: University of Rochester Press.

Coie, J. D., Cillessen, A. H. N., Dodge, K. A., Hubbard, J. A., Schwartz, D., Lemerise, E., et al. (1999). It takes two to fight: A test of relational factors and a method for assessing aggressive dyads. *Developmental Psychology, 35,* 1–10.

Coie, J. D., & Dodge, K. A. (1983). Continuities and change in children's social status: A five-year longitudinal study. *Merrill-Palmer Quarterly, 29,* 261–282.

Coie, J. D., & Dodge, K. A. (1998). The development of aggression and antisocial behavior. In W. V. Damon (Series Ed.) & N. Eisenberg (Vol. Ed.), *Handbook of Child Psychology, Vol. 3: Social, emotional, and personality development* (5th ed., pp. 779–861). New York: Wiley.

Coie, J. D., Dodge, K. A., & Coppotelli, H. (1982). Dimensions and types of social status: A cross-age perspective. *Developmental Psychology, 18,* 557–570.

Coie, J. D., Dodge, K. A., & Kupersmidt, J. B. (1990). Peer group behavior and social status. In S. R. Asher & J. D. Coie (Eds.), *Peer rejection in childhood.* Cambridge, England: Cambridge University Press.

Coie, J. D., Dodge, K. A., Terry, R., & Wright, V. (1991). The role of aggression in peer relations: An analysis of aggression episodes in boys' play groups. *Child Development, 62,* 812–826.

Coie, J. D., & Krehbiel, G. (1984). Effects of academic tutoring on the social status of low-achieving, socially-rejected children. *Child Development, 55,* 1465–1478.

Coie, J. D., & Kupersmidt, J. B. (1983). A behavioral analysis of emerging social status in boys' groups. *Child Development, 54,* 1400–1416.

Coie, J. D., Lochman, J. E., Terry, R., & Hyman, C. (1992). Predicting adolescent disorder from childhood aggression and peer rejection. *Journal of Clinical and Consulting Psychology, 60,* 783–792.

Coie, J. D., & Miller-Johnson, S. (2001). Peer factors. In R. Loeber & D. P. Farrington (Eds.), *Child delinquents: Development, intervention and service needs* (pp. 191–209). Thousand Oaks, CA: Sage.

Coie, J. D., Miller-Johnson, S., Maumary-Gremaud, A., & Lochman, J. E. (2001, April). Does the early-late starter model of adolescent delinquency apply to contemporary African American, urban youth? In J. D. Coie (Chair), *Evaluating early versus late starter delinquency theory with recent data on young adults from four diverse longitudinal samples.* Symposium conducted at the biennial meetings of the Society for Research on Child and Adolescent Development, Minneapolis, MN.

Coie, J. D., Terry, R., Lenox, K. F., Lochman, J. E., & Hyman, C. (1995). Peer rejection and aggression as predictors of stable risk across adolescence. *Development and Psychopathology, 7,* 697–713.

Coie, J. D., Watt, N. F., West, S., Hawkins, J. D., Asarnow, J., Markman, H., et al. (1993). The science of prevention: A conceptual framework and some directions for a national research program. *American Psychologist, 48,* 1013–1033.

Conduct Problems Prevention Research Group. (1992). A developmental and clinical model for the prevention of conduct disorders: The Fast Track Program. *Development and Psychopathology, 4,* 509–527.

Conduct Problems Prevention Research Group. (2002). Evaluation of the first three years of the Fast Track prevention trial with children at high risk for adolescent conduct problems. *Journal of Abnormal Child Psychology, 30,* 19–35.

Cowen, E. L., Pederson, A., Babigian, H., Izzo, L. D., & Trost, M. A. (1973). Long-term follow-up of early detected vulnerable children. *Journal of Consulting and Clinical Psychology, 41,* 438–446.

Crick, N. R., & Dodge, K. A. (1994). A review and reformulation of social-information processing mechanisms in children's social adjustment. *Psychological Bulletin, 115,* 74–101.

Dishion, T. J., Patterson, G. R., & Griesler, P. C. (1994). Peer adaptations in the development of antisocial behavior. In L. R. Huesmann (Ed.), *Aggressive behavior: Current perspectives* (pp. 61–95). New York: Plenum.

Dodge, K. A. (1980). Social cognition and children's behavior. *Child Development, 51,* 162–170.

Dodge, K. A. (1983). Behavioral antecedents of peer social status. *Child Development, 54,* 1386–1399.

Dodge, K. A. (1993). Social-cognitive mechanisms in the development of conduct disorder and depression. *Annual Review of Psychology, 44,* 559–584.

Dodge, K. A., Coie, J. D., & Brakke, N. P. (1982). Behavior patterns of socially rejected and neglected preadolescents: The roles of social approach and aggression. *Journal of Abnormal Child Psychology, 10,* 389–410.

Dodge, K. A., Coie, J. D., Pettit, G. S., & Price, J. M. (1990). Peer status and aggression: Developmental and contextual analyses. *Child Development, 61,* 1289–1309.

Dodge, K. A., Price, J. M., Coie, J. D., & Christopoulos, C. (1990). On the development of dyadic aggressive relationships in boys' peer groups. *Human Development, 33,* 260–270.

Elliot, D. S., Huizinga, D., & Ageton, S. S. (1985). *Explaining delinquency and drug use.* Newbury Park, CA: Sage.

Elliott, D. S., & Menard, S. (1996). Delinquent friends and delinquent behavior: Temporal and developmental patterns. In J. D. Hawkins (Ed.), *Delinquency and crime: Current theories* (pp. 28–67). New York: Cambridge University Press.

Erhardt, D., & Hinshaw, S.P. (1994). Initial sociometric impressions of attention-deficit hyperactivity disorder and comparison boys: Predictions from social behavior and from nonbehavioral variables. *Journal of Consulting and Clinical Psychology, 62,* 833–842.

Felner, R. D., Jason, L. A., Moritsugu, J., & Farber, S. S. (1983). Preventive psychology: Evolution and current status. In R. D. Felner, L. A. Jason, J. N. Moritsugu, & S. S. Farber (Eds.), *Preventive psychology: Theory, research, and practice* (pp. 3–10). New York: Pergamon Press.

Harris, J. R. (1995). Where is the child's environment? A group socialization theory of development. *Psychological Review, 102,* 458–489.

Hodges, K. (1987). Assessing children with a clinical interview: The Child Assessment Schedule. In R. J. Prinz (Ed.), *Advances in behavioral assessment of children and families* (pp. 203–233). Greenwich, CT: JAI Press.

Hollander, E. P. (1958). Conformity, status, and idiosyncrasy credit. *Psychological Review, 65,* 117–127.

Hubbard, J. A., Dodge, K. A., Coie, J. D., Cillessen, A. H. N., & Schwartz, D. (2001). The dyadic nature of social information processing in boys' reactive and proactive aggression. *Journal of Personality and Social Psychology, 80,* 268–280.

Hudley, C., & Graham, S. (1993). An attributional intervention to reduce peer-directed aggression among African-American boys. *Child Development, 64,* 124–138.

Hymel, S., & Franke, S. (1985). Children's peer relations: Assessing self-perceptions. In B. H. Schneider, K. H. Rubin, & J. E. Ledingham (Eds), *Children's peer relations: Issues in assessment and intervention* (pp. 75–91). New York: Springer-Verlag.

Kohlberg, L., LaCrosse, J., & Ricks, D. (1972). The predictability of adult mental health from childhood behavior. In B. Wolman (Ed.), *Manual of child psychopathology* (pp. 1217–1284). New York: McGraw-Hill.

Kuklinski, M. R., & Weinstein, R. S. (2000). Classroom and grade level differences in the stability of teacher expectations and perceived differential teacher treatment. *Learning Environments Research, 3,* 1–34.

Kupersmidt, J. B., & Coie, J. D. (1990). Preadolescent peer status and aggression as predictors of externalizing problems in adolescence. *Child Development, 61,* 1350–1362.

Kusche, C. A., & Greenberg, M. T. (1994). *The PATHS curriculum.* Seattle, WA: Developmental Research and Programs.

Ladd, G. W. (1983). Social networks of popular, average, and rejected children in school settings. *Merrill-Palmer Quarterly, 29,* 283–308.

Ladd, G. W., Kochenderfer, B. J., & Coleman, C. C. (1997). Classroom peer acceptance, friendship, and victimization: Distinct relational systems that contribute uniquely to children's school adjustment? *Child Development, 68,* 1181–1197.

Lochman, J. E., Coie, J. D., Underwood, M., & Terry, R. (1993). Effectiveness of a social relations intervention program for aggressive and non-aggressive rejected children. *Journal of Consulting and Clinical Psychology, 61,* 1053–1058.

Lochman, J. E., & the Conduct Problems Prevention Research Group (J. D. Coie, member). (1995). Screening of child behavior problems for prevention programs at school entry: Gender and race effects. *Journal of Consulting and Clinical Psychology, 63,* 549–559.

McFall, R. M. (1982). A review and reformulation of the concept of social skills. *Behavioral Assessment, 4,* 1–35.

Miller-Johnson, S., Coie, J. D., Maumary-Gremaud, A., Bierman, K. B., & the Conduct Problems Prevention Research Group. (2002). Peer rejection and aggression and early starter models of conduct disorder. *Journal of Abnormal Child Psychology, 30,* 217–230.

Miller-Johnson, S., Coie, J. D., Maumary-Gremaud, A., Lochman, J. E., & Terry, R. (1999). Peer rejection and aggression in childhood and severity and type of delinquency during adolescence among African-American youth. *Journal of Emotional and Behavioral Disorders, 7,* 137–146.

Moffitt, T. E. (1993). Adolescence-limited and life-course-persistent antisocial behavior: A development taxonomy. *Psychological Review, 100,* 674–701.

Mrazek, P. G., & Haggerty, R. J. (Eds.). (1994). *Reducing risks for mental disorders: Frontiers for preventive intervention research.* Washington, DC: National Academy Press.

MTA Cooperative Group. (1999). A 14-month randomized clinical trial of treatment strategies for attention-deficit/hyperactivity disorder. *Archives of General Psychiatry, 56,* 1073–1086.

Parker, J. G., & Asher, S. R. (1987). Peer relations and later personal adjustment: Are low-accepted children at risk? *Psychological Bulletin, 102,* 357–389.

Patterson, G. R., Capaldi, D. M., & Bank, L. (1991). An early-starter model for predicting delinquency. In D. J. Pepler & K. H. Rubin (Eds.), *The development and treatment of childhood aggression* (pp. 139–168). Hillsdale, NJ: Erlbaum.

Patterson, G. R., Reid, J. B., & Dishion, T.J. (1992). *Antisocial boys: A social interactional approach.* Eugene, OR: Castalia.

Rabiner, D., & Coie, J. D. (1989). The effect of expectancy inductions on the social entry of rejected and popular children. *Developmental Psychology, 25,* 450–457.

Rabiner, K. L., Coie, J. D., Miller-Johnson, S., & Lochman, J. E. (2001). *Predicting the persistence vs. desistance of aggressive and non-aggressive offending*. Manuscript submitted for publication.

Roff, M., Sells, S. B., & Golden, M. M. (1972). *Social adjustment and personality development in children*. Minneapolis: University of Minnesota Press.

Rudolph, K. D., & Asher, S. R. (2000). Adaptation and maladaptation in the peer system. Developmental processes and outcomes. In A. J. Sameroff, M. Lewis, & S. Z. Miller (Eds.), *Handbook of developmental psychopathology* (pp. 157–175). New York: Kluwer Academic/Plenum.

Sameroff, A., & Chandler, M. J. (1975). Reproductive risk and continuum of caretaking casualty. In F. D. Horowitz (Ed.), *Review of child development research* (Vol. 4, pp. 187–244). Chicago: University of Chicago Press.

Sarason, S. B., Levine, M., Goldenberg, I., Cherlin, D. I., & Bennett, E. M. (1966). *Psychology in community settings*. New York: Wiley.

Snyder, H. N. (2001). Epidemiology of official offending. In R. Loeber & D. P. Farrington (Eds.), *Child delinquents: Development, intervention and service needs* (pp. 25–66). Thousand Oaks, CA: Sage.

Sullivan, H. S. (1953). *The interpersonal theory of psychiatry*. New York: Norton.

Thornberry, T. P., Huizinga, D., & Loeber, R. (1995). The prevention of serious delinquency and violence: Implications from the program of research on the causes and correlates of delinquency. In J. C. Howell, B. Krisberg, J. D. Hawkins, & J. J. Wilson (Eds.), *Sourcebook on serious violent and chronic juvenile offenders* (pp. 147–166). Thousand Oaks, CA: Sage.

Thornberry, T. P., Krohn, M., Lizotte, A. J., & Chard-Wierschem, D. (1993). The role of juvenile gangs in facilitating delinquent behavior. *Journal of Research in Crime and Delinquency, 30*, 55–87.

Author Index

Numbers in italics refer to listings in the reference sections.

Subject Index

Abbey, B. B., 87
Aber, L. J., 145
Ablow, J., 164
Academic achievement, 191
Academic skills interventions, 186
Acceptance, 38, 106–109, 211. *See also*
  popularity
Achenbach, T. M., 165
Acknowledgment issues, in community
  partnerships, 234
Activities
  communal, 27
  joint, 24
Activity preferences, boys', 24
Adaptation process, 111–115
Adaptive Behavior Inventory, 165
Adolescent offenders, 46–47
Adolescents, 12, 15. *See also* high school;
  middle school
  in Fast Track Project, 196–198
  peer-based interventions, 209–220
Adult Attachment Interview (AAI), 143–144
Adult interaction, 6
Adult role model, 192
Affect induction techniques, 69
Affective social competence (ASC), 81. *See
  also* ASC model
African Americans, 14–15, 50, 133, 149, 184,
  187, 192, 211–212, 217, 224, 245–246,
  249
Age, and status-behavior link, 5, 15
Age groups, 30
Aggression, 4–6, 14–15, 28, 31–32, 39–42, 65,
  161–163, 166, 183–184, 211, 244, 246–
  247, 250–252
  boys and, 5, 14–16, 28, 250–254
  dyadic, 15–16, 75–76, 255
  and gender, 14, 70–72
  gender-atypical, 71
  and peer rejection, 104–107, 110–111, 121,
  124, 160–161, 172, 184–186, 244–246,
  263–264
  physical, 6
  proactive, 74–76
  reactive, 74–76, 255–256
  relational, 31–32, 53, 71
  and SIP, 68, 74–76
Aggression beliefs, 65–66, 68, 70
Aggressive-behavior interventions, 186–187
Antisocial behaviors, 12, 37–53, 159–175,
  210–213, 243–264
  early starters, 182–183, 210, 246–250

and emotion, 86–87, 89–90, 92–96
late starters, 182–183, 210, 246–250
middle and high school, 190–193
in middle childhood, 159–175
and peer rejection, 173, 252–254, 256–257,
  262–264
in preschool and elementary-school years,
  188–190
Anxiety, 6, 73–74, 127
Appraisal process, 113–114
Arnold, D. H., 231
ASC model, 82–97
Asher, S., 65, 81, 101, 104–105, 108, 113, 119,
  160, 172, 244, 253
Attachment, 143–145
Attachment theory, 143–145, 147, 151,
  153–154
Attention-deficit/hyperactivity disorder
  (ADHD), 41, 247, 251–252, 261
Attribution of peer problems, 105–106
Aumiller, K., 10, 250
Authority stars, 217–219

Babigian, H., 243
Bagwell, C. L., 22, 258
Baker, B. L., 165
Ballard, M., 89
Balthazor, M., 107
Bates, J., 64, 120
Beauvais, F., 226
Beckwith, L., 144
Behavior, aggressive-disruptive. *See*
  aggression
Behavior, disruptive. *See* aggression; anti-
  social behaviors
Behavior, withdrawn. *See* withdrawal
Behavioral characteristics, and rejection
  experience, 104–105
Behavioral similarity, 43
Behavior observation, 7–8. *See also* observa-
  tion studies
Bellmore, A. D., 108
Belsky, J., 141, 145
Berkeley Guidance Study, 143
Berndt, T. J., 26, 45
Bernzweig, J., 92
Best friendship, 26, 31, 42, 122, 152
Bierman, K. L., 10, 15, 159–160, 184–185,
  187–188, 250–252
Blame, externalizing, 106
Bodenhausen, D., 69
Boivin, M., 103, 110, 113

About the Editors

Janis B. Kupersmidt, PhD, is an associate professor of psychology at the University of North Carolina at Chapel Hill. She is also the president of Innovation Research and Training, a research organization devoted to bridging the gaps between science, practice, and policy, particularly in the areas of child mental health, developmental disabilities, and substance abuse services. Dr. Kupersmidt has published over 50 scientific papers in areas of peer rejection, friendship, and peer victimization in childhood as well as aggression and delinquency. Most recently, she has been developing, implementing, and evaluating an intervention program to enhance kindergarten readiness, with a particular focus on the adjustment of aggressive preschoolers. She earned her bachelors degree at Douglass College of Rutgers University in 1978 and her PhD in clinical psychology at Duke University in 1985, where her research advisor was Dr. John D. Coie. Dr. Kupersmidt was honored with a William T. Grant Faculty Scholars Award. As principal investigator or coprincipal investigator, she has been involved in a number of research efforts funded by federal agencies such as the National Institute of Mental Health, the National Institute on Drug Abuse, the National Institute on Child Health and Human Development, and the Center on Substance Abuse Prevention.

Kenneth A. Dodge, PhD, is the William McDougall Professor of Public Policy and of Psychology at Duke University. He directs the Center for Child and Family Policy, which is devoted to finding solutions to problems facing children in contemporary society through research, policy engagement, service, and education. Professor Dodge earned his bachelors degree at Northwestern University in 1975 and his PhD in clinical psychology at Duke University in 1978, where he worked under the tutelage of Dr. John D. Coie. Professor Dodge is interested in how problem behaviors such as violence and drug use develop across the life span, how they can be prevented in high-risk children, and how communities can implement policies to prevent these outcomes. He has teamed up with colleagues to create, implement, and evaluate the Fast Track Program to prevent chronic violence in high-risk children. Professor Dodge has been honored with the Distinguished Scientific Contribution Award from the American Psychological Association, the Boyd McCandless Award, and the Senior Scientist Award from the National Institutes of Health. He is a fellow of the American Association for the Advancement of Science, the Academy of Experimental Criminology, the American Psychological Society, and the American Psychological Association. He has authored over 200 scientific articles, and his research is funded by the National Institute of Mental Health, the National Institute on Drug Abuse, the Spencer Foundation, the William T. Grant Foundation, the Duke Endowment, and the Centers for Disease Control and Prevention.